W9-BYG-220

Contents

Colour section 1

Introduction 4
What to see 6
When to go 8
Things not to miss 9

Basics 17

Getting there 19
Arrival 23
Getting around 25
The media 31
Festivals 32
Culture and etiquette 34
Travelling with children 35
Travel essentials 35

The City 43

1. The Belváros 45
2. Lipótváros and Újlipótváros 53
3. Terézváros and Erzsébetváros 63
4. The Városliget and the stadium district 73
5. Józsefváros and Ferencváros 81
6. Várhegy and central Buda 90
7. Gellért-hegy and the Tabán 108
8. Óbuda and Margit-sziget 114
9. The Buda Hills 121
10. The city limits 125
11. Excursions from Budapest 129

Listings 147

12. Accommodation 149
13. Restaurants 157
14. Coffee houses and patisseries 167
15. Bars and clubs 170
16. Gay Budapest 175
17. Entertainment 177
18. Sports 185
19. Baths and pools 188
20. Kids' Budapest 193
21. Shopping 197

Contexts 205

History 207
Books 215

Language 221

Travel store 235

Small print & Index 245

Budapest's Art Nouveau colour section following p.80

Hungarian music colour section following p.176

Colour maps following p.256

◀◀ Parliament viewed from across the River Danube ◀ Gellért Baths

Introduction to Budapest

With a wonderful natural setting straddling the River Danube, beautiful architecture and flavoursome Magyar cuisine, Budapest is one of the most rewarding cities in Europe to visit. Its magnificent waterfront and boulevards invite comparisons with Paris, Prague and Vienna – as do many features of its cultural life, from coffee houses and a love of opera to its wine-producing tradition. However, the city is also distinctively Hungarian, its inhabitants displaying fierce pride in their Magyar ancestry. Their language, too, whose nearest European relative is Finnish, underlines the difference.

Ironically, provincial Hungarians have long regarded Budapest as a hotbed of alien values and loose morals – a charge that misses the point. Foreigners have played a major role in the city since its inception, and the Chinese and Arab communities established since the end of Communism simply bring Budapest up to date as an international capital. Even the sex trade that has earned it the reputation of the "Bangkok of Europe" is nothing new, having been a feature of life during Habsburg times. In politics, art and much else, Budapest is not only the capital but a catalyst for the country, without which Hungary would be a far duller place.

Fundamental to the city's layout and history, the **River Danube** (Duna) – which is seldom blue – separates **Buda** on the hilly west bank from **Pest** on the eastern plain. Until 1873 these were separate cities, and they still retain a different feel. Buda is older and more dignified: dominated by Várhegy (Castle Hill), a mile-long long plateau overlooking the Danube, it was the capital of medieval monarchs and the seat of power for successive occupying powers. Built during the city's golden age in the late nineteenth century, with boulevards of Haussmann-like apartment blocks sweeping out from the old medieval centre, **Pest** holds most of the capital's

The **Rough Guide** to

Budapest

written and researched by

Charles Hebbert and Dan Richardson

NEW YORK • LONDON • DELHI

www.roughguides.com

▶ St Stephen's Basilica, Lipótváros

magnificent Art Nouveau edifices and has a noisy, bustling feel. Following construction of the first permanent bridge between the two cities in 1845, power gradually moved across the river, culminating in the building of the grandiose Parliament on the Pest side. The two halves of the city still retain their differences, but as a whole Budapest is a vibrant place today, never in danger of being overwhelmed by tourism but nonetheless offering plenty for visitors to enjoy.

One of Budapest's strongest suits is its **restaurants**, with places to suit all pockets and tastes. As well as the richly sauced meat and fish dishes of Hungarian food, you'll find Indian, Chinese, Italian and Middle Eastern cooking alongside plenty of options for vegetarians – and though it's often overlooked abroad, Hungarian **wine** makes a delightful accompaniment to any meal. Catering for a wide range of tastes, Budapest's **nightlife** is also very much of a draw. Generally trouble-free, welcoming and accessible, it ranges from outdoor nightclubs and backstreet music bars to *táncház* (dance houses) where Hungarians of all ages perform wild stamping movements to the rhythms of darkest Transylvania, and internationally renowned artists such as Márta Sebestyén appear in an informal setting.

There's plenty to offer in terms of **classical music and opera**, too: world-class ensembles and soloists can be enjoyed in the Palace of Arts' state-of-the-art concert hall or the grander, older settings of the Music Academy and State Opera House. For fans of **pop**, **rock** and **world music**, the two big events are the Budapesti Bucsú, first held to celebrate the departure of Soviet troops in 1991, and the huge **Sziget Festival**, which attracts many international stars.

A tribal nation

As a small, landlocked country whose language sets it apart from its neighbours, Hungary is a tribal nation, whose citizens still identify with their remote ancestors, pagan Magyar tribes from the Eurasian steppes who conquered the Carpathian Basin in 896 AD. Since the epochal Christmas Day when the Magyar ruler Vajk was baptized and crowned as King Stephen by a papal envoy, Hungary has identified itself with Europe whilst simultaneously remaining aware of its "otherness" – a sentiment reinforced by successive foreign occupations and the loss of much of its territory to neighbouring states: "this nation has already paid for its sins, past and future", asserts the national anthem.

The symbol of statehood is **St Stephen's Crown**, whose distinctive bent cross – caused by it being squashed in the eighteenth century – is a cherished sign of the vicissitudes that Hungary has endured, and features on the national **coat of arms** that you'll see everywhere in Budapest, from bridges and public buildings to posters and bumper stickers. The shield beneath the crown bears a Catholic cross of Lorraine, and the red and white "Árpád stripes" of the early Magyar tribal kings; today, the latter signify far-right loyalties, having formerly been employed as the flag of the Fascist Arrow Cross. Under Communism, the historic coat of arms was replaced by a Soviet star and ears of wheat; in the 1956 Uprising, people cut the hated symbol from Hungarian flags and proudly flew them with holes – something that still occurs at protests and commemorative ceremonies. When the People's Republic was renamed the Republic of Hungary in 1989, St Stephen's Crown returned to the coat of arms, but not to the national **flag** – which is a simple red, white and green tricolour with no ideological baggage.

What to see

Pest is where you're likely to spend most of your time, enjoying the streetlife, bars and shops within the **Belváros** (Inner City) and the surrounding districts. These surrounding areas are defined by two semicircular boulevards – the **Kiskörút** (Small Boulevard) and the **Nagykörút** (Great Boulevard) – and radial avenues such as Andrássy út and Rákóczi út. Exploring the area between them can easily occupy you for several days. In the financial and government centre of **Lipótváros**, interest lies in St Stephen's Basilica and the monumental Parliament building, which rivals the grand structures across the Danube. In **Terézváros**, Andrássy út leads out past the grandiose Opera House and the House of Terror to Hősök tere (Heroes' Square), a magnificent imperial set-piece where the Fine Arts Museum displays a first-rate collection of old European masters. Beyond, the **Városliget** (City Park) holds one of the finest zoos in Europe, both in terms of its animals and its architecture, as well as the hugely popular Széchenyi Baths, served by its own thermal springs.

Of Pest's remaining inner-city districts, **Erzsébetváros** and **Józsefváros** hold the most appeal. The former is Budapest's old Jewish quarter, with a rich and tragic history that's still palpable in the bullet-scarred backstreets behind the great synagogue on Dohány utca. From here, it's not far to the National Museum, a well-presented introduction to Hungarian history, and to the Great Market Hall, further round in **Ferencváros**, whose hinterland harbours the Applied Arts Museum and Holocaust Memorial Centre.

Várhegy (Castle Hill) on the **Buda** side was once the seat of Hungary's monarchs, and its palace, museums, churches and Baroque streets offer some absorbing sightseeing; the historic Turkish baths along the banks of the Danube are also well worth experiencing. In fine weather, people flock to **Margit-sziget**, the large, leafy island mid-river between Buda and Pest, to swim and sunbathe at enormous lidos and party through the night. Encircling the city to the west, the **Buda Hills** have a different kind of allure, with fun rides on the Cogwheel and Children's railways and chairlift, and intriguing caves to be visited. **Further out**, the steam trains of the Hungarian Railway History Park and the redundant Communist monuments within the Memento Park rate as major attractions.

◀ Applied Arts Museum

There is plenty to see on **excursions** from Budapest. Szentendre is a picturesque artists' colony with a superb open-air ethnographic museum. Further upriver, the Danube Bend offers gorgeous scenery, a Renaissance palace and citadel and an amazing treetop zip-ride at Visegrád, while Esztergom boasts its Basilica and medieval castle, a deluxe aqua-centre and a raft of festivals. Classical-music lovers will also enjoy concerts in the former Habsburg palace of Gödöllő, to the east of Budapest.

When to go

▼ View from Vár

The best times to visit Budapest are **spring** (late March to the end of May) and **autumn** (Sept–Oct), when the weather is mild and there are fewer tourists (though things tend to get busy during the **Budapest Spring Festival** in late March/early April). The majority of visitors come in the summer, when many residents decamp to Lake Balaton and those who remain flock to the city's pools and parks to escape the heat and dust. Though some concert halls are closed over summer, there are all kinds of outdoor events to compensate – especially in August, when the **Budapest Plázs** (Budapest Beach) turns one side of the Danube into a sandy resort, and the Sziget Festival and Formula One Grand Prix take place. Winter is cold and may be snowy, but you can still enjoy all the city's sights and cultural attractions (as well as trying roasted chestnuts from street vendors), while the thermal baths take on an extra allure. It's wise to book accommodation in advance for Christmas, New Year, the Spring Festival and Grand Prix.

Average daytime temperature, and average monthly rainfall

	Jan	Feb	Mar	Apr	May	June	July	Aug	Sept	Oct	Nov	Dec
°F	29	32	42	53	61	68	72	70	63	52	42	34
°C	-2	0	6	12	16	20	22	21	17	11	6	1
mm	37	44	38	45	72	69	56	47	33	57	70	46

things not to miss

It's not possible to see everything that Budapest has to offer in one trip – and we don't suggest you try. What follows is a selective taste of the region's highlights: magnificent Art Nouveau treasures, unique thermal baths, and world-class concerts and festivals. They're arranged in five colour-coded categories, which you can browse through to find the very best things to see and experience. All highlights have a page reference to take you straight into the Guide, where you can find out more.

01 Memento Park Page **126** • Imre Varga's revolutionary sailor is one of the highlights of the city's Communist statuary, now laid out in a park on the outskirts of Budapest.

02 Thermal baths Page **188** • Bathe in splendour at the city's spas, which are fed by hot springs.

03 Hospital in the Rock Page **97** • Revisit the Cold War in a nuclear bunker beneath Várhegy, formerly attached to a World War II field hospital.

04 Folk music Page **180** • Catch the irrepressible sounds of Muzsikás and other top bands on Budapest's dynamic folk circuit.

05 Coffee houses Page **167** • Ponder the world over a coffee and cake – after all, it's an old Central European tradition.

06 Gresham Palace Page **53** • Savour a cocktail or an apricot brandy amid the Art Nouveau elegance of this landmark hotel's foyer.

08 No. 2 tram ride Page **28** • This route along the Pest embankment affords stunning views of Buda.

07 Budapest Spring Festival Page **32** • The biggest arts event of the year includes music, dancing and theatre, as well as a grand parade.

09 Hungarian National Gallery Page **99** • Showcased In the imposing Buda Palace, this is Hungary's premier collection of home-grown art, from Gothic altar-pieces to Art Nouveau and abstract expressionism.

10 Margit-sziget Page **118** • A car-free refuge from the hustle of the city: go swimming, jogging or picnic on the grass during the day, or hit the island's outdoor bars after dark.

11 Wine Page **158** • Every region of Hungary has its own variety, to be enjoyed in bars or cafés, or at the round of annual wine festivals, where it's sold by the cask or jerry-can as well as by bottle.

12 Sikló funicular Page **104** • Take the scenic way up to Várhegy and watch the views unfold as you rise above the rooftops.

13 Hungarian Railway History Park Page **125** • Both children and adults will enjoy this extensive collection of vintage trains – you can even drive a steam locomotive.

14 Sziget Festival Page **180** • Hungary's Glastonbury, the mid-August festival on Óbudai-sziget draws music fans from across Europe.

15 House of Terror Page **66** • A dramatic memorial-museum to the victims of state repression, occupying the former headquarters of the Fascist and Communist secret police.

16 Libegő chairlift

Page **123** • A unique and wonderfully silent way to ride up the Buda Hills, with great views over the city from the top.

17 Holocaust Memorial Centre Page **88** • Harrowing audiovisual material and artefacts attesting to the persecution of Jews and Roma from 1920 to 1945.

18 Várhegy Page **92** • Its medieval Mátyás Church, Baroque houses and Buda Palace make Castle Hill a must-see for any visitor.

19 Classical concerts Page **178** • High-class musicianship throughout the year, often in dramatic venues.

20 Budapest's cemeteries Pages **85**, **86**, **124** & **126** • A wander through the tombs offers such rewards as the hideously ugly Pantheon of the Working Class at Kerepesi and the gorgeous azure-tiled Schmidl tomb in the Jewish Cemetery.

21 Budapest Zoo Page **80** • Feed the giraffes, tickle the rhinos and marvel at the magnificent Art Nouveau buildings – the Elephant and Palm Houses are particularly impressive.

22 Fun Extreme Canopy Page **139** • Zip-wire down through the forested Visegrád Hills to a cluster of "organic" buildings.

23 Jewish quarter Page **68** • Atmospheric Erzsébetváros, with its synagogues and kosher businesses, is still the city's Jewish quarter.

24 Food markets Page **198** • Stock up on paprika, sausages and salami at Budapest's atmospheric market halls.

25 Museum of Fine Arts Page **75** • El Greco, Raphael, Gauguin and Austrian Symbolists – this museum of pan-European art has them all.

Basics

Basics

Getting there 19

Arrival 23

Getting around 25

The media 31

Festivals 32

Culture and etiquette 34

Travelling with children 35

Travel essentials 35

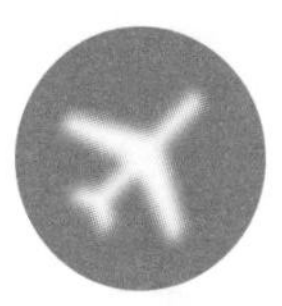

Getting there

Budapest is an extremely popular city-break destination, with a growing number of operators offering trips; it's also included on some two- or three-centre itineraries, usually combined with Prague and Vienna. Several airlines fly to Budapest from airports in the UK and Ireland, and there are also nonstop flights from the US and Canada. Travelling overland from the UK takes around a day by train, or a day and a half by bus.

Airfares always depend on the **season**, with the highest fares from June to August, when the weather is best. You'll get the best prices during the low season, November to February (excluding Christmas and New Year when prices are hiked up and seats are at a premium).

Flights from the US and Canada

Delta fly **nonstop** to Budapest from New York all year round, with flights lasting around eight and a half hours. Other European carriers will get you to Budapest via their hub city, so it's easy to connect with Budapest flights from elsewhere within the US or Canada.

Fares from the **US** to Budapest are typically US$750 from New York and US$900 from west coast cities in low season, rising by around $600 in high season. From **Canada**, fares rise from Can$1000 to at least Can$1600 in high season. Flights take around twelve hours in low season with at least one change.

Flights from the UK and Ireland

The cost of flying to Budapest **from the UK** has been sharply reduced since several **low-cost operators** – easyJet, Jet2, Ryanair and the Hungarian Wizz Air at the time of writing – started direct flights to the city. Tickets with these airlines go for around £50 return, or sometimes even less, including tax. As flights fill up quickly, you'll need to book a couple of months ahead during summer; moreover, the earlier you book, the cheaper the ticket is likely to be.

British Airways and Malév fly direct daily from Heathrow and Gatwick in two hours forty minutes. EasyJet goes from Gatwick and Luton, and Wizz Air from Luton only. Ryanair has flights from Bristol, East Midlands, Glasgow Prestwick and Liverpool – but note that their flights from Stansted go to Balaton airport, a good two-hour drive away from central Budapest. Jet2 has summer-only flights from Manchester. You can also get good deals by flying via cities in Europe with carriers such as Lufthansa and KLM – especially if you're leaving from regional airports in the UK. From Ireland, Aer Lingus and Malév fly daily between Dublin and Budapest, and Ryanair has five flights a week from Dublin – flights take three hours.

Scheduled fares from London (flight time 2hr 30min) start at around £200 in high season and £120 in low season, and from **Ireland** (3hr) at around €150 in low season.

Flights from Australia, New Zealand and South Africa

There are no direct flights to Hungary from Australia, New Zealand or South Africa; the best option is to fly to a western European gateway and get a connecting flight from there. A standard return **fare** to Budapest with Qantas from eastern **Australia** via Frankfurt is around A$2600 in low season, rising to A$3500 in high season. From **New Zealand**, a standard return ticket via London with Air New Zealand costs around NZ$3500 in low season, NZ$4000 in high season. Flying from South Africa, you can get return flights for R8900 in low season and R9600 in high season.

Fly less – stay longer! Travel and climate change

Climate change is perhaps the single biggest issue facing our planet. It is caused by a build-up in the atmosphere of carbon dioxide and other greenhouse gases, which are emitted by many sources – including planes. Already, **flights** account for three to four percent of human-induced global warming: that figure may sound small, but it is rising year on year and threatens to counteract the progress made by reducing greenhouse emissions in other areas.

Rough Guides regard travel as a **global benefit**, and feel strongly that the advantages to developing economies are important, as are the opportunities for greater contact and awareness among peoples. But we also believe in travelling responsibly, which includes giving thought to how often we fly and what we can do to redress any harm that our trips may create.

We can travel less or simply reduce the amount we travel by air (taking fewer trips and staying longer, or taking the train if there is one); we can avoid night flights (which are more damaging); and we can make the trips we do take "climate neutral" via a carbon offset scheme. **Offset schemes** run by climatecare.org, carbonneutral .com and others allow you to "neutralize" the greenhouse gases that you are responsible for releasing. Their websites have simple calculators that let you work out the impact of any flight – as does our own. Once that's done, you can pay to fund projects that will reduce future emissions by an equivalent amount. Please take the time to visit our website and make your trip climate neutral, or get a copy of the *Rough Guide to Climate Change* for more detail on the subject.

www.roughguides.com/climatechange

Trains

Getting to Budapest by **train** is likely to be considerably more expensive than flying, and the shortest journey from London's St Pancras International to Budapest is nineteen hours. This is with Eurostar to Paris and then by TGV on to Munich – it's slightly more expensive but involves the fewest changes. A standard second-class **return ticket** on this route costs around £350, but booking ahead can reduce it to less than £200; there are discounts for students, and those under 26 or over 60. Going via Brussels and Cologne is slightly cheaper: it involves more changing trains and takes up to 24 hours but the views along the Rhine Valley are delightful. Deutsche Bahn is the best option for making seat reservations on continental trains and its website (see p.22) is an excellent resource for checking railway timetables, while the website of The Man in Seat Sixty-One is an excellent source of information on most aspects of rail travel in Europe.

A **train pass from** Inter-Rail (Ⓦwww .interrail.net) or Eurail (Ⓦwww.eurail.com) – both cover Hungary – makes it convenient to take in the country as part of a wider rail trip around Europe.

Bus and coach

The **bus** journey to Budapest from London takes 24–27 hours. A standard return fare (valid for six months) with Eurolines costs around £110, but regular promotional offers can bring this down to as low as £70. The Eurolines buses are air-conditioned and have on-board toilets. The usual route is to take the ferry across the Channel to Calais and then on via Brussels and Vienna.

By car

Driving to Hungary from the UK can be a pleasant proposition if you want to make stops in other places along the way. The most direct route to Budapest is through the Channel Tunnel and then on motorways through Brussels, Aachen, Cologne, Frankfurt, Nürnberg, Linz and Vienna. It's a distance of 1500km. Some people drive it nonstop in 24 hours but you are better off planning on at least two days in case you meet delays. The days of rigorous border checks as you cross over from Austria at Hegyeshalom are long gone – normally you just have to slow down to 50kmh as you drive past the old checkpoints. However, there are delays at peak times – such as during the Grand Prix in August or when guest workers are returning home from Germany to southeast Europe. The main cause for the queues is the need to buy a motorway sticker (*matrica*) – compulsory if you are driving on Hungarian motorways and costing from 1200Ft in low season, October–April, and 2530Ft otherwise, for four days; Ⓦwww.motorway.hu. Fines start at 15,300Ft if you don't have one. You can buy the sticker online ahead of travelling, or at one of the petrol stations in Austria before you cross the border, which should reduce any waiting. See p.29 for- information on driving in Budapest.

Online booking

Ⓦ**www.expedia.co.uk** (in UK), Ⓦ**www.expedia.com** (in US), Ⓦ**www.expedia.ca** (in Canada)
Ⓦ**www.lastminute.com** (in UK)
Ⓦ**www.opodo.co.uk** (in UK)
Ⓦ**www.orbitz.com** (in US)
Ⓦ**www.travelocity.co.uk** (in UK), Ⓦ**www.travelocity.com** (in US), Ⓦ**www.travelocity.ca** (in Canada), Ⓦ**www.travelocity.co.nz** (in New Zealand)
Ⓦ**www.travelonline.co.za** (in South Africa)
Ⓦ**www.zuji.com.au** (in Australia)

Airlines

Aer Lingus Republic of Ireland Ⓣ0818/365 000, New Zealand Ⓣ1649/308 3355, South Africa Ⓣ1-272/2168-32838, UK Ⓣ0870/876 5000, US & Canada Ⓣ1-800/IRISH-AIR; Ⓦwww.aerlingus.com.
Air France US Ⓣ1-800/237-2747, Canada Ⓣ1-800/667-2747, UK Ⓣ0870/142 4343, Australia Ⓣ1300/390 190, South Africa Ⓣ0861/340 340; Ⓦwww.airfrance.com.
Air New Zealand Ⓣ0800/737 000, Australia Ⓣ0800/132 476, UK Ⓣ0800/028 4149, Republic of Ireland Ⓣ1800/551 447, USA Ⓣ1-800/262-1234, Canada Ⓣ1-800/663-5494; Ⓦwww.airnz.co.nz.
British Airways US & Canada Ⓣ1-800/AIRWAYS, UK Ⓣ0844/493 0787, Republic of Ireland Ⓣ1890/626 747, Australia Ⓣ1300/767 177, New Zealand Ⓣ09/966 9777, South Africa Ⓣ114/418 600; Ⓦwww.ba.com.
Delta US & Canada Ⓣ1-800/221-1212, UK Ⓣ0845/600 0950, Republic of Ireland Ⓣ1850/882 031 or 01/407 3165, Australia Ⓣ1300/302 849, New Zealand Ⓣ09/977 2232; Ⓦwww.delta.com.
easyJet UK Ⓣ0905/821 0905, Ⓦwww.easyjet.com.
Jet2 UK Ⓣ0871/226 1737, Republic of Ireland Ⓣ0818/200 017; Ⓦwww.jet2.com.
KLM (Royal Dutch Airlines) US & Canada Ⓣ1-800/225-2525, UK Ⓣ0870/507 4074, Republic of Ireland Ⓣ1850/747 400, Australia Ⓣ1300/392 192, New Zealand Ⓣ09/921 6040, South Africa Ⓣ0860/247 747; Ⓦwww.klm.com.
Lufthansa US Ⓣ1-800/399-5838, Canada Ⓣ1-800/563-5954, UK Ⓣ0871/945 9747, Republic of Ireland Ⓣ01/844 5544, Australia Ⓣ1300/655 727, New Zealand Ⓣ0800/945 220, South Africa Ⓣ0861/842 538; Ⓦwww.lufthansa.com.
Malév Hungarian Airlines US Ⓣ1-800/223-6884, Canada Ⓣ11-866/379-7313, UK Ⓣ0870/909 0577, Republic of Ireland Ⓣ0818/555 577; Ⓦwww.malev.hu.
Qantas Airways US & Canada Ⓣ1-800/227-4500, UK Ⓣ0845/774 7767, Republic of Ireland Ⓣ01/407 3278, Australia Ⓣ13 13 13, New Zealand Ⓣ0800/808 767 or 09/357 8900, South Africa Ⓣ11/441 8550; Ⓦwww.qantas.com.
Ryanair UK Ⓣ0871/246 0000, Republic of Ireland Ⓣ0818/303 030, Ⓦwww.ryanair.com.
South African AirwaysⓉ11/978 1111, US & Canada Ⓣ1-800/722-9675, UK Ⓣ0870/747 1111, Australia Ⓣ1300/435 972, New Zealand Ⓣ09/977 2237; Ⓦwww.flysaa.com.
Wizz Air UK Ⓣ 0904/475 9500, Republic of Ireland Ⓣ1550/475 970; Ⓦwizzair.com.

Agents and operators

Cox & Kings UK Ⓣ020/7873 5000, Ⓦwww.coxandkings.co.uk. Upmarket cultural trips to Budapest staying in five-star hotels: a four-night break starts at £520 including flights, transfers and breakfast (£170 more for three nights in the Four Seasons hotel), and there's a ten-night trip (from £2345, including flights, transfers and breakfast) that also takes in Vienna and Prague.
Danube Travel Australia Ⓣ03/9530 0888, Ⓦwww.danubetravel.com.au. Regional specialists whose offers include spa packages from Australia to Budapest, two-night breaks from A$272 per person, one week from A$699 per person (prices include half board and some treatments but not flights).
ebookers UK Ⓣ0871/223 5000, Republic of Ireland Ⓣ01/431 1311, Ⓦwww.ebookers.com; www.ebookers.ie. Low fares on an extensive selection of scheduled flights and package deals.
Forum International Travel US Ⓣ1-800/252-4475, Ⓦwww.foruminternational.com. Easy seven-day self-guided cycling tours from Vienna to Budapest staying in family pensions and hotels (from US$655

including bicycle rental and accommodation but no flights), and a Danube Bike and River Cruise (Passau–Vienna–Budapest; from US$630). Available April/May to Sept.

Great Escapes ⓣ0845/330 2084 ⓦwww.greatescapes.co.uk. Good-value city breaks in a range of hotels, starting at £280 for a four-night trip including flights from the UK.

Kirker Holidays UK ⓣ020/7593 2288, ⓦwww.kirkerholidays.co.uk. Three-night cultural breaks in a four-star hotel from £423 per person, including flights from the UK. They can reserve opera tickets and arrange walking tours of the city.

Martin Randall Travel UK ⓣ020/8742 3355, ⓦwww.martinrandall.com. Well-respected art, architecture and music tours led by a lecturer covering, for example, the Spring Festival and Budapest at Christmas. Prices for a seven-day trip are from around £1500, which includes flights from the UK, hotels, transfers, excursions, concert tickets and some meals.

North South Travel UK ⓣ01245/608 291, ⓦwww.northsouthtravel.co.uk. Friendly, competitive travel agency, offering discounted fares worldwide. Profits are used to support projects in the developing world, especially the promotion of sustainable tourism.

Osprey City Holidays UK ⓣ0845/310 3031, ⓦwww.ospreyholidays.com. Two-night breaks in one of three excellent and central hotels from £240 per person, including travel from London Heathrow.

Page & Moy UK ⓣ0116/217 8006, ⓦwww.pageandmoy.com/motorracing. Organizes breaks to see the Hungarian Grand Prix in Aug – three nights from £699 per person, including flights from the UK.

Regent Holidays UK ⓣ0117/921 1711, ⓦwww.regent-holidays.co.uk. Eastern European specialists offering three-night city breaks (from £292, including flights from the UK) and tailor-made itineraries.

Stag Republic UK ⓣ0800/027 4836, ⓦwww.stagrepublic.co.uk. A Budapest-based operation that arranges stag packages that can include Trabant treks, quad biking, visits to the baths and stag dinners. Prices start from £99 per person for a minimum of six people for two nights (including accommodation, transfers and pub crawl but not flights and activities).

STA Travel US ⓣ1-800/781-4040, UK ⓣ0871/230 0040, Australia ⓣ13 47 82, New Zealand ⓣ0800/474 400, South Africa ⓣ0861/781 781; ⓦwww.statravel.com. Worldwide specialists in independent travel; also student IDs, travel insurance, car rental, rail passes, and more. Good discounts for students and under-26s.

Thermalia Travel UK ⓣ0870/165 9420, ⓦwww.thermalia.co.uk. Spa holiday specialists offering stays centred around health and fitness at four-star thermal resorts in Budapest. Prices from around £720 for seven nights, including flights from the UK and Ireland.

Trailfinders UK ⓣ0845/058 5858, Republic of Ireland ⓣ01/677 7888; ⓦwww.trailfinders.com. One of the best-informed and most efficient agents for independent travellers.

Rail contacts

Deutsche Bahn UK ⓣ0871/880 8066, ⓦwww.bahn.co.uk.

European Rail UK ⓣ020/7619 1083, ⓦwww.europeanrail.com.

Eurostar UK ⓣ0870/518 6186, outside UK ⓣ0044/12336 17575, ⓦwww.eurostar.com.

The Man in Seat 61 ⓦwww.seat61.com.

Rail Europe US ⓣ1-888/382-7245, Canada ⓣ1-800/361-7245, UK ⓣ0844/848 4064, Australia ⓣ03/9642 8644, South Africa ⓣ11/628 2319, ⓦwww.raileurope.co.uk.

Bus contacts

Eurolines UK ⓣ0871/781 8181, ⓦwww.nationalexpress.com/eurolines.

Arrival

Other than the airport, all points of arrival are fairly central; most are within walking distance or just a few stops by metro from downtown Pest. There are accommodation-booking services at the airport and the Keleti train station.

Budapest's excellent **public transport** system ensures that few parts of the city are more than thirty-minutes' journey from the centre; many places can be reached in half that time. The city's three metro lines and three main roads meet at the major junction of Deák tér in Pest, making this the main transport hub of the city (a **transport map** appears at the back of this book).

By air

Ferihegy Airport, 20km southeast of the centre, has three passenger terminals. Ferihegy 1 has been renovated and now serves as the terminal for no-frills airlines. Ferihegy 2A and 2B are the other side of the airport, ten-minutes' drive further out: Terminal 2A serves countries covered by the Schengen Agreement (including Austria, Belgium, Denmark, Finland, France, Germany, Iceland, Italy, Greece, Luxembourg, Netherlands, Norway, Portugal, Spain and Sweden), while Ferihegy 2B covers the rest of the world (the UK, USA, Romania, etc). Terminal 1 handles both Schengen and non-Schengen traffic. Before leaving, it is worth checking which terminal you're flying from, as the Schengen divide was introduced in March 2008 and might be subject to revision. There are **ATMs** and tourist information desks in all the terminal buildings.

The easiest – and most expensive – way to get into the centre is an **airport taxi**. Now run by Zóna taxi, these charge a fixed fee to different zones (you'll pay around 5300Ft or €25 to the centre), and also offer return fares. Alternatively, Ferihegy's Tourinform offices (daily 8am–11pm) can help with booking an ordinary city cab around 5000Ft). A cheaper option is the **Airport Shuttle** (ⓣ1/296-8555, ⓦwww.airportshuttle.hu) minibus, which will take you directly to any address in the city. Tickets (2990Ft single, 4990Ft return; discounts available for groups of two or more) can be bought in the luggage claim hall while you are waiting for your bags, or in the main concourse; you give the address you're heading to and then have to wait five to twenty minutes until the driver calls your destination.

Public transport might be more inconvenient but it's not much slower, and it's certainly cheaper. Bus #200 departs every fifteen minutes from the stop between terminals 2A and 2B via terminal 1 to Kőbánya-Kispest metro station; from here, you can switch to the blue metro line to get to the centre. Total journey time is about thirty minutes from terminal 1 and 45 minutes from 2A and 2B, and both bus and metro tickets cost 270Ft each if bought from the newsagents in the terminals or from the machine by the bus stop. Buying a bus ticket from the driver on board will cost you 350Ft.

The quickest and cheapest route into the centre is to catch a mainline train from the station across the road from Ferihegy 1, which takes you to Nyugati Station for a mere 300Ft (discounts with Budapest Card); journey time is 22 minutes. You buy tickets at the Tourinform desk inside the terminal building, and trains go every half hour. Trains from Nyugati Station to the airport leave on the hour and 35 past the hour. You can get tickets – ask for tickets to Ferihegy – from the ticket offices by platform 13; the information window should be able to say which platform to go to. You'll want a train to Monor, Cegléd and Szolnok. Ferihegy 1 is the stop after Kőbánya-Kispest, and is poorly signed. You should also note that if the lifts are not working it is fifty steps up and down to get over the tracks to terminal 1 (and the stop for bus #200 if you're departing from 2A or 2B).

By train

The Hungarian word *pályaudvar* (abbreviated "*pu.*" in writing) is used to designate a **train station**. Of the six in Budapest, only three are important for tourists, but note that their names, which are sometimes translated into English, refer to the direction of services handled rather than their location.

Most international trains terminate at Pest's **Keleti Station**, on Baross tér in the VIII district. It's something of a hangout for thieves and hustlers, and there are often police about checking people's ID. There are usually plenty of touts offering accommodation as international trains arrive. The most reliable of several hostel-booking agencies here is Mellow Mood (daily: June–Aug 7am–midnight; Sept–May 7am–8pm; ⓣ1/343-0748 or 1/413-2062, ⓦwww.mellowmood.hu), whose offices are to the right of the big glass doorways at the far end of the station. They also organize transport to their hostels, and should be able to offer other city information, too. Otherwise, head for the Tourinform office at Deák tér (see p.41). Unmarked **taxis** lining the road outside the doors of the Keleti Station are worth avoiding, especially if their drivers are wearing badges saying "official taxi", as these are the most likely to rip off unsuspecting tourists. Instead, look out for taxis from the companies listed on p.29, such as Fotaxi, which you can find by going out of the main doors and turning right. In summer there are long queues at the 24-hour left-luggage office by platform 6 (300Ft or 600Ft for 24hr depending on bag size, half that amount for six hours); the lockers there (300Ft for 24hr) are a better bet if they are not closed for security reasons.

Nyugati Station, north of central Pest in the VI district, is the mainline link to Ferihegy airport. It has a 24-hour left-luggage office (300Ft or 600Ft for 24hr) next to the ticket office beside platform 13. To reach Deák tér, take the blue metro line two stops in the direction of Kőbánya-Kispest.

Some trains from Vienna arrive at **Déli Station**, 500m behind the Vár in Buda, which has left-luggage facilities but no tourist office. It's four stops from Deák tér on the red metro line.

By bus or hydrofoil

International buses and services from the Great Plain and Transdanubia terminate at the **Népliget bus station**, 5km southeast of the centre at Üllői út 131 in the IX district. Adjacent to Népliget train station, the bus station is six stops from Deák tér on the blue metro line. If you are taking a taxi, your best bet is one of the taxi companies listed on p.29, as unmarked taxis are more likely to rip you off. There is no tourist office here but the station staff should be able to help you order a regular taxi, which will cost around 2000Ft to the centre – there is no fixed tariff for the ride from here.

Of the other bus stations, the **Árpád híd** in the XIII district (on the blue metro line) is the jumping-off point for buses to and from Szentendre and the Danube Bend; the **Stadion bus station** in the XIV district (on the red metro line) serves the Northern Uplands and the **Etele tér bus station** in the XI district (take buses #7 or #7E to the centre) serves the Buda hinterland. None of the city's bus stations has any tourist facilities.

Hydrofoils (Mahart ⓣ1/484-4010 or 4050, ⓦwww.mahartpassnave.hu) from Vienna (April–Oct) dock at the **international landing stage**, on the Belgrád rakpart (embankment), near downtown Pest.

By car

Most drivers enter Budapest along the M1 motorway from Vienna via Hegyeshalom, which is a busy road, heavily policed to fine speeding foreigners. It approaches Budapest from the southwest, and goes straight through to Erzsébet híd in the centre, with turn-offs signed to Petőfi híd in the south of the centre, and Moszkva tér and Margít híd to the north.

Getting around

Budapest's metro trains, buses and trams reach most areas of interest to tourists, while the outer suburbs are well served by the overground HÉV rail network. Services operate generally between 5am and 11pm, and there are also night-time buses covering much of the city. Locals will tell you that standards are falling, and more cuts in services are certainly expected, but public transport is still efficient and covers most of the city.

At the time of writing there is a whole array of **tickets** available for use on public transport, but since validating your ticket can be complex and is easy to forget, it's best to get a **travel pass** if you're staying for more than half a day. The ticket system is expected to be radically changed from January 2009, with new tickets and higher prices so it is worth checking the wesite of the **Budapest Transport Company** (BKV; Ⓦwww.bkv.hu) for information on routes and prices before travelling.

Budapest addresses

Finding your way around Budapest is easier than the welter of names might suggest. Districts and streets are well signposted, and those in Pest conform to an overall plan based on radial avenues and semicircular boulevards.

Budapest is divided into 23 districts, numbered using Roman numerals. Except when addressing letters, a Budapest **address** always begins with the district number, a system used throughout this book. On letters, a four-digit **postal code** is used instead, the middle two digits indicating the district (so that 1054 refers to a place in the V district). For ease of reference, we list below the district numbers you're most likely to encounter, along with some of the areas within those districts that represent the ones which you're most likely to be visiting:

I	Várhegy and Viziváros
II	Rószadomb and Hűvösvölgy
III	Óbuda and Aquincum
IV	Újpest
V	Belváros and Lipótváros
VI	Terézváros
VII	Erzsébetváros
VIII	Józsefváros
IX	Ferencváros
X	Kőbánya
XI	The area south and east of Gellért-hegy
XII	The area from Várhegy west into the Buda Hills
XIII	Újlipótváros and Angyalföld
XIV	Városliget and Zugló
XXII	Budafok and Nagytétény

As a rule of thumb, **street numbers** ascend away from the north–south axis of the River Danube and the east–west axis of Rákóczi út/Kossuth utca/Hegyalja út. Even numbers are generally on the left-hand side as you head outwards from these axes, odd numbers on the right. One number may refer to several premises or an entire apartment building, while an additional combination of numerals denotes the floor and number of individual **apartments** (eg Kossuth utca 14.III.24). Confusingly, some old buildings in Pest are designated as having a half-floor (*félemelet*) or upper ground floor (*magas földszint*) between the ground (*földszint*) and first floor (*elsőemelet*) proper – so that what the British would call the second floor, and Americans the third, Hungarians might describe as the first. This stems from a nineteenth-century taxation fiddle, whereby landlords avoided the higher tax on buildings with more than three floors.

Tickets and passes

Standard single **tickets** valid for the metro, buses, trams, trolleybuses, the Cogwheel Railway (see p.121) and suburban HÉV lines (up to the edge of the city) cost 270Ft per journey and are sold at metro stations, newspaper kiosks and tobacconists. Metro tickets also come in a variety of other types, depending on whether you are changing trains and how many stops you want to go: a metro section ticket (220Ft) takes you three stops on the same line; a metro transfer ticket (420Ft) is valid for as many stops as you like with one line change. Tickets bought on board buses and trolleybuses (*helyszini vonaljegy*) cost 350Ft.

The standard single ticket is not valid on night buses: you have to buy a 350Ft *helyszini vonaljegy* separately – on board or from a ticket machine – unless you have a day or weekly pass (see below). Books of ten standard single tickets (*tíz-darabos gyüjtőjegy* – 2350Ft) are also available – these are still valid if torn out of the book but cannot be used on night services.

Tickets must be **validated** when you use them. On the metro and HÉV you punch them in the machines at station entrances (remember to validate a new ticket if you change lines, unless you have a metro transfer ticket); on trams, buses and trolleybuses, you punch the tickets on board in the small red or orange machines.

Day **passes** (*napijegy*) cost 1550Ft and are valid for unlimited travel from midnight to midnight on the metro, buses, trams, trolleybuses, the Cogwheel Railway and suburban HÉV lines; three-day passes cost 3400Ft and weekly passes 4000Ft. **Season tickets** cost 5300Ft for two weeks and 8250Ft for a month, and are available from metro stations, but you'll need a passport photo for the accompanying photocard; there are photo booths inside the entrance of Deák tér and Moszkva tér stations.

Children up to the age of 6 travel free on all public transport. EU citizens over the age of 65 also travel free, but must show proof of age if challenged by inspectors, who may not understand if you simply tell them that you don't need a ticket.

Bear in mind that there are active **pickpocket** battalions on the metro (especially the yellow line) and the city buses and trams. Gangs distract their victims by pushing them or blocking their way, and empty their pockets or bags at the same time. Also beware of bogus ticket inspectors "working" the transport system and demanding money from passengers. Genuine inspectors wear blue armbands and usually work in twos or threes.

The metro

The Budapest **metro** has three lines, usually referred to by their colour and shown on the colour map at the end of this book; they intersect at Deák tér in downtown Pest. A fourth line is under construction between Keleti Station and Etele tér: its completion is scheduled for 2012, but few expect it to be ready in time. Trains run at two- to twelve-minute intervals. There's little risk of going astray once you've learned to recognize the signs *bejárat* (entrance), *kijárat* (exit), *vonal* (line) and *felé* (towards). The train's direction

Just the ticket

It's worth bearing in mind that **ticket regulations** on Budapest's public transport are subject to regular changes, and the myriad rules make it easy to catch foreigners out – many readers have complained about the treatment meted out by inspectors (who wear blue armbands saying *jegyellenőr*), who can be unpleasant and tend to be strict in levying 6000Ft fines for travelling without a valid ticket. The easiest way to get fined is to fail to validate your ticket at metro entrances or when changing lines. If you have a season ticket but are not carrying it when stopped, the fine is higher, though most of it is refunded upon presentation of the season ticket within three days at the BKV office at VII, Akácfa utca 22 (but only if your pass is valid for the day before and the day after the day you were fined). If you feel you've been fined unfairly you can try taking your complaint to the office at Akácfa utca 18 (Mon–Fri 8am–5pm, Wed open till 6pm).

Budapest Card

Your tourist pass for 48 or 72 hours

- unlimited travel on public transport
- free or discounted admission to 60+ museums and selected sights
- discounted admission to selected cultural and folklore programmes
- discounted city sightseeing tours
- discounted admission or reductions to thermal baths, in restaurants, shops and numerous other services

The Budapest Card is on sale in hotels, tourist information offices, travel agencies, and main underground ticket offices.

Purchase your Budapest Card online at **www.budapestinfo.hu**

is indicated by the name of the station at the end of the line, and drivers announce the next stop between stations.

Buses, trams and trolleybuses

There is a good **bus** (*autóbusz*) network across the city, especially in Buda, where Moszkva tér (on the red metro line) and Móricz Zsigmond körtér (southwest of Gellért-hegy) are the main terminals. Bus stops are marked by a picture of a bus on a white background in a blue frame, and have timetables underneath; most buses run every ten to twenty minutes (*utolsó kocsi indul* … means "the last one leaves …"). On busier lines express buses – with an E at the end of the number – run along the same route making fewer stops: for example, the bus #7E that runs along most of the route of the #7. **Night buses** have three-digit numbers beginning with a 9 and run every hour or half-hour from around midnight or whenever the service they replace finishes: so the #906 follows the route of the #6 tram on the Nagykörút from half past midnight, when the tram stops, until 4.15am.

The network of yellow (or the newer orange) **trams** (*villamos*) is smaller, but they provide a crucial service round the Nagykörút

Useful bus, tram and trolleybus routes (listed with key stops)

Buses

#7 Bosnyák tér–Keleti Station–Móricz Zsigmond körtér (via Rákóczi út, Ferenciek tere, *Gellért Hotel*, Rudas Baths).

#16A Moszkva tér–Dísz tér (Castle District).

#16 Erzsébet tér–Dísz tér (Castle District)–Bécsi kapu tér–Moszkva tér.

#26 Nyugati Station–Szent István körút–Margit-sziget–Árpád híd metro station.

#27 Móricz Zsigmond körtér–Gellért-hegy.

#56 Moszkva tér–Szilágyi Erzsébet fasor–Huvősvölgy.

#65 Kolosy tér–Pálvölgyi Caves–Fenyőgyöngye restaurant at the bottom of Hármashatár-hegy.

#86 Southern Buda–Gellért tér–the Víziváros–Flórián tér (Óbuda).

#105 Apor Vilmos tér–Lanchíd–Deák tér–Gyöngyösi utca.

#116 Fény utca market–Moszkva tér– Dísz tér (Castle District).

Night buses

#906 Moszkva tér–Margit-sziget–Nyugati Station–Great Boulevard–Móricz Zsigmond körtér.

#907 Örs vezér tere–Bosnyák tér–Keleti Station–Erzsébet híd–Etele tér (Kelenföld).

#914 and **#950** Kispest (Határ út metro station)–Deák tér–Lehel tér–Újpest, along the route of the blue metro and on to the north and south.

Trams

#2 Margit Bridge–Petőfi híd (along embankment)–Közvágóhíd HÉV Station.

#4 Moszkva tér–Margit-sziget–Nyugati Station–Nagykörut–Petőfi Bridge–Október 23 utca.

#6 Moszkva tér–Margit-sziget–Nyugati Station–Great Boulevard–Petőfi híd–Móricz Zsigmond körtér.

#19 Batthyány tér–the Víziváros–Kelenföld Station.

#47 Deák tér–Szabadság híd–*Gellért Hotel*–Móricz Zsigmond körtér–Budafok.

#56 Móricz Zsigmond körtér–Villányi út–Moszkva tér–Huvősvölgy.

Trolleybuses

#72 Arany János utca metro station–Nyugati Station–Zoo–Széchenyi Baths–Petőfi Csarnok–Thököly út.

#74 Dohány utca (outside the Main Synagogue)–Városliget.

and along the Pest embankment. **Trolleybuses** (*trolibusz*) mostly operate northeast of the centre near the Városliget. Interestingly, their route numbers start at 70 because the first trolleybus line was inaugurated on Stalin's 70th birthday in 1949. Trolleybus #83 was started in 1961, when Stalin would have been 83.

To get off buses, trams and trolleybuses, press the button above the door or on the handrail beside the door before the bus reaches the stop, which alerts the driver to open the door. On a very few trams, such as #2, you may have to open the doors yourself, pressing the button by the doors.

Most modern buses, trams and trolleybuses have dot displays that tell you the name of the next stop, and the driver may also mumble it.

See p.42 and 35 for information on disabled access and travelling with pushchairs.

HÉV trains

The green overground **HÉV trains** provide easy access to Budapest's suburbs, running at least four times an hour between 6.30am and 11pm. As far as tourists are concerned, the most useful line is the one from **Batthyány tér** (on the red metro line) out to **Szentendre**, which passes through Óbuda, Aquincum and Rómaifürdő. The other lines originate in Pest, with one running northeast from **Örs vezér tere** (also on the red metro line) to **Gödölllő** via the Formula One racing track at Mogyoród; another southwards from Boráros tér at the Pest end of Petőfi híd to Csepel; and the third from **Közvagóhíd** (bus #23 or #54 from Boráros tér) to **Ráckeve**.

Ferries and other transport

Although **ferries** play little useful part in Budapest's transport system, they do offer an enjoyable ride. From May to September there are boats along the Danube between Boráros tér (by Petőfi híd) and Batthyány tér up to Jászai Mari tér and Rómaifürdő. These run every fifteen to thirty minutes between 7am and 7pm, and cost between 200Ft (for going from Pest across to the Margit-sziget) and 600Ft. Ferry tickets can be obtained from kiosks (where timetables are posted) or machines at the docks.

In the Buda Hills, there's also the **Cogwheel Railway** (Fogaskerekűvasút, now officially designated as tram #60), the **Children's Railway** (Gyermekvasút), and the **chairlift** (*libegő*) between Zugliget and János-hegy; see chapter 9 for details. Note that BKV tickets and passes are valid only for the Cogwheel Railway – for the others, you'll need to buy tickets at the point of departure or on board.

Taxis

Budapest's registered **taxis** are cheap and plentiful, and are recognizable by their yellow number plates; make sure your taxi has a meter that is visible and switched on when you get in, and that the rates are clearly displayed. **Fares** begin at 300Ft, and the price per-kilometre is around 250Ft.

Taxis can be flagged down on the street, and there are **ranks** throughout the city; you can hop into whichever cab you choose – don't feel you have to opt for the one at the front of the line if it looks at all dodgy. For a cheaper rate, order a cab by phone. The best companies are the established ones: Citytaxi (ⓣ1/211-1111, ⓦwww.citytaxi.hu), whose cars have yellow shield logos; Főtaxi (ⓣ1/222-2222), with red-and-white chequerboard and oval lights on their car roofs; Tele-5-taxi (ⓣ1/355-5555) and Volántaxi (ⓣ1/466-6666); the first two are the most likely to have English-speaking dispatchers.

Foreigners are easy prey for **rogue taxi drivers**, so avoid unmarked private cars, and drivers hanging around the stations and airport. There are also a few fake Fő- and Citytaxis, sporting poor copies of their logos.

Driving

All things considered, **driving** in Budapest can't be recommended. Road manners are nonexistent, parking spaces are scarce and traffic jams are frequent, while the Pest side of the Lánchíd (Chain Bridge) and the roundabout before the tunnel under the Vár are notorious for collisions – and careering trams, bumpy cobbles, swerving lane markings and unexpected one-way systems make things worse. In addition, access to the Castle District and parts of the Belváros are strictly limited.

If you do decide to take the plunge, there are a few **rules of the road** to bear in mind.

City tours

If you're hard-pressed for time, you might appreciate a two- to three-hour **city bus tour**. These generally take you past the Parliament, along Andrássy út, across to the Várhegy and up to Gellért-hegy for panoramic photo opportunities. Of the many on offer, Ibusz runs three-hour trips for 6000Ft, and for 9200Ft will add on a visit to the Parliament building; tickets are sold at V, Ferenciek tere 10, in the centre (or online Ⓦwww.ibusz.hu). Buda Tours (Ⓣ1/374-7070, Ⓦwww.budatours.hu) has a two-hour tour for 4000Ft, and in summer uses open-top buses; you buy tickets at VI, Andrássy út 2.

Most of Budapest's backstreets and historic quarters are eminently suited to walking, and this is much the best way to appreciate their character. Traffic is restricted in downtown Pest and around the Vár in Buda, and fairly light in the residential backstreets off the main boulevards, which are the nicest areas to wander around. For a range of **walking tours**, including some which take in less obvious attractions such as Communist Budapest or the city's bars, try the Discover Hungary offices (see p.42) – prices from 4000Ft for three and a half hour tours (Ⓦwww.absolutetours.com). The same office handles **bike tours** (Ⓦwww.yellowzebrabikes.com), and tours on the strange-looking two-wheel segway (Ⓦwww.citysegwaytours.com; you can also hire segways). All tours cost 4000–5000Ft – you need book ahead only for the segway trips.

See p.68 for information on guided tours around the old Jewish area behind the Dohány utca synagogue, and p.186 for information on cave tours.

Under the Hungarian Highway Code, you must give way to cars on your right if there are no road markings to indicate otherwise; and at night, many traffic lights go into flashing orange mode, which means that priority is given to the right. The rules on drink-driving are very strict – do not consume any alcohol before getting behind the wheel. It's illegal to use a hand-held mobile phone while driving. The speed limit in built-up areas is 50kph (30mph), and 90kph (60mph) outside built-up areas. On main roads, it's 110kph (68mph), and on motorways 130kph (80mph).

In terms of **parking**, you might be better off leaving your car outside the centre and using public transport to travel in – there are park and ride facilities at most metro termini. If you must park in the centre, the best option are the underground car parks in Szent István tér by the Basilica and underneath Szabadsag tér, both in Lipótváros. Parking on the street in the central districts costs 120–440Ft – you get a ticket from the nearest machine.

Renting a car is easy provided you're 21 or older and hold a valid driving licence that's at least one year old. Rental **costs** are not particularly cheap – expect to pay around €100 upwards for a day's hire (unlimited mileage) and at least €260 per week. When checking prices make sure the price quoted includes the 20 percent ÁFA (VAT). You'll usually have to leave a deposit by way of a credit card imprint. Before signing, check on mileage limits and any other restrictions or extras, as well as what you're liable for in the event of an accident.

Car rental companies

All these companies listed have offices at the airport.

Avis V, Szervita tér 8, by the petrol station under the multistorey car park Ⓣ1/318-4240, Ⓦwww.avis.hu.

Budget Hotel Mercure Buda, I, Krisztina körút 41–43 Ⓣ1/214-0420, Ⓦwww.budget.hu.

Europcar V, Erzsébet tér 9–10 Ⓣ1/505-4400, Ⓦwww.europcar.hu.

Hertz V, Váci utca 19–21 Ⓣ1/296-0999, Ⓦwww.hertz.hu.

Cycling

Cycling is finally catching on in Budapest – cyclist numbers have risen sharply and cycle lanes are slowly appearing. It isn't easy riding: drivers are only beginning to be aware of cyclists and you also have to contend with sunken tram-lines and bumpy cobbles and bad air pollution. Bikes are banned from the major thoroughfares and the **cycle routes** are still patchy – they don't link up to form a network yet. However, there are also good routes out of town, such as along the Buda bank of the Danube to Szentendre and on up towards Slovakia. Tourinform has free cycling maps of Budapest. Bicycles can be carried on HÉV trains and the Cogwheel Railway for the price of a single ticket, but not on buses or trams. For trail-biking in the Buda Hills, see p.121

Bike shops that do repairs include Nella Bikes, off Bajcsy-Zsilinszky út at V, Kálmán Imre utca 23 (ⓣ1/331-3184, ⓦwww.nella.hu); and the Bike Store, VI, Nagymező utca 43 (ⓣ1/312-5073).

Bike rental companies

Bikebase VI, Podmaniczky utca 19 (moves to no.15 in winter) ⓣ1/269-5983, ⓦwww.bikebase.hu. An excellent operation near Nyugati Station, with friendly staff who dole out maps and advise on cycling routes. They hold a service session every afternoon at 3pm. Daily 9am–7pm.

Yellow Zebra V, Sütő utca 2, in a courtyard by Deák tér ⓣ1/266-8777, ⓦwww.yellowzebrabikes.com. Daily 9.30am–6.30pm. Bike rental and cycling tours of the city. Daily 9.30am–6.30pm.

Budapest Bike Szóda bar, VII, Wesselényi utca 18 ⓣ06-30/944-5533, ⓦwww.budapestbike.hu. Rents bicycles and mopeds, and also organizes bike tours. Daily 9am–midnight.

The media

There are several broadsheets available in Hungary, plenty of tabloids doing the daily rounds of sensationalism, and a handful of local English-language papers. Television differs little from that in other European countries, with foreign cable and satellite television having made huge inroads in recent years.

Newspapers and magazines

You can buy foreign **newspapers**, usually one day old, from some newsagents and street kiosks – those at stations and shopping malls are always a good bet – as well as Bestsellers bookshop (see p.200); Immedio, V, Városháza utca 3, just off Kossuth Lajos utca, has an excellent range of foreign newspapers and magazines. You can sometimes find them for free in the lobbies of larger hotels, which also have copies of Budapest-based **English-language weeklies** such as the *Budapest Sun* (ⓦwww.budapestsun.com), a lightweight, newsy rag with entertainment and events listings; and the *Budapest Business Journal* (ⓦwww.bbj.hu), which covers mainly business and politics. The best source of in-depth information about Hungary and its culture is *The Hungarian Quarterly* (ⓦwww.hungarianquarterly.com), a periodical that has presented Hungarian literature and essays to English readers for more than seventy years.

Television

Generally speaking, Hungarian **television** is pretty dismal, with state TV (MTV) screening a dreary diet of gameshows and low-budget soaps from morning to night. In addition, there are numerous commercial channels such as TV2, the RTL Klub and Duna TV, a state-supported channel geared to Hungarian minorities abroad, though these are little better. For this reason many Hungarians subscribe to satellite channels, with whole apartment blocks sharing the cost of installation. Most half-decent hotels have access to foreign channels, though in some cases they will be German channels only, while the better hotels will have the full satellite package.

Listings magazines

There are several sources of English-language **listings information**: the fortnightly *Budapest Funzine*, distributed free in cafés and bars, is aimed at the expat market and has good background information on events, as well as listings for the art-house cinemas. The weekly *Budapest Sun* has a more comprehensive set of film listings in English and the free monthly magazine *Where Budapest* (available in hotels) has information on current events. The widely available Hungarian-language listings bible *Pesti Est* has extensive details of film and music events, and sometimes has an English section in the summer.

Festivals

Whatever time of the year you visit Budapest, there's almost certain to be something happening. The biggest events are the Spring Festival in late March/early April, and the Autumn Festival from late September to late October, both of which feature music, ballet and drama, including star acts from abroad.

Many theatres, concert halls and dance houses close down during the long, hot months of July and August, when open-air performances are staged instead. The city's population returns from the countryside for the fireworks on August 20, and life returns to normal as school starts the following week. The new arts season kicks off in the last week of September with a rash of music festivals and political anniversaries. The opening performance of the season in September at the State Opera House is traditionally *Bánk Bán*, by Ferenc Erkel.

January and February

Farsang Jan 6 to Ash Wednesday. Held in the run-up to Lent, this Hungarian carnival sees revellers taking to the streets in fancy dress, parading across the Lánchíd and down to Vörösmarty tér. Unfortunately the inclement weather at this time of year often dampens the event's spirit.

Hungarian Film Festival (Magyar Filmszemle) Two weeks of the latest films from Hungarian studios. See p.182 for more information.

March and April

Declaration of Independence of 1848 March 15. A public holiday in honour of the 1848 Revolution, which began with Petőfi's declaration of the *National Song* from the steps of the National Museum. Budapest decks itself out with Hungarian tricolours (red, white and green), and there are speeches and gatherings outside the museum and by Petőfi's statue on Marcius 15 tér. The more patriotic citizens wear little cockades in the national colours pinned to their lapels.

Budapest Spring Festival (Budapest Tavaszi Fesztivál) late March/early April; ⓦwww.btf.hu. The city's major arts festival. It comprises classical-music concerts in venues across the city, as well as some jazz and folk; exhibitions, including the World Press Photos show; theatre and cinema, with a series of Hungarian films with English subtitles; and dance, including a big folk dance gathering and market (*Országos Táncháztalálkozó és Kirakodóvásár*, ⓦwww.tanchaz.hu).

Easter (Húsvét) late March/early April. Easter has strong folk traditions in Hungary. In the city this is limited to some processions in churches Easter Saturday, while on Easter Monday *locsolkodás* (splashing) takes place, when men and boys visit female friends to spray them with cologne in a tamer version of an older village tradition where a bucket of water was used instead of the perfume bottle. Kids get a painted egg or money in return for splashing, while the men receive *pálinka* (schnapps). The weeks preceding Easter see arts and craft fairs in the Museum of Ethnography (p.61) and the Hungarian Open-Air Museum in Szentendre (p.133), with traditional folk skills like egg painting on display; and performances of the Bach Passions in the big, yellow Lutheran church on Deák tér.

Titanic International Film Festival An annual show of independent films staged over ten days in April. See p.182 for more information.

May, June and July

Labour Day May 1. These days, Budapest's citizens are no longer obliged to parade past the Lenin statue that once stood behind the Műcsarnok; instead, the major trade unions put on a big do in the park, with shows, games, talks and food and drink in large quantities.

Book Week (Könyvhét) early June. Hungarian writers gather from neighbouring countries and further afield, stalls line Vörösmarty tér and Szent István tér in front of the Basilica. Authors sign books for the punters – politicians have now joined the book circus, competing to see who can attract the largest crowd – and there's singing and dancing on the temporary stages in the two squares. It has been going since 1929 and is as popular as ever.

Athe Sam Roma Arts Festival mid-June; Ⓦwww.godorklub.hu. Big international event in the Gödör Klub in central Pest (see p.52) that showcases Roma music, art, theatre and film. "We are Here", as the festival translates in Romany, started in 2007 but has grown rapidly, attracting an increasing number of foreign artists too. Most events are free.

Bridge Festival (Hídünnep) mid-June; Ⓦwww.btf.hu. The commemoration of the building of the Lánchíd in the 1840s marks the start of Summer on the Chain Bridge, a two-month long festival that sees the Lánchíd closed to cars each weekend until the middle of Aug to make way for music, food and craft stalls and jugglers and dancers. Each weekend has a different theme, from theatre to world music or jazz.

Gay Pride Budapest late June or early July (see p.175). The largest event in the gay calendar, this is a four-day festival culminating in a march along Andrássy út to the Városliget.

August

Sziget Festival mid-Aug; Ⓦwww.sziget.hu. One of the biggest rock and pop festivals in Europe, staged on Óbudai sziget, an island north of the centre. Over the week it features rock, pop and world music, dance, theatre, films and children's events.

Festival of Crafts (Mesterségek Ünnepe) In the days leading up to Aug 20, the Várhegy is taken over by a huge festival of traditional crafts, accompanied by folk music and dancing.

Red Bull Air Race Aug 19 & 20; Ⓦwww.redbullairrace.com. The Budapest leg of the international race sends the dare-devil pilots speeding under the Danube bridges.

St Stephen's Day Aug 20. A public holiday in honour of Hungary's national saint and founder, with day-long rites at his Basilica, and a spectacular fireworks display fired off between the Erzsébet and Margit bridges at 9pm, watched by over a million people who line the Danube; the traffic jam that follows is equally mind-blowing. Restaurants are packed that night, so book well ahead if you want to eat out.

Jewish Summer Festival end of Aug; Ⓦwww.jewishfestival.hu. Attracts an international range of classical, jazz and *klezmer* music performances, films and exhibitions.

September and October

Budapest Wine Festival (Budapest Bor Fesztivál) early Sept; Ⓦwww.winefestival.hu. Centred around Vörösmarty tér, with wine stalls offering tasting and buying. The country's top producers set out their wares on the terrace of the Royal Palace in the Castle District: for the price of a day ticket (2200Ft, 6000Ft for a five-day pass) you get a glass and a couple of free tastings.

European Heritage Days (Kulturális Örökség Napjai) late Sept. A Council of Europe initiative which sees public buildings all over Europe opened up for a weekend. Tours (in Hungarian) take you round the Art Nouveau Geological Institute on Stefánia út, and the Interior Ministry on Roosevelt tér.

Budapest Autumn Festival (Budapest Őszi Fesztivál) late Sept to mid-Oct; Ⓦwww.bof.hu. Smaller than its spring counterpart, but stronger on contemporary music, with exhibitions as well as operatic and theatre performances.

Budapest Music Weeks (Zenei hetek) late Sept to early Nov. City-wide music events starting around the anniversary of Bartók's death on Sept 25.

Music of Our Time early Oct. Two weeks of contemporary music concerts from Hungarian and foreign artists.

Anniversary of the Arad Martyrs Oct 6. Commemoration of the shooting of the thirteen Hungarian generals in 1849 in Arad (Nagyvárad) in present-day Romania, when the 1848 revolution was crushed by the Austrians with Russian help. Wreaths are laid at the Eternal Flame (see p.58).

Commemoration of the 1956 Uprising Oct 23. A national holiday to mark the 1956 Uprising and the declaration of the Republic in 1990. Ceremonies take place in Kossuth tér, by the nearby Nagy Imre statue, and at Nagy's grave in the New Public Cemetery. Bear in mind that 1956 has left a divided inheritance and tempers can flare; see p.36 for more information.

November and December

All Saints' Day (Mindenszentek napja) Nov 1. Cemeteries stay open late and candles are lit in memory of departed souls, making for an incredible sight as darkness falls.
St Nicholas's Day (Mikulás) Dec 5 & 6. On Dec 5, children clean their shoes and put them in the window for "Mikulás", the Santa Claus figure, to fill with sweets; naughty children are warned that if they behave badly, all they will get is *virgács*, a gold-painted bunch of twigs from Mikulás's little helpers.
Christmas (Karácsony) Dec 24 & 25. The main celebration is on Dec 24, when the city becomes eerily silent by late afternoon. Children are taken out while their parents decorate the Christmas tree (until then the trees are stored outside, and on housing estates you can often see them dangling from windows). When the kids return home, they wait outside until the bell rings, which tells them that "little Jesus" (Jézuska) has come. Inside, they sing carols by the tree, open presents, and start the big Christmas meal, which traditionally includes spicy fish soup. In the preceding weeks there are Christmas fairs in several locations around town, the best being in the Museum of Ethnography, where traditional crafts are demonstrated.
New Year's Eve (Szilveszter) Dec 31. Revellers gather on the Nagykörút during the evening, engaging in paper trumpet battles at the junction with Rákóczi út.

Culture and etiquette

Forty years of communism swept away Hungary's archaic semi-feudal society but you can still find remnants of the old ways, for instance in the language. As a foreigner, you are not obliged to know these details, but Hungarians will love it if you can get them right.

Hungarians preserve certain formalities in meeting and greeting. Young people will go usually straight into the informal form of address with each other (the Hungarian equivalent of the French "*tu*" is to use the second person), but with their elders or in the more formal settings of work or school they would use the formal mode, talking to people in the third person, until invited to use the **informal** mode. So "*Hogy vagy?*" is the informal "how are you?", "*Hogy van?*" is the **formal** – and then to be awfully polite, talking to someone's granny for instance, you can say "*Hogy tetszik lenni?*" (literally, "How does it please you to be?").

When introduced to someone you shake hands and say your name. You would usually **shake hands** when meeting people, though between friends kissing on both cheeks is the norm – between men, too. Some older men still bow to kiss a woman's hand – but it looks rather affected when anyone else does it, so it is best not to try. You will hear an echo of this social convention in the greeting "*Csókolom*", which means "I kiss [your hand]". Children will say this to adults and adults will say it to elderly ladies – responding in kind is an easy error to make and will provoke much laughter.

The formal salutation – to say hello or goodbye – is "*Jó napot*" (or "*Jó reggelt*" before 9am) while with friends "*Szia*", "*Szervusz*" or even "*Helló*" is normal. For more on language see p.223.

A sense of social formality is preserved in other ways too. When visiting someone at home, taking flowers is always acceptable: there are many complex rules and codes in flower-giving that you need not worry about – but do take an odd number of flowers (not 13, though).

Two other useful points when visiting: it is common to take off your shoes when you go in to people's houses; and if eating at someone's house it is customary to complement the host(ess) on the food early on after the first couple of mouthfuls.

Smoking is pretty universal in Budapest – though in someone's home, of course, it is polite to ask if it is permitted. Outside the home, anything goes. In restaurants and bars smoking and no-smoking sections are often hardly separated – a law banning smoking in public places is expected, but no one knows when it will come. Smoking is banned on public transport.

Travelling with children

Budapest is a child-friendly city, with plenty to entertain young ones – see chapter 20 for details. Hungarians tend to be welcoming to kids without making them the centre of attention as you might find in, say, Italy.

Facilities are a bit patchy, though; while the network of playgrounds is marvellous, nappy-changing facilities (*pelenkázó*) are hard to find – they're mostly concentrated in big shopping malls. Buildings don't tend to be very accessible if you're pushing a buggy, but help is usually quickly forthcoming when you're trying to negotiate stairs. On public transport people will readily give up seats to pregnant women and to parents with babies. They will also happily chat to children – the flipside is that old ladies may also loudly berate parents for not looking after their babies "properly", such as for not putting a hat on a baby even in the mildest of weather.

Shopping for babies has become much easier in recent years – the big malls (see p.199) are the best bet for nappies, baby toiletries and clothes. Many also have indoor play areas. Restaurants usually have high chairs and some even put on activities for children (see p.193), and although there isn't a culture of whole families dining out in the evening, waiting staff (even in smart places) are usually accommodating. In many places you can ask for small child's portions – *kisadag*.

Travel essentials

Costs

Hefty price rises over the past few years – especially in restaurants – mean that Hungary is not the bargain destination it once was, although it's still good value on the whole. If you're on a pretty tight **budget**, you could get by on 9000Ft (around £30/$60/€40) a day, staying in a hostel (around 4000Ft), eating in cheap diners (1000–2000Ft per meal) and using public transport. Staying in a three-star hotel will double your accommodation costs, and eating in better restaurants will more than double your meal costs.

Foreigners are easy targets for overcharging, so it is always worth checking the price of what you are buying ("*Mennyibe kerül?*" means "how much is it?"). One hidden extra is the ÁFA or sales tax (the equivalent of VAT in Britain) of up to 25

The Budapest card

If you're doing a lot of sightseeing, you might be tempted to buy a **Budapest Card**. For 6500Ft (48hr) or 8000Ft (72hr), it covers travel in most of the city, entry to over sixty museums, and affords discounts of up to fifty percent in some shops and restaurants as well as on some sightseeing programmes and cultural and folklore events. The card is available from tourist offices, hotels, central metro stations and at the airport, and comes with a booklet explaining where it can be used. Note that it's not valid for the Airport Shuttle minibus, the funicular that goes up to the castle or for tours of Parliament, but as most museums in Budapest now charge admission, it can represent good value. ⓦwww.budapestinfo.hu/en has more information.

percent, which can hike up the cost of hired cars and hotels, for example: look out for the phrase "*az árak nem tartalmaznak Áfát*", meaning "prices do not include tax". There is also a three percent tourist tax on hotel prices, and it is worth checking that both taxes are included in any prices quoted. The simplest way to ask is "*Ez az ár bruttó vagy nettó*?" – "Is this price with or without tax?".

Tipping is standard practice when paying for meals, drinks, and taxi fares (though not when paying for drinks at a bar counter); ten percent or thereabouts is fine, unless the service was not worth it. In restaurants, include the tip when you are paying the bill – say the amount you want to pay and they will give you the change – or give the tip to the staff rather than leaving it on the table. Note that ten percent may have quietly been added to the bill, in which case you don't have to leave more. It's also customary to tip bath attendants who unlock your cubicle (100–200Ft is usual), and even medical staff in hospital.

If you expect change back, don't say *köszönöm* (thank you) when handing over payment, as it will be assumed that you want the change to be kept.

Crime and personal safety

Hungary is one of the safest European countries, and there's little reason to worry about your personal security whilst visiting. However, although violent crime is extremely rare, the rate of **theft** is growing, with Budapest a prime area for pickpocketing, car theft and scams directed at tourists. Unfortunately, the incidence of racist attacks is also increasing, with the Hungarian Roma bearing the brunt of physical assaults.

Since the 2006 riots that made international headlines (see p.213), a small nationalist (even neo-Nazi) hardcore has made regular appearances on Budapest's streets in protests against the Socialist government. In 2007 and 2008 they attacked the Gay Pride march, and their red and white striped flags, the fascist *Árpád sáv*, are seen on the fringe of demonstrations held on national holidays, especially March 15 and October 23, when they often head towards the hated state TV building on Szabadság tér, where the Soviet war memorial whips up their fury (see p.57).

The police

The Hungarian **police** (*rendőrség*) have a milder reputation than their counterparts in other Eastern Bloc states, and are generally keen to present a favourable image. During the summer, **tourist police** patrol the streets and metro stations mainly to act as a deterrent against thieves, and to assist in any problems tourists may encounter. As police occasionally ask to inspect **passports and visas**, you should carry your documents with you.

Most Hungarian police have at least a smattering of German, but rarely speak any other foreign language. To contact the police, call ⓣ107; they have a setup with Tourinform to provide translators should this be necessary.

Scams

Parts of Budapest, notably Váci utca in the Belváros, are notorious for "**consume girls**", who target solo male foreigners. A couple of attractive young women (they're not difficult to spot) will approach you, get talking and, without wasting any time, "invite" you to a bar of their choice. A few drinks later, you'll find yourself presented with a bill somewhat bigger than you bargained for and be strong-armed into paying up. The bars, and the waiters who work in them, are an integral part of the scam, so bids for escape or complaint are futile, but if ever you do find yourself caught up in such a situation then report it to the police.

Even if you disregard pick-ups and avoid places offering the "companionship of lovely ladies", there's a risk of **gross overcharging** at restaurants or bars which don't list their prices. Be cautious, and always check how much things cost before ordering. If you get stung, try insisting that you'll only pay in the presence of the police.

Electricity

The Hungarian system runs on 220 volts. Round two-pin plugs are used. A standard continental adapter allows the use of 13-amp square-pin plugs.

Embassies and consulates

Australia XII, Királyhágó tér 8–9 ⓣ1/457-9777, ⓦwww.ausembbp.hu.
Canada XII, Budakeszi út 32 ⓣ1/392-3360, ⓦwww.kanada.hu.
France VI, 27 Lendvay utca ⓣ1/374-1100, ⓦwww.ambafrance.hu.
Germany I, Úri utca 64 ⓣ1/488-3500, ⓦwww.deutschebotschaft-budapest.hu.
Ireland V, Szabadság tér 7, Bank Center, seventh floor ⓣ1/302-9600.
UK V, Harmincad utca 6 ⓣ1/266-2888, ⓦwww.britishembassy.hu.
USA V, Szabadság tér 12 ⓣ1/475-4400, ⓦwww.usembassy.hu.

Entry requirements

Since Hungary signed up to the Schengen agreement in 2007, citizens of the 24 Schengen states can enter Hungary with just an ID card and stay for up to ninety days. Citizens of the UK, Ireland, US, Canada, Australia and New Zealand, and most other European countries, can enter Hungary with just a passport and stay for the same period. South African citizens will need to apply to their local Hungarian consulate for a visa (€60), though note that visas valid for another Schengen country is also valid for Hungary.

Hungarian embassies and consulates abroad

Australia and New Zealand Embassy: 17 Beale Crescent, Deakin, Canberra, ACT 2600 ⓣ02/6282 3226, ⓦwww.mfa.gov.hu/emb/canberra; consulate: Suite 405 Edgecliffe Centre, 203–233 New South Head Rd, Edgecliffe, Sydney, NSW 2027 ⓣ02/9328 7859, ⓦwww.mfa.gov.hu/cons/sydney.
Canada Embassy: 299 Waverley St, Ottawa, Ontario, K2P 0V9 ⓣ613/230-2717; consulate: 425 Bloor St East, Suite 501, Toronto M4W 3R4 ⓣ416/923-8981, ⓦwww.mfa.gov.hu/emb/ottawa.
Ireland Embassy: 2 Fitzwilliam Place, Dublin 2 ⓣ01/661-2902, ⓦwww.mfa.gov.hu/emb/dublin.
South Africa Embassy: 959 Arcadia St, Hatfield, Pretoria 0083 ⓣ012/342-3288, ⓦwww.mfa.gov.hu/emb/pretoria.
UK Embassy 35b Eaton Place, London SW1 8BY ⓣ020/7235-2664, ⓦwww.mfa.gov.hu/kulkepviselet/uk/hu.
US Embassy: 3910 Shoemaker St NW, Washington DC 20008 ⓣ202/362-6730, ⓦwww.huembwas.org/; visa enquiries ⓣ202/362-6737. Consulate: 223 East 52nd St, New York, NY 10022.

Customs

Visitors over the age of 16 are allowed to bring 200 cigarettes (or 250g of tobacco, or fifty cigars), one litre of wine and one litre of spirits into Hungary. There is no **import duty** on personal effects, though items like laptop computers and video cameras, which are judged to have a high resale value, are liable to customs duty and 25 percent VAT unless you can prove that they are for personal use. Duty-free export limits for tobacco and alcohol are the same as the import limits.

Health

No inoculations are required for Hungary. Standards of public health are good, and tap water is safe to drink. All towns and some villages have **pharmacies** (*gyógyszertár* or *patika*), which normally open Monday to Friday from 9am to 6pm, and on Saturday from 9am until noon or 1pm; signs in the window give the location or telephone number of the nearest all-night (*éjjeli* or *ügyeleti szolgálat*) pharmacy.

In **emergencies**, dial ⓣ104 for the Mentok ambulance service, or get a taxi to the nearest **hospital** (*kórház*). Hungary's national health service (OTBF) provides free emergency treatment in any hospital or doctor's office for citizens of the EU who have the free European Health Insurance Card (EHIC; ⓦwww.ehic.org.uk), but there is a charge for drugs and non-emergency care. Unfortunately, the standard of hospitals varies enormously. Low morale among medical staff and shortages of beds testify to poor wages and the general underfunding of the health service. It is standard practice to tip doctors and medical staff, and unfortunately this is sometimes the best way of ensuring good treatment.

For non-urgent treatment, tourist offices can direct you to a local **medical centre** or doctors' surgery (*orvosi rendelő*), and your embassy in Budapest will have the addresses of foreign-language-speaking **doctors** and **dentists**, who will probably be in private (*magán*) practice.

Sunburn (*napszúrás*) and insect bites (*rovarcsípés*) are the most common **minor complaints** for travellers; sunscreen and repellent are available locally. Mosquitoes can be annoying, but the bug to beware of in forests around Budapest is the *kullancs*, a tick which bites and then burrows into human skin, causing inflammation of the brain. The risk of one biting you is fairly small, but if you get a bite which seems particularly painful, or are suffering from a high temperature and stiff neck following a bite, it's worth having it checked out as quickly as possible.

Insurance

You'd do well to take out an insurance policy before travelling to cover against theft, loss and illness or injury. Specialist travel insurance companies offer various levels of cover, or consider the travel insurance deal we offer (see below).

If you need to make a **claim**, you should keep receipts for medicines and medical treatment, and in the event you have anything stolen, you must obtain an official statement from the police.

Internet

Wireless hotspots are easy to find; the website ⓦwww.hotspotter.hu/en lists places offering access both for free (*ingyenes*) and for a fee (*térítéses*), as do listings magazines such as *Pesti Est*, and the *Dining Guide* publication that you can find in cafés and restaurants. There are **internet cafés** all over Budapest, though the speed of connections varies and not many have keyboards labelled in English. Expect to pay 300–500Ft per hour online, more in central locations such as Váci utca.

Laundry

Laundry Irisz Szalon (V, Városház utca 3–5; Mon–Fri 7am–7pm, Sat 7am–1pm) is one of the few self-service launderettes left in the city; or you can get washing done in the small Laundromat Mosómata at Ó utca 24–26 (Mon–Fri 9am–7pm, Sat–Sun 10am–4pm) near the Basilica, where a wash and dry costs 1600Ft.

Rough Guides travel insurance

Rough Guides has teamed up with Columbus Direct to offer you **travel insurance** that can be tailored to suit your needs. Products include a low-cost **backpacker** option for long stays; a **short break** option for city getaways; a typical **holiday package** option; and others. There are also annual **multi-trip** policies for those who travel regularly. Different sports and activities (trekking, skiing, etc) can usually be covered if required.

See our website (ⓦwww.roughguides.com//shop) or call UK ⓣ0870/033 9988, Australia ⓣ1300/669 999, New Zealand ⓣ0800/559 911, or worldwide ⓣ+44 870/890 2843.

Living in Budapest

Teaching English has traditionally been the main opportunity for **work** in Hungary, and it remains a big business, with many native speakers working in Budapest and a growing number of schools in and around the capital. The most reputable **language school** is International House, whose Budapest branch is at I, Vérmező út 4 (ⓣ1/212-4010, ⓦwww.ih.hu); their minimum requirement is a CELTA or TESOL qualification, and preferably one year's experience. Salaries work out at about 120,000–150,000Ft for a 22-hour week, and some schools (including International House) will help arrange accommodation and offer some transport allowances, as well as one return flight. Although most language schools recruit year-round, the majority of teachers are in place by September. Another option is to give **private lessons**, the going rate for which is anywhere between 2500Ft and 4000Ft for a 45-minute lesson.

Although teaching in a **primary or secondary school** pays much less (around 70,000Ft per month), the deal usually includes subsidized or free accommodation. Expect to teach around twenty 45-minute periods a week, with a timetable that may also include exam preparation, marking, invigilation and the like. Primary schools may take anyone whose native language is English and who seems capable and enthusiastic, though you are likely to require at least a certificate in TEFL and/or a PGCE.

Study, work and exchange programmes

Several schools in Budapest cater for foreigners wishing to **learn Hungarian**, the best of which is the Hungarian Language School at VIII, Bródy Sándor utca 4 (ⓣ1/266-2617, ⓦwww.magyar-iskola.hu. The school runs a comprehensive range of short- and long-term courses, from beginners to advanced, as well as organizing cultural programmes and workshops.

The Debrecen Summer School, which has been going for decades in eastern Hungary, is now running courses in Budapest all year. However the teaching methods are pretty old-school (V, Báthory utca 4.II.1 ⓣ1/320-5751, ⓦwww.summerschool.hu/bp).

There are also several organizations arranging summer **work camps** or **exchange programmes** in Hungary for people from a large number of countries.

Lost property

For items left on public transport go to the BKV office at VII, Akácfa utca 18 (ⓣ1/267-5299; Mon, Tues & Thurs 7.30am–3pm, Wed 7.30am–7pm, Fri 7.30am–2pm). Lost or stolen passports should be reported to the police station in the district where they were lost.

Mail

Post offices (*posta*) are usually open Monday to Friday 8am to 5pm. The city's main post office at V, Petőfi Sándor utca 13, stays open a little later (Mon–Fri 8am–8pm, Sat 8am–2pm), and there are several open even longer hours; one is by Keleti Station at VIII, Baross tér 11c (Mon–Fri 7am–9pm, Sat 8am–2pm), another by Nyugati Station at VI, Teréz körút 51 (Mon–Fri 7am–8pm, Sat 8am–6pm). The post office at the Mammut Mall by Moszkva tér is open 8am to 8pm on weekdays and 9am to 2pm on Sundays, while the branch in the Tesco at XIV, Pillangó utca 15 near the Pillangó utca stop on the red metro is open 24 hours a day. **Stamps** (*bélyeg*) can be bought at tobacconists or post offices, though the latter are usually pretty crowded and very few staff speak English. Stamps cost 150Ft for postcards within Europe, 170Ft for further afield, while stamps for letters up to 20g cost 200Ft and 220Ft respectively. Note that letters and postcards have different rates, so don't buy a job lot of stamps.

Maps

The maps in this guide, together with the small freebies supplied by tourist offices and hotels, should be sufficient to help you find your way around. Larger folding maps are sold all over the place, but their size makes them cumbersome. For total coverage you can't beat the wirebound **Budapest Atlasz**, available in bookshops in a range of sizes, which shows every street, bus and tram route, and the location of restaurants, museums and such like. It also contains enlarged maps of the Vár, central Pest, Margit-sziget and the Városliget, plus a comprehensive index.

Money

Hungary's unit of currency is the **forint** (Ft or HUF). The forint comes in notes of 200, 500, 1000, 2000, 5000, 10,000 and 20,000Ft, with 5, 10, 20, 50 and 100Ft coins (1Ft and 2Ft coins were withdrawn from circulation in 2008 and amounts are rounded up – or down).

At the time of writing, the **exchange rate** was around 300Ft to the pound sterling, 270Ft to the euro and around 200Ft to the US dollar. It's easy to get forints before you travel – you can buy them at exchange offices, or in the UK at post offices, but you may have to order them in advance.

Euros are the most widely accepted foreign currency in shops and restaurants, though the exchange rate is unlikely to be favourable. Banks (generally open Mon–Thurs 8am–4pm, Fri 8am–3pm) and large hotels will change most hard currencies and **traveller's cheques**. The advantages of changing money on the illegal black market are negligible and, in any case, scalpers are skilled at cheating, so you're best off avoiding them. There are also an increasing number of **Automatic Currency Exchange Machines** outside banks, into which you insert foreign currency in return for forints; the exchange rate is usually the same as that offered in the bank itself. The private exchange offices in Váci utca and Vörösmarty tér tend to offer poorer rates.

MasterCard, Visa and American Express **credit cards** are widely accepted, but it is worth checking in advance, as even some smart restaurants don't take them. There are cash machines (**ATMs**) all over the city; if your debit card won't work in a particular ATM, it is worth trying another – not all of the smaller banks are connected to the right global clearing system.

Names

Surnames precede forenames in Hungary, to the confusion of foreigners. In this book, the names of historical personages are rendered in the Western fashion, for instance, Lajos Kossuth rather than Kossuth Lajos (Hungarian-style), except when referring to the names of buildings, streets, etc. (The Hungarian order has a clear logic: in Hungarian the stress in any word always comes on the first syllable; since Hungarian, like most other languages, puts the main stress on the family name when saying a person's name, that means putting the family name first.)

Opening hours and public holidays

Shops are generally open Monday to Friday from 10am to 6pm, and on Saturdays from 10am to 1pm; grocery stores and supermarkets open slightly longer hours at both ends of the day. The shopping malls are open Monday to Saturday 10am to 8pm or 9pm, and Sunday 10am to 6pm. There are also a growing number of 24-hour shops (signed "non-stop", "0–24" or "*éjjel-nappali*").

Most **museums** open Tuesday to Sunday 10am to 6pm (5pm in winter). Office hours are usually Monday to Friday from 8am to 4pm.

Most things in Hungary shut down on the **public holidays** listed below. When these fall on a Tuesday or Thursday, the Monday before or the Friday after may also become a holiday, and the previous or next Saturday a working day to make up the lost day.

Phones

If you want to use your home mobile phone in Budapest, check with your phone provider whether it will work in Hungary,

Public holidays

January 1 New Year's Day
March 15 Independence Day
March/April (variable) Easter Monday
May 1 Labour Day
August 20 St Stephen's Day
October 23 National holiday
November 1 All Saints' Day
December 25 Christmas. (Since celebrations start on Christmas Eve, many shops will be closed the whole day, and by the afternoon everything closes down.)
December 26

Calling home from Hungary

Note that the initial zero is omitted from the area code when dialling the UK, Ireland, Australia and New Zealand from abroad.

Australia international access code + 61 + city code.

New Zealand international access code + 64 + city code.

Republic of Ireland international access code + 353 + city code.

South Africa international access code + 27 + city code.

UK international access code + 44 + city code.

US and Canada international access code + 1 + area code.

and what the call charges will be; US cell phones need to be tri-band to work. If you want to buy a Hungarian **SIM card** (they cost about 1500Ft) try outlets such as T-Mobile or Vodafone, which both have pay-as-you-go offers – you can find them in most malls (see p.199).

When **calling Hungary** from abroad, dial your international access code, then 36 for Hungary, then the area code (omitting the initial zero where present) and the number. If the Hungarian number begins with 06, omit these two digits.

Hungarian **mobile phone** numbers begin with ⓣ06-20, 06-30, 06-60 or 06-70, followed by seven digits. Calling a mobile phone number, you have to dial all the numbers, unless you are calling from a phone on the same network, when you drop the first four digits.

Within Hungary, directory enquiries is on ⓣ198, international directory enquiries on ⓣ199. To make another part of Hungary, dial ⓣ06 (which gives a burring tone), followed by the area code and the subscriber's number.

Religion

The majority of the Hungarian population is officially Roman Catholic, with the remainder comprising Calvinists, smaller numbers of Lutherans and Jews and even smaller groups such as Serb and Greek Orthodox.

As in other former eastern bloc countries, the church was very strong before the Second World War, and some people believe it should once again be a powerful force. In Hungary, their number is small: there has been a steady rise in religious interest, with the church playing a more visible role in everyday life, although, Christmas and Easter aside, it's rare to see churches full.

Hungary has a rich Jewish heritage and is today the focus of huge donations aiming to build up communities and restore buildings that were devastated in the Holocaust. Budapest still retains a sizeable and increasingly active Jewish community, which is far more visible than it was before 1989.

Getting into **churches** may be problematic: the really important ones charge a small fee to see their crypts and treasures, and may prohibit sightseeing during services (*mise* or *istentisztelet*, or *Gottesdienst* in German). Visitors are expected to wear "decorous" dress – that is, no shorts or sleeveless tops. Several churches offer religious services in English: Anglican: Sunday 10.30am, VII, Almássy utca 6 ⓣ06-23/452-023; Baptist: Sunday 10.30am, International Baptist Church, II, Törökvész út 48–54 (Móricz Zsigmond Gimnázium) ⓣ1/319-8525; Roman Catholic: Saturday 5pm, Pesti Jézus Szíve Templom, VIII, Mária utca 25 ⓣ1/318-3479.

Time

Hungary is one hour ahead of GMT, six hours ahead of Eastern Standard Time and nine ahead of Pacific Standard Time. A word of caution: Hungarians express time in a way that might confuse the Anglophone traveller. As in German, 10.30am is expressed as "half eleven" (written 1/2 11 or f11), 10.45am is "three-quarter-eleven" (3/4 11 or h11), and 10.15am is "a quarter of eleven" (1/4 11 or n11).

Tourist information

The best source of **tourist information** in Budapest is Tourinform (ⓦwww.tourinform.hu), the National Tourist Office. The most central office at V, Sütő utca 2, just around the corner from Deák tér metro (daily 8am–8pm; ⓣ1/438-8080), has multilingual staff who can answer just about any question on Budapest or Hungary in general. However, the office is often packed and the staff are overstretched, so you might get more attention at the friendly, privately run **Yellow Zebra**, inside the courtyard behind Tourinform at V, Sütő utca 2 (daily 9.30am–6.30pm; ⓣ1/266-8777 ⓦwww.discoverhungary.com), which can help with all kinds of practical information. The same company has another office behind the Opera House (Discover Hungary, Lázár utca 16, Mon–Fri 9.30am–6.30pm, Sat–Sun 10am–4pm). Alternatively, head for the Tourinform offices at VI, Liszt Ferenc tér 11 (daily: May–Sept 10am–10pm; Oct–April 10am–6pm; ⓣ1/322-4098); and in the Vár on Szentháromság tér (daily 8am–8pm; ⓣ1/488-0475), which are both run by the Budapest Tourism Office (ⓦwww.budapestinfo.hu). There are also Tourinform offices in all three airport terminals.

Hungarian tourist offices abroad

UK **Hungarian National Tourist Office, 46 Eaton Place, London SW1 8AL ⓣ020/7823 1055, ⓦwww.gotohungary.co.uk.** There is also a free tourist hotline or information about the city: ⓣ0800 360 0000.

US **Hungarian National Tourist Office, Commercial Counsellor's Office, 350 Fifth Ave, Suite 7107, New York, NY 10118 ⓣ212/695-1221, ⓦwww.gotohungary.com.**

Websites

Usefully, plenty of Hungarian sights and tourist amenities make it a point to have an English version of their **website**. The list below features websites of general interest; websites on specific themes, such as accommodation or gay life, are covered in the appropriate section of this book.

ⓦwww.caboodle.hu English-language news and listings website aimed at the expat community.

ⓦwww.hvg.eu One of the best sources of news about Hungary in English, this is the website of the excellent Hungarian weekly *HVG*.

ⓦwww.hungary.org.uk The website of the Hungarian Cultural Centre in London is a useful place to keep up Hungarian links after your visit.

ⓦwww.met.hu Daily weather bulletins and forecasts.

ⓦwww.pestiside.hu Irreverent but informed expat-run website on the Budapest scene.

Travellers with disabilities

Hungary has been painfully slow to acknowledge the needs of the disabled traveller, and while progress is being made, don't expect much in the way of special facilities. In Budapest, however, a number of hotels offer specially designed rooms, and an increasing number of museums provide ramps for wheelchairs. The website of the **Hungarian Disabled Association** or Meosz, San Marco utca 76, 1032 Budapest (ⓣ1/388-5529, ⓦwww.meosz.hu), has information about access to museums, hotels and public transport. It is generally useful, though not entirely up to date. For information on public transport accessibility, check the "Passengers with disabilities" section of the Budapest transport website, ⓦwww.bkv.hu, which lists routes where modern low-floored buses operate. The only accessible trams are the #4 and #6 on the Nagykörút. The Airport Shuttle from the airport is also accessible.

Meosz also operates its own special transport service in Budapest whereby, for a fixed payment, a bus equipped with lift or ramp can take you to your chosen destination.

The City

The City

1 The Belváros ... 45

2 Lipótváros and Újlipótváros ... 53

3 Terézváros and Erzsébetváros ... 63

4 The Városliget and the stadium district ... 73

5 Józsefváros and Ferencváros ... 81

6 Várhegy and central Buda ... 90

7 Gellért-hegy and the Tabán ... 108

8 Óbuda and Margit-sziget ... 114

9 The Buda Hills ... 121

10 The city limits ... 125

11 Excursions from Budapest ... 129

The Belváros

A buzz with pavement cafés, street artists, vendors, boutiques and nightclubs, the **Belváros** or Inner City is the hub of Pest and, for tourists at least, the epicentre of what's happening. Commerce and pleasure have been its lifeblood as long as Pest has existed, first as a medieval market town and later as the kernel of a city whose *belle époque* rivalled Vienna's. Since their fates diverged, the Belváros has lagged far behind Vienna's Centrum in prosperity, but the gap is fast being narrowed, at least superficially. It's now increasingly like any Western city in its consumer culture, but you can still get a sense of the old atmosphere, especially in the quieter backstreets south of Kossuth utca.

The **Kiskörút** (Small Boulevard; comprising Károly körút, Múzeum körút and Vámház körút) that surrounds the Belváros follows the course of the medieval walls of Pest, showing how compact it was before the phenomenal expansion of the nineteenth century. However, little remains from further back than the eighteenth century, as the "liberation" of Pest by the Habsburgs in 1686 left the town in ruins. Some Baroque churches and the former Greek and Serbian quarters attest to its revival by settlers from other parts of the Habsburg empire, but most of the **architecture** dates from the era when Budapest asserted its right to be an imperial capital, between 1860 and 1918. Today, first-time visitors are struck by the statues, domes and mosaics on the Neoclassical and Art Nouveau piles, which are reflected in the mirrored banks and luxury hotels that symbolize the post-Communist era.

After a stroll along **Váci utca** from **Vörösmarty tér** and a look at the splendid view of Várhegy from the **embankment**, the best way to appreciate the Belváros is by simply wandering around. People-watching and window-shopping are the most enjoyable activities, and though prices are above average for Budapest, any visitor should be able to afford to sample the **cafés**. Shops are another matter – there are few bargains – and nightclubs are a trap for the unwary, but there's nothing to stop you from enjoying the **cultural life**, from performances by jazz musicians and violinists to world-class conductors and soloists.

Vörösmarty tér

Vörösmarty tér, the leafy centre of the Belváros, is a good starting point for exploring the area. Crowds eddy around the portraitists, conjurers and saxophonists, and the craft stalls that are set up over summer, Christmas and the wine festival. While children play in the fountains, teenagers lounge around the

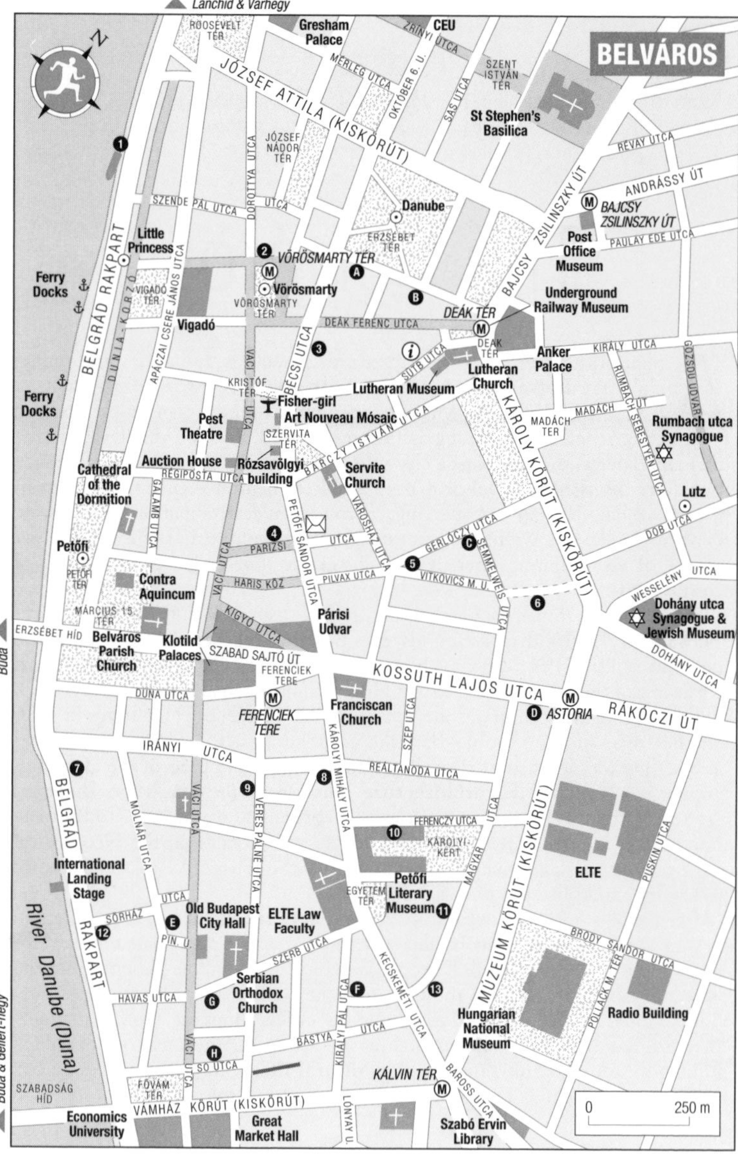

ACCOMMODATION		RESTAURANTS, CAFÉS & BARS			
Art (Best Western)	F	Action	13	Gerlóczy	5
Astoria	D	Amstel River Café	4	Károlyi	10
ELTE Peregrinus Vendégház	G	Astoria Kávéház	D	Mélypont	11
Green Bridge	E	Azték	6	Rézkakas	9
Kempinski Corvinus	A	Capella	7	Spoon	1
Le Méridien	B	Centrál Kávéház	8	Trattoria Toscana	12
Red Bus	C	Gerbeaud	2	Vapiano	3
Zara	H				

statue of Mihály Vörösmarty (1800–50), a poet and translator whose hymn to Magyar identity, *Szózat* ("Appeal"), is publicly declaimed at moments of national crisis. Its opening line "Be faithful to your land forever, Oh Hungarians" is carved on the statue's pedestal. Made of Carrara marble, the statue has to be wrapped in plastic sheeting each winter to prevent it from cracking. The black spot below the inscription is reputedly a "lucky" coin donated by a beggar towards the cost of the monument.

On the north side of the square is the **Gerbeaud patisserie**, Budapest's most famous confectioners. Founded in 1858 by Henrik Kugler, it was bought in 1884 by the Swiss confectioner Emile Gerbeaud, who invented the *konyakos meggy* (cognac-cherry bonbon) – still a popular sweet with Hungarians. He sold top-class cakes at reasonable prices, making the Gerbeaud a popular rendezvous for the middle classes. His portrait hangs in one of the rooms, whose gilded ceilings and china recall the *belle époque*.

From the terrace outside you can observe the entrance to the **Underground Railway** (Földalattivasút, the yellow line), whose vaguely Art Nouveau cast-iron fixtures and elegant tilework stamp it as decades older than the other metro lines. For its centenary in 1996, the line was equipped with the latest technology and its stations restored to their original decor. If you're curious to know more about its history, visit the Underground Railway Museum at Deák tér (see p.52). The Underground Railway's route along Andrássy út is covered in Chapter 3, with Hősök tere described in Chapter 4.

Otherwise, take a look at the two fine Art Nouveau buildings facing the square. Directly behind Vörösmarty's statue stands the erstwhile **Luxus department store**, its facade adorned with bronze panels with plant motifs. The square's southwest corner is dominated by the (sadly derelict) former **Bank Palace**, built between 1913 and 1915, in the heyday of Hungarian self-confidence, by Ignác Alpár, who also designed the prewar Stock Exchange on Szabadság tér (see p.57). Count Mihály Károlyi, the radical liberal who became Prime Minister in 1918, had an office in the building across the street and used to address crowds from its balcony.

Váci utca

Váci utca has been famous for its shops and **korzó** (promenade) since the eighteenth century. During the 1980s, its vivid streetlife became a symbol of the "consumer socialism" that distinguished Hungary from other Eastern Bloc states. Since 1989 it has been a tourist haunt, with endless souvenir shops and rip-off bars where unsuspecting visitors would be tricked into paying huge bills. Today the northern half of the street, down to Ferenciek tere, has at least gained a touch of style from a number of outlets for big Western designer names. A few landmarks along the way might catch your eye: the scantily-clad **Fisher-girl fountain** on **Kristóf tér**; the **Pest Theatre** (no. 9) on the site of the *Inn of the Seven Electors*, where the 12-year-old Liszt performed in 1823; and the former **Auction House** (no. 11A), with its neo-Gothic facade of majolica tiles and toothy wrought-ironwork.

An underpass further south brings you out on Március 15 tér, where a weird stone **monument** resembling a giant cactus flower commemorates the 125th anniversary of the unification of Buda and Pest. Beyond here, the pedestrianized continuation of Váci is infested with tourist-trap restaurants and shops, but retains some imposing architecture: worth a look are the prewar **Officers' Casino** (no. 38) guarded by statues of halberdiers (now a bank's headquarters), and the sculptural **plaque** on the wall of no. 47, commemorating the fact that the Swedish King Charles XII stayed here during his lightning fourteen-day horse-ride from Turkey to Sweden, in 1714. Further along at nos. 62–64 looms the griffon and majolica-encrusted **Old Budapest City Hall**, where the city council still meets.

Shortly after this, an eastward turn into Szerb utca will bring you to the **Serbian Orthodox Church** (daily 10am–4pm; 500Ft), built by the Serbian artisans and merchants who settled here after the Turks were driven out. Secluded in a high-walled garden, it's best visited during High Mass on Sunday (10.30–11.45am), when the singing of the liturgy, the clouds of incense and flickering candles create an unearthly atmosphere. A block or so south of the church, part of the **medieval wall** of Pest can be seen behind a children's playground on the corner of Bástya utca and Vernes Pálné utca.

Szervita tér to Kálvin tér

If you want to linger longer amidst Váci utca's hustle, head back north towards **Szervita tér** – named after the eighteenth-century **Servite Church**, whose facade bears a relief of an angel cradling a dying horseman, in memory of the Seventh Kaiser Wilhelm Hussars killed in World War I. Across the way are two remarkable buildings from the golden age of Hungarian architecture. No. 3 has a gable aglow with a superb **Art Nouveau mosaic** of *Patrona Hungariae* (Our Lady) flanked by shepherds and angels, one of the finest works of Miksa Róth (see p.72). The **Rózsavölgyi Building**, next door but one, was built a little later (between 1910 and 1913) by the "father" of Hungarian Modernism, **Béla Lajta**, whose earlier association with the National Romantic school is evident from the majolica bands on its upper storeys, typical of the style. On the ground floor is the Rózsavölgyi music shop, one of the oldest and best in the city.

Beside the church, the aluminium-ribbed, Brutalist-style T-pont phone, fax and email centre is an equally striking if less attractive presence on **Petőfi Sándor utca**, the street running parallel to Váci utca between Vörösmarty and **Ferenciek tere** (Franciscans' Square). The square itself has been swallowed up by the expansion of the huge road leading down from the Erzsébet bridge. The six or so lanes squeeze down between a pair of imposing *fin-de-siècle* office buildings, named the **Klotild Palaces** after the Habsburg princess who commissioned them – they are sometimes mistakenly called the Klotild and Matilde palaces, though no one is certain which is which.

The most notable building on Ferenciek tere is the **Párisi Udvar**, a flamboyantly eclectic shopping arcade completed in 1915. Its fifty naked statues above the third floor were deemed incompatible with its intended role as a savings bank, symbolized by images of bees throughout the building. The neglected arcade, with its hexagonal dome designed by Miksa Róth, is as dark as an Andalusian mosque and twice as ornate, and cries out for restoration.

The eastern side of Ferenciek tere seamlessly becomes **Kossuth Lajos utca**, which passes the **Franciscan Church** that gave the square its name. The relief on the church's wall recalls the great flood of 1838, in which over four hundred citizens were killed; it depicts the heroic efforts of Baron Miklós Wesselényi, who personally rescued scores of people in his boat. The junction of Kossuth

▲ Art Nouveau mosaic of Our Lady of Hungary, Szervita tér

Lajos utca with the Kiskörút is named after the **Astoria Hotel** on the corner, a prewar haunt of spies and journalists that was commandeered as an HQ by the Nazis in 1944 and the Soviets after the 1956 Uprising. Today, its Neoclassical coffee lounge is redolent of Stalinist chic.

Károlyi Mihály utca

Walking southwards from the Franciscan Church past the coloured dome of the university library, you come to another thoroughfare, named after Count Mihály Károlyi, the liberal politician who briefly led the government after World War I. Immediately to the right, on the corner, is the **Centrál Kávéház**, one of Pest's grand old coffee houses where, in the early twentieth century, writers and intellectuals lingered day and night.

Today, Károlyi's birthplace at no. 16 houses the **Petőfi Literary Museum** (Petőfi Irodalmi Múzeum; Tues–Sun 10am–6pm; 600Ft; ⓦwww.pim.hu), showcasing the personal effects of Sándor Petőfi, the nineteenth-century revolutionary poet (see box, p.51), and of later Hungarian writers, including Endre Ady's fedora and Mihály Babit's bomb-flattened typewriter. Captions are in Hungarian only. More accessible for foreigners is the mansion's garden, the **Károlyi-kert**, a delightful haven within the Belváros with an agreeable restaurant (see p.161). It was here that Lajos Batthyány, head of the independent Hungarian government following the 1848 revolution, was arrested in 1849, and General Haynau, the "Butcher of Vienna", signed the death warrants of Batthyány and other rebel leaders after finishing his morning exercises.

Along the embankment

The **Belgrád rakpart** (Belgrade Embankment) bore the brunt of the fighting in 1944–45, when the Nazis and the Red Army exchanged salvos across the Danube. As with the Várhegy in Buda, postwar clearances exposed historic sites and provided an opportunity to integrate them into the environment – but the magnificent **view** of Buda Palace and Gellért-hegy is hardly matched by the row of modern hotels on the Pest side. While such historic architecture as remains can be seen in a fifteen-minute stroll between the Erzsébet híd and the Lánchíd, **tram #2** enables you to see a longer stretch of the waterfront between Szabadság híd and Kossuth tér in the north, periodically interrupted by a tunnel that's the first to be flooded if the Danube overflows its embankments, as sometimes happens in the summer.

The bold white pylons and cables of the **Erzsébet híd** (Elizabeth Bridge) are as cherished a feature of the panorama as the stone Lánchíd to the north or the wrought-iron Szabadság híd to the south. Of all the Danube bridges blown up by the Germans as they retreated to Buda in January 1945, the Erzsébet híd was the only one not rebuilt in its original form. In fact it was not replaced until 1964 – and even then had to be closed down immediately due to faulty engineering.

In the shadow of the approach ramp, the grimy facade of the **Belváros Parish Church** (Belvárosi Plébánia Templom; Mon–Sat 7am–7pm, Sun 8am–7pm; free) masks its origins as the oldest church in Pest. Founded in 1046 as the burial place of St Gellért (see p.108), it was rebuilt as a Gothic hall church in the fifteenth century (his remains had been long shipped off to Venice), turned into a mosque by the Turks and then reconstructed as a church in the eighteenth century. This history is reflected in the interior, and after Latin Mass at 10am on Sunday you can see the Gothic sedilia and Turkish *mihrab* (prayer niche) behind the high altar, which are otherwise out of bounds. The vaulted nave and side chapels are Baroque.

Március 15 tér and Petőfi tér

On the square beside the Belváros Parish Church, a sunken enclosure exposes the remains of **Contra-Aquincum**, a Roman fort that was an outpost of the settlement at Óbuda at the end of the third century. More pertinently to Hungarian history, the name of the square, **Március 15 tér**, refers to March 15, 1848, when the anti-Habsburg Revolution began, while the adjacent **Petőfi tér** is named after Sándor Petőfi, whose poem *National Song* – the anthem of 1848 – and romantic death in battle the following year

Sándor Petőfi

Born on New Year's Eve, 1822, of a Slovak mother and a southern Slav butcher-innkeeper father, **Sándor Petőfi** was to become obsessed by acting and by poetry, which he started to write at the age of 15. As a strolling player, soldier and labourer, he absorbed the language of working people and composed his lyrical poetry in the vernacular, to the outrage of critics. Moving to Budapest in 1844, he fell in with the young radical intellectuals who met at the *Pilvax Café* (its modern embodiment on Pilvax utca, off Váci utca, fails to capture the rebellious spirit), and embarked on his career as a revolutionary hero. He declaimed his *National Song* from the steps of the National Museum on the first day of the 1848 Revolution, and fought in the War of Independence with General Bem in Transylvania, where he disappeared during the battle of Segesvár in 1849. Though he was most likely trampled beyond recognition by the Cossacks' horses (as predicted in one of his poems), Petőfi was long rumoured to have survived as a prisoner. In 1990, a Hungarian entrepreneur sponsored an expedition to Siberia to uncover the putative grave, but it turned out to be that of a woman.

made him a patriotic icon (see box above). Erected in 1882, the square's **Petőfi statue** has long been a focus for demonstrations as well as patriotic displays – especially on March 15, when the statue is bedecked with flags and flowers. Beyond it looms the Greek Orthodox **Cathedral of the Dormition**, built by the Greek community in the 1790s and, more recently, the object of a tug-of-war between the Patriarchate of Moscow that gained control of it after 1945 and the Orthodox Church in Greece that previously owned it. The cathedral admits sightseers (Wed 2–5pm, Fri 1–5pm, Sat 3–8pm, Sun noon–5pm), and has services in Hungarian, accompanied by singing in the Orthodox fashion.

Just north of Petőfi tér, the gigantic **Marriott Hotel** is situated between the embankment and the street running parallel, Apáczai Csere János utca. Inaugurated as the *Duna Intercontinental* in 1969, it was the first hotel in the Eastern Bloc managed in partnership with a Western firm and the model for others on the embankment. On the Danube side of the *Marriott*, the concrete esplanade is a sterile attempt at recreating the prewar **Duna-korzó**, the most informal of Budapest's promenades, where it was socially acceptable for strangers to approach celebrities and stroll beside them. The outdoor cafés here, which boast wonderful views, charge premium rates.

The Vigadó

Vigadó tér is an elegant square named after the **Vigadó** concert hall, whose name translates as "having a ball" or "making merry". Inaugurated in 1865, this Romantic pile by Frigyes Feszl is encrusted with statues of the Muses and plaques recalling performances by Liszt, Mahler, Wagner, von Karajan and other renowned artists. Badly damaged in World War II, it didn't reopen until 1980, such was the care taken to recreate its sumptuous decor. At the time of writing, the hall was once again closed for refurbishment.

Don't overlook the statue of the impish **Little Princess**, which has been sitting on the railings by the tram line since 1990. After dusk, you'll hardly notice that she isn't a person, if you notice her at all. By day, she looks like a cross-dressing boy in a Tinkerbell hat. Prince Charles was so taken by her that he invited her creator, László Marton, to hold an exhibition of his work in Britain.

Deák tér and Erzsébet tér

Three metro lines and several important roads meet at **Deák tér** and **Erzsébet tér** – two squares that merge into one another (making local addresses extremely confusing) to form a jumping-off point for the Belváros and Lipótváros. You'll recognize the area by two landmarks: the vast mustard-coloured **Anker Palace** on the Kiskörút and, by the metro pavilion on the edge of the Belváros, the **Lutheran Church**, which hosts some excellent concerts that include Bach's *St John Passion* over the fortnight before Easter. Next door, the **Lutheran Museum** (Evangélikus Múzeum; Tues–Sun 10am–6pm; 500Ft) displays a facsimile of Martin Luther's last will and testament, and a copy of the first book printed in Hungarian, a New Testament from 1541.

Erzsébet tér, once the site of a cemetery beyond the medieval city walls, has gone through many names since then, notably Sztálin tér from 1946 until 1953, when it became Engels tér, before getting its older name back. The statue in the middle of the park is of **Old Father Danube** with his three tributaries, the Dráva, Száva and Tisza, and was designed in 1880 by Miklós Ybl. The long low functionalist building behind the trees housed the main bus station until it moved out to the stadium district (see p.80), and much to the ire of locals, is protected by a conservation order so cannot be demolished. In the 1990s, Mayor Demszky's plan to build a new National Theatre on the adjacent car park was thwarted by the government, leaving a vast pit dubbed the "National Hole". Eventually filled in and tidied up, it now houses the *Gödör Klub*, an underground concert and exhibition venue, visible from above through a glass-bottomed pool.

Underground Railway Museum

Accessible via the upper sub-level of Deák tér metro, the **Underground Railway Museum** (Földalattivasút Múzeum; Tues–Sun 10am–5pm; 270Ft or one BKV ticket) extols the history of Budapest's original metro. The exhibits include two elegant wooden carriages (one used up until 1973) and period fixtures and posters, which enhance the museum's nostalgic appeal.

The metro's genesis was a treatise by Mór Balazs, proposing a steam-driven tram network starting with a route along Andrássy út, an underground line being suggested as a fallback in case the overground option was rejected. Completed in under two years, it was inaugurated in 1896 – in time for the Millennial Exhibition – by Emperor Franz Josef, who agreed to allow it to bear his name, which it kept until 1918. The metro was the first on the European continent and the second in the world (after London's Metropolitan line), and originally ran from Vörösmarty tér as far as the Millennial Exhibition grounds at Hősök tere.

2

Lipótváros and Újlipótváros

Lipótváros (Leopold Town), lying to the north of the Belváros, started to develop in the late eighteenth century, first as a financial centre and later as the seat of government and bureaucracy. Several institutions of national significance are found here, including **Parliament**, **St Stephen's Basilica**, the **National Bank** and the Television headquarters. Though part of the V District, as is the Belváros, Lipótváros has quite a different ambience, with sombre streets of Neoclassical buildings interrupted by squares flanked by monumental Art Nouveau or neo-Renaissance piles. It's busy with office workers by day, but used to be dead in the evenings and at weekends until good restaurants brought some life to the area in the 1990s. Another source of vitality is the Central European University (CEU), funded by the Hungarian-born billionaire financier George Soros.

It makes sense to start a Lipótváros visit either with Roosevelt tér, just inland of the Lánchíd, or St Stephen's Basilica, two-minutes' walk from Erzsébet tér. Most of the streets between them lead towards the set-piece expanse of **Szabadság tér**, whence you can head on towards Parliament – though the Kossuth tér metro station or tram #2 from the Belgrád rakpart will provide quicker access.

Across the Nagykörút lies **Újlipótváros** (New Leopold Town; the XIII district), stretching from the bustling Pozsonyi út through quieter residential streets to another focus of activity, **Lehel tér**. The way to get here is either by tram #4 or #6 along the Nagykörút or on the blue metro line to the Lehel tér stop.

Roosevelt tér

At the Pest end of the Lánchíd, **Roosevelt tér** is blitzed by traffic, making it difficult to stand back and admire the magnificent Art Nouveau **Gresham Palace** on the eastern side of the square. Commissioned by a British insurance company in 1904, it's named after the financier Sir Thomas Gresham, the author of Gresham's law that bad money drives out good, whereby the circulation of coins of equal face value but different metals leads to those made of more valuable metal being hoarded and disappearing from use.

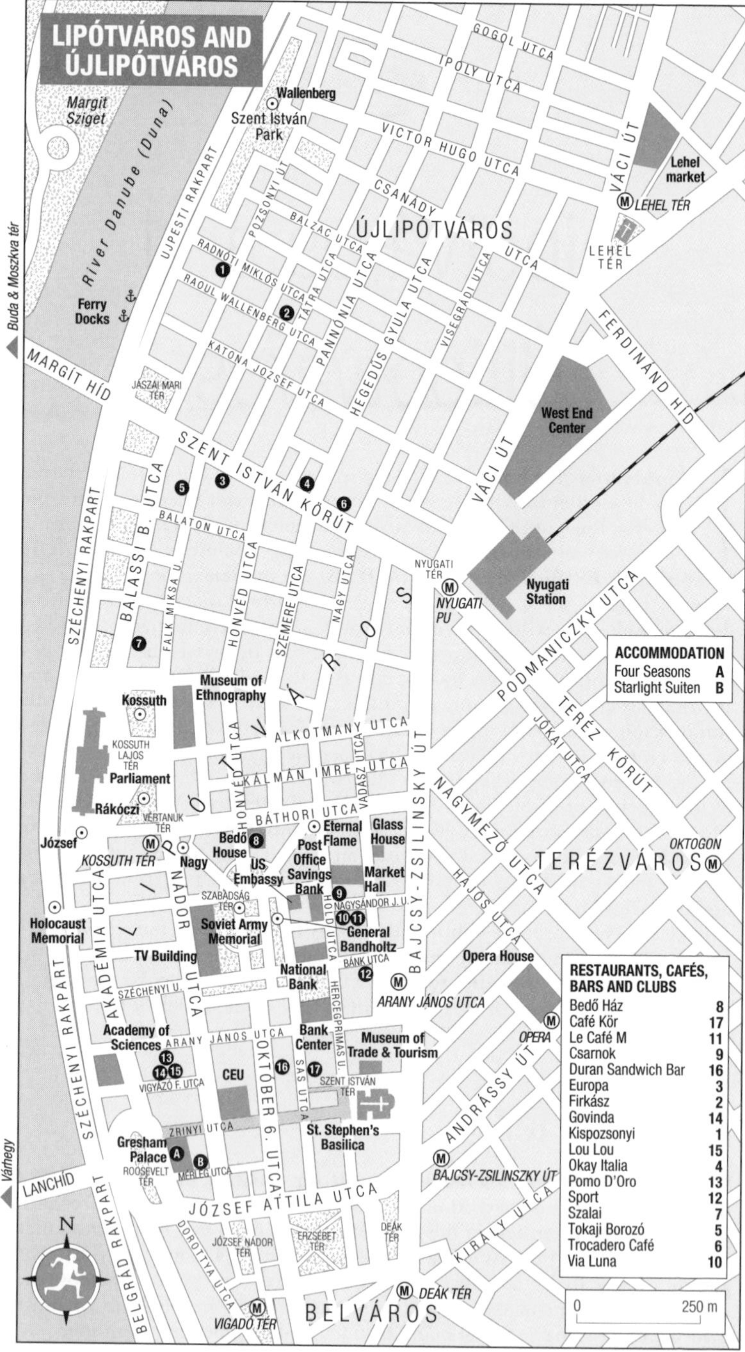

LIPÓTVÁROS AND ÚJLIPÓTVÁROS
Margit Sziget
River Danube (Duna)
Ferry Docks
Buda & Moszkva tér
MARGÍT HÍD
Wallenberg
Szent István Park
ÚJPESTI RAKPART
POZSONYI ÚT
GOGOL UTCA
IPOLY UTCA
VICTOR HUGO UTCA
CSANÁDY UTCA
BALZAC UTCA
RADNÓTI MIKLÓS UTCA
RAOUL WALLENBERG UTCA
KATONA JÓZSEF UTCA
TÁTRA UTCA
PANNÓNIA UTCA
HEGEDŰS GYULA UTCA
VISEGRÁDI UTCA
ÚJLIPÓTVÁROS
VÁCI ÚT
Lehel market
LEHEL TÉR
FERDINÁND HÍD
West End Center
JÁSZAI MARI TÉR
SZENT ISTVÁN KÖRÚT
BALATON UTCA
BALASSI B. UTCA
FALK MIKSA U.
HONVÉD UTCA
SZEMERE UTCA
NAGY UTCA
NYUGATI TÉR
NYUGATI PU
Nyugati Station
PODMANICZKY UTCA
TERÉZ KÖRÚT
JÓKAI UTCA
SZÉCHENYI RAKPART
LIPÓTVÁROS
Museum of Ethnography
Kossuth
KOSSUTH LAJOS TÉR
Parliament
Rákóczi
VÉRTANUK TÉR
ALKOTMÁNY UTCA
KÁLMÁN IMRE UTCA
VADÁSZ UTCA
BÁTHORI UTCA
Eternal Flame
Glass House
Bedő House
Post Office Savings Bank
US Embassy
Market Hall
József
KOSSUTH TÉR
Nagy
NÁDOR UTCA
SZABADSÁG TÉR
Soviet Army Memorial
NAGYSÁNDOR J. U.
HOLD UTCA
General Bandholtz
BANK UTCA
BAJCSY-ZSILINSKY ÚT
NAGYMEZŐ UTCA
HAJÓS UTCA
TERÉZVÁROS
OKTOGON
Opera House
OPERA
ANDRÁSSY ÚT
Holocaust Memorial
AKADÉMIA UTCA
TV Building
National Bank
ARANY JÁNOS UTCA
SZÉCHENYI U.
HERCEGPRIMÁS U.
Academy of Sciences
Bank Center
Museum of Trade & Tourism
CEU
OKTÓBER 6. UTCA
SAS UTCA
VIGYÁZÓ F. UTCA
SZENT ISTVÁN TÉR
ZRÍNYI UTCA
St. Stephen's Basilica
Gresham Palace
ROOSEVELT TÉR
MÉRLEG UTCA
BAJCSY-ZSILINSZKY ÚT
Várhegy
LANCHÍD
JÓZSEF ATTILA UTCA
KIRÁLY UTCA
BELGRÁD RAKPART
DOROTTYA UTCA
JÓZSEF NÁDOR TÉR
ERZSÉBET TÉR
DEÁK TÉR
VIGADÓ TÉR
BELVÁROS
N
0 250 m
ACCOMMODATION
Four Seasons A
Starlight Suiten B
RESTAURANTS, CAFÉS, BARS AND CLUBS
Bedő Ház 8
Café Kör 17
Le Café M 11
Csarnok 9
Duran Sandwich Bar 16
Europa 3
Firkász 2
Govinda 14
Kispozsonyi 1
Lou Lou 15
Okay Italia 4
Pomo D'Oro 13
Sport 12
Szalai 7
Tokaji Borozó 5
Trocadero Café 6
Via Luna 10

The building was in an awful state when it was acquired by the Four Seasons hotel chain in 2001, but fears of a crass refurbishment have been dispelled by a loving restoration: authentic materials and even the original workshops were sought out to do the job. Today you can once again see Gresham's bust high up on the facade, and members of the public may walk in to admire the subtle hues of the tiled lobby and glass-roofed arcade, with wrought-iron peacock gates and stained-glass windows by Miksa Róth.

Statues of Count Széchenyi (see p.104) and Ferenc Deák, another major nineteenth-century politician, stand at opposite ends of the square. The statue of the former isn't far from the **Hungarian Academy of Sciences** (Magyar Tudományos Akadémia), founded after Széchenyi pledged a year's income from his estates towards its establishment in 1825 – as depicted on a relief on the wall facing Akadémia utca.

While the Academy and the Lánchíd are tangible reminders of Széchenyi's enterprise, there is no reminder of Deák's achievement in forging an *Ausgleich* (Compromise) with the Habsburgs. This was symbolized by the crowning of Emperor Franz Josef as King of Hungary in 1867, when soil from every corner of the nation was piled into a Coronation Hill, on the site of the present square. Here the emperor flourished the sword of St Stephen and promised to defend Hungary against all its enemies – a pledge that proved almost as ephemeral as the hill itself. Eighty years later, the square was renamed Roosevelt tér in honour of the late US president – a rare example of Cold War courtesy that was never revoked.

St Stephen's Basilica and Bajcsy-Zsilinszky út

St Stephen's Basilica (Szent István-Bazilika; Mon–Fri 9am–5.15pm & 7–7.30pm, Sat 9am–1pm & 7–7.30pm, Sun 1–5pm; free) took so long to build that Budapestis once joked, when borrowing money, "I'll pay you back when the basilica is finished". Work began in 1851 under the supervision of József Hild, continued after his death under Miklós Ybl, and was finally completed by Joseph Krauser in 1905. At the inaugural ceremony Emperor Franz Josef was seen to glance anxiously at the dome, whose collapse during a storm in 1868 had set progress back. At 96m, it is exactly the same height as the dome of the Parliament building – both allude to the putative date of the Magyars' arrival in Hungary (896 AD). After recent restoration work that seemed to take as long as the original construction, the Basilica looks fabulous today. It is best visited when the interior is open for sightseeing, as its beauty lies in the carvings, frescoes and chapels, the variegated marble, gilded stucco and bronze mouldings, and the splendid **organ** above the doorway.

In the second chapel to the right is a painting of King Stephen offering the Crown of Hungary to the Virgin (see p.94), while a statue of him haloed as a saint (but with a sword at his side) forms the centrepiece of the altar. In a **chapel** (April–Sept Mon–Fri 9.30am–4.30pm, Sun 1–4.30pm; Oct–March Mon–Fri 10am–4pm, Sun 1–4.30pm; free) to the left at the back is the gnarled **mummified hand of St Stephen**, Hungary's holiest relic. The Szent Jobb (literally, "holy right") is paraded with great pomp through the surrounding streets on August 20, the anniversary of his death, but at other times you can see it in the chapel by inserting 100Ft to illuminate the casket.

Although the **treasury** (same hours; 400Ft) is paltry compared to that at Esztergom's Basilica, you shouldn't miss the so-called **Panorama Tower** (daily: April–May 10am–4pm; June–Aug 9.30am–6.30pm; Sept–Oct 10am–7.30pm; 500Ft), reached by a lift to the base of the cupola, 65m up, and then another lift or a spiral stairway (mind your head on the joists) to the external walkway, which offers a grand **view** over the city, as well as the option of walking back down 302 stone steps. **Mass** is held in the basilica on weekdays (7am, 8am & 6pm) and Sundays (8am, 9am, 10am, noon, 6pm & 7.30pm).

Museum of Trade and Tourism

At Szent István tér 15, on the north side of the Basilica, a pea-green majolica facade of entwined fishes with bronze peacock motifs beneath its portal harbours the **Museum of Trade and Tourism** (Kereskedelmi és Vendéglátóipari Múzeum; daily except Tues 11am–7pm; 600Ft; Ⓦwww.mkvm.hu). Besides temporary exhibitions, there are several rooms devoted to fashions and ephemera from the *belle époque* and interwar eras, and a spacious upper floor where musical, theatrical and culinary events are held – ask in the lobby or check the website for details of what's on. At some point in the future, the museum hopes to be able to afford to display more items currently in storage, such as a model dog that rapped shop windows with its paws to draw in passers-by, and a reconstructed prewar bedroom from the *Gellért Hotel*.

Bajcsy-Zsilinszky út

While Stephen is revered as the founder and patron saint of Hungary, the pantheon of national heroes includes a niche for Endre Bajcsy-Zsilinszky (1866–1944), after whom the avenue that runs past the Basilica is named. Originally a right-winger, he ended up an outspoken critic of Fascism, was arrested in Parliament and shot as the Russians approached. **Bajcsy-Zsilinszky út** is the demarcation line between the Lipótváros and Terézváros districts, running northwards to **Nyugati Station**, an elegant, iron-beamed terminal built in 1874–77 by the Eiffel Company of Paris. Beside the station, the **WestEnd City Center** is one of Budapest's largest malls, boasting four hundred outlets and an artificial waterfall three storeys high. For some years it was also the launch-pad for a hot-air balloon offering a bird's eye view of the city. This no longer operates, but the mall's rooftop now holds an equally popular **ice-skating rink** (daily 8am–10pm, Fri & Sat till midnight; 800–1000Ft depending on the time and day; Ⓦwww.jegterasz.hu).

Szabadság tér and around

For over a century, Lipótváros was dominated by a gigantic barracks where scores of Hungarians were imprisoned or executed, until this symbol of Habsburg tyranny was demolished in 1897 and the site redeveloped as **Szabadság tér** (Liberty Square). Invested with significance from the outset, it became a kind of record of the vicissitudes of modern Hungarian history, where each regime added or removed **monuments**, according to their political complexion. For an excellent vantage point from which to admire the square's buildings, head to the café pavilion in the centre of the square.

The Stock Exchange and National Bank

In the early twentieth century, Hungary's burgeoning prosperity was expressed by two monumental temples to capitalism on opposite sides of the square. To the west stood the **Stock Exchange** (Tőzsde), one of the grandest buildings in Budapest. Designed by Ignác Alpár, it has blended motifs from Greek and Assyrian architecture and is crowned with twin towers resembling Khmer temples. After the Communists closed down the Exchange in 1948, it became the headquarters of Hungarian Television.

Alpár also designed the **National Bank** (Magyar Nemzeti Bank), which still functions as such and is notable for the bas-reliefs on its exterior, representing such diverse aspects of wealth creation as Magyars ploughing and herding, ancient Egyptians harvesting wheat, and Vikings loading longships with loot. The stones for its columns were hauled all the way from Transylvania by oxen. An entrance at Szabadság tér 8 leads to a stylish **Visitor Centre** (Mon–Fri 9am–4pm; free; Ⓦ www.lk.mnb.hu) featuring curiosities like the "Kossuth" banknotes that were issued in America during the politician's exile after the failed War of Independence, and notes denominated in billions of forints from the period of hyper-inflation in 1946. Look out too for the stained-glass windows on the stairs. Across the way outside, the mirrored-glass and granite **Bank Centre** is a triumphant affirmation of the fact that Hungary has rejoined the capitalist system.

Szabadság tér's monuments

From 1921 to 1945, the square was dominated by the Monument to Hungarian Grief – consisting of a flag at half mast and four statues called North, South, East and West – in protest at the 1920 Treaty of Trianon, which awarded two-thirds of Hungary's territory and a third of its Magyar population to the "Successor States" of Romania, Czechoslovakia and Yugoslavia. After World War II, this was replaced by a **Soviet Army Memorial** commemorating the liberation of Budapest from the Nazis, with bas-reliefs of Red Army troops and tanks advancing on Ferenciek tere and Parliament. Today, the Soviet obelisk is fenced off to protect it from vandalism by right-wing nationalists, who periodically erect a tent nearby, emblazoned with "Give us back our flag!", coyly neglecting to mention the revanchist impulse behind the original monument.

Ironically, the Soviet memorial and the protest tent stand near the former headquarters of the Fascist Arrow Cross, and the **US Embassy** (now cordoned off for security); for fifteen years, the latter sheltered Cardinal Mindszenty, the Primate of Hungary's Catholic Church, in the aftermath of the 1956 Uprising. Later, however, the US became embarrassed by his presence, as did the Vatican, which finally persuaded him to leave for Austria in 1971 (see box p.142). Nearby is a statue of **General Harry Bandholtz** of the US army, who intervened with a dogwhip to stop Romanian troops from looting the Hungarian National Museum in 1919. The statue was erected in the 1930s, removed after World War II, and reinstated by the Communists prior to President George Bush's visit in 1989.

The Bedő House and Post Office Savings Bank

On Honvéd utca, behind the Soviet memorial, look out for the pistachio facade of the **Bedő House** (no. 3), a superb example of Hungarian Art Nouveau architecture, built by Emil Vidor in 1903. Recently restored after decades of neglect, it now holds the **Museum of Hungarian Art Nouveau** (Magyar Szecesszió Háza; Tues–Sun 10am–5pm; 1100Ft), displaying furniture, graphics and interior design (check out the toilets in the basement), and with a shop selling reproduction and original pieces, and the *Art Nouveau Café*. For more in a similar vein, turn right onto Báthori utca and right again onto Hold utca, where you can't miss the former **Post Office Savings Bank** (Postatakarék-pénztár), its tiled facade patterned like a quilt, with swarms of bees (symbolizing savings) ascending to the polychromatic roof, which is the wildest part of the building. Its architect, Ödön Lechner, once asked why birds shouldn't enjoy his buildings too, and amazing roofs are a feature of his other masterpieces in Budapest, the Applied Arts Museum and the Geological Institute (see *Budapest's Art Nouveau* colour section). Now an annex of the National Bank, its foyer is accessible during banking hours but the rest of the interior is only open to the public on European Heritage Day sometime in September (ask Tourinform for details).

The Market Hall and Glass House

Diagonally across the street from the Savings Bank is a wrought-iron **market hall** (Mon 6am–5pm, Tues–Fri 6am–6pm, Sat 6am–3pm); one of five opened on a single day in 1896, and which still serve the centre of Pest, it's much less touristy than the Great Market Hall on Vámház körút (see p.87). Its rear entrance will bring you out on Vadász utca, not far from one of Budapest's least-known memorials to the Holocaust. Across the street at no. 29, the **Glass House** (Üvegház; daily 1–4pm; free) was named both for the extensive use of glass in its Modernist design and for its erstwhile role as a glass showroom. From 1944 to 1945, it was one of many properties in Budapest that was designated as neutral territory by the Swiss consul Carl Lutz (see p.71), serving as a refuge for 3000 Jews and the underground Zionist Youth organization. An **exhibition** (entered to the right of the courtyard) explains how Lutz, Wallenberg and other "Righteous Gentiles" managed to save thousands of Jews from the SS and Arrow Cross death squads. While their co-religionists from the provinces were transported en masse to Auschwitz, the Jews of Budapest faced random executions in the heart of the capital, within full view of Parliament (see p.59) and their gentile compatriots, who seemed more offended by the bloodshed than outraged by their murder.

The Batthyány and Nagy Monuments

A few blocks from the Glass House, at the junction of Hold utca and Báthori utca, a lantern on a plinth flickers with an **Eternal Flame** commemorating Count Lajos Batthyány, the Prime Minister of the short-lived republic declared after the 1848 War of Independence, whom the Habsburgs executed on this spot on October 6, 1849. As a staunch patriot – but not a revolutionary – Batthyány is a hero for conservative nationalists, and his monument is the destination of annual marches on October 6.

The refrains and paradoxes of Hungarian history are echoed on Vértanuk tér (Martyrs' Square), between Szabadság tér and Kossuth tér, where a **statue of Imre Nagy** – the reform Communist who became Prime Minister during the 1956 Uprising and was shot in secret two years afterwards – stands on a footbridge, gazing towards Parliament. With his raincoat, trilby and umbrella hooked over his arm, Nagy cuts an all-too-human, flawed figure – and is scorned by those who pay homage to Batthyány.

Kossuth tér

The apotheosis of the government district and Hungary's romantic self-image comes at **Kossuth tér**, with its colossal Parliament building and memorials to national heroes and epic moments in Hungarian history. The square is named after **Lajos Kossuth**, the leader of the 1848 Revolution against the Habsburgs (see box, p.60), who was originally represented by a sculptural tableau showing him and his ministers downcast by their defeat in 1849. However, the Communists replaced it with a more "heroic" **statue** of Kossuth rousing the nation to arms, by Kisfaludy-Strobl (see p.110). The dramatic equestrian statue is of **Prince Ferenc Rákóczi II**, an earlier hero of the struggle for Hungarian independence, whose plinth is inscribed with the words "The wounds of the noble Hungarian nation burst open!" This is a reference to the anti-Habsburg war of 1703–11, but also perfectly describes the evening of October 23, 1956, when crowds filled the square, chanting anti-Stalinist slogans at Parliament – the prelude to the Uprising that night. Directly opposite Parliament, a black pillar upholds an **Eternal Flame** (sometimes extinguished), in memory of those who died on Kossuth tér on October 25, when ÁVO snipers opened fire on a peaceful crowd that was fraternizing with Soviet tank-crews.

Two more notable monuments can be seen in the vicinity. Immediately south of Parliament sits the brooding figure of **Attila József**, one of Hungary's finest poets, who was expelled from the Communist Party for trying to reconcile Marx and Freud, and committed suicide in 1937 after being rejected by his lover. His powerful, turbulent verse has never lost its popularity, and he earns his place here for his poem *By the Danube*. Further south beside the river is a poignant **Holocaust Memorial**: dozens of shoes cast in iron, marking the spot where hundreds of Jewish adults and children were machine-gunned by the Arrow Cross and their bodies thrown into the Danube. Before being massacred, they were made to remove their coats and footwear, which were earmarked for use by German civilians.

▲ Cast-iron shoes commemorating the massacre of Jews by the Danube

Lajos Kossuth

Lajos Kossuth was the incarnation of post-Napoleonic bourgeois nationalism. Born into landless gentry in 1802, he began his career as a lawyer, representing absentee magnates in Parliament. His Parliamentary reports, which advocated greater liberalism than the Habsburgs would tolerate, became widely influential during the Reform era, and he was jailed for sedition. While in prison, Kossuth taught himself English by reading Shakespeare. Released in 1840, he became editor of the radical *Pesti Hírlap*, was elected to Parliament and took the helm during the 1848 Revolution.

After Serbs, Croats and Romanians rebelled against Magyar rule and the Habsburgs invaded Hungary, the Hungarians proclaimed a republic with Kossuth as de facto dictator. After the Hungarians surrendered in August 1849, Kossuth escaped to Turkey and later toured Britain and America, espousing liberty and trying to win support for the Hungarian cause. So eloquent were his denunciations of Habsburg tyranny that London brewery workers attacked General Haynau, the "Butcher of Vienna", when he visited the city. One man who did his best to undermine Kossuth's efforts was Karl Marx, who loathed Kossuth as a bourgeois radical and wrote hostile articles in the New York *Herald Tribune* and the London *Times*.

As a friend of the Italian patriot Mazzini, Kossuth spent his last years in Turin, where he died in 1894. His remains now lie in the Kerepesi Cemetery (see p.85).

Parliament

The Hungarian **Parliament** building (Országház; Ⓦwww.mkogy.hu) makes the Houses of Parliament in London look humble, its architect Imre Steindl having larded Pugin's Gothic Revival style with Renaissance and Baroque flourishes. Sprawling for 268m along the embankment, its symmetrical wings bristle with finials and 88 statues of Hungarian rulers, surmounted by a dome 96m high (alluding to the date of the Magyar conquest; see p.73). Though most people are impressed by the building, the poet and writer Gyula Illyés once famously dismissed it as "no more than a Turkish bath crossed with a Gothic chapel" – albeit one that cost 38,000,000 gold forints. One weakness in the design was the white limestone of the exterior, which has been degraded by the elements and pollution; since 1925 it has required almost constant cleaning and replacement.

For centuries, Hungarian assemblies convened wherever they could, and it wasn't until 1843 that it was resolved to build a permanent "House of the Motherland" in Pest-Buda (as the city was then called). By the time work began in 1885, the concept of Parliament had changed insofar as the middle classes were now represented as well, though over ninety percent of the population still lacked the right to vote. Gains were made in 1918, but they were soon curtailed under the Horthy regime, just as the attainment of universal adult suffrage in 1945 was rendered meaningless after 1948 by a Communist dictatorship. The introduction of multiparty democracy in 1990 was symbolized by the removal of the red star from Parliament's dome and the replacement of Communist emblems by the traditional coat of arms featuring the crown of King Stephen – whose Coronation Regalia is now on show in the building's Cupola Hall.

The interior – and the Coronation Regalia

Tickets for **tours** of the interior in English (daily at 10am, noon & 2pm; free for EU citizens with passport, otherwise 2640Ft) and other languages sell out fast after the ticket office opens at 8am. It's situated by Gate X on the Kossuth tér side, beyond the rope near the Eternal Flame, where visitors with tickets wait to be admitted; you'll need to ask the guards to let you cross the barrier. Having passed through a security check, the extent to which the interior is accessible depends on Parliament's activities, but you can be sure of seeing the main staircase, the Cupola Hall and the Lords Chamber, if nothing else.

Despite its archaic style the building was high-tech for its time, being air-conditioned via blocks of ice in the basement that kept it at the constant temperature of 25°C which the architect reckoned was most conducive to thought – since modern air-conditioning was installed, MPs have complained of back pains. Statues, carvings, gilding and mosaics are ten a penny, lit by lamps worthy of the Winter Palace – but there are also cosy touches such as the individually numbered brass ashtrays where peers left their cigars smouldering in the lounge while they popped back into the chamber to hear someone speak; a good speaker was said to be "worth a Havana".

Guards holding drawn sabres flank the **Coronation Regalia**, whose centrepiece, **St Stephen's Crown**, has symbolized Hungarian statehood for over a thousand years. It consists of two crowns joined together: the cruciform crown that was sent as a gift by Pope Sylvester II to Stephen for his coronation in 1000, and a circlet given by the Byzantine monarch to King Géza I. The distinctive bent cross was caused by the crown being squashed as it was smuggled out of a palace in a baby's cradle. At other times it has been hidden in a hay-cart or buried in Transylvania, abducted to Germany by Hungarian Fascists and thence taken to the US, where it reposed in Fort Knox until its return home in 1978, together with Stephen's crystal-headed sceptre, a fourteenth-century gold-plated orb and a sixteenth-century sword made in Vienna, used by his successors. Under the Dual Monarchy, Habsburg emperors ruled Hungary in the name of St Stephen, and travelled to Budapest for a special coronation ceremony, traditionally held in the Mátyás Church on Várhegy.

On a humbler note, you'll be shown a **scale model** of Parliament made of 100,000 matchsticks, built by a patriotic family over three years.

Museum of Ethnography

Across the road from Kossuth's statue stands a neo-Renaissance building housing the **Museum of Ethnography** (Néprajzi Múzeum; Tues–Sun 10am–6pm; 800Ft; Ⓦwww.neprajz.hu). Little visited by tourists, it's actually one of the finest museums in Budapest, originally built as the Palace of the Supreme Court; petitioners would have been overawed by its lofty, gilded main hall, whose ceiling bears a fresco of the goddess Justitia surrounded by allegories of Justice, Peace, Revenge and Sin.

The museum's permanent exhibition on Hungarian folk culture occupies thirteen rooms on the first floor (off the left-hand staircase) and is fully captioned in English, with an excellent catalogue available. Habsburg-ruled Hungary comprised a dozen ethnic groups, represented by exhibits arranged under headings such as "Institutions" and "Peasant Work"; the only groups not represented are the Jews and the Gypsies. Though the beautiful costumes and objects on display are no longer part of everyday life in Hungary, you can still see them in parts of Romania, such as Maramureş and the Kalotaszeg, which belonged to Hungary before 1920.

Temporary exhibitions (on the ground and second floors) cover anything from Hindu rituals to musical instruments from around the world, while over Easter and Christmas there are **concerts** of Hungarian folk music and dancing, and **craft fairs**.

Újlipótváros

Szent István körút, the section of the Nagykörút running from Nyugati Station to the Danube, marks the end of Lipótváros – but there are a few sights further out in **Újlipótváros** (the XIII District) that are worth a mention. The bank of the Danube north of the Margit híd is the site of the summertime **Budapest Beach** (Budapest Plázs), which takes its cue from the Paris original. From late May onwards the 1500-metre stretch of the Újpesti rakpart is closed to traffic and covered in sand and palm trees, recreating a seaside feel, and there are stages, live music, children's programmes and numerous food stalls, bars and restaurants to keep beach-goers happy.

Running up from the körút parallel to the beach is Pozsonyi út, a bustling tree-lined street leading to **Szent István Park**, the prewar social hub of a wealthy Jewish neighbourhood. It's an apt site for a **monument to Raoul Wallenberg**, who gave up a playboy life in neutral Sweden to help the Jews of Budapest in 1944 (see p.69). The monument was constructed in the 1950s but "exiled" to Debrecen in eastern Hungary before being stashed away for decades, only taking its rightful place in Budapest in 1999.

Heading 500m eastwards along Csanádi utca will take you to **Lehel tér**, notable for its picturesque 1930s reconstruction of the ruined **Romanesque church** at Zsámbék, west of Budapest. Beyond lies the **Lehel tér market hall** (Lehel Csarnok; Mon 6am–5pm, Tues–Fri 6am–6pm, Sat 6am–3pm), which may look like a stylistic mish-mash but has an excellent range of food stalls inside.

3

Terézváros and Erzsébetváros

Terézváros (Theresa Town, the VI District) is home to the **State Opera House**, the **Academy of Music** and the Hungarian equivalent of Broadway, making it one of the most vibrant parts of the city. Its main thoroughfare, **Andrássy út**, marking the border between it and Lipótváros, is Budapest's longest, grandest avenue, running in a perfect straight line for two and a half kilometres up to Hősök tere and the Városliget, covered in chapter 4. With its coffee houses and grey stone edifices laden with dryads, not to mention the Opera House, the avenue retains something of the style that made it so fashionable in the 1890s, when "Bertie" the Prince of Wales drove its length in a landau, offering flowers to women as he passed.

To the south of Király utca, the mainly residential **Erzsébetváros** (Elizabeth Town, the VII District) is composed of nineteenth-century buildings whose bullet-scarred facades, adorned with fancy wrought-ironwork, conceal a warren of dwellings and leafy courtyards. It is also traditionally the **Jewish quarter** of the city, which was transformed into a ghetto during the Nazi occupation and almost wiped out in 1944–45, but has miraculously retained its cultural identity. Its current resurgence owes much to increased contacts with international Jewry, and a revival of interest in their religion and roots among the eighty-thousand-strong Jewish community of Budapest, which had previously tended towards assimilation, reluctant to proclaim itself in a country where anti-Semitic prejudices linger. There is no better part of Pest to wander around, soaking up the atmosphere.

The stretch of Andrássy út up to the Oktogon – where it meets the Nagykörút (Great Boulevard) – is within walking distance of Deák tér, and the whole length of the boulevard is served by the metro. Trams and buses circle the Nagykörút almost 24 hours, and several trolleybus lines run through the two districts out to the Városliget.

Terézváros

Laid out in the late nineteenth century, **Terézváros** was heavily influenced by Haussmann's redevelopment of Paris, and at that time it was one of the smartest districts in the city. Under Communism, the area became pretty run-down, but

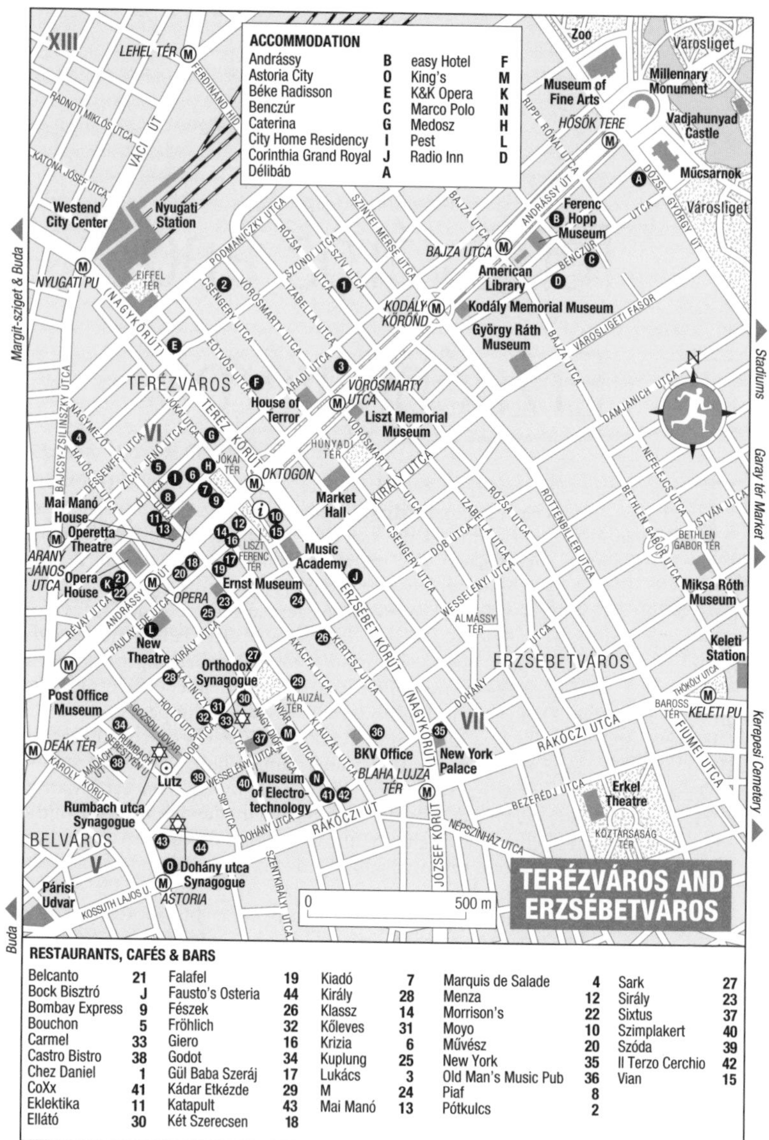

the appeal of the old apartment blocks lining its streets is now bringing in the middle classes; the villas near the park have recovered their value and café society flourishes around Liszt Ferenc tér.

Andrássy út was inaugurated in 1884 as the Sugár (Radial) út, but was soon renamed after the statesman Count Gyula Andrássy, and it was this name which stayed in popular use throughout the years when this was officially Stalin Avenue (1949–56) or the Avenue of the People's Republic (1957–89). The first point of interest as you head out along the boulevard is at no. 3, where the **Post Office Museum** (Posta Múzeum; Tues–Sun 10am–6pm; 500Ft) occupies a fabulous old apartment complete with parquet floors, marble fireplaces, Venetian mirrors and frescoes by Károly Lotz; its owners fled to the US in 1938. Besides offering a window into how wealthy Budapestis lived before World War II, it also features a wealth of postal exhibits including a compressed-air mail tube, vintage delivery vehicles and a display on the inventor and telephone pioneer Tivadar Puskás, a colleague of Thomas Edison. Press #10 on the entry-phone to gain access to the building.

The State Opera House and New Theatre

The **State Opera House** (Állami Operaház; Ⓦwww.opera.hu) was founded by Ferenc Erkel, the composer of Hungary's national anthem, and occupies a magnificent neo-Renaissance pile built in 1875–84 by Miklós Ybl. It can boast of being directed by Mahler (who was driven out by the anti-Semitism he experienced in the city), hosting performances conducted by Otto Klemperer and Antal Doráti, and sheltering two hundred local residents (including Kodály) in its cellars during the siege of Budapest. The 1260-seat auditorium was the first in Europe to feature an iron fire curtain (installed after a blaze at the Vienna Opera House), underfloor heating and air-conditioning. Its chandelier weighs three tonnes, and 2.7 kilos of gold were used to gild the fixtures. To the left of the stage is the box used by Emperor Franz Josef's wife, Sissi (see p.112), who loved Hungarian opera as much as he detested it. The upstairs reception rooms and downstairs foyer are equally lavish, festooned with portraits and busts of Hungarian divas and composers. Tickets for English-language **tours** of the interior (daily 3 & 4pm; 2600Ft) are available from the shop to the left of the foyer; see p.178 regarding tickets for performances.

In a similar vein, on Paulay Ede utca, off the opposite side of Andrássy, stands the **New Theatre** (Új Színház), whose blue and gold Art Nouveau facade and foyer (by Béla Lajta) look superb. Continuing north along Andrássy, you'll pass another of Budapest's venerable coffee houses, the *Mővész* (no. 29), where the magnificent interior is more enticing than the cakes or service.

Nagymező utca

One block beyond the Opera, Andrássy út is crossed by **Nagymező utca** – nicknamed "**Broadway**" because of its theatres and nightclubs. During the interwar years, the best-known club was the *Arizona*, run by Sándor Rozsnyai and his wife Miss Arizona (which inspired Pal Sándor's 1988 film of the same name, starring Hanna Schygulla and Marcello Mastroianni); the Rozsnyais were murdered by the Arrow Cross in 1944. Their club was at Nagymező utca 20, in the former home of the Habsburg court photographer who lends his name to the bottle-green tiled **Mai Manó House** (Mai Mano Ház; Mon–Fri 2–7pm, Sat, Sun & holidays 11am–7pm; 700Ft; Ⓦwww.maimano.hu), which features temporary photographic exhibitions in three separate galleries, and an excellent photographic bookshop on the first floor. Across the street, take a look at the **statue** of the composer **Imre Kálmán**, lounging on a bench outside the Operetta Theatre.

At Nagymező utca 8, on the far side of Andrássy, the **Ernst Museum** (Ernst Múzeum; Tues–Sun 11am–7pm; 600Ft; Ⓦwww.mucsarnok.hu) is another venue for temporary exhibitions, affiliated to the Műcsarnok on Hősök tere (see p.74). It's worth a peek inside purely to see the Art Nouveau features by

József Rippl-Rónai and Ödön Lechner; take a look at the Art Deco lobby of the Tivoli theatre next door, too.

The Oktogon and around

Further up Andrássy, two elongated squares lined with pavement **cafés** provide a vibrant interlude. On the left (north of Andrássy út) is **Jókai tér**, with a large statue of the novelist Mór Jókai, while across the road on **Liszt Ferenc tér**, the composer Liszt hammers an imaginary keyboard with his vast hands, blind to the drinkers and diners surrounding him. At the far end of the square, the **Music Academy** that bears his name (no. 8) contains a magnificent Art Nouveau entrance hall designed by Aladár Körösfői Kriesch, and two gilded auditoriums whose glorious decor matches the quality of the music played there.

Continuing up Andrássy út, you meet the Nagykörút at the **Oktogon**, an eight-sided square flanked by eclectic buildings. With 24-hour fast-food chains ensconced in two of them, and buses and taxis running along the Nagykörút through to the small hours, the Oktogon never sleeps. During the Horthy era it rejoiced in the name of Mussolini tér, while under the Communists it was called November 7 tér after the date of the Bolshevik revolution.

The House of Terror

You can't miss the **House of Terror** (Terror Háza; Tues–Fri 10am–6pm, Sat & Sun 10am–7.30pm; 1500Ft; Ⓦwww.terrorhaza.hu), at Andrássy út 60, due to the ominous black frame that surmounts the building, once the dreaded headquarters of the secret police. Dubbed the "House of Loyalty" by the Fascist Arrow Cross during World War II, it was subsequently used for the same purpose by the Communist ÁVO (see box below). When captured by insurgents in 1956, no trace was found of the giant meat-grinder rumoured to have been used to dispose of corpses; after the re-imposition of Soviet rule, the building was thoroughly sanitized before being handed over to the Communist Youth organization.

Opened in 2002 as a cross between a museum and a memorial, the House of Terror has been criticised by some for glossing over Hungary's role in the invasion of the Soviet Union, and its emphasis on Stalinist terror compared to the Holocaust (a subject treated in far more depth at the Holocaust Memorial Centre; see p.88). A video in the lobby repeatedly plays the image of a man weeping at the execution of 1956 insurgents, saying "this was their socialism". Perhaps balance is impossible in such a sensitive area, and the public treatment of the Stalinist years is at least a much-needed, if simplified, beginning.

The ÁVO

The **Communist secret police** began as the party's private security section during the Horthy era, when its chief, **Gábor Péter**, betrayed Trotskyites to the police to take the heat off their Stalinist comrades. After World War II it became the 9000-strong Államvédelmi Osztály or **ÁVO** (State Security Department), its growing power implicit in a change of name in 1948 – to the State Security Authority or **ÁVH** (though the old acronym stuck). Ex-Nazi torturers were easily persuaded to apply their skills on its behalf, and its network of 41,000 informers permeated society. So hated was the ÁVO that any members caught during the Uprising were summarily killed, and their mouths stuffed with banknotes (secret policemen earned more than anyone else).

The moment you step in through the spooky automatic door you're bombarded with funereal sounds and powerful images, starting with a Soviet tank and photos of ÁVO victims in the courtyard. An audioguide (1000Ft) can save you the trouble of reading the English-language sheets in each room, but the latter pack far more information. The displays begin on the second floor (you take the lift, then work downwards) with a couple of rooms dealing briskly with the murder of 600,000 Jews and Gypsies in the Holocaust, before moving on to the Soviet "liberation", deportations of "class enemies", rigged elections, collectivization, and other themes. The most harrowing part is the **basement**, with its reconstructed torture chamber and cells, where the music mercifully stops and the exhibits are allowed to speak for themselves.

The Liszt Memorial Museum and around

A little further up Andrássy on the opposite side, the Old Music Academy at no. 67 harbours the **Liszt Memorial Museum** (Liszt Ferenc Emlékmúzeum; Mon–Fri 10am–6pm, Sat 9am–5pm; closed on national holidays; 600Ft; ⓦwww.lisztmuseum.hu), entered from around the corner at Vörösmarty utca 35, where the composer – who was the first president of the Academy – lived from 1881 until his death in 1886. His glass piano and travelling keyboard are the highlights of an extensive collection of memorabilia and scores. **Concerts** are performed here by young pianists every Saturday at 11am (600Ft; Budapest Card covers entry to the museum but concert tickets must be bought separately).

Just down to the right (south) from the museum along Vörösmarty utca lies **Hunyadi tér**, which has a fine old market hall that has not yet been modernized, and some fruit and vegetable stalls in the square itself.

Kodály körönd to Hősök tere

Kodály körönd, named after the composer Zoltán Kodály, is one of Budapest's most elegant squares, flanked by four neo-Renaissance mansions. At no. 1 on the northeast corner, the ground-floor flat where he lived until his death in 1967 is a **Kodály Memorial Museum** (Kodály Emlékmúzeum; Wed 10am–4pm, Thurs–Sat 10am–6pm, Sun 10am–2pm; 600Ft; ⓦwww.kodaly-inst.hu), preserving his library, salon, dining room and folk-art collection – press the buzzer for apartment 11 to get in. During World War II the körönd was named Hitler tér, prompting the émigré Bartók to vow that he would not be buried in Hungary so long as anywhere in the country was named after Hitler or Mussolini.

Two fine collections of Asian art lurk just beyond the körönd. The **György Ráth Museum** (Tues–Sun 10am–6pm; 600Ft) displays artefacts from the vast collection amassed by the optician and art collector Ferenc Hopp (1833–1919), drawn from all the great Eastern civilizations. The museum is in an Art Nouveau villa at Városligeti fasor 12, on an avenue parallel to Andrássy. The statue in the garden of a Buddhist monk actually depicts Sándor Kőrösi-Csoma, a Hungarian who achieved fame by compiling the first English–Tibetan dictionary, though his real goal was a vain search for the ancestors of the Hungarian people. Nearby, the **Ferenc Hopp Museum** (same hours; 600Ft; ⓦwww.hoppmuzeum.hu) at Andrássy út 103 presents temporary displays of works from the same collection; you can buy a combined ticket for both for 1000Ft.

From here, the final stretch of Andrássy út up to Hősök tere is lined with spacious villas set back from the avenue, mostly housing embassies.

Erzsébetváros

The official boundary between Terézváros and **Erzsébetváros** runs down the middle of **Király utca**, which used to be a main thoroughfare before Andrássy út was built. In the 1870s the street contained 14 of the 58 licensed brothels in Budapest, and as late as 1934 Patrick Leigh Fermor was told that "any man could be a cavalier for five pengöes" here. After decades of shabby respectability under Communism the street is undergoing a revival, with numerous cafés, bars and restaurants, plus interior design and furniture boutiques. Though not the most logical place to start exploring the Jewish quarter, the route here from the direction of Andrássy út makes a wonderful approach, as you zigzag down through the backstreets. However, if you approach the area from the **Kiskörút**, as most people do, then the Dohány utca Synagogue is the obvious first objective.

English-language **guided walking tours** of the area, run by Aviv (Ⓣ1/462 0477, Ⓦwww.aviv.hu), depart from the Dohány utca Synagogue (daily except Sat at 10.30am, 11.30am, 12.30pm & 1.30pm; April–Oct also 2.30pm & 3.30pm). The cheapest tour (1900Ft) simply covers the synagogue and memorial garden; another (2250Ft) includes the Jewish Museum, while the most expensive (2600Ft) also features the Rumbach utca Synagogue. For a fascinating personalized walking tour of the entire quarter, contact Eszter Gömöri (Ⓔbp.cityguide@gmail.com), who charges €25 an hour. None of the prices cited include admission charges, where these apply.

The Dohány utca Synagogue

The splendid **Dohány utca Synagogue** (Dohány utcai Zsinagóga; April–Oct Mon–Thurs 10am–5pm, Fri 10am–3pm, Sun 10am–6pm; Nov–March Mon–Thurs 10am–3pm, Fri & Sun 10am–2pm; 1600Ft including the Jewish Museum) is one of the landmarks of Pest. Located only five-minutes' walk from Deák tér, just off Károly körút, it is Europe's largest synagogue and the second biggest in the world after the Temple Emmanuel in New York, with 3600 seats and a total capacity for over 5000 worshippers. It belongs to the **Neolog** community, a Hungarian denomination combining elements of Reform and Orthodox Judaism. Today, eighty percent of Hungarian Jewry are Neologs, but their numbers amounted to only twenty percent before the Holocaust, which virtually wiped out the Orthodox and Hassid communities in the provinces. Neolog worship includes features that are anathema to other denominations, not least organ music during services.

Designed by a Viennese Gentile, Ludwig Förster, the building epitomizes the so-called Byzantine-Moorish style that was popular in the 1850s, and attests to the patriotism of Hungarian Jewry – the colours of its brickwork (yellow, red and blue) being those of Budapest's coat of arms. In the 1990s the synagogue was restored at a cost of over $40 million; the work was funded by the Hungarian government and the Hungarian-Jewish diaspora, notably the Emmanuel Foundation, fronted by the Hollywood actor Tony Curtis who was born of 1920s emigrants.

You have time to admire the gilded onion-domed towers while waiting to pass through a security check, before entering the magnificent **interior** by Frigyes Feszl, the architect of the Vigadó concert hall. Arabesques and Stars of David decorate the ceiling, the balconies for female worshippers are surmounted by gilded arches, and the floor is inset with eight-pointed stars. The layout reflects the synagogue's Neolog identity, with the *bemah*, or Ark of the Torah, at one end, in the Reform fashion, but with men and women seated apart, according to Orthodox tradition. On Jewish festivals, the place is filled to the rafters with Jews from all over Hungary, whose chattering disturbs their more devout co-religionists. At other times, the hall is used for concerts of classical or klezmer music, as advertised outside and on Ⓦwww.jewishfestival.hu.

The **cemetery** behind the synagogue only exists at this spot because the Nazis forbade Jews from being buried elsewhere – one of many calculated humiliations inflicted on the Jewish quarter (by then a walled ghetto) by the local SS commander, Eichmann. Some 2281 Jews are interred beneath simple headstones, erected immediately after the Red Army's liberation of the ghetto on January 18, 1945. Beyond the cemetery looms the cuboid, domed **Heroes' Temple**, erected in 1929–31 in honour of the 10,000 Jewish soldiers who died fighting for Hungary during World War I. These days it serves as a synagogue for everyday use and is not open to tourists.

The Jewish Museum

Heading upstairs to the **Jewish Museum** (Zsidó Múzeum), to the left of the main synagogue entrance, note a relief of Tivadar (Theodor) Herzl, the founder of modern Zionism, who was born and taught on this site. In the foyer is a gravestone inscribed with a menorah (seven-branched candlestick) from the third century AD – proof that there were Jews living in Hungary six hundred years before the Magyars arrived. The first three rooms are devoted to Jewish festivals, with beautifully crafted objects such as Sabbath lamps and bowls for the Seder festival, some from medieval times. The final room covers the Holocaust in Hungary, with chilling photos and examples of anti-Semitic propaganda. Oddly, the museum says nothing about the huge contribution that Jews have made to Hungarian society, in every field from medicine to poetry.

Upon leaving, turn the corner on to Wesselényi utca and enter the **Raoul Wallenberg Memorial Garden**, named after the Swedish consul who saved 20,000 Jews during World War II. Armed with diplomatic status and money for bribing officials, Wallenberg and his assistants plucked thousands from the cattle trucks and lodged them in "safe houses", manoeuvring to buy time until the Russians arrived. He was last seen alive the day before the Red Army liberated the ghetto; arrested by the Soviets on suspicion of espionage, he died in the Gulag. The park's centrepiece is a **Holocaust Memorial** by Imre Varga, shaped like a weeping willow, each leaf engraved with the names of a family killed by the Nazis. On the plinth are testimonials from their relatives living in Israel, America and Russia. Behind it, glass panels by the artist Klára Szilárd commemorate the sixtieth anniversary of the Goldmark Hall, named after Károly Goldmark, the composer of the opera *The Queen of Sheba*.

Other sights in the Jewish quarter

Fanning out behind the synagogue is what was once the Jewish **ghetto**, created by the Nazis in April 1944. Initially, the Hungarian government feared that concentrating all the Jews within one area would expose the rest of Budapest to Allied bombing raids, but by November such considerations were forgotten, and all Jews living outside the ghetto were compelled to move there. As their menfolk had already been conscripted into labour battalions intended to kill them from overwork, the 70,000 inhabitants of the ghetto were largely women,

▲ Rumbach utca Synagogue

children and old folk, crammed into 162 blocks of flats, with over 50,000 of them (in buildings meant for 15,000) around Klauzál tér alone.

In happier times, each Jewish community within the quarter had their own place of worship, with a *yeshiva* (religious school) and other facilities within an enclosed courtyard invisible from the surrounding streets – as epitomized by the **Rumbach utca Synagogue** (Mon–Thurs 10am–4.30pm, Fri 10am–2.30pm, Sun 10am–5.30pm; 800Ft), five-minutes' walk from the Dohány Synagogue. Built by Otto Wagner in 1872, for the so-called "Status Quo" or middling-conservative Jews, it now belongs to the Neolog community and is slated to be turned into a museum or cultural centre. Decorated in violet, crimson and gold, its octagonal Moorish interior has yet to be fully restored after being ruined during the war. As a plaque outside notes, the building served as a detention barracks in August 1941, from where up to 1800 Slovak and Polish refugees were deported to the Nazi death camps.

En route from Dohány utca to the Rumbach Synagogue you'll cross Dob utca, where you'll see a **monument to Carl Lutz**, the Swiss consul who began issuing Schutzpasses to Jews, attesting that they were Swiss or Swedish citizens – a ruse subsequently used by Wallenberg. After the war he was criticized for abusing Swiss law and, feeling slighted, proposed himself for the Nobel Peace Prize. His monument – a gilded angel swooping down to help a prostrate victim – is locally known as "the figure jumping out of a window".

Just beyond Lutz's memorial, a grey stone portal at no. 16 leads into the **Gozsdu-udvar**, a 200-metre-long passageway built in 1904 and running through to Király utca 11. Connecting seven courtyards, it was a hive of life and activity before the Holocaust; after many years of dereliction, has now been redeveloped as a luxury plaza containing flats and shops.

The kosher *Fröhlich* patisserie at Dob utca 22 is one of several Jewish businesses around **Kazinczy utca**, the centre of the 3000-strong Orthodox community, where Yiddish can still be heard. There's a butcher's in the yard of Dob utca 35, with wigmakers at nos. 31 and 46, while down to the right at Kazinczy utca 28 are a kosher baker and pizzeria, opposite the kosher *Carmel* restaurant. Almost next door to the last stands the **Orthodox Synagogue** (Mon–Thurs 10am–4.30pm, Fri 10am–2.30pm, Sun 10am–5.30pm; 800Ft), built by Béla and Sándor Löffler in 1913 in the Art Nouveau style, with a facade melding into the curve of the street, and an interior with painted rather than moulded motifs. A smaller wood-panelled synagogue for winter use, a *yeshiva* and the *Hanna* Orthodox kosher restaurant are all contained within an L-shaped courtyard that can also be entered via an arcade on Dob utca.

The Museum of Electrotechnology

For something quite different, visit the **Museum of Electrotechnology** (Magyar Elektrotechnikai Múzeum; Tues–Fri 10am–5pm, Sat 9am–6pm; 400Ft; Ⓦwww.emuzeum.hu), set in a former electricity substation at Kazinczy utca 21, down the road from the Orthodox Synagogue. Its curators can demonstrate the world's first dynamo (invented in 1859 by Áynos Jedlik, a Benedictine monk) and other devices in rooms devoted to such topics as the history of light bulbs and the Hungarian section of the **Iron Curtain**, along the border with Austria. Though the current was too weak to kill and the minefields were removed in 1965, patrols kept it inviolate until 1989, when the Hungarians ceased shooting escapees, thereby spelling the end of the Iron Curtain as a whole.

Beyond the Nagykörút

Pressing on along Dohány utca, you come to another piece of old Budapest that for many years lay derelict. Like the Gresham Palace on Roosevelt tér (see p.53), the **New York Palace** on the corner of the Nagykörút is a Budapest landmark also associated with an insurance company, in this case the New York, which commissioned the building in 1895 and included in the plans a magnificent coffee house, which became one of the great literary cafés of interwar Budapest. Under Communism the edifice housed a publishers, and its Beaux Arts façade – with a small Statue of Liberty high up on the corner – survived being rammed by a tank in 1956. Now reopened as a luxury hotel, its gilded and frescoed restaurant-cum-coffee house is worth a look, even if you don't want to fork out to eat there.

Further along Dohány utca the district changes, becoming more working class and tinged with Arab and Chinese influences as you near the "**Garment District**" around **Garay tér**. The bustling **market hall** on the square is a lunch spot for workers from the sweatshops in a neighbourhood where wholesalers do business in a dozen languages and travel agents offer trips to Mecca. A few blocks from Keleti Station (you can also take the metro to Keleti pu. if you want to avoid the walk), the **Miksa Róth Museum** (Róth Miksa Múzeum; Tues–Sun 2–6pm; 600Ft), in the backstreets behind Keleti at Nefelejcs utca 26, showcases the work of a leading figure in the Hungarian Art Nouveau movement. Located in Róth's former home, the museum reveals the diversity of his work – both in stained glass and in mosaics – which can also be seen in the Parliament, the Gresham Palace, the Music Academy and the Jewish Museum.

4

The Városliget and the stadium district

Both **Hősök tere** (Heroes' Square) and the **Városliget** (City Park), at the end of Andrassy út, were created in the late nineteenth century for the nationwide celebrations of the millennium of the Magyar conquest of Hungary, but as neither was ready on time the anniversary was rescheduled for the following year. Historians revised the date of the conquest accordingly and have stuck to 896 ever since. The millennial celebrations were unashamedly nationalistic but full of contradictions, as the Dual Monarchy tried to flatter Hungarians without alienating other ethnic groups that resented Magyar chauvinism, so each was represented at the exhibition. Today, the chief attractions are the **Museum of Fine Arts** and the romantic **Vajdahunyad Castle**, followed by a wallow in the **Széchenyi Baths**. Budapest's **zoo**, **circus** and amusement park are also located in the vicinity, together with two of the city's classiest restaurants, and a handful of other museums. Nearby are several indoor and outdoor **stadiums** that host sporting competitions, concerts and other events, and one of Budapest's Art Nouveau masterpieces, the **Geological Institute**.

The best ways to reach the Városliget from the centre are on the yellow metro line or bus #4, but trolleybus #74 from the Dohány utca Synagogue and #72 from Arany János utca metro station are also useful. To reach the stadium district, catch trolleybus #75 from Hősök tere or the red metro from the centre of town to Stadionok Station.

Hősök tere and the Museum of Fine Arts

The enormous ceremonial plaza of **Hősök tere** is flanked by two galleries resembling Greek temples. At its centre is the **Millenary Monument** – Budapest's answer to London's Nelson's Column – consisting of a 36-metre-high column topped by the figure of the Archangel Gabriel who, according to legend, appeared to Stephen in a dream and offered him the crown of Hungary. Around the base are figures of Prince Árpád and his chieftains, who led the seven Magyar tribes into the Carpathian Basin. They look like a wild bunch; one of the chieftains, Huba, even has stag's antlers strapped to his horse's head. As a backdrop

VÁROSLIGET AND THE STADIUMS

to this, a semicircular colonnade displays statues of Hungary's most illustrious leaders, from King Stephen to Kossuth.

During the brief Republic of Councils in 1919, when the country was governed by revolutionary Soviets, the square was decked out in red banners and the column enclosed in a red obelisk bearing a relief of Marx. In 1989, it was the setting for the ceremonial reburial of Imre Nagy and other murdered leaders of the 1956 Uprising (plus an empty coffin representing the "unknown insurgent") – an event which symbolized the dawning of a new era in Hungary. Today it's more likely to be filled with rollerbladers and skateboarders – for whom the smooth surface is ideal – or for hosting **events** such as the National Gallop or Army Day in May.

On the south side of the square is the **Műcsarnok** (Exhibition Hall; Tues, Wed & Fri–Sun 10am–6pm, Thurs noon–8pm; 1200Ft; Ⓦwww.mucsarnok.hu), also called the Palace of Art (not to be confused with the Palace of Arts, covered on p.89). A Grecian pile with gilded columns and a mosaic of St Stephen as patron of the arts, it was inaugurated in 1895. Its magnificent facade and foyer are in contrast to the four austere rooms used for **temporary exhibitions** (two or three at a time), often of modern art. It's possible to buy a combined ticket (1400Ft) valid for a month, which also covers exhibitions at the Ernst Museum on Nagymező utca (see p.65).

Dózsa György út, the wide avenue running off alongside the Városliget, serves as the setting for occasional **fairs** and **concerts**. In Communist times it was here that Party leaders reviewed parades from a grandstand, beneath a 25-metre-high statue of Stalin that was torn down during the Uprising, dragged to the Nagykörút and hammered into bits for souvenirs. After the re-imposition of Communist rule a statue of Lenin was erected in its place, which remained until it was taken away "for structural repairs" in 1989 and finally ended up in the Memento Park (see p.126).

Today, three monuments mark the distance that Hungary has travelled since then. The **Timewheel** is the world's largest hourglass, a metal canister eight metres in diameter that rotates 180° on the last day of each year, symbolizing

Hungary's accession to the European Union in 2004. Where the Stalin statue once stood, the **Monument to the Uprising** is a forest of oxidized columns merging into a stainless steel wedge, beside a Hungarian flag with a circle cut out, recalling the excision of the hated Soviet symbol in 1956. Beyond this, a crucifix rises over the foundations of the **Virgin Mary Church** that the Communists demolished in 1951.

Museum of Fine Arts

To the north of the square, the **Museum of Fine Arts** (Szépművészeti Múzeum; Tues–Sun 10am–5.30pm; 1200Ft; Ⓦwww.szepmuveszeti.hu) is the pan-European equivalent of the Hungarian National Gallery, housed in an imposing Neoclassical building completed in 1906. Most exhibits are labelled in English and a free floor-plan is available, but if you want more information you should go on an English-language **tour** (Tues–Sat 11am & 2pm from the lobby; free) or hire an **audioguide** (1000Ft). Besides its permanent collection, there are regular **temporary exhibitions** (1400–3200Ft; combined ticket 3600Ft) and cultural **events** on Thursdays (6–10pm; 3000Ft), as advertised. Art historians may be drawn to the **library** (Mon–Fri 9am–5pm), a treasure trove of information in various languages, housed nearby at VI, Szondi utca 77.

Lower ground floor

In the museum's bowels, a hippopotamus-tusk wand carved with spells to protect a child presages the small but choice **Egyptian Collection**, chiefly from the Late Period and Greco-Roman eras of Egyptian civilization. The highlights of the first room are four huge painted coffins and a child-sized one from Gamhud in Middle Egypt; *shabti* figures, intended to perform menial tasks in the afterlife; and mummified crocodiles and other creatures from the Late Period, when animal cults reached their apogee. In the second room, look out for the sculpted heads of a priestess of Hathor and a bewigged youth from the New Kingdom, the painted coffin of a priestess of Amun (bearing an uncanny resemblance to Julia Roberts), and a tautly poised bronze of the cat goddess Bastet.

Across the basement lobby, the section entitled **Art around 1900** starts with **Symbolist** and **Decadent** works such as Franz von Stuck's *The Kiss of the Sphinx*, Arnold Böcklin's *Spring*, and Hans Makart's *Nessus carries off Deianeira*. The remainder musters a few works by the Hungarian **Art Nouveau** masters József Rippl-Rónai and Károly Ferenczy (better showcased in the National Gallery; see pp.101–102), an Utrillo street scene, some dull Bonnards and two iconic images by **Oscar Kokoschka**: *Veronica's Veil* and the poster *Der Sturm*.

Ground floor

In the entrance lobby, take a look at the larger-than-life **statue of Maria Theresa** that the Communists removed from the pantheon of Hungarian leaders on Hősök tere in 1957, as a tit-for-tat for the demolition of Stalin's statue. Across the lobby are several rooms devoted to **ancient Mediterranean cultures** from Etruria to Athens, mainly represented by jugs and vases. Highlights include a pair of bronze shin-guards decorated with rams' heads, terracotta tiles portraying bestial deities, a man's torso and head from the pediment of a Campanian temple, lifelike busts of Roman worthies, and an Attic marble sarcophagus carved with hunting scenes.

Across the ground-floor lobby is an excellent **bookshop** (where you can have a poster of any picture in the museum printed for 9000Ft), leading to a wing used for **temporary exhibitions** (requiring a separate ticket). Before heading upstairs, visit the grand **Renaissance Hall**, used for hanging large allegorical or religious works on loan from other museums; the **Baroque** Hall (often used for televised events), and the **Prints and Drawings Room** at the far end on the right, mounting temporary displays (free) drawn from the museum's holdings of works by Raphael, Leonardo, Rembrandt, Rubens, Dürer, Picasso and Chagall.

First floor

The museum's forte is its hoard of **Old Masters**, based on the collection of Count Miklós Esterházy, which he sold to the state in 1871. The paintings are organized into eight sections – four on each side at the top of the stairs – and are harder to navigate than you'd imagine due to the system of numbering main rooms with Roman numerals and smaller ones with Arabic digits. Happily, the current director has reversed his predecessor's policy of stacking pictures one above another (which made it hard to appreciate ones far above eye-level), allowing the pieces more space.

The **Spanish Collection** of seventy works is arguably the best in the world outside Spain. Located off to the right at the top of the stairs, it kicks off with vivid altarpieces by unknown Catalonians, such as the *Bishop-Saint Enthroned* (whose bewilderment belies his magnificent attire) in room II. Room V, beyond, has seven **El Greco**s – including *The Disrobing of Christ*, *The Agony in the Garden*, *The Apostle St Andrew* and *The Penitent Magdalene* – and a superb *Adoration of the Magi* by Eugenio Cajes. **Murillo**'s *Flight into Egypt* and *Holy Family with the Infant St John the Baptist* hang beside a tender *Holy Family* and celestial *Virgin Immaculate* by **Zubaran** in room IV, leading to five **Goya**s (room III) ranging from war scenes (*2nd of May*) to portraits of the rich (*Señora Ceán Bermudez*) and humble (*The Knife-Grinder*). **Velázquez**'s *Peasants at Table* and **Ribera**'s gory *Martyrdom of St Andrew* are the highlights of room VI; with an annex of Habsburg court portraits by Juan Martinez (room 1).

Entering the adjacent **Flemish Collection**, Snyders' gigantic *Hawk in the Barnyard* and Van Valkenborch's nocturnal *Pilgrims Before a Forest* in room VII are overshadowed by room VIII, where the serenity of **Van Dyck**'s *St John the Evangelist* contrasts with the melodrama of **Rubens**' *Mucius Scaevola before Porsenna* and **Jordeans**' *The Satyr and the Peasant.*

Room IX segues into the **Dutch Collection** with an array of **Brueghels**, from Pieter the Elder's *Sermon of St John the Baptist* to Pieter the Younger's *Blind Hurdy-Gurdy Player* and Jan's *Paradise Landscape* and *Garden of Eden with the Fall of Man*. A copy of **Bosch**'s *The Bacchus Singers* (featuring a man making himself vomit) hangs in room 7. The rest of the Dutch collection is on the floor above, reached by stairs (or a lift) off room IX. There you'll find the *Parable of the Hidden Treasure* by **Rembrandt** and his pupil Gerard Dou and other works from his studio in room XVIII to the right, with portraits by **Hals** and wildlife scenes by **Melchior de Houdeleoter** in rooms XXVII and XXVI, off to the left.

Back on the first floor, in room X, the **German Collection** opens with **Angelika Kauffann**'s *The Wife of Count Esterházy as Venus* – a strumpet with her jewellery box – and darkly Gothic works by **Cranach** the Elder, such as *Christ and the Adulteress* and *The Lamentation* (room XI). In *Salome with the Head of St John the Baptist*, Salome displays his head on a platter with the nonchalance of a hostess bringing out the roast. Every emotion from awe to jealousy appears on the faces in **Holbein**'s *Dormition of the Virgin*, at the far end of the room. Don't overlook **Dürer**'s *Young Man* with an enigmatic smile, sharing room 14 with pictures by **Altdorfer**.

For a change of mood, cross the lobby and enter **From Romanticism to Postimpressionism**, where Room XII displays **Courbet**'s wild landscapes and life-sized *Wrestlers*, **Corot**'s *Remembrance of Coubrou* and **Rodin**'s sculpture *The Brazen Age*. Tucked away elsewhere you'll find *Lady with a Fan* by **Manet** (room 20), orchards and river-views by **Renoir**, **Monet** and **Pissaro** (room 21), **Toulouse-Lautrec**'s *Ladies* and a little-known **Gauguin**, *Black Pigs*, from his Tahitian period (room 22). Teutonic Romanticism rules in room XIII, with Von Lenbach's *The Triumphal Arch of Titus in Rome* and Böcklin's *Centaur at a Forge*.

The single room (XIV) devoted to **English art** musters a dullish portrait apiece by Hogarth, Reynolds and Gainsborough, and a melodramatic theatre scene by Zoffany – put to shame by the display of **French art until 1800** that fills room XVI (beyond the cloakroom), whose highlight is *The Rest on the Flight into Egypt* by **Poussin**.

The superb **Italian Collection** occupies nine rooms and can be viewed in chronological order by entering from the lobby opposite the Spanish section, or in reverse from the English or French rooms; some backtracking is inevitable. A tradition of gilded altarpieces such as *The Mystic Marriage of St Catherine* (room XXIV) gave rise to **Boccacio**'s masterpiece *The Adoration of the Infant Christ*, displayed in room XII near **Titian**'s *Madonna and Child with St Paul* and a watchful Venetian Doge by **Tintoretto** (who is also represented by a *Portrait of a Lady* and *Hercules Expelling the Faun from Omphale's Bed* in room XX). Look out for **Raphael**'s exquisite *Esterházy Madonna* – a Virgin and Child with the infant St John – and a self-portrait by **Giorgione** in room XIX; a **Veronese** grandee in an ermine-trimmed robe (room XVII); **Bellini**'s pig-eyed *Queen of Cyprus* (room XXIII); and the Biblical epic *Jael and Sara*, by **Artemisia Gentileschi** (room XVIII).

The Városliget

The **Városliget** (City Park) starts just behind Hősök tere, where the fairy-tale towers of **Vajdahunyad Castle** rear above an island girdled by an artificial lake that's used for **boating** in the summer and transformed into a splendid outdoor **ice-rink** in winter. Like the park, the castle was created for the Millenary Anniversary celebrations of 1896, proving so popular that the temporarystructures were replaced by permanent ones. Vajdahunyad is a catalogue in stone of architectural styles from the kingdom of Hungary, incorporating parts of two Transylvanian castles and a replica of the Romanesque **chapel at Ják** (May–Sept daily 10am–8pm; 100Ft), with a splendidly carved portal and a Renaissance courtyard that makes a romantic setting for evening **concerts** from July to mid-August.

In the main wing of the castle, the **Agriculture Museum** (Mezőgazdasági Múzeum; Tues–Sun 10am–5pm; 500Ft; Ⓦwww.mezogazdasagimuzeum.hu) traces the history of hunting and farming in Hungary. Its most interesting sections relate to the early Magyars and such typically Hungarian breeds of livestock as long-horned grey cattle (favoured for their draught power rather than their milk) and woolly pigs. Upstairs, the hunting section is notable for a prehistoric dugout boat carved from a single piece of oak, which was found at

▲ Statue of Anonymous, Városliget

Lake Balaton southwest of the capital, and antique crossbows and rifles exquisitely inlaid with leaping hares and other prey.

Even if you decide to skip the museum, don't miss the hooded **statue of Anonymous** outside. This nameless chronicler to King Béla is the prime source of information about early medieval Hungary, though the existence of several monarchs of that name during the twelfth and thirteenth centuries makes it hard to date him (or his chronicles) with any accuracy. Further into the park roughly midway between the Castle and the Timewheel, a monument to **George Washington** erected in 1906 by immigrant Hungarians attests to the patriotism of the Magyar diaspora.

The Petőfi Csarnok and Transport Museum

Leaving Vajdahunyad island by the causeway at the rear, you're ten-minutes' walk from the **Petőfi Csarnok** (Petőfi Hall; ⓣ1/363-3730 or ⓦwww.petoficsarnok.hu for information), a 1970s "Metropolitan Youth Centre" that regularly hosts concerts (outdoors in summer), films and parties, and a fine

flea market at weekends. Trolleybuses #70, #72 and #74 from the centre of town all go near the hall. At the back of the building is a stairway leading to the **Aviation and Space Flight Exhibition** (Repüléstörténeti és Űrhajózási kiállítás; April–Nov Tues–Fri 10am–5pm, Sat & Sun 10am–6pm; 800Ft) which, among other items, contains the space capsule used by Hungary's first astronaut, Bertalan Farkas and his Soviet colleague on the Soyuz-35 mission of 1980; and an L-2 monoplane sporting an Italian Fascist symbol, which broke world speed records in the Budapest–Rome races of 1927 and 1930. Alas, there seems to be nothing about Count **László Almássy**, Hungary's foremost aviator of that time, now better known abroad as the hero of the book and film *The English Patient*.

Not far away is the **Transport Museum** (Közlekedési Múzeum; Tues–Fri 10am–5pm, Sat & Sun 10am–6pm; 800Ft) on the edge of the park, of which the aviation exhibition is an outgrowth (a combined ticket for both costs 1100Ft). Captions in English explain that the Hungarian transport network of the 1890s was among the most sophisticated in Europe; despite the country starting from a low technological base, railways, canals, trams and a metro had all been created within fifty years. Displays include vintage locomotives and scale models of steamboats, and a wonderful collection of Hungarian Railways posters from 1900 to 1980. The model train set on the floor above the foyer attracts a crowd when it's switched on – for fifteen minutes every hour, on the hour. Collectors can buy Hungarian model trains in the museum shop. Outside the building are remnants of two of the Danube bridges that were wrecked in 1945: the cast-iron Erzsébet híd (replaced by a new bridge) and a few links of the original chains from the Lánchíd, which is now supported by cables.

The Széchenyi Baths

On the far side of the park's main axis, Kós Károly sétány, the **Széchenyi Baths** (Széchenyi Gyógyfürdő; see p.192 for details) could be mistaken for a palace, so grand is its facade. Outside is a statue of the geologist Zsigmondy Vilmos, who discovered the thermal spring that feeds its outdoor pool and Turkish baths. This is perhaps the best venue for mixed-sex bathing, and in one of the large outdoor pools you can enjoy the surreal spectacle of people playing **chess** while immersed up to their chests in steaming water – so hot that you shouldn't stay in for more than twenty minutes. The best players sit at tables around the pool's edge (the late former world champion **Bobby Fischer** among them in the 1980s); bring your own set if you wish to participate. Come evening, the pool is a popular spot for **parties** (see p.170).

The Circus, Vidám Park and the Zoo

Beyond the baths, on the far side of Állatkerti körút, the **Municipal Circus** (Fővárosi Nagycirkusz; all year except Sept Wed, Fri & Sun 3pm & 7pm, Thurs 3pm, Sat 10am, 3pm & 7pm; 1200–1900Ft; Ⓦwww.maciva.hu) traces its origins back to 1783, when the Hetz Theatre played to spectators on what is now Deák tér. To the right is **Vidám Park**, an old-fashioned fairground known as the "English Park" before the war (daily 11am–6pm, till 8pm July–Aug; weekdays adult/child 3900/2500Ft, weekends & holidays 3900/2900Ft, free for children under 100cm in height; Ⓦwww.vidampark.hu). The funfair was the setting for Ferenc Molnár's play *Liliom*, which inspired the musical *Carousel*. The gilded merry-go-round to the left of the entrance and the wooden switchback at the back of the fairground both predate World War II.

Further down towards Hősök tere you'll find the delightful Elephant Gates of Budapest's **Zoo** (Állatkert; Jan, Feb, Nov & Dec daily 9am–3pm; March & Oct Mon–Thurs 9am–4.30pm, Fri–Sun 9am–5pm; April & Sept Mon–Thurs 9am–4.30pm, Fri–Sun 9am–5.30pm; May–Aug Mon–Thurs 9am–6pm, Fri–Sun 9am–6.30pm; 1690Ft, family 4800Ft; ⓦwww.zoobudapest.com), which opened its doors in 1866. Its Art Nouveau pavilions by Károly Kós (dating from 1911) seemed the last word in zoological architecture, but it slowly stagnated until the 1990s, when a new director aided by private sponsors began long-overdue improvements to give the animals better habitats and make the zoo more visitor-friendly. In 2007, it proudly announced the world's first birth of a rhino conceived by artificial insemination, which has been one of its top attractions ever since. Don't miss the exotic **Elephant House**, resembling a Central Asian mosque, the **Palm House** with its magnificent **aquarium** below, or the **Bonsai garden**. Look out also for children's events and evening concerts, as advertised outside the main entrance. The children's corner is signposted "Állatóvoda", to the left from the entrance past the Palm House. Note that the animal houses open one hour later and close thirty minutes before the zoo itself.

The stadium district

The **stadium district**, 1km south of Vajdahunyad Castle, is chiefly notable for the **Puskás Ferenc Stadium**, where league championship and international **football** matches, **concerts** by foreign rock stars and events such as the national dog show are held. Originally known as Népstadion ("People's Stadium") and built in the early 1950s by fifty thousand Budapestis who "volunteered" their labour, unpaid, on Soviet-style "free Saturdays", it was renamed in 2002 after the legendary footballer and manager Ferenc Puskás (1927–2006), who captained the Mighty Magyars in their stunning triumph over England at Wembley Stadium in 1953 (a team that went unbeaten for a world record of 32 consecutive games), before defecting to forge a second career at Real Madrid.

To the west of the stadium is the smaller Kisstadion, while to the east Stalinist statues of healthy proletarian youth line the court that leads to the indoor **Papp László Sportaréna** (or Aréna), a mushroom-shaped silver structure which also hosts concerts and sporting events – Papp was the first boxer to win three Olympic gold medals (1948, 1952 and 1956). The Stadion **bus station** completes this concrete ensemble.

Catching trolleybus #75 along Stefánia út, past the Aréna, you can admire the **Geological Institute** at no. 14, one of the major edifices in Budapest designed by Ödön Lechner. The exterior is as striking as his Post Office Savings Bank (see p.58) and Applied Arts Museum (p.87), with a gingerbread facade, scrolled gables and steeply pitched Transylvanian roofs patterned in bright-blue tiles, crowned by figures holding globes on their backs. By visiting its small **Geological Museum** (Földani Múzeum; Thurs, Sat & Sun 10am–4pm; 400Ft), you can also see something of the interior, with its gingerbread stucco and faux lapis lazuli stairways.

Budapest's Art Nouveau

From swirling maidens and foliage on apartment block balustrades to the sumptuous facades and rooftops of iconic edifices such as the Gresham Palace and Post Office Savings Bank, Art Nouveau can be seen all over Budapest. Tombs in the Jewish Cemetery, stained glass in shopping arcades and gilded mosaics in theatres – even humble bus terminals exude the spirit of Hungarian Art Nouveau, which locals call *Magyar szecesszió* to distinguish it from the Vienna Secession and Jugendstil movements that flourished at the same time in Austria and Germany.

Zsolnay tilework, portico of the Applied Arts Museum ▲

Hűvösvölgy bus terminus ▼

Stained-glass window, Miksa Róth Museum ▼

Life as a work of art

Conceived as an all-encompassing style in which architecture, fine art and design worked in harmony to elevate the mundane objects and activities of modern life to a "total work of art", **Art Nouveau** spread across Europe and the world in the late 1880s and 1890s before abruptly falling from fashion – all within 25 years. Budapest was no exception, with the city's Art Nouveau **architecture** acquiring a distinctively Magyar flavour thanks to **Ödön Lechner** (1845–1914). He eschewed the linear "whiplash" motif of the Viennese Secessionists in favour of vibrant ornamentation that blended Magyar and Turkic folk designs with Mogul elements. In the 1890s Lechner used new materials such as reinforced concrete and glazed Zsolnay tiles from Pécs in southern Hungary to create such flamboyant public buildings as the **Post Office Savings Bank**, the **Applied Arts Museum** and the **Geological Institute**.

Though Lechner's creations were too weird for official tastes, they influenced a generation of architects who left their mark on Budapest in the 1900s. **Béla Lajta** (1873–1920) collaborated with Lechner on the exotic **Schmidl tomb** in the Jewish Cemetery before pursuing a more Modernist style. Others remained closer to Lechner's vision of a "national" style, drawing on the medieval village architecture of Transylvania for inspiration. The **National Romantic** school of Károly Kós (1883–1977) for example imagined a Magyar arcadia of garden cities and model villages, as seen in the Arts and Crafts-style homes on the **Napraforgó utca housing estate**, the medieval-esque **Hűvösvölgy bus terminus** and the **Bird House** in Budapest's Zoo.

In and out of style

Despite its claim to be a style for all, the ideal of a totally Art Nouveau environment was only attained in grand apartments and villas. Emil Vidor's **Bedő House** is a treasure-trove of Art Nouveau furniture, glassware, cutlery, jewellery and fashion, behind a *Hansel-and-Gretel*-on-acid facade. In contrast, the relatively austere work of **Miksa Róth** (1865–1944), a prolific **stained-glass** painter and designer, graces the interiors of the **Gresham Palace**, Parliament, the Applied Arts Museum and the Parizsi udvar shopping arcade – not to mention his own house, preserved as a museum.

Róth was greatly influenced by the English Pre-Raphaelites, as was the **Gödöllő artists' colony**, whose pictorial version of National Romanticism – all Magyar maidens, knights and peasants – ennobles many of Budapest's theatres and concert halls.

In the graphic arts, the impression left by the Gödöllő artists proved short-lived beside that of **József Rippl-Rónai** (1861–1927), who painted and drew everyday life in a style which greatly influenced post-war artists, and was only later deemed to be Art Nouveau. You can see his portraits in the **Hungarian National Gallery**. In architecture, the triumph of Modernism was writ large under Communism but the work of the National Romantics would inspire Hungary's best known contemporary architect, **Imre Makovecz**, whose "**organic architecture**" is in the same tradition. Don't miss his gullet-like crypt at **Farkasréti Cemetery** and wooden buildings in the Visegrád Hills from the 1980s, when Makovecz was a rebel against the system.

▲ Bedő House

▼ Bedő House, interior

Post Office Savings Bank, detail of facade ▲

Geological Institute ▼

Budapest's Art Nouveau highlights

▸▸ **Post Office Savings Bank** Ödön Lechner at his best, with a green-and-gold tiled facade decorated with bees (symbolizing saving). Sadly, the interior is off-limits. See p.58

▸▸ **Gresham Palace** The foyer of this deluxe hotel is exquisitely tiled in subtle greys, with wrought-iron peacock gates by Miksa Róth. See p.53

▸▸ **Bedő House** A fantastic museum of Art Nouveau furniture, silver and other pieces, set in a recently restored 1900s residential block with a groovy pistachio facade. See p.57

▸▸ **Budapest Zoo** An outstanding collection of buildings in different styles – check out the Bird, Monkey and Elephant Houses, and the Aquarium beneath the Palm House. See p.80

▸▸ **Music Academy** The spectacular gilded auditoria and Babylonian foyer can only be seen when you attend a concert, but the music is wonderful, too. See p.66

▸▸ **Applied Arts Museum** Buttercup tiling spangled with Turkic motifs, a magnificent majolica dome and a pure white Mogul interior make this Lechner's masterpiece. See p.87

▸▸ **Kerepesi Cemetery** Two funerary colonnades with gilded mosaics by Körösfői-Kriesch, and heaps of other Art Nouveau statuary. See p.85

▸▸ **Gellért Baths** Bathe like a Roman emperor in a sumptuous pool surrounded by majolica creatures and columns. See p.109

▸▸ **Geological Institute** Unmistakeably by Lechner, with a zany Transylvanian skyline and an interior verging on the psychedelic. See p.80

▸▸ **Hűvösvölgy bus terminus** Turreted ticket offices and sweeping covered stairways make commuters feel that they've walked on stage. See p.123

5

Józsefváros and Ferencváros

Separated from Erzsébetváros by Rákóczi út, which runs out to Keleti Station, **Józsefváros** (the VIII District) is an amalgam of high and low life. While the **Hungarian National Museum**, Eötvös Loránd University and the Szabó Ervin Library on Múzeum körút make for a lively **student quarter**, its seedier hinterland beyond the Nagykörút district – nicknamed "Chicago" between the wars – is still associated with vice and crime, despite efforts to clean it up. You can wander safely anywhere in Józsefváros by day, and between the Kiskörút and Nagykörút in the small hours, but elsewhere stick to main roads and avoid pedestrian underpasses after midnight – particularly around Keleti Station, where **Kerepesi Cemetery** and the **Police History Museum** are worth a visit by day.

Üllői út – leading to the airport – marks the boundary of the adjacent **Ferencváros** (Franz Town, the IX District), once the most solidly working class of the inner city districts. Today, **Ráday utca** and the backstreets behind the wonderful **Great Market Hall** on Vámház körút are full of hip restaurants and bars; luxury condos rise where teenage insurgents once fought, and the district's historic far-right sympathies are challenged by a **Holocaust Memorial Centre**. For culture, there's the **Palace of Arts** complex by the river, while football fans will want to see Fradi in action at the **FTC Stadium**, and children enjoy the **Natural History Museum**.

Transport for the two districts include the red and blue metro lines, trams #4 and #6 along the Nagykörút and tram #2, which runs down the Pest bank of the Danube to the Palace of Arts.

Józsefváros

Part of the Kiskörút, **Múzeum körút** separates the Belváros and Józsefváros. Aside from being curved rather than straight, it resembles Andrássy út in miniature, lined with trees, shops and grandiose buildings. Immediately beyond the East–West Business Centre by the Astoria junction stands the old faculty of the **Eötvös Loránd Science University** (known by its Hungarian initials as ELTE). It's named after the physicist Loránd Eötvös, whose pupils included

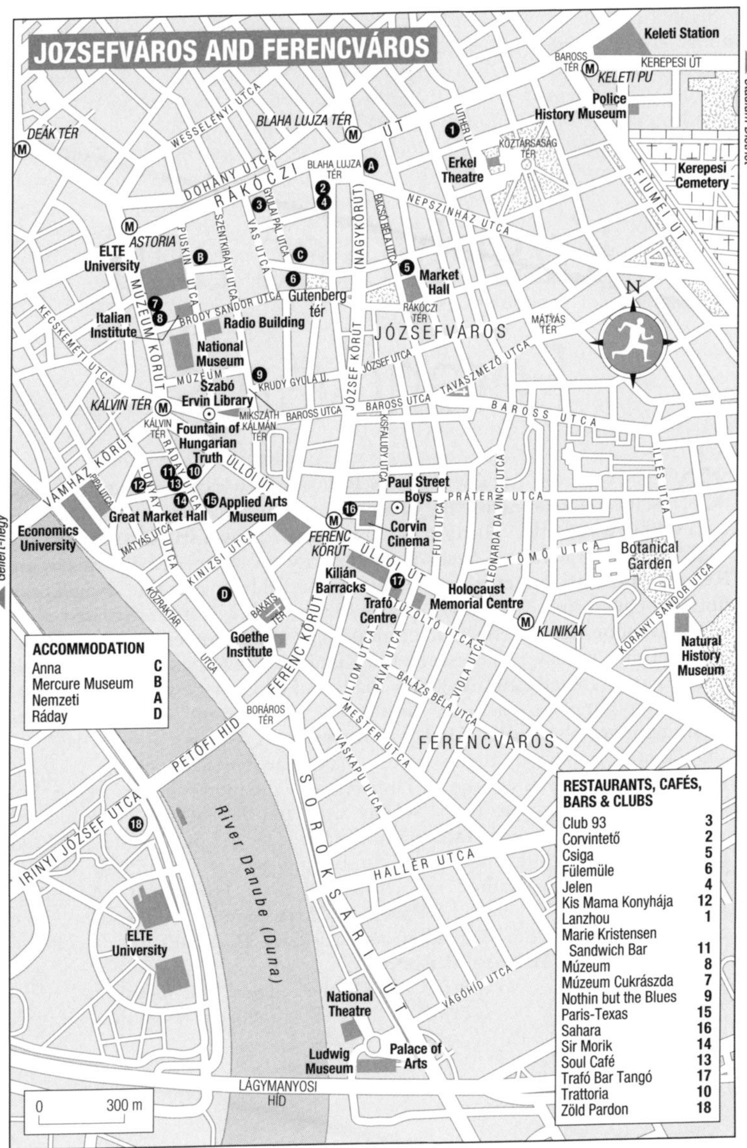

many of the scientists who later developed the US atomic bombs at Los Alamos, including Edward Teller, "Father of the Hydrogen Bomb".

Across the street, on Ferenczy utca, you can see a small crenellated section of the **medieval wall of Pest**. Originally 2km long and 8m high, the walls gradually disappeared as the city was built up on either side, but fragments remain here and there – a larger freestanding chunk lurks in the courtyard of no. 21.

Staying on the outer edge of Múzeum körút, you'll find the **Múzeum** at no. 12, which was one of the earliest coffee houses in Pest. Its original frescoes and Zsolnay ceramic reliefs dating from 1885 still grace what has long since become a restaurant (see p.164). From here, you can wander down **Bródy Sándor utca**, which runs along the garden of the Hungarian National Museum. The Renaissance-style mansion at no. 8 housed the lower chamber of the Hungarian Parliament from 1867 until its present building was completed, and is now home to the **Italian Institute**. Diagonally across the street at nos. 5–7 is the **Radio Building**, from which ÁVO guards fired upon students demanding access to the airwaves, an act which turned the hitherto peaceful protests of October 23, 1956 into an uprising against the secret police and other manifestations of Stalinism.

Hungarian National Museum

Like the National Library on Várhegy, the **Hungarian National Museum** (Magyar Nemzeti Múzeum; Tues–Sun 10am–6pm; 1000Ft; free on March 15, Aug 20 & Oct 23; Ⓦwww.hnm.hu) was the brainchild of Count Ferenc Széchenyi (father of István), who donated thousands of prints and manuscripts to form the basis of its collection. Housed in a Grecian-style edifice by Mihály Pollack, it was only the fourth such museum in the world when it opened in 1847, and soon afterwards became the stage for a famous event in the **1848 Revolution**, when Sándor Petőfi (see p.51) first declaimed the *National Song* from its steps, with its rousing refrain "Choose! Now is the time! Shall we be slaves or shall we be free?" ("Some noisy mob had their hurly-burly outside so I left for home," complained the museum's director.) Ever since, March 15 has been commemorated here with flags and speeches.

The basement and ground floor

By way of amends for losing the Coronation Regalia in 2000 (now on display in Parliament – see p.61), the National Museum has undergone a major refit, resulting in two new subterranean levels devoted to **medieval and Roman stonework** – the latter starring a second-century AD mosaic floor from a villa at Nemesvámos-Baláca in western Hungary. To the left of the ground-floor foyer, a darkened room displays King Stephen's exquisite Byzantine silk **coronation mantle**, which is far too fragile to be exhibited in the Parliament building.

Equally impressive is the section to the right of the foyer, called **On the East-West Frontier**, which covers the pre-Hungarian peoples of the Carpathian Basin. Besides life-size models of a Palaeolithic cave dwelling and a 6000-year-old house, its highlights include three skeletons and grave goods from a 1600 BC cemetery at Tiszafüred, gold Germanic bangles and the **Nagyszentmiklós treasure**, a gorgeous 23-piece gold dinner service belonging to an Avar chieftain.

While all the sections so far described are fully captioned in English, the same can't be said of the exhibits upstairs, so you may wish to rent an **audioguide** (750Ft per hour) from the museum shop before proceeding any further.

Upstairs

The main exhibition on the upper floor traces **Hungarian history** from the Árpád dynasty to the end of Communism, starting on the left side of the rotunda at the top of the stairs. Room 1 contains Béla III's crown, sceptre and

sword, and in room 2, there's a gilded reliquary bust of St László and a wall fountain from the royal palace at Visegrád (see p.137). Don't miss the ivory saddles inlaid with hunting scenes in room 3, the suit of armour of the child-king Sigismund II in room 5, or the huge carved Renaissance pew in room 6. Turkish weaponry and the ornate tomb of Count György Apafi in room 7 speak of the 150 years when Hungary was divided and its destiny decided by intriguers and warlords, including the Forgáchs and Nádasdys depicted in the oldest **portraits** in Hungary, hung in room 8 – except for the infamous "Blood Countess" Erzsébet Báthori, whose picture is kept in storage. As the widow of national hero Ferenc Nádasdy, charged with torturing six hundred women to death and reputedly bathing in their blood to preserve her beauty, she was walled up in her castle and the atrocity hushed up.

From here, proceed back across the rotunda to find the Reform era and the *belle époque*, covered in rooms 11–18, followed by World War II and the Communist era in room 20. The last features newsreel footage and such items as a radio set dedicated to Stalin's 70th birthday, a scaled-down model of the Stalin statue torn down by crowds in 1956, and kitsch tributes to János Kádár, who reimposed Communist rule with a vengeance, but later liberalized it to the point that his successors felt able to abandon it entirely. Not to be missed are the **propaganda** films from the Horthy, Fascist and Stalinist eras, whose resemblance to each other makes the point.

Kálvin tér

Múzeum körút ends at **Kálvin tér**, a busy intersection with roads going to the airport, the east and westwards across the river. In 1956, street fighting was especially fierce here as insurgents battled tanks rumbling in from the Soviet base on Csepel Island. It seems almost miraculous that the ornate reading rooms of the **Szabó Ervin Library** (Mon–Fri 10am–8pm, Sat 10am–4pm, closed July, reduced hours in Aug; free), on the corner of Baross utca, survived unscathed. Built in 1887 by the Wenckheim family – who enjoyed a near-monopoly on Hungary's onion crop – the library has come through a thorough modernization in sparkling form. At the main entrance on Reviczky utca, you can ask at the information desk about visiting the fourth floor reading rooms, reached by a lovely wooden staircase. Staff may ask you to register but will probably just wave you through.

Outside the library and facing Kálvin tér stands one of the few surviving monuments marking the hated Treaty of Trianon (see p.57): the so-called **Fountain of Hungarian Truth** (Magyar Igazság kútja). Erected in 1928, it honours the British press magnate Lord Rothermere, whose campaign against the treaty in the *Daily Mail* was so appreciated that he was offered the Hungarian crown. On June 4, the anniversary of the treaty's signing, nationalist and Fascist groups gather to pay their respects.

To the Nagykörút and Keleti Station

Behind the library lies an atmospheric quarter of small squares and parochial schools; formerly shabby, it's now buzzing with cafés and bars popular with students, and is promoted by the local council as "**Budapest's Soho**". Having face-lifted **Mikszáth Kálmán tér** and much of Krudy utca, the process of gentrification is set to cross the **József körút** – one of the sleazier arcs of the Nagykörút – to embrace **Rákóczi tér**, the focus of street prostitution until it was outlawed in 1999. At the time of writing, the square was fenced off for refurbishment, with its

market hall a place for locals to shop and a centre for Chinese wholesalers – but the whole area may well move upmarket in the future.

While theatregoers bestow bourgeois respectability upon **Köztársaság tér** – the home of Budapest's "second" opera house, the **Erkel Theatre** (named after the composer of the national anthem, Ferenc Erkel) – the grittier side of life prevails at **Keleti Station** on Baross tér. As the station is Budapest's "gateway to the east", it's not surprising that Chinese takeaways and Arab shops are a feature of the area – as are frequent ID checks by the **police**, who patrol here in threes ("One can read, one can write, and the third one keeps an eye on the two intellectuals", as the old joke has it).

The Police History Museum

Handily for the police, their precinct HQ is only two blocks from the station, on Mosonyi utca. Tourists who'd never go there otherwise can visit the **Police History Museum** (Rendőrség-Történeti Múzeum; Tues–Sun 9am–5pm; free; Ⓦwww.policehistorymus.com) next door at no. 7, guarded by a dummy sentry. Since the exhibits are largely captioned in Hungarian only, you can easily miss the ideological cast of the display of uniforms and memorabilia going back to Habsburg times, which harbours a tribute to the Communist border guards and militia, and CIA leaflets inciting the Uprising. Be thankful you're not an exhibit in the other hall, where many displays depict murders and mutilations in horrific detail, unlike the staged – and very Sixties – crime scene with a sign listing key points for trainee investigators. Stuff on forgery and art theft in the 1980s begs the question why there's nothing about crime in Hungary nowadays. The show ends with a fraternal display of police uniforms from fellow forces in the EU, and there's also a shop selling police memorabilia, where you can have your fingerprints taken as a souvenir.

Kerepesi Cemetery

Five-minutes' walk from the museum, along Fiumei út, you'll find **Kerepesi Cemetery** (Kerepesi temető; daily: April & Aug 7am–7pm, May–July 7am–8pm, Sept 7am–6pm, Oct 7am–5pm, Nov–March 7.30am–5pm; free), the Père Lachaise of Budapest, where the famous, great and not-so-good are buried. Vintage hearses and mourning regalia in the **Funerary Museum** (Kegyeleti Múzeum; Mon–Thurs 10am–3pm, Fri 10am–1pm; free) near the main gates illuminate the Hungarian way of death and set the stage for the necropolis. In Communist times, Party members killed during the Uprising were buried in a prominent position near the entrance and government ministers in honourable proximity to Kossuth, while leaders and martyrs who "Lived for Communism and the People" were enshrined in a starkly ugly **Pantheon of the Working Class Movement**; some have been removed by their relatives since the demise of Communism. Party leader János Kádár – who ruled Hungary from 1956 to 1988 – rates a separate grave, still heaped with wreaths from admirers.

Further in lie the florid **nineteenth-century mausoleums** of Kossuth, Batthyány, Deák and Petőfi (whose family tomb is here, though his own body was never found). Don't miss the Art Nouveau funerary arcades between Batthyány's and the novelist Jókai's mausoleums, nor the nearby tomb of the diva Lujza Blaha, the "Nation's Nightingale", whose effigy is surrounded by statues of serenading figures. Other notables include the composer Erkel, the confectioner Gerbeaud and three chess grandmasters whose tombs are engraved with the chess moves that won them their titles. A more recent addition is

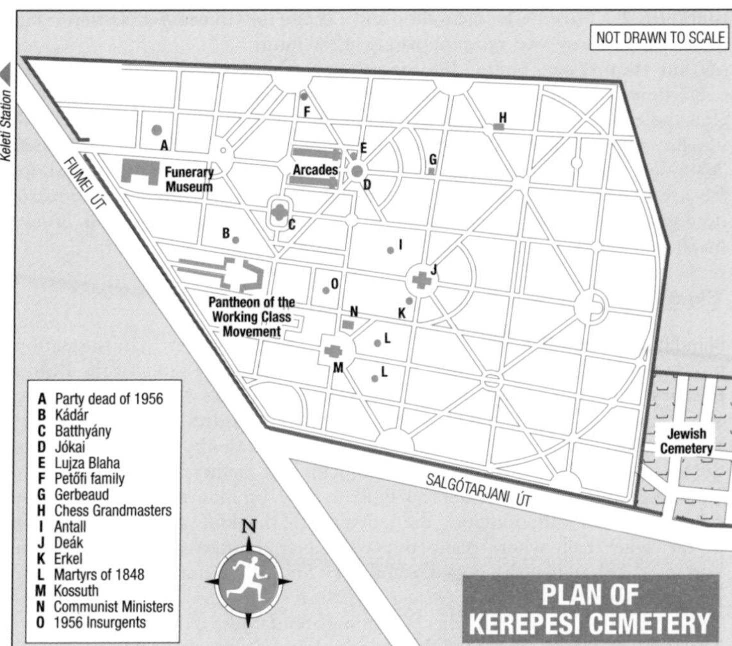

József Antall, the first post-Communist prime minister of Hungary, honoured by an allegorical monument with horses struggling to burst free of a sheet.

Next to Kerepesi lies an overgrown **Jewish cemetery** (Izraelita temető; Mon–Fri & Sun 8am–2pm; free), with some beautiful Art Nouveau tombs of artists, politicians and industrialists, several designed by the brilliant architect Béla Lajta. That of **Manfred Weiss**, founder of the Csepel ironworks that once dominated the industrial island south of the city centre, is still maintained by Csepel's council, in gratitude and by way of apology for the fact that Weiss had to sign his factory over to the government in return for being allowed to leave Hungary with his family in 1944. The cemetery gates are on Salgótarján utca, about ten-minutes' walk from the main entrance to Kerepesi.

Ferencváros

Ferencváros was developed to house workers in the latter half of the nineteenth century, on the same lines as the more bourgeois Józsefváros. During the 1930s and 1940s, its population confounded Marxist orthodoxy by voting for the extreme right, who returned the favour by supporting the local football team **FTC** – popularly known as "**Fradi**" – which became the unofficial team of the opposition under Communism, subsequently known for its hooligan "ultras". The club's green and white colours can be seen throughout the district; its stadium is way out along Üllői út. (See p.185 for more on Fradi and the football scene in general.)

Initially, Ferencváros takes its tone from two institutions on Vámház körút, the section of Kiskörút that separates it from the Belváros. The wrought-iron **Great Market Hall** (Nagycsarnok; Mon 6am–5pm, Tues–Fri 6am–6pm, Sat 6am–3pm) is as famous for its ambience as for its produce, with tanks of live fish and stalls festooned with strings of paprika downstairs and cheap eateries upstairs.

Nearer the Danube, the **Economics University** (named after Karl Marx during Communist times) makes a fine sight from Buda at night, reflected in the river, and adds to the liveliness of the area by day. The building was originally Budapest's main Customs House (Vámház) – hence the name of the körút. A freestanding section of the **medieval walls** of Pest can be found off Vámház körút in the courtyard of no. 16, if the door is open.

Further inland off Kálvin tér (see p.84), **Ráday utca** hums with restaurants, cafés and bars, their pavement tables packed till after midnight and occasionally frequented by raucous stag partygoers (see p.174). In late June/early July, the **Ferencváros festival** (FETE) sees concerts on Bakáts tér at the far end of Ráday, and other events in the neighbourhood; while the **Goethe-Institut** at no. 58 has its own programme of events throughout the year.

Along Üllői út: the Applied Arts Museum and Corvin Cinema

Grey, polluted **Üllői út** isn't an obvious place to linger, but there's much to see within a few blocks' radius of Ferenc körút metro. Take the signposted exit in the underpass to marvel at the **Applied Arts Museum** (Iparművészeti Múzeum; Tues–Sun 10am–6pm; 600Ft; ⓦwww.imm.hu), the most flamboyant creation of Ödön Lechner, who strove to create a uniquely Hungarian form of architecture emphasizing the Magyars' Ugric roots, but was also influenced by Art Nouveau. Inaugurated by Emperor Franz Josef during the 1896 Millennial celebrations, it has a vast dome tiled in green and yellow and a portico with ceramic Turkic motifs on an egg-yolk-coloured background, from the Zsolnay porcelain factory in Pécs. By contrast, the all-white interior is reminiscent of Mogul architecture: at one time it was thought that the Magyars came from India. The museum has a large collection but no permanent displays, instead mounting small exhibitions of its own material and major shows drawn from other collections.

Returning to the subway and crossing the Nagykörút, duck into **Corvin köz**, a U-shaped Art Deco maze of passages and apartment blocks surrounding the **Corvin Cinema**, from which teenage guerrillas (some as young as 12) sallied forth to battle Soviet tanks in 1956. Since the fall of Communism, they have been honoured by a statue of a young insurgent outside the cinema. Its auditoriums are named after illustrious Hungarian actors or directors such as Alexander Korda – one of many Magyars who made it in Hollywood (see p.182).

Having renovated Corvin köz, developers have upped the stakes with the Corvin Promenade – a spa, mall and luxury apartment complex stretching back between Üllői út and Práter utca, set to open in 2010. Meanwhile, you can walk around the corner to find a delightful statue of the **Paul Street Boys** – the heroes of Ferenc Molnár's eponymous 1906 novel – portraying the moment they are caught playing marbles in the yard of their enemies, the Redshirts. The most widely-sold and translated Hungarian book ever, it's both a universal tale of childhood and a satire on extreme nationalism.

If you're wondering how locals were able to fight so well in 1956, the answer lies across Üllői út, where the Hungarian garrison of the **Kilián Barracks** was the first to join the insurgents, organizing youths already aware of street-fighting tactics due to an obligatory diet of films about Soviet partisans. It was in

▲ Paul Street Boys, Práter utca

Budapest that the Molotov cocktail proved lethal to T-54s, as the "Corvin Boys" trapped columns in the backstreets by firebombing the front and rear tanks. Memorial plaques honour Colonel Pál Maleter and others who directed fighting from the Corvin Cinema.

The Holocaust Memorial Centre

One block past the barracks, a right turn into Páva utca brings you to the **Holocaust Memorial Centre** (Holocaust Emlékközpont; Tues–Sun 10am–6pm; 1000Ft; Ⓦwww.hdke.hu), more chilling than the House of Terror (see p.66); think twice about bringing children here. Like Libeskind's Jewish Holocaust Museum in Berlin, the building is distorted and oppressive; darkened ramps resounding to the crunch of jackboots and the shuffle of feet lead to artefacts, newsreels and audio-visual testimonies relating the slide from "deprivation of rights to genocide". From 1920 onwards, Jews were systematically stripped of their assets by right-wing regimes with the participation of local citizens, and Gypsies forced into work gangs. The family stories and newsreel footage of the death camps after liberation are truly harrowing, accompanied by the roar and clang of a furnace being stoked. Visitors emerge from the bowels of hell to find themselves within a glorious and sunlit Art Deco **synagogue**, built by Leopold Baumhorn in the 1920s, which has been restored and incorporated in the memorial centre, itself designed by István Mányi.

On your way back to the metro, it's worth a detour onto Liliom utca to see another striking building – an old transformer plant turned into an outstanding contemporary arts centre, **Trafó** (see p.178 for details).

The Natural History Museum

A kilometre further down Üllői út just past the Klinikák metro stop, a left turn up Korányi Sándor utca brings you to the revamped **Hungarian Natural History Museum** (Magyar Természettudományi Múzeum; daily except Tues 10am–6pm; 600Ft, 1000Ft for temporary displays; Ⓦwww.nhmus.hu). Though

slightly out on a limb, it's worth the hike, especially if you have children: the presentation is captivating, with lots of colour, wide open spaces, explanations in English and, for the weary, benches made from huge tree trunks.

From the entrance hall, dominated by a whale skeleton, you walk through to a fantastic **underwater room**, which has colourful fish in sea- and freshwater aquariums – the mock seabed under the glass floor makes you feel as if you're walking on water. The first floor has lots of interesting displays of animals around the world, recreating their habitats, while the top floor is a Noah's Ark, focusing on animals under threat and what Hungary is doing for the environment. The shop downstairs by the entrance sells an excellent range of animal-related souvenirs, from fridge magnets to games and books.

Across the road is a small **Botanical Garden** (Fűvészkert; daily 9am–5pm, greenhouses closed noon–1pm and from 4pm; 800Ft). Delightfully jungle-like, it derives part of its appeal from its rather run-down state.

The National Theatre and Palace of Arts

Spectacularly floodlit in blue and gold on the banks of the Danube, the National Theatre and Palace of Arts complex looks like the crowning jewel of Budapest's cultural life from a distance, being a 3km ride from Deák tér (take tram #2 to the penultimate stop, Vágóhíd utca). Though still isolated by tracts of wasteland, the landscaping, outdoor bars and hip warehouse developments are colonizing the riverside from the Petőfi bridge outwards, gradually creating a whole new arts and leisure zone.

The **National Theatre** (Nemzeti Szinház; Ⓦwww.nemzetiszinhaz.hu) resembles a Ceauşescu folly, its exterior and environs strewn with random architectural references and statuary. The Classical facade is a replica of the frontage of the original theatre on Blaha Lujza tér, torn down to build the metro in 1964 – a Communist plot to undermine Hungary's identity, many said – which condemned the company to a dump in the backstreets of Pest while the debate continued as to where this national institution should be housed. The fiasco of the "National Hole" on Erzsébet tér (see p.52) was followed by a scandal over the existing site, when it emerged that the minister in charge awarded the contract to the architect of his holiday home. Lacklustre performances since the theatre opened haven't helped.

Next door is the **Palace of Arts** (Művészetek Palotája; Ⓦwww.mupa.hu), a vast edifice that is the new home of the excellent Philharmonic Orchestra and National Dance Theatre. Resembling a dull office block by day, it comes alive each evening with snazzy lighting and events – from world music and dance to Philip Glass's latest composition. No expense has been spared to make this a top venue; particularly in the concert hall, whose acoustics are so sharp that some orchestras are said to dislike it, as you can hear their mistakes.

The Palace also encompasses the **Ludwig Museum** or Museum of Contemporary Art (Kortárs Művészti Múzeum; Tues–Sun 10am–8pm; 1000Ft; Ⓦwww.ludwigmuseum.hu), established in 1996 to build upon an earlier bequest by the German industrialist Peter Ludwig, which was formerly housed on Várhegy. The collection includes US pop art such as Warhol's *Single Elvis* and Lichtenstein's *Vicki*, as well as Picasso's *Musketeer with a Sword* and a *Sealed Letter* by Beuys, but most of the recent acquisitions are works by lesser-known Europeans, in such styles as Hyper-Realism and Neo-Primitivism. It also hosts **temporary exhibitions** by international artists, who may personally conduct guided tours (Thurs from 7pm and Sat at 5pm; 1000Ft for under ten people; reserve 14 days ahead Ⓣ1/555-3469, Ⓔguidedtour@lumu.hu).

6

Várhegy and central Buda

Várhegy (Castle Hill), often referred to simply as the **Vár**, is Buda's most prominent feature. A 1500-metre-long plateau encrusted with bastions, mansions and a huge palace, it dominates both the Víziváros below and Pest, over the river, making this stretch of the river one of the grandest, loveliest urban waterfronts in Europe. The hill is studded with interesting museums, from the **National Gallery** and the **Budapest History Museum** in the **Royal Palace** to the **Golden Eagle Pharmacy** and the **Telephone Museum**, but it's equally enjoyable just walking the streets and admiring such florid creations as the **Mátyás Church** and the **Fishermen's Bastion**, or exploring the World War II **Hospital in the Rock** and the surrounding nuclear **bunkers** and labyrinth of **caves** that lie beneath the hill

Between the castle and the river, the **Víziváros** is something of a quiet residential backwater in the heart of Buda, with a distinctive atmosphere but few specific sights other than the Lánchíd and the Sikló funicular at the southern end, the **Church of St Anne** on **Batthyány tér** in the middle, and the **Király Baths** further up.

The area to the **north of Várhegy** has a variety of attractions in the backstreets off Margit körút: a lively **market** and the **Millenaris Park**, a major concert venue, exhibition centre and children's playground all in one. Further north, on the edge of the affluent Rószadomb district, is one of Budapest's Turkish remnants, **Gül Baba's tomb**.

The simplest and most novel approach to Várhegy is to ride up to the palace by the aforementioned **Sikló**, a renovated nineteenth-century **funicular** that runs from Clark Ádám tér by the Lánchíd. From Pest, the most direct approach is to get bus #16 from Erzsébet tér across the Lánchíd to the lower terminal of the Sikló, or straight up to Várhegy. From Moszkva tér (on the red metro line) you can take **buses** #16, #16A or #116 from the raised side of Moszkva tér, as far as the palace, or walk uphill to the Vienna Gate at the northern end of the Castle District. Walking from Batthyány tér via the steep flights of steps (*lépcső*) off Fő utca involves more effort, but the dramatic stairway up to the Fishermen's Bastion is worth the sweat. The red metro line and bus #16 will also get you to the Víziváros, while the southern Rószadomb is skirted by trams #4 and #6 between Pest and Moszkva tér.

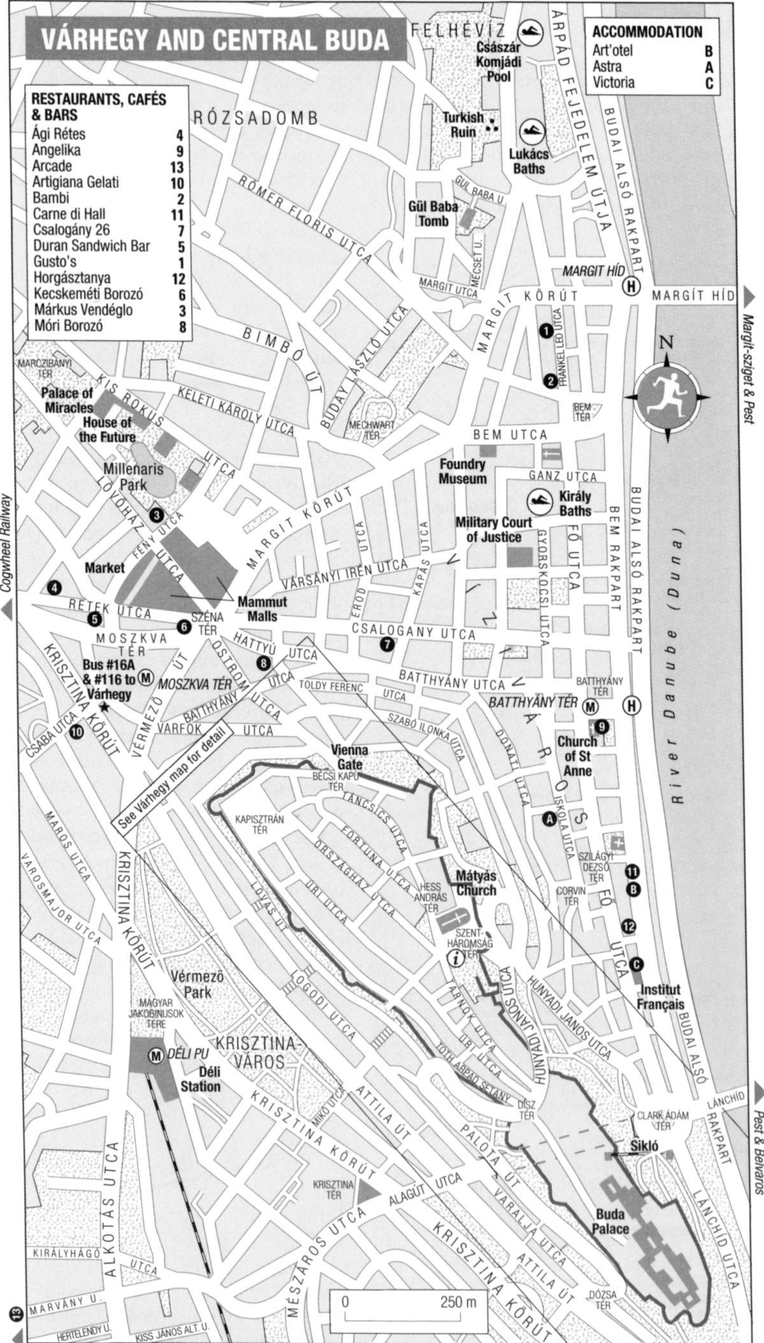
VÁRHEGY AND CENTRAL BUDA
RESTAURANTS, CAFÉS & BARS
Ági Rétes 4
Angelika 9
Arcade 13
Artigiana Gelati 10
Bambi 2
Carne di Hall 11
Csalogány 26 7
Duran Sandwich Bar 5
Gusto's 1
Horgásztanya 12
Kecskeméti Borozó 6
Márkus Vendéglo 3
Móri Borozó 8
ACCOMMODATION
Art'otel B
Astra A
Victoria C
FELHÉVIZ
Császár Komjádi Pool
RÓZSADOMB
Turkish Ruin
Lukács Baths
ÁRPÁD FEJEDELEM ÚTJA
BUDAI ALSÓ RAKPART
RÓMER FLÓRIS UTCA
Gül Baba Tomb
GÜL BABA U.
MECSET U.
MARGIT UTCA
MARGIT HÍD
MARGIT KÖRÚT
MARGÍT HÍD
Margit-sziget & Pest
BIMBÓ ÚT
BUDAY LÁSZLÓ UTCA
FRANKEL LEO UTCA
MARCZIBÁNYI TÉR
Palace of Miracles
KIS ROKUS UTCA
KELETI KÁROLY UTCA
House of the Future
MECHWART TÉR
BEM TÉR
BEM UTCA
Millenáris Park
LÖVŐHÁZ UTCA
Foundry Museum
GANZ UTCA
Király Baths
BEM RAKPART
Military Court of Justice
GYORSKOCSI UTCA
FŐ UTCA
FÉNY UTCA
Market
VÁRSÁNYI IRÉN UTCA
KAPÁS UTCA
ERŐD UTCA
Cogwheel Railway
RETEK UTCA
Mammut Malls
SZÉNA TÉR
MOSZKVA TÉR
CSALOGÁNY UTCA
HATTYÚ UTCA
OSTROM UTCA
KRISZTINA KÖRÚT
Bus #16A & #116 to Várhegy
MOSZKVA TÉR
VÉRMEZŐ ÚT
BATTHYÁNY UTCA
TOLDY FERENC UTCA
BATTHYÁNY TÉR
River Danube (Duna)
VÍZIVÁROS
CSABA UTCA
VARFOK UTCA
SZABÓ ILONKA UTCA
DONÁTI UTCA
Church of St Anne
See Várhegy map for detail
Vienna Gate
BÉCSI KAPU TÉR
KAPISZTRÁN TÉR
TÁNCSICS UTCA
ISKOLA UTCA
MAROS UTCA
FORTUNA UTCA
ORSZÁGHÁZ UTCA
SZILÁGYI DEZSŐ TÉR
VÁROSMAJOR UTCA
ÚRI UTCA
Mátyás Church
HESS ANDRÁS TÉR
CORVIN TÉR
LOVAS ÚT
SZENTHÁROMSÁG TÉR
Vérmező Park
LOGODI UTCA
ÁRNYOK UTCA
ORSZÁGHÁZ UTCA
HUNYADI JÁNOS UTCA
Institut Français
BUDAI ALSÓ
MAGYAR JAKOBINUSOK TERE
DÉLI PU
Déli Station
KRISZTINA-VÁROS
TÓTH ÁRPÁD SÉTÁNY
DÍSZ TÉR
LÁNCHÍD
CLARK ÁDÁM TÉR
RAKPART
Pest & Belváros
MIKÓ UTCA
ATTILA ÚT
PALOTA ÚT
Sikló
KRISZTINA TÉR
ALAGÚT UTCA
VÁRALJA UTCA
Buda Palace
LÁNCHÍD UTCA
ALKOTÁS UTCA
KIRÁLYHÁGÓ UTCA
MÉSZÁROS UTCA
ATTILA ÚT
KRISZTINA KÖRÚT
DÓZSA TÉR
MÁRVÁNY U.
HERTELENDY U.
KISS JÁNOS ALT. U.
0 250 m
Mom Park Mall & Budapest Convention Centre

Várhegy

Várhegy's striking location and its strategic utility have long gone hand in hand: Hungarian kings built their palaces here because it was easy to defend, a fact appreciated by the Turks, Habsburgs and other occupiers. **Buda Palace** serves as a reminder of this past, rising like a house of cards at the southern end of the hill, as proud yet insubstantial as those who ruled there while Hungary's fate was determined by mightier forces.

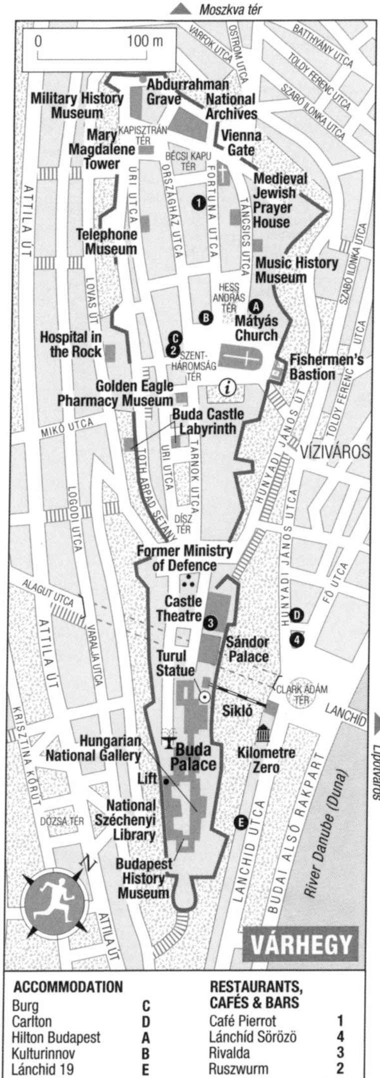

The hill's buildings have been almost wholly reconstructed from the rubble of 1945, when the Wehrmacht and the Red Army battled over the hill while Buda's inhabitants cowered underground. This was the eighty-sixth time that Várhegy had been ravaged and rebuilt over seven centuries, rivalling the devastation caused by the recapture of Buda from the Turks in 1686. It was this repeated destruction that caused the melange of styles characterizing the hill. While the palace is a faithful postwar reconstruction of the Habsburg behemoth that bestrode the ruins of earlier palaces, the Neo-Gothic **Mátyás Church** and **Fishermen's Bastion** are romantic nineteenth-century evocations of medieval glories, interweaving past and present national fixations.

The streets of the **Várnegyed** (Castle District), the residential area to the north of the palace, still follow their medieval courses, with Gothic arches and stone carvings half-concealed in the courtyards and passages of eighteenth-century Baroque houses, whose facades are embellished with fancy ironwork grilles. For many centuries, residence here was a privilege granted to religious or ethnic groups, each occupying a specific street. This pattern persisted through the 145-year-long Turkish occupation, when Armenians, Circassians and Sephardic Jews established themselves under the relatively tolerant Ottomans. The liberation of Buda by a multinational Christian

army under Habsburg command was followed by a pogrom and ordinances restricting the right of residence to Catholics and Germans, which remained in force for nearly a century. Almost every building here displays a stone *műemlék* (listed) plaque giving details of its history (in Hungarian), and a surprising number are still homes rather than embassies or boutiques – there are even a couple of schools and corner shops. At dusk, when most of the tourists have left, pensioners walk their dogs and toddlers play in the long shadows of Hungarian history.

Szentháromság tér

The obvious starting point is **Szentháromság tér** (Holy Trinity Square), the historic heart of the district, named after an ornate **Trinity Column** erected in 1713 in thanksgiving for the abatement of a plague; a scene showing people dying from the Black Death appears on the plinth. To the southwest stands the former **Town Hall**, Buda having been a municipality until its unification with Pest and Óbuda in 1873; note the corner statue of Pallas Athene, bearing Buda's coat of arms on her shield.

Down the road at Szentháromság utca 7, the tiny **Ruszwurm patisserie** has been a pastry shop and café since 1827 and was a gingerbread shop in the Middle Ages. Its Empire-style decor looks much the same as it would have done under Vilmos Ruszwurm, who ran the patisserie for nearly four decades from 1884.

In the small park by the square, Tourinform can supply a free map of Várhegy and rent an **audioguide** for self-guided walks (3000Ft/3hr). Nearby is a touch-friendly **scale model** of the Mátyás Church and Fishermen's Bastion, labelled in Braille for blind visitors.

Mátyás Church

The square's most prominent feature is the Neo-Gothic **Mátyás Church** (Mátyás templom; daily 9am–5pm; 700Ft; audioguide 400Ft), with its wildly asymmetrical diamond-patterned roofs and toothy spires. Officially dedicated to Our Lady but popularly named after "Good King Mátyás", the building is a late nineteenth-century recreation by architect Frigyes Schulek, grafted onto those portions of the original thirteenth-century church that survived the siege of 1686. Ravaged yet again in World War II, the church was laboriously restored by a Communist regime keen to show its patriotic credentials, and the transition to democracy in 1989–90 saw the sanctity of this "ancient shrine of the Hungarian people" reaffirmed – which means that visitors are expected to be properly dressed and respectfully behaved.

As you enter the church through its twin-spired **Mary Portal**, the richness of the interior is overwhelming. Painted leaves and geometric motifs run up columns and under vaulting, while shafts of light fall through rose windows onto gilded altars and statues with stunning effect. Most of the **frescoes** were executed by Károly Lotz or Bertalan Székely, the foremost historical painters of the nineteenth century. The **coat of arms of King Mátyás** can be seen on the wall to your left, just inside; his family name, Corvinus, comes from the raven (*corvus* in Latin) that appeared on his heraldry and on every volume in his famed Corvin Library.

Around the corner, beneath the south tower, is the **Loreto Chapel**, containing a Baroque Madonna, while in the bay beneath the **Béla Tower** you can see two medieval capitals, one carved with monsters fighting a dragon, the other with two bearded figures reading a book. The tower is named after Béla IV, who founded the church, rather than his predecessor in the second chapel along, who shares a **double sarcophagus** with Anne of Chatillon. The tomb,

originally located in the old capital, Székesfehérvár, 60km southwest of Budapest, was moved here after its discovery in 1848. Although Hungary's medieval kings were crowned at Székesfehérvár, it was customary to make a prior appearance in Buda – hence the sobriquet, the "Coronation Church".

The church also has a small collection of **ecclesiastical treasures** and relics, including the right foot of St János. The **crypt**, normally reserved for prayer, contains the red-marble tombstone of a nameless Árpád prince. Otherwise, climb a spiral staircase to the **Royal Oratory** overlooking the stained-glass windows and embossed vaulting of the nave; here votive figures and vestments presage a **replica of the Coronation Regalia**, whose attached exhibition is more informative about the provenance of St Stephen's Crown than that accompanying the originals, on display in Parliament (see p.61).

Mass is celebrated in the Mátyás Church daily at 7am, 8.30am and 6pm, and at 10am and noon on Sundays and public holidays. The 10am mass on Sunday is in Latin with a full choir. The church is also a superb venue for **concerts** during the festival seasons, and evening organ recitals throughout the year. Details appear in listings magazines and on the church's own website, Ⓦwww.matyas-templom.hu. Tickets are available from any booking agency (see p.177).

Fishermen's Bastion

After the Mátyás Church, the most impressive sight in Várhegy is the **Fishermen's Bastion** (Halászbástya) just beyond. An undulating white rampart of cloisters and stairways intersecting at seven tent-like turrets (symbolizing the Magyar tribes that conquered the Carpathian Basin), it looks as though it was dreamt up by the illusionist artist Escher, but was actually designed by Schulek as a foil to the Mátyás Church. Although fishermen from the Víziváros reputedly defended this part of the hill during the Middle Ages, the bastion is purely decorative. The **view** of Pest across the river, framed by the bastion, is only

King Stephen

If you commit just one figure from Hungarian history to memory, make it **King Stephen**, for it was he who welded the tribal Magyar fiefdoms into a state and won recognition from Christendom. Born Vajk, son of Grand Duke Géza, he emulated his father's policy of trying to convert the pagan Magyars and develop Hungary with the help of foreign preachers, craftsmen and merchants. By marrying Gizella of Bavaria in 996, he was able to use her father's knights to crush a pagan revolt after Géza's death, and subsequently received an apostolic cross and crown from Pope Sylvester II for his coronation on Christmas Day, 1000 AD, when he took the name Stephen (István in Hungarian).

Though noted for his enlightened views (such as the need for tolerance and the desirability of multiracial nations), he could act ruthlessly when necessary. After his only son Imre died in an accident and a pagan seemed likely to inherit, Stephen had the man blinded and poured molten lead into his ears. Naming his successor, he symbolically offered his crown to the Virgin Mary rather than the Holy Roman Emperor or the pope; ever since, she has been considered the Patroness of Hungary. Swiftly canonized after his death in 1038, **St Stephen** became a national talisman, his mummified right hand a holy relic, and his coronation regalia the symbol of statehood. Despite playing down his cult for decades, even the Communists eventually embraced it in a bid for some legitimacy, while nobody in post-Communist Hungary thinks it odd that the symbol of the republic should be the crown and cross of King Stephen.

surpassed by the vistas from the terrace of Buda Palace, and the Citadella on Gellért-hegy. However, you might baulk at paying 400Ft to go up to the top level – tickets from the machine nearby (students and OAPs get their half-price tickets from an office beside Tourinform) – as the free view from the lower level is just as good.

Between the bastion and the church, an equestrian **statue of King Stephen** honours the founder of the Hungarian nation, whose conversion to Christianity and coronation with a crown sent by the pope presaged the Magyars' integration into European civilization (see box, p.85). The relief at the back of the plinth depicts Schulek offering a model of the church to Stephen. Like the church and the bastion, his statue is reflected in the copper-glass facade of the **Budapest Hilton**, incorporating chunks of a medieval Dominican church and monastery on the side facing the river, and an eighteenth-century Jesuit college on the other, which bears a copy of the **Mátyás Relief** from Bautzen in Germany that's regarded as the only true likeness of Hungary's Renaissance monarch.

Along Táncsics Mihály utca

In the fifteenth century, when both Ashkenazi and Sephardic Jews lived here, Táncsics Mihály utca was known as Zsidó utca (Jewish Street). The Ashkenazi community was established in 1251 in the reign of Béla IV, but was completely wiped out when Buda was captured from the Ottomans in 1686. The Jews, who had fared well under Turkish rule, assisted in the defence of Buda, and those who had not fled or died in the siege were carted away as prisoners by the victorious Christian army. After several name changes, the street was renamed in 1948 after **Mihály Táncsics**, a radical Hungarian politician of the 1848 uprising who was imprisoned here. As it happens, Táncsics, though not Jewish, joined a Jewish platoon of the National Guard in protest against anti-Semitism.

The **Music History Museum** (Zenetörténeti Múzeum; Tues–Sun 10am–4pm; 1000Ft; Ⓦwww.zti.hu) at no. 7 occupies the Baroque Erdödy Palace where Beethoven was a guest in 1800, and where Bartók once had a workshop before he emigrated. The collection ranges from a Holczman harp made for Marie Antoinette and a unique tongue-shaped violin in the classical section to hurdy-gurdies, zithers, cowhorns and bagpipes, as well as many Bartók scores and jottings. On your way out, have a look at no. 9 next door, which was once the Joseph Barracks where the Habsburgs jailed Hungarian radicals such as Táncsics.

Evidence of Buda's Jewish past can be found at no. 26, which contains a **Medieval Jewish Prayer House** (Középkori Zsidó Imaház; May–Oct Tues–Sun 10am–6pm; 400Ft). Around 1470, King Mátyás allowed the Jews to build a synagogue and appointed a Jewish council led by Jacobus Mendel; part of Mendel's house survives in the entrance to the prayer house. All that remains of its original decor are two Cabbalistic symbols painted on a wall, and though the museum does its best to flesh out the history of the community with maps and prints, all the real treasures are in the Jewish Museum in Pest (see p.69).

Kapisztrán tér

At the end of Táncsics Mihály utca lies **Bécsi kapu tér**, named after the **Vienna Gate** (Bécsi kapu) that was erected on the 250th anniversary of the recapture of Buda. Beside it, the forbidding-looking Neo-Romanesque **National Archives** (no admission) guard the way to **Kapisztrán tér**, a larger

square centred on the **Mary Magdalene Tower** (Magdolna-torony), whose accompanying church was wrecked in World War II. In medieval times this was where Hungarian residents worshipped (Germans used the Mátyás Church), so its reconstruction is occasionally mooted by nationalist politicians. Today the tower boasts a peal of ornamental bells that jingles through a medley composed by the jazz pianist György Szabados, including Hungarian folk tunes, Chopin *Études* and the theme from *Bridge over the River Kwai.*

Beyond the tower is a statue of **Friar John Capistranus**, who exhorted the Hungarians to victory at the siege of Belgrade in 1456, a triumph which the pope hailed by ordering church bells to be rung at noon throughout Europe. The statue, showing Capistranus bestriding a dead Turk, is aptly sited outside the Military History Museum.

The Military History Museum

The **Military History Museum** (Hadtörténeti Múzeum; April–Sept 10am–6pm; Oct–March 10am–4pm; closed Mon; 700Ft), in a former barracks on the north side of the square, has gung-ho exhibitions on the history of hand weapons from ancient times till the advent of firearms, and the birth and campaigns of the Honvéd (national army) during the 1848–49 War of Independence. However, what sticks in the memory are the sections on the Hungarian Second Army that was decimated at Stalingrad (ask to see newsreel footage as there are no regular shows). In the courtyard are post-Communist memorials to the POWs who never returned from the Gulag.

The entrance to the museum is on **Tóth Árpád sétány**, a promenade lined with cannons and chestnut trees on the western side of the hill, looking across to the Buda Hills. At its northern end it turns east, past a giant **flagpole** striped in Hungarian colours, to the symbolic **grave of Abdurrahman**, the last Turkish Pasha of Buda, who died on the walls in 1686 – a "valiant foe", according to the inscription.

Országház utca and Úri utca

Back towards Szentháromság tér, there's more to be seen on **Országház utca**, which was the district's main thoroughfare in the Middle Ages and was known as the "street of baths" during Turkish times. Its present name, Parliament Street, recalls the sessions of the Diet held in the 1790s in a former Poor Clares' cloister at no. 28, where the Gestapo imprisoned 350 Hungarians and foreigners in 1945. No. 17, over the road, consists of two medieval houses joined together and has a relief of a croissant on its keystone, from the time when it was a bakery. A few doors down from the old parliament building, Renaissance graffiti survive on the underside of the bay window of no. 22 and a Gothic trefoil-arched cornice on the house next door, while the one beyond has been rebuilt in its original fifteenth-century form.

Úri utca (Gentleman Street) also boasts historic associations, for it was at the former Franciscan monastery at no. 51 that the five Hungarian Jacobins were held before being beheaded on the "Blood Meadow" below the hill in 1795. Next door is a wing of the Poor Clares' cloister that served as a postwar telephone exchange before being turned into a **Telephone Museum** (Telefónia Múzeum; Tues–Sun 10am–4pm; 400Ft), entered from Országház utca 30 on weekends and holidays. The curator strives to explain the development of telephone exchanges since their introduction to Budapest in the early 1900s – activating a noisy rotary one that's stood here since the 1930s – and you're invited to dial up commentaries in English or songs in Hungarian, check out

the webcam and internet facilities, and admire the personal phones of Emperor Franz Josef, Admiral Horthy and the Communist leader János Kádár.

Further down the street, on either side, notice the statues of the four seasons in the first-floor niches at nos. 54–56, Gothic sedilia in the gateway of nos. 48–50, and three arched windows and two diamond-shaped ones from the fourteenth and fifteenth centuries at no. 31.

The Hospital in the Rock and Buda Castle Labyrinth

Some six to fourteen metres beneath the Várhegy's streets lie 10km of galleries formed by hot springs and cellars dug since medieval times. In 1941, a section was converted into a military hospital staffed from the civilian Szent János hospital, which doubled as an air-raid shelter after the Red Army broke through the Attila Line and encircled Budapest in December 1944. In the 1950s, a nuclear bunker was added to the complex and was maintained in readiness until 2000, a time capsule of the Cold War. English-language tours of the **Hospital in the Rock** (Sziklakórház; Tues–Sun 10am–7pm; Ⓦwww.sziklakorhaz.hu) run every hour till 6pm; one limited to the hospital (40min; 2600Ft), the other also featuring the bunkers (1hr; 4000Ft). Ramped throughout for wheelchairs and trolleys, its operating theatres contain 1930s X-ray and anaesthetic machines (used in the film *Evita*) and gory waxworks; bed-sheets in the wards were changed every fortnight until 2000.

The ventilation system is run by generators installed in the **nuclear bunker** built in 1953, with charcoal air-filters, a laboratory for detecting toxins, atropine ampoules to be injected against nerve gas, and an airlock fitted when the bunker was enlarged between 1958 and 1962. To preserve its secrecy, fuel was delivered by trucks pretending to "water" flower beds on the surface, via a concealed pipeline. The entrance to the hospital is at Lovas út 4/b, on the rear hillside beyond the castle walls, reached by descending the steps at the end of Szentháromság utca and then walking 50m uphill.

Just downhill from the steps at Lovas út 4/a is a wheelchair-accessible entrance to the **Buda Castle Labyrinth** (Budavári Labirintus; daily 9.30am–7.30pm; 1500Ft; Ⓦwww.labirintus.com), a separate maze of **caves** that most visitors enter from Úri utca 9, at the top of Várhegy. The displays include copies of the cave paintings of Lascaux (Buda's caves also sheltered prehistoric hunters), and a "bravery labyrinth", where you have to make your way through a section of cave in total darkness. Masked figures and a giant head sunken into the floor enliven other dank chambers. There's a cup of warming tea at the end of the optional 25-minute tour.

The Golden Eagle Pharmacy

Heading south from Szentháromság tér towards the palace, check out the **Golden Eagle Pharmacy Museum** (Arany Sas Patikamúzeum; Mon 10.30am–5.30pm, Tues–Sun 10.30am–6.30pm; 500Ft) at Tárnok utca 18. The Golden Eagle was the first pharmacy in Buda, established after the expulsion of the Turks, and moved to its present site in the eighteenth century. Its original murals and furnishings lend authenticity to dubious nostrums, including the skull of a mummy used to make Mumia powder to treat epilepsy; there's also a reconstruction of an alchemist's laboratory, complete with dried bats and crocodiles, and other obscure exhibits such as the small, long-necked Roman glass vessel for collecting widows' tears. The museum has no handouts in English, but

the staff can usually explain the more interesting bits. Notice the portrait of the Dominican nun pharmacist – it was common practice for nuns and monks in the Middle Ages to double up as apothecaries. The *Tárnok* coffee house, next door but one, occupies a medieval building with a Renaissance graffiti facade of red and yellow checks and roundels and, like the street, is named after the royal treasurers who once lived there.

Dísz tér and the Turul statue

Both Tárnok utca and Úri utca end in **Dísz tér** (Parade Square), whose cobbled expanses are guarded by a mournful Honvéd memorial to the dead of 1848–49. To the south lies the scarred hulk of the old **Ministry of Defence**, to the east of which stands the **Castle Theatre** (Várszínház), which was a Carmelite church until the order was dissolved by Josef II; its conversion was supervised by Farkas Kempelen, inventor of a chess-playing automaton. It was here that the first-ever play in Hungarian was staged in 1790, and where Beethoven performed in 1808; today it is used by the National Dance Theatre. The last building in the row is the **Sándor Palace** (Sándor Palota), formerly the prime minister's residence, where Premier Teleki shot himself in protest at Hungary joining the Nazi invasion of Yugoslavia. It is now the residence of the country's president, a figurehead who is elected by parliament rather than the electorate.

Next door to Sándor Palace, the upper terminal of the **Sikló** funicular (see p.104) is separated from the terrace of Buda Palace by stately railings and the ferocious-looking **Turul statue** – a giant bronze eagle clasping a sword in its talons, which is visible from across the river. In Magyar mythology, the Turul sired the first dynasty of Hungarian kings by raping the grandmother of Prince Árpád, who led the tribes into the Carpathian Basin. The Turul also accompanied their raids on Europe, bearing the sword of Attila the Hun in its talons. During the nineteenth century it became a symbol of Hungarian identity in the face of Austrian culture, but wound up being co-opted by the Habsburgs, who cast Emperor Franz Josef as a latter-day Árpád for the next millennium. Today, the Turul has been adopted as an emblem by Hungary's skinheads.

From here, you can go through the wrought-iron gates and down some steps to the **terrace** of the palace, commanding a sweeping **view** of Pest. Beyond the souvenir stalls prances an equestrian **statue of Prince Eugene of Savoy**, who captured Buda from the Ottomans in 1686. The smaller bronze statues nearby represent **Csongor and Tünde**, the lovers in the play of the same name, by Vörösmarty.

Buda Palace

As befits a former royal residence, the lineage of **Buda Palace** (Budavári palota) can be traced back to medieval times, the rise and fall of various palaces on the hill reflecting the changing fortunes of the Hungarian state. The first fortifications and dwellings, hastily erected by Béla IV after the Mongol invasion of 1241–42, were replaced by the grander palaces of the Angevin kings, who ruled in more prosperous and stable times. This process of rebuilding reached its zenith in the reign of Mátyás Corvinus (1458–90), whose palace was a Renaissance extravaganza to which artists and scholars from all over Europe were drawn by the blandishments of Queen Beatrice and the prospect of lavish hospitality. The rooms had hot and cold running water, and during celebrations the fountains and gargoyles flowed with wine. After the Turkish occupation and

the long siege that ended it, only ruins were left – which the Habsburgs, Hungary's new rulers, levelled to build a palace of their own.

From modest beginnings under Empress Maria Theresa (when there were a mere 203 rooms, which she never saw completed), the palace expanded inexorably throughout the nineteenth century, though no monarch ever dwelt here, only the Habsburg palatine (viceroy). After the collapse of the empire following World War I, Admiral Horthy inhabited the building with all the pomp of monarchy until he was deposed by a German coup in October 1944. The palace was left unoccupied, and it wasn't long before the siege of Buda once again resulted in total devastation. Reconstruction work began in the 1950s in tandem with excavations of the medieval substrata beneath the rubble. The medieval section was incorporated into the new building, whose interior is far less elegant than the prewar version, being designed to accommodate cultural institutions.

The complex houses the **Hungarian National Gallery** (Wings A, B, C and D), the **Budapest History Museum** (E) and the **National Széchenyi Library** (F) – the first two of which are definitely worth seeing and could easily take an afternoon. There are separate entrances for each.

The Hungarian National Gallery

Most people's first port of call is the **Hungarian National Gallery** (Magyar Nemzeti Galéria; Tues–Sun 10am–6pm; 800Ft for permanent displays, 800Ft for visiting shows; Ⓦwww.mng.hu), devoted to Hungarian art from the Middle Ages to the present. It contains much that's superb, but the vastness of the collection and the confusing layout can be fatiguing. Though all the paintings are labelled in English, other details are scanty, so it's worth investing in a guidebook (3500Ft) or guided tour (3200Ft for up to five people; book a couple of days in advance on Ⓣ06-20/4397-326). The main entrance is on the eastern side of Wing C, overlooking the river, behind the statue of Eugene of Savoy. Don't buy a special ticket (500Ft) to see the separate **Habsburg crypt**, containing the tombs of several Habsburgs who ruled as palatines of Hungary up until 1849, until you've checked that a tour is scheduled, as they require at least 25 people (Ⓣ06-20/4397-331).

Through the shop to the left of the ticket office, a lovely **wooden ceiling** from a sixteenth-century church and marble reliefs of knightly tombs are the highlights of a **Medieval and Renaissance Lapidarium**. Between the two, doors on the left lead to the fantastic collection of fifteenth-century **Gothic altarpieces** and panels at the rear of Wing D. Salvaged from churches great and small that escaped destruction by the Turks, some are artful and others rustic, but all are full of character and detail: notice the varied reactions expressed within the *Death of the Virgin* from Kassa (Kosice, a Slovakian centre of altar-painting) and the gloating spectators in the Jánosrét *Passion* in the second room. From the same church comes a *St Nicholas* altar as long as a limo and lurid as a comic strip, whose final scene shows cripples being cured by the saint's corpse. Also strange to modern eyes are *The Expulsion of St Adalbert*, who seems blithely oblivious to the demolition of his church, and the woodcarving of *St Anthony the Hermit*, carrying a hill upon his back. The pointed finials on the high altar from Liptószentmária (Liptovská Mara in Slovakia) anticipate the winged altarpieces of the sixteenth century on the floor above. To get there without returning to the foyer, use the small staircase outside the doors to this section and turn left, left and left again at the top.

The **first floor** covers the widest range of art and is likely to engage you the longest. It picks up where the ground floor left off in the former Throne

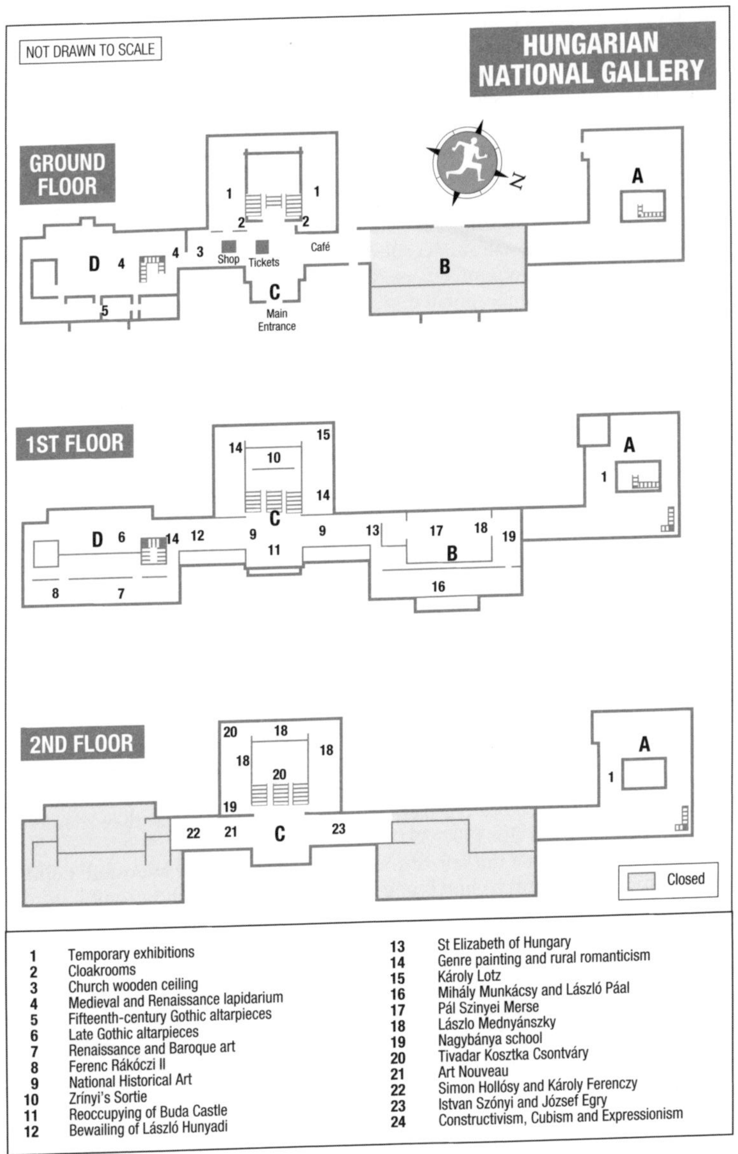

Room, where **late Gothic altarpieces** with soaring pinnacles and carved surrounds are displayed. Most of them come from churches now in Slovakia or Romania, such as the Annunciation altarpiece from Csíkmenaság (now Armaseni in Romania) or the homely St Anne altarpiece from Kisszeben (Sabinov, Slovakia), which looks like a medieval playgroup. On an altar from Berki (Rokycany, Slovakia), Mary Magdalene is raptured by angels as bishops

are impaled, while another piece from Liptószentandrás (Liptovsky Ondrej, Slovakia) shows St Andrew clutching the poles for his crucifixion. Also look out for *The Visitation* by the anonymous "Master MS", in the anteroom, and the coffered **ceiling** from Gogánváralija (Gogan-Varolea, Romania), in the room behind the Kisszeben Annunciation altarpiece.

Many of the works in the adjacent section on **Baroque art** once belonged to Count Miklós Esterházy (including his portrait), or were confiscated from private owners in the 1950s. The prolific Austrian **Anton Maulbertsch**, who executed scores of altars and murals reminiscent of Caravaggio, is represented here by works such as *The Death of St Joseph*. On the back of one panel running across the room, don't miss **Ádám Mányoki**'s portrait of Ferenc Rákóczi II from 1712, a sober study of a national hero that foreshadowed a new artistic genre of **National Historical art** in the nineteenth century.

People coming up the **main stairs** from the ticket office will find, at the rear of the mid-floor landing, two vast canvases by **Peter Krafft**. *Zrínyi's Sortie* depicts the suicidal sally by the defenders of Szigetvár against a Turkish army fifty times their number; not a drop of blood spatters the melee, as Count Zrínyi leads the charge across the bridge. The other shows Franz Josef being crowned King of Hungary in equally slavish detail. Facing you in the large first-floor **atrium** is **Gyula Benczúr**'s *Reoccupying of Buda Castle*, whose portrayal of Eugene of Savoy and Karl of Lotharingia suggests a mere exchange of Turkish rulers for Habsburg ones, while *The Bewailing of László Hunyadi* by **Viktor Madarász** (hung off towards Wing D) would have been read as an allusion to the execution of Hungarian patriots after the War of Independence. At the other end, near Wing B, you'll find **Sándor Lilzen-Mayer**'s *St Elizabeth of Hungary* offering her ermine cape to a ragged mother and child, and two iconic scenes by **Bertalan Székely**: *The Battle of Mohács*, a shattering defeat for the Hungarians in 1526; and *The Women of Eger*, exalting their defiance of the Turks in 1552.

The remainder of the first floor illustrates other trends in nineteenth-century Hungarian art, namely genre painting, **rural romanticism** and Impressionism. On the Buda side of Wing C, *Thunderstorm on the Puszta* and *Horses at the Watering Place* evoke the hazy skies and manly world of the Hungarian "Wild West" – the Great Plain southeast of Budapest. Both are by **Károly Lotz**, better known for his frescoes around the city, such as in the Mátyás Church, Opera House and Parliament. Wing B devotes a section to works by **Mihály Munkácsy** and **László Paál**, exhibited together since both painted landscapes – though Paál did little else, whereas Munkácsy was internationally renowned for pictures with a social message (*The Last Day of a Condemned Man*, *Tramps of the Night*) and bravura historical works like *The Conquest* (in the Parliament building). Many canvases have suffered from his use of bitumen in mixing paint, which has caused them to darken and crack.

Impressionism was introduced to Hungary by **Pál Szinyei Merse**, whose models and subjects – such as in *A Picnic in May* – were cheerfully bourgeois. Nearby you'll find two luminous landscapes by the prolific **László Mednyánszky** – *Watering-place* and *Fishing on the Tisza* – and paintings from the **Nagybánya school**, an influential artists' colony in what is now Baia Mare in Romania. Look out for peasants discussing *The Country's Troubles*, by the school's guru, **Simon Hollósy**, who quit during a spiritual crisis; a cheerful *Drying the Laundry*, by his successor **Béla Iványi Grünwald**; and *Boys Throwing Pebbles*, by the school's most adept pupil, **Károly Ferenczy**.

There's more of their work on the next floor, off towards Wing D. Midway up the **stairs** hang three canvases by the visionary **Tivadar Kosztka**

Csontváry, whose obsession with the Holy Land and the "path of the sun" inspired scenes such as *Pilgrimage to the Cedars in Lebanon* and the vast *Ruins of the Greek Theatre at Taormina*, with its magical twilight colours. When Picasso saw an exhibition of his works years later, he remarked: "And I thought I was the only great painter of our century."

The **second floor** covers **twentieth-century Hungarian art up to 1945**, starting with the vibrant **Art Nouveau** movement off to the right of the atrium. Pictures by **János Vaszary** (*Golden Age*) and **Aladár Körösfői Kriesch** (founder of the Gödöllő artists' colony – see p.146) are set in richly hand-carved frames, an integral part of their composition. **József Rippl-Rónai** was a pupil of Munkácsy whose portraits such as *Woman in a White-dotted Dress* went mostly unrecognized in his lifetime – they're now regarded as Art Nouveau classics. Here you'll also find Csontváry's magically lit *Coaching in Athens at the Full Moon*, and more works by Hollósy (*Rákóczi March*) and Ferenczy (*Morning Sunshine*).

Across the atrium, **István Szónyi**'s wintry *Burial at Zebegény*, and **József Egry**'s watery *St John the Baptist* have simple lines and muddy colours in common. Both belonged to a generation of artists whose sympathies were on the left in largely right-wing times: Constructivists such as **Béla Uitz**, Cubists **János Kmetty** and **Gyula Derkovits**, the Expressionist **Vilmos Aba-Novák** and the "Hungarian Chagall", **Imre Ámos** (who died in a Nazi death camp) are all represented in Wing C off the stairs.

Climbing the **stairs** to the **third floor**, **Tamás Lossonczy**'s abstract-surrealistic *Cleansing Storm*, **Béla Kondor**'s whimsical *The Genius of Mechanical Flying* and a wire sculpture by Tibor Vilt portraying the awful fate of the peasant rebel leader Dózsa presage the section on **Hungarian art since 1945**. Exhibits are rotated to showcase the museum's collection of work by modern artists such as Endre Bálint, Attila Szűcs, Sándor Altorjai and Erzsébet Schaár. On fine days, visitors can ascend to the palace's **dome** for a **view** of the city.

The Mátyás Fountain, Lion Courtyard and the National Library

The square outside the museum is flanked on three sides by the palace and overlooks Buda to the west, though the **view** is marred by the MTI (Hungarian News Agency) building on Nap-hegy. By the far wall stands the flamboyant **Mátyás Fountain**, whose bronze figures recall the legend of Szép Ilonka. This beautiful peasant girl met the king while he was hunting incognito, fell in love with him, and died of a broken heart after discovering his identity and realizing the futility of her hopes. The man with a falcon is the king's Italian chronicler, who recorded the story for posterity (it is also enshrined in a poem by Vörösmarty).

A gateway guarded by lions leads into the **Lion Courtyard**, totally enclosed by further wings. To the right is the **National Széchenyi Library** (Országos Széchenyi Könyvtár; Tues–Sat 10am–8pm, closed mid-July to late Aug), occupying the nineteenth-century Ybl block, whose full size is only apparent from the far side of the hill, where it looms over Dózsa tér like a mountain. The library was founded in 1802 on the initiative of Count Ferenc Széchenyi, the father of István (see p.104). A repository for publications in Hungarian and material relating to the country from around the world, by law it receives a copy of every book, newspaper and magazine that is published in Hungary. You can only visit the reading room on guided tours (200Ft; call ☎1/487-8657) or with a reader's pass (6000Ft; passport required to apply). During library hours, a passenger **lift** (100Ft) in the adjacent building by the Lion Gateway – open to all – provides direct access to and from Dózsa tér, at the foot of Várhegy.

▲ Mátyás Fountain, Várhegy

The Budapest History Museum

On the far side of the Lion Courtyard, the **Budapest History Museum** (Budapest Történeti Múzeum; mid-March to mid-Sept daily 10am–6pm; mid-Sept to Oct 10am–6pm; Nov to mid-March daily except Tues 10am–4pm; 1600Ft, audioguide 850Ft; Ⓦwww.btm.hu) covers two millennia of history on three floors, and descends into original vaulted, flagstoned halls from the Renaissance and medieval palaces unearthed during excavations. It's worth starting with **prehistory**, on the top floor, to find out about the ancient Magyars. Here you can see the artefacts of their nomadic precursors who overran the Pannonian Plain after the Romans left, such as a gold bridle and stirrup fastenings in a zoomorphic style from Avar burial mounds. Owing to the ravages inflicted by the Mongols and the Turks, there's little to show from the time of the Conquest or Hungary's medieval civilization, so most of the second floor is occupied by **Budapest in Modern Times**, an exhibition giving insight into urban planning, fashions, trade and vices, from 1686 onwards. At either end of the section, two life-sized replicas of the lions on the Lánchíd bracket the period starting with the hopes of the Reform era in the 1840s and ending with the devastated city of 1945. Other items range from an 1880s barrel organ to one of the Swedish Red Cross notices affixed to Jewish safe houses by Wallenberg (see p.69).

The **remains of the medieval palace** are reached from the basement via an eighteenth-century cellar spanning two medieval yards on a lower level. A wing of the ground floor of King Sigismund's palace and the cellars beneath the Corvin Library form an intermediate stratum overlaying the cross-vaulted crypt of the **Royal Chapel** and a **Gothic Hall** displaying statues from later in the fourteenth century (found in 1974), where lute **concerts** are held. In another chamber are portions of red marble fireplaces and a massive portal carved with cherubs and flowers from the palace of King Mátyás. Emerging into daylight, bear left and up the stairs to reach another imposing hall, with a view over the castle ramparts.

The Sikló and the Lánchíd

Between the Buda Palace and the Sándor Palace stands the upper station of the **Sikló** (daily 7.30am–10pm, closed every other Monday; 700Ft one-way, 1300Ft return; Budapest Card not valid), a nineteenth-century **funicular** that takes you down to the river and the Lánchíd. Constructed on the initiative of Ödön Széchenyi, whose father built the bridge below, it was only the second funicular in the world when it was inaugurated in 1870, and functioned without a hitch until wrecked by a shell in 1945. The wooden carriages, replicas of the originals, are now lifted by an electric winch rather than a steam engine; they're divided into three sections at different heights to give as many people as possible a view (the bottom compartment gives the most unimpeded views). Capacity is limited, however, so in summer you can expect to queue to go up. In the small park at the foot of the Sikló stands **Kilometre Zero**, a zero-shaped monument from where all distances from Budapest are measured.

The Széchenyi Lánchíd

The majestic **Lánchíd** (Chain Bridge) has a special place in the history of Budapest and in the hearts of its citizens. As the first permanent link between Buda and Pest (replacing seasonal pontoon bridges and ferries), it was a tremendous spur to the country's economic growth and eventual unification, linking the rural hinterland to European civilization so that Budapest became a commercial centre and transport hub. The bridge symbolized the abolition of feudal privilege, as nobles (hitherto exempt from taxes) were obliged to pay the toll to cross it. It also embodied civic endurance, having been inaugurated only weeks after Hungary lost the 1849 War of Independence, when Austrian troops tried and failed to destroy it.

However, in 1945, the Wehrmacht dynamited all of Budapest's bridges in a bid to check the Red Army. Their reconstruction was one of the first tasks of the postwar era, and the reopening of the Lánchíd on the centenary of its inauguration (Nov 21) was heralded as proof that life was returning to normal, even as Hungary was becoming a Communist dictatorship. Today, the bridge is once again adorned with the national coat of arms rather than Soviet symbols.

Count Széchenyi

Count István Széchenyi (1791–1860) was the outstanding figure of Hungary's Reform era. As a young aide-de-camp he cut a dash at the Congress of Vienna and did the rounds of stately homes across Europe. While in England, he steeplechased hell-for-leather, but still found time to examine factories and steam trains, providing Bernard Shaw with the inspiration for the "odious Zoltán Karpathy" of *Pygmalion* (and the musical *My Fair Lady*). Back in Hungary, he pondered solutions to his homeland's backwardness and offered a year's income from his estates towards the establishment of a Hungarian Academy. In 1830 he published *Hitel* (Credit), a hard-headed critique of the nation's feudal society.

Though politically conservative, Széchenyi was obsessed with **modernization**. A passionate convert to steam power after riding on the Manchester–Liverpool railway, he invited Britons to Hungary to build rail lines and the Lánchíd. He also imported steamships and dredgers, promoted horsebreeding and silk-making, and initiated the dredging of the River Tisza and the blasting of a road through the Iron Gates of the Danube. Alas, his achievements were rewarded by a melancholy end. The 1848 Revolution and the short-lived triumph of the radical party led by his *bête noire*, Kossuth, triggered a nervous breakdown, and Széchenyi eventually shot himself.

A positive development in recent years has been its closing to traffic for up to ten weekends over the summer for popular festivities, notably the **Bridge Festival** (Hídünnep; see p.33) in June.

The idea for a bridge came to **Count István Széchenyi** after he was late for his father's funeral in 1820 because bad weather had made the Danube uncrossable. Turning his idea into reality was to preoccupy him for two decades, and it became the centrepiece of a grand plan to modernize Hungary's communications. Owing to Britain's industrial pre-eminence and Széchenyi's Anglophilia, the bridge was designed by **William Tierney Clark** (who based it on his earlier plan for Hammersmith Bridge in London) and constructed under the supervision of a Scottish engineer, **Adam Clark** (no relation), from components cast in Britain. Besides the technical problems of erecting what was then the longest bridge in Europe (nearly 380m), there was also the attempt by the Austrians to blow it up – which Adam Clark personally thwarted by flooding its chain-lockers. He also dissuaded a Hungarian general from setting it alight in 1849.

Whereas Széchenyi died in an asylum, Clark settled happily in Budapest with his Hungarian wife. After his death, he was buried on the spot that now bears his name, though his remains were subsequently moved to Kerepesi Cemetery. Adam Clark also built the **tunnel** (*alagút*) under Várhegy – another Széchenyi project – which Budapestis joked could be used to store the new bridge when it rained.

The Víziváros

Inhabited by fishermen, craftsmen and their families in medieval times, the **Víziváros** ("Watertown"), between Várhegy and the Danube, became depopulated during the seventeenth century, and was resettled by Habsburg mercenaries and their camp followers after the Turks were driven out. The following century saw the neighbourhood gradually gentrified, with solid apartment blocks meeting at odd angles on the hillside, reached by alleys which mostly consist of steps rising from the main street, **Fő utca**. Some of these are still lit by gas lamps and look quite Dickensian on misty evenings.

If you head north past the **Institut Français** at Fő utca 17 and a former Capuchin church featuring Turkish window arches at no. 30, you come to **Szilágyi Desző tér**, a square infamous for the events that occurred here in January 1945. When Eichmann and the SS had already fled, the Arrow Cross massacred hundreds of Budapest's Jews and dumped their bodies in the river; an inconspicuous plaque commemorates the victims. From here, you can make a brief detour left up Vám utca, just north of the square, to see the **Iron Block**, a replica of a wooden block into which itinerant apprentices once hammered nails for good luck (the original is in a museum).

Batthyány tér

The main square and social hub of the Víziváros, **Batthyány tér** is named after the nineteenth-century prime minister, Lajos Batthyány, but started out as Bomba tér (Bomb Square) after an ammunition depot sited here for the defence of the Danube. Today, it's busy with shoppers visiting the supermarket in an old market hall on the western side of the square, and commuters using

the underground metro/HÉV interchange. The sunken two-storey building to the right of the market used to be the *White Cross Inn*, where Casanova reputedly once stayed. Many of the older buildings in this area are sunken in this way owing to the ground level being raised several feet in the nineteenth century to combat flooding.

The twin-towered **Church of St Anne** (Szent Anna templom) on the southern corner of Fő utca is one of the finest Baroque buildings in Budapest. Commissioned by the Jesuits in 1740, it wasn't consecrated until 1805 owing to financial problems, the abolition of the Jesuit order in 1773, and an earthquake. During Communist times there were plans to demolish the building, as it was feared that the metro would undermine its foundations, but these, fortunately, came to nothing. Figures of Faith, Hope and Charity hover above the entrance, and in the middle of the facade St Anne cherishes the child Mary, while God's eye surmounts the Buda coat of arms on its tympanum. The interior is ornate yet homely, the high altar festooned with statues of St Anne presenting Mary to the Temple in Jerusalem, accompanied by a host of cherubim and angels, while chintzy bouquets and potted trees welcome shoppers dropping in to say their prayers.

In the northern corner of the square, the **Church of the St Elizabeth Nuns** is worth a look inside for its fresco of St Florian protecting the faithful during the 1810 fire of Tabán.

Bem tér and around

Fő utca terminates at **Bem tér**, named after the Polish general Joseph Bem, who fought for the Hungarians in the War of Independence, and was revered by his men as "Father". A **statue of Bem** with his arm in a sling recalls him leading them into battle at Piski, crying "I shall recapture the bridge or die! Forward Hungarians! If we do not have the bridge we do not have the country." Traditionally a site for demonstrations, it was here that the crowds assembled prior to marching on Parliament at the beginning of the 1956 Uprising. In the northwest corner, at the junction of Frankel Leó utca, stands a Budapest institution, the *Bambi* – one of the few unreformed café-bars that retains its 1970s furnishing and fierce waitresses.

You can identify the **Király Baths** nearby (Király gyógyfürdő; see p.191 for details) by the four copper cupolas, shaped like tortoise shells, poking from its eighteenth-century facade. Together with the Rudas, this is the finest of Budapest's Turkish baths, whose octagonal pool, lit by star-shaped apertures in the dome, was built in 1570 for the Buda garrison. The baths' name, meaning "king", comes from that of the König family who owned them in the eighteenth century.

If you approach the baths from the south, you'll pass the hulking Fascist-style **Military Court of Justice** at Fő utca 70–72, where Imre Nagy and other leaders of the 1956 Uprising were secretly tried and executed in 1958. The square outside has now been renamed after Nagy, whose body lay in an unmarked grave in the New Public Cemetery for over thirty years (see p.126).

A century ago, the neighbourhood surrounding Bem tér was dominated by a foundry established by the Swiss ironworker Abrahám Ganz, which grew into the mighty Ganz Machine Works. The original ironworks only ceased operation in 1964, when it was turned into a **Foundry Museum** (Öntödei Múzeum; Tues–Sun 9am–4pm; 400Ft). You can still see the old wooden structure and the foundry's huge ladles and cranes *in situ*, together with a collection of cast-iron stoves, tram wheels, lamp posts and other exhibits. The museum is located at Bem utca 20, 200m from Bem tér, or barely a block from Margit körút.

Moszkva tér to Rószadomb

The area immediately north of Várhegy is defined by the transport hub of **Moszkva tér** (Moscow Square), which has kept its name owing to the sheer cost of renaming all the vehicles, maps and signs on which it appears. To the north, the **Mammut mall** (fronted by a statue of the woolly beast) is a magnet for shoppers, as is the lively Fény utca **market**. Further down Fény utca lies the main attraction of the area, where the site of the former Ganz Machine Works has been transformed into the **Millenaris Park** (daily 6am–11pm; free) with water features, vineyards and plots of corn to represent different regions of Hungary. Kids can be let loose on the fantastic **playground**, and visitors of all ages can enjoy the **performances** at the outdoor theatre, indoor and outdoor concerts and an ever-changing rota of **events** in the converted factory buildings; get details from the information centre (daily 10am–6pm; ⓣ1/336-4057, ⓦwww.millenaris.hu) in Building G.

A big draw for those with kids or an interest in science is the **Palace of Miracles** (Csodák palotája; mid-June to late Aug daily 10am–6pm; rest of the year Mon–Fri 9am–5pm, Sat & Sun 10am–6pm; 1090Ft, family 2990Ft; ⓦwww.csodapalota.hu) in Building D. This interactive playhouse is the brainchild of two Hungarian physicists and aims to explain scientific principles to 6- to 12-year-olds, using devices such as optical illusions, a bed of nails, a simulated low-gravity "moonwalk" and a "miracle bicycle" on a tightrope. Nearby in Building B, the **House of the Future** (Tues–Fri 9am–5pm, Sat & Sun 10am–6pm; 1500Ft, family 4500Ft) offers digital-based temporary exhibitions on futuristic themes.

The park provides a cultural focal point, augmenting the longstanding tourist attraction of Gül Baba's tomb, on the lower slopes of Rószadomb. Otherwise, Moszkva tér is the place to catch buses to the Cogwheel Railway (see p.121) or the Farkasréti Cemetery (see p.124), as well as trams #4 or #6 to Pest.

Gül Baba's tomb and Rószadomb

The smoggy arc of **Margit körút** underlines the gulf between the polluted inner city and the breeze-freshened heights of Budapest's most affluent neighbourhood, **Rószadomb** (Rose Hill). The hill is named after the flowers that were reputedly introduced to Hungary by a revered Sufi dervish, Gül Baba, the "Father of the Roses", who participated in the Turkish capture of Buda but died during the thanksgiving service afterwards. The **Tomb of Gül Baba** (Tues–Sun: May–Sept 10am–6pm; Oct–April 10am–4pm; 500Ft) is located on Mecset utca (Mosque Street), five-minutes' walk uphill from Margit körút via Margit utca. Restored with funds donated by the Turkish government, its octagonal shrine is adorned with Arabic calligraphy and Turkish carpets, and is surrounded by a colonnaded parapet with fine views and a pristine park with rose bushes and marble fountains decorated with tiles.

The Rószadomb itself is as much a social category as a neighbourhood: a list of residents would read like a Hungarian *Who's Who*. During the Communist era this included the top Party *funcionárusok*, whose homes featured secret exits that enabled ÁVO chiefs to escape lynching during the Uprising. Nowadays, wealthy film directors and entrepreneurs predominate, and the sloping streets are lined with spacious villas and flashy cars.

The area north of the Margit híd contains two noteworthy baths, the Neoclassical **Lukács Baths**, harbouring a thermal pool, a small swimming pool and whirlpools, and slightly further north up the road, the modern **Császár Komjádi Pool** (see pp.191–192), past a ruined Turkish bath to the left.

7

Gellért-hegy and the Tabán

Gellért-hegy, a craggy dolomite hill rearing 130m above the embankment, is one area you'd be foolish to miss: it offers a fabulous view of the city and is as much a feature of Budapest's waterfront panorama as Várhegy and the Parliament building. At its foot, meanwhile, the *Gellért hotel* is famous for its Art Nouveau thermal baths and summer terrace. North of Gellért-hegy, the **Tabán**, once Buda's artisan quarter, now has more roads than buildings and makes an incongruous setting for one of Budapest's most historic and magical Turkish baths, the **Rudas**.

Transport to the district is plentiful: bus #7 and trams # 47 and #49 go from Pest to Gellért tér and Móricz Zsigmond körtér, while tram #18 from Moszkva tér and tram #19 from Batthyány tér via the Tabán serve the same points.

Gellért-hegy

Surmounted by the Liberation Monument and the Citadella, **Gellért-hegy** makes a distinctive contribution to Budapest's skyline. The hill is named after the Italian missionary Ghirardus (Gellért in Hungarian), who converted pagan Magyars to Christianity at the behest of King Stephen. After his royal protector's demise, vengeful heathens strapped Gellért to a barrow and toppled him off the cliff, where a larger-than-life **statue of St Gellért** now stands astride an artificial waterfall facing the Erzsébet híd, his crucifix raised as if in admonition to motorists.

The Gellért Hotel and Baths

At the foot of the hill, the graceful wrought-iron **Szabadság híd** (Liberty Bridge) links the inner boulevard of Pest to Szent Gellért tér on the Buda side, dominated by the Art Nouveau **Gellért Hotel**. Opened in 1918, it was commandeered as a staff headquarters by the Reds, the Romanian army, and finally by Admiral Horthy, following his triumphal entry into "sinful Budapest" in 1920 – in his eyes it was a decadent, communist and, above all, a Jewish city. During the 1930s and 1940s, the hotel's balls were the highlight of Budapest's

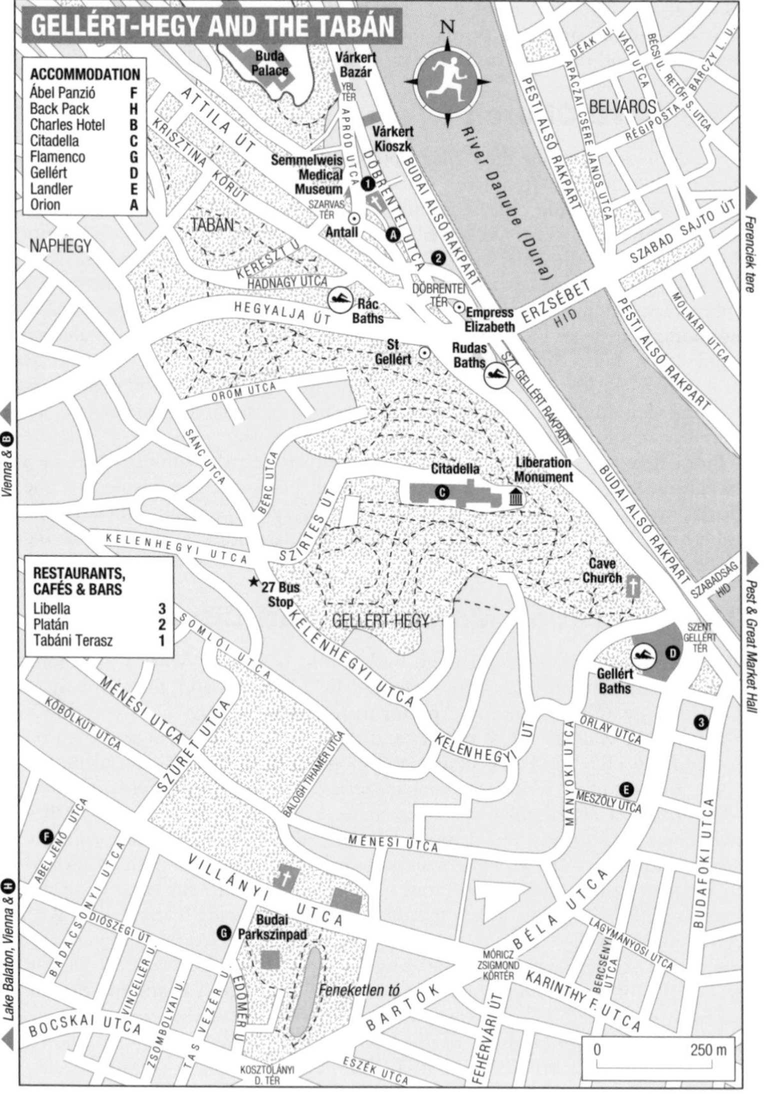

social calendar, when debutantes danced on a glass floor laid over its pool. The ostentatious domed **drinking fountain** in front of the hotel has been the source of some controversy: symbolizing the eight springs of Budapest, it was erected without planning permission, and the city authorities toyed with the idea of pulling it down before relenting.

The attached **Gellért Baths** (entered from Kelenhegyi út to the right of the main entrance, though hotel guests can go down in the lift in their bathrobes) are magnificently appointed with majolica tiles and mosaics, and a columned,

Roman-style **thermal pool**, with lion-headed spouts. In the summer visitors can also use the **outdoor pools**, including one with a wave machine, on the terraces behind the main baths. For more details, see p.191.

The Cave Church

On the hillside opposite the *Gellért Hotel* you'll find the **Cave Church** (Sziklatemplom; daily 8am–9pm; free), where masses are conducted by white-robed monks of the Pauline order, the only religious order indigenous to Hungary. Founded in 1256, its monks served as confessors to the Hungarian kings until Josef II dissolved the order in 1773, though it was re-established 150 years later. The church itself was created in the 1930s by monks from the nearby Pauline monastery, and functioned until the whole community was arrested by the ÁVO at midnight mass on Easter Monday, 1951, whereupon the chapel was sealed up until 1989. Flickering candles and mournful organ music create an eerie atmosphere during services (daily 8.30–9.30am, 11am–noon, 4.30–6.30pm & 8–9pm), but tourists are only allowed to enter between times. Outside the entrance stands a **statue of St Stephen** with his horse.

From here, you can follow one of the footpaths to the summit – about a twenty-minute climb. The hillside, which still bears fig trees planted by the Turks, was covered in vineyards until a phylloxera epidemic struck in the nineteenth century. Kids will enjoy the long tubular **slides** on the hotel-facing slopes of the hill.

The Liberation Monument and Citadella

Whether you walk up or get there by bus (bus #27 from Móricz Zsigmond körtér to the Busuló Juhász stop, followed by a 10min walk), the **summit** of Gellért-hegy affords a stunning **panoramic view**, drawing one's eye slowly along the curving river, past bridges and monumental landmarks, and then on to the Buda Hills and Pest's suburbs, merging hazily with the distant plain.

On the summit, beside the citadel, stands the **Liberation Monument** (Felszabadulási emlékmű) – a female figure brandishing the palm of victory over 30m aloft. There is a famous tale that the monument was originally commissioned by Admiral Horthy in memory of his son István (who was killed in a plane crash on the Eastern Front in 1942), and that, by substituting a palm branch for the propeller it was meant to hold and placing a statue of a Red Army soldier at the base, the monument was deftly recycled to commemorate the Soviet soldiers who died liberating Budapest from the Nazis. While the story may not be true, the monument's sculptor, **Zsigmond Kisfaludi-Strobl**, certainly succeeded in winning approval as a "Proletarian Artist", despite having previously specialized in busts of the aristocracy – and was henceforth known by his compatriots as "Kisfaludi-Strébel" (*strébel* meaning "to climb" or "step from side to side"). The monument survived calls for its removal following the end of Communism, but its inscription was rewritten to honour those who died for "Hungary's prosperity", and the Soviet soldier was banished to the Memento Park on the outskirts of Budapest (p.126).

The **Citadella** behind the monument was built by the Habsburgs to dominate the city in the aftermath of the 1848–49 Revolution; ironically, both its architects were Hungarians. When the historic Compromise was reached in 1867, citizens breached the walls to affirm that it no longer posed a threat to them – though in fact an SS regiment did later hole up in the citadel during World War II. Today it has been usurped by a private company, which charges

▲ The Liberation Monument on Gellért-hegy

visitors 1200Ft to set foot inside the walls (daily 8am–dusk) and view an outdoor exhibition on the hill's history since the Celtic Eravisci lived here two thousand years ago; there's also a dull recreation of a **Nazi bunker** in a concrete cellar. The *Citadella Hotel* (see p.153) is reached by a separate entrance.

The Tabán

The **Tabán** district, bordering the northern end of Gellért-hegy, chiefly consists of arterial roads built in Communist times on land left vacant by the prewar demolition of a quarter renowned for its drinking dens and open sewers. Traditionally this was inhabited by Serbs (Rác in Hungarian), who settled here en masse after the Turks were expelled, though in a typically Balkan paradox, some were present earlier, working in the Ottoman gunpowder factories which

may have been the origin of the name Tabán (from *tabahane*, the Turkish for "armoury"). Thankfully, the slum-clearance and motorway building spared Tabán's historic Turkish baths, and its traditions of lusty nightlife are kept alive by summertime concerts in the park.

The Rudas Baths

The relaxing and curative effects of Buda's **mineral springs** have been appreciated for two thousand years. The Romans built splendid bathhouses at Aquincum (see p.117) and, while these declined with their empire, interest in bathing revived after the Knights of St John built a hospice on the site of the present Rudas Baths, near where St Elizabeth cured lepers in the springs below Gellért-hegy. However, it was the Turks who consolidated the habit of bathing (as Muslims, they were obliged to wash five times daily in preparation for prayer) and constructed proper bathhouses which function to this day – though their surroundings and exteriors give little clue to what's inside.

The **Rudas Baths** (Rudas Gyógyfürdő), in the shadow of Gellért-hegy, harbour a fantastic octagonal pool constructed in 1556 on the orders of Pasha Sokoli Mustapha. Bathers wallow amid shafts of light pouring in from the star-shaped apertures in the domed ceiling, surrounded by stone pillars with iron tie-beams and a nest of smaller pools for parboiling oneself or cooling down; for more details, see p.192.

Walking north from the Rudas Baths, you'll pass the **Drinking Hall** (Ivócsarnok; Mon, Wed & Fri 11am–6pm, Tues & Thurs 7am–2pm), nestling beneath the road to the bridge, which sells inexpensive mineral water from three nearby springs by the tumbler. Regular imbibers bring bottles or jerrycans to fill.

The Rác Baths

Retaining an octagonal stone pool from Turkish times, the **Rác Baths** (Rác Gyógyfürdő) are tucked away beneath Hegyalja út, which leads uphill away from the bridgehead of the Erzsébet híd. At the time of writing, the baths were closed as part of a major redevelopment that will turn them into a luxury spa hotel complex, set to open in 2009. A cuboid **memorial stone** outside commemorates the 51st Esperanto Congress held in Budapest in 1966 – an event that would have been inconceivable in Stalin's day, when Esperanto was forbidden for conflicting with his thesis that the time for an international language had yet to come.

Nearby, on one of the grassy areas that comprise Döbrentei tér, is a seated **statue of Empress Elizabeth** (1837–98), after whom the Erzsébet híd (Elizabeth Bridge) is named. She endeared herself to Hungarians by learning their language and refusing to be stifled by her crusty husband, Franz Josef. Assassinated by an anarchist in Switzerland, she was widely mourned in Hungary and is still fondly known by her nickname, Sissi.

The Semmelweis Medical Museum

Often overlooked by tourists, the **Semmelweis Medical Museum** (Semmelweis Orvostörténeti Múzeum; Tues–Sun: mid-March to Oct 10.30am–6pm, Nov to mid-March 10.30am–4pm; 700Ft Ⓦ www.semmelweis.museum.hu), at Apród utca 1–3, contains a fascinating collection of artefacts relating to the history of medicine, with mummified limbs from ancient Egypt, and a

shrunken head used by Borneo witchdoctors giving an international dimension to the display. Other exhibits – including a medieval chastity belt, trepanning drills, a lifesize wax model of a dissected female cadaver, and a sewing machine with what looks like a bicycle chain attached, for closing stomach incisions – all give an idea of the centuries of misconceptions and the slow progress of medicine through fatal errors.

Dr Ignác Semmelweis (1818–65), who lived in this house until he was 5, discovered the cause of puerperal fever – a form of blood poisoning contracted in childbirth, which was usually fatal. While serving in Vienna's public hospitals in the 1840s, he noticed that deaths were ten times lower on the wards where only midwives worked than on the ones attended by doctors and students, who went from dissecting corpses to delivering babies with only a perfunctory wash. His solution was to sterilize hands, clothes and instruments between operations – an idea dismissed as preposterous by the hospital, which fired him. Embittered, he wrote open letters to obstetricians, accusing them of being murderers, and was sent to an asylum where he died within a couple of weeks. Only after Pasteur's germ theory was accepted was Semmelweis hailed as the "saviour of mothers". The good doctor is buried in the garden.

The museum also contains the 1876 **Holy Ghost Pharmacy**, transplanted here from Király utca, and a collection of portraits, including one of Vilma Hugonai, Hungary's first woman doctor, and one of Kossuth's sister, Zsuzsanna, who founded the army medical corps during the War of Independence.

Just around the corner is **Szarvas tér** (Stag Square), named after the eighteenth-century *Stag House* inn at no. 1, which functions as a restaurant to this day. In between the museum and the restaurant stands a bust of **Dr József Antall** (1931–93), the first democratically elected prime minister of Hungary after the fall of Communism. For many years, while working as the director of the Semmelweis Museum, he had been dreaming of the chance to emerge from the political shadows, and as prime minister he skilfully ran his centre-right coalition to give Hungary a stable start, though his social conservatism was loathed by his opponents. He died in office and is buried in the Kerepesi Cemetery (see p.80).

Past the museum and by the riverbank on **Ybl Miklós tér** are two buildings designed by Miklós Ybl, the man behind the Opera House and other major works. To the left of the road, the grand facade and terraces of the **Várkert Bazár** stand in deep decay, awaiting a saviour. Designed as the grand entrance to the Várkert, the park running up to the palace, with shops either side of the steps, the Bazár was damaged in the war and used as artists' studios until it was purchased by foreign investors soon after the millennium, but the promised restoration has yet to materialise. Some insignificant-looking stones in the gardens behind (accessible from Szarvas tér) are actually Turkish gravestones. By the river across the road is the **Várkert Kioszk**, a former pumping station with an ornate interior and Ybl's statue standing in front.

8

Óbuda and Margit-sziget

Óbuda is the oldest part of Budapest, though that's hardly the impression given by the factories and high-rises that dominate the district today, hiding such ancient ruins as remain. Nonetheless, it was here that the Romans built a legionary camp and a civilian town, later taken over by the Huns. Under the Hungarian Árpád dynasty this developed into an important town, but in the fifteenth century it was eclipsed by Várhegy. The original settlement became known as Óbuda (Old Buda) and was incorporated into the newly formed Budapest in 1873. The tiny old town centre is as pretty as Várhegy, with several **museums** worth seeing, but to find the best-preserved **Roman ruins** you'll have to go to the **Rómaifürdő** district, further out. To the west, there is a pair of striking **caves** near the valley of Szépvölgy, a visit to which can be combined with the **Kiscelli Museum**, with its interesting collection of furniture and interior furnishings in a former monastery.

In the middle of the Danube, leafy **Margit-sziget** is a haven from the noise and pollution of the city. One of Budapest's favourite parks and summer pleasure-grounds, the island is part of its grand waterfront panorama – unlike shabby **Óbudai-sziget** just north which, like Cinderella, gets but one chance to have fun, by hosting Hungary's equivalent of Glastonbury, the **Sziget festival**, each August (see p.190).

The HÉV from Batthyány tér (see p.105) provides easy **access** to riverside Óbuda, while a variety of trams and buses serve Margit-sziget. You can also reach Margit-sziget on one of the ferries which zigzag up the river from Boráros tér; see p.29 for details.

Óbuda

After its incorporation within the city, **Óbuda** became a popular place to eat, drink and make merry, with garden restaurants and taverns serving fish and wine from the locality. Some of the most famous establishments still exist around **Fő tér**, the heart of eighteenth-century Óbuda, with its ornate Trinity Column. While there's no denying the charm of their Baroque facades and

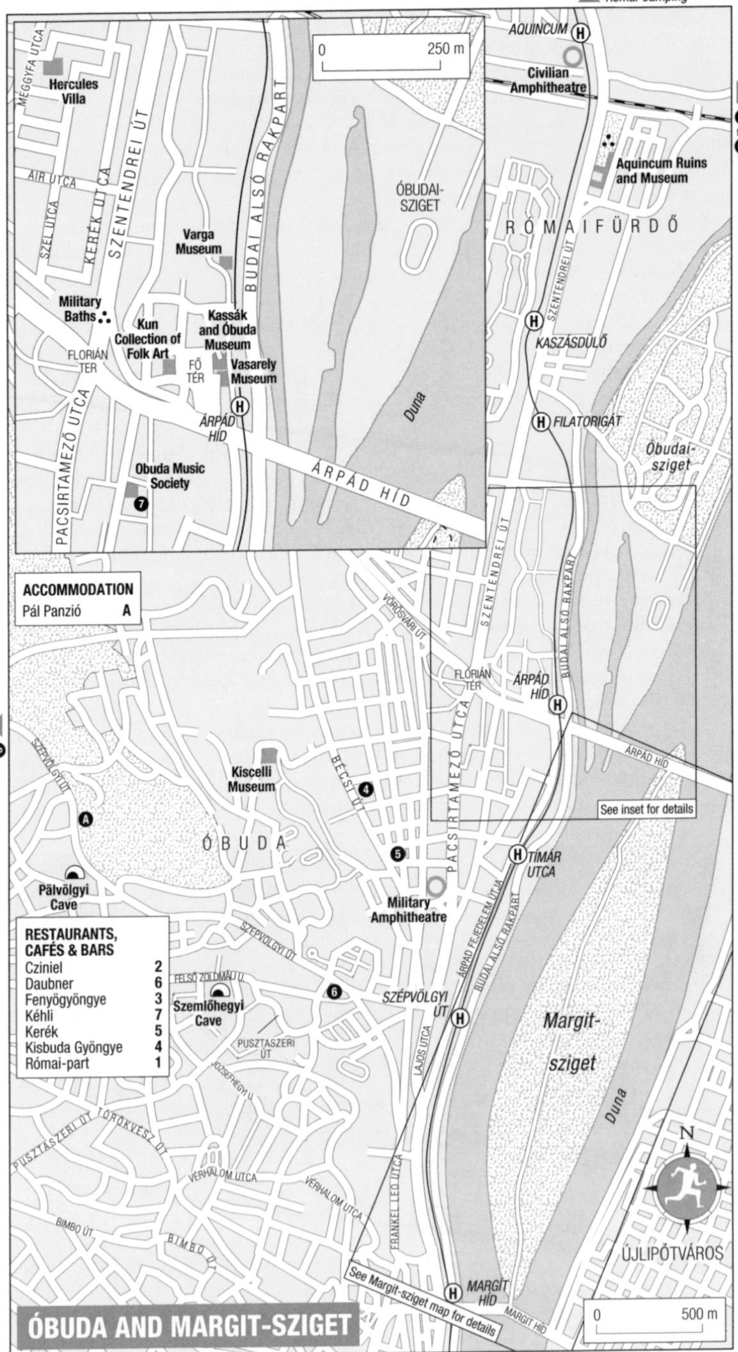

ÓBUDA AND MARGIT-SZIGET

wrought-iron lamps, many are simply trading on past glories; see p.166 for our pick of Óbuda's eating places.

There's more to enjoy from a cultural standpoint. Directly opposite the Árpád híd HÉV exit at Szentlélek tér 6, the **Vasarely Museum** (Vasarely Múzeum; Tues–Sun 10am–5.30pm; 800Ft; Ⓦwww.vasarely.tvn.hu) displays eyeball-throbbing Op Art works by Viktor Vasarely (1906–99), the founder of the genre, who was born in Pécs in southern Hungary, emigrated to Paris in 1930 and spent the rest of his life in France.

Around the corner at Fő tér 1, the Baroque Zichy mansion contains a courtyard seemingly unchanged since Habsburg times, at the back of which is the **Kassák Museum** (Kassák Múzeum; Wed–Sun 10am–5pm; 300Ft), dedicated to the Hungarian Constructivist Lajos Kassák (1887–1967) and featuring his paintings, magazine designs, publications and possessions. A self-taught artist and publisher who devoted much of his younger life to the socialist cause (publishing work by Cocteau and Le Corbusier), Kassák's avant-garde style had little in common with Socialist Realism and he was not allowed to exhibit in his last years.

Another door off the courtyard leads to the **Óbuda Museum** (Óbudai Múzeum; Tues–Sun 10am–6pm; 300Ft), a fascinating local history collection with reconstructed living-rooms and workshops, one from the Sváb (German) community on the northern edge of Buda – including a pre-electric washing machine – and one from a middle-class household where Art Nouveau holds sway. There's also a cute collection of antique toys.

Across the square at no. 4, another Baroque mansion houses the charming **Kun Collection of Folk Art** (Kun Zsigmond Népművészéti Gyűjtemeny; Tues–Sun 10am–5pm; 300Ft): peasant furniture, ceramics and textiles collected by "Uncle Zsigmond", as he was fondly known, who lived to the ripe old age of 107; the museum was his former apartment.

Whatever the weather, you'll see several figures sheltering beneath umbrellas just off Fő tér, life-sized sculptures by Imre Varga, Hungary's best known living artist, whose oeuvre is the subject of the nearby **Varga Museum** (Varga Imre Múzeum; Tues–Sun 10am–6pm; 500Ft) at Laktanya utca 7. Pathos and humour

▲ Fő tér, Óbuda

pervades his sheet-metal, iron and bronze effigies of famous personages, including Pope John Paul II and Bartók. Varga's career has spanned the eras of "goulash socialism" and democracy – evinced by state-commissioned monuments to Béla Kun (in the Memento Park, see p.126) and Imre Nagy (near Parliament; p.58) – but nobody accuses him of being a hack like Kisfaludi-Strobl (see p.110).

Roman remains

Óbuda's Roman remains lurk in a concrete jungle. On Flórián tér, 500m west of Fő tér, weathered columns rise amid a shopping plaza, while the old **military baths** (*thermae maiores*) are exposed in the pedestrian underpass beneath the Szentendrei út flyover. The largest ruin is a weed-choked, crumbling **military amphitheatre** (*amfiteátrum*) which once seated up to 13,000 spectators, at the junction of Pacsirtamező utca and Nagyszombat utca, 800m further south – accessible by bus #86 or by walking 400m from Kolosy tér, near the Szépvölgyi út HÉV stop. A more elusive relic – only viewable by pre-arrangement – is the **Hercules Villa** (Ⓣ1/250-1650; minimum six people, 500Ft each) at Meggyfa utca 19–21 (take bus #86 to the Bogdan utca stop). The villa was discovered when the neighbouring secondary school was built, yielding a superb **mosaic floor** from the third century AD. Its central composition (from the villa's main room) depicts the centaur Nessus abducting Deianeira, whom Hercules had to rescue as one of his twelve labours. All that can be seen now is a photograph, since the mosaic was moved to the Aquincum Museum (see below), but a fragment of another mosaic remains in situ, featuring a delightfully rendered tiger and Hercules about to vomit at a wine festival.

North of Óbuda, the riverside factory belt merges into the **Rómaifürdő** (Roman Bath) district, harbouring a campsite, a lido and the ruins of **Aquincum**. Originally a settlement of camp followers spawned by the legionary garrison, Aquincum eventually became a *municipium* and then a *colonia*, the provincial capital of Pannonia Inferior. The **ruins** (Tues–Sun: May–Sept 9am–6pm; late April & Oct 9am–5pm; Nov 10am–4pm; 900Ft; Ⓦwww.aquincum.hu) are visible from the Aquincum HÉV stop, from where a brief walk south under the mainline rail bridge brings you to the site itself. Enough of the foundation walls and underground piping survives to give a fair idea of the town's layout, with its forum and law courts, its sanctuaries of the goddesses Epona and Fortuna Augusta, and the *collegia* and bathhouses where fraternal societies met. Its bare bones are given substance by an excellent **museum** (opens at 10am, same ticket) and smaller exhibitions around the site. Its star exhibit is the **mosaic** of Nessus abducting Deianeira, from the Hercules Villa (see above), which originally consisted of sixty thousand stones, selected and arranged in Alexandria before shipment to Europe. Other highlights include a mummy preserved in natron, a cult-relief of the god Mithras and a reconstructed water-organ. The **Floralia Festival** (May 17–18) and **Aquincum Summer** (mid-May to mid-Sept at weekends) see theatrical performances, crafts-making displays, mock gladiator battles and other events staged here, rather than in the ancient **civilian amphitheatre** near the HÉV stop, which once seated up to seven thousand spectators.

The caves

The hills rising to the west of Óbuda feature a network of caves that are unique for having been formed by thermal waters rising up from below, rather than by rainwater. Two of the sites have been accessible to the public since the 1980s, with

guided tours (some English spoken) every hour on the hour, if there are five people. In both cases the starting point is **Kolosy tér** in Óbuda (accessible by bus #86 from Flórián tér or Batthyány tér, or bus #6 from Nyugati tér in Pest), from where you catch bus #65 five stops to the Pálvölgyi Cave, or bus #29 four stops to the Szemlőhegyi Cave. As the two caves are ten-minutes' walk apart, it's possible to dash from one to the other and catch both tours within two hours.

The **Pálvölgyi Stalactite Cave** (Pálvölgyi cseppkőbarlang; tours hourly Tues–Sun 10am–4pm; 1250Ft) at Szépvölgyi út 162 is the more spectacular of the two labyrinths; part of the longest of the cave systems in the Buda Hills, it is still being explored by speleologists. It was discovered in 1904 by a quarryman searching for a sheep that disappeared when the floor of the quarry fell in. Tours, on which you negotiate hundreds of steps and dank constricted passages, last about half an hour. You start on the lowest level, which boasts rock formations such as the "Organ Pipes" and "Beehive". From "John's Lookout" in the largest chamber, you ascend a crevice onto the upper level, there to enter "Fairyland" and finally "Paradise", overlooking the hellish "Radium Hall" 50m below.

Quite different is the **Szemlőhegyi Cave** (Szemlőhegyi barlang; tours hourly Mon & Wed–Sun 10am–4pm; 1250Ft) at Pusztaszeri út 35, with less convoluted and claustrophobic passages and no stalactites. Instead, the walls are encrusted with cauliflower- or popcorn-textured precipitates. Discovered in 1930, the cave has exceptionally clean air, and its lowest level is used as a respiratory sanatorium. After the tour you can view a museum of cave finds and plans from all over Hungary.

For refreshment after the caves you should schedule in a stop at the *Daubner* patisserie at Szépvölgyi út 29 (near the bottom of the hill), which does some of the most delicious cakes in the city, and attracts huge queues at weekends. Alternatively, you can combine a visit to the Szemlőhegyi Cave with the Bartók Memorial House (see p.123) or the Kiscelli Museum.

The Kiscelli Museum

On a hillside above Óbuda, fifteen-minutes' walk north of the Szemlőhegyi Cave, the **Kiscelli Museum** (Kiscelli Múzeum; Tues–Sun: April–Oct 10am–6pm; Nov–March 10am–4pm; 700Ft; Ⓦwww.btmfk.iif.hu) occupies a former Trinitarian monastery in a beautiful wooded setting at Kiscelli utca 108. The museum's collection includes antique printing presses and the 1830 Biedermeier furnishings of the Golden Lion pharmacy, which used to stand on Kálvin tér. Also on show are carved shop signs, the Budapest Municipal Gallery's collection of sculptures and graphics by twentieth-century Hungarian artists, and antique furniture exhibited in the blackened shell of the monastery's Gothic church, which makes a dramatic backdrop for classical **concerts**, animated film shows and other events (see Ⓦwww.kiscell.org). The museum can be reached by bus #165 from Kolosy tér or bus #60 from Batthyány tér.

Margit-sziget

There's a saying that "love begins and ends on **Margit-sziget**", for this verdant island has been a favourite meeting place for lovers since the nineteenth century (though before 1945 a stiff admission charge deterred the poor). A royal game reserve under the Árpáds and a monastic colony until the Turkish conquest,

today Margit-sziget has two public baths fed by thermal springs, an outdoor theatre and other amenities.

The island was named at the end of the nineteenth century after Princess **Margit** (Margaret), the daughter of Béla IV. Legend has it that he vowed to bring her up as a nun if Hungary survived the Mongol invasion, and duly confined the 9-year-old in a convent when it did. She apparently made the best of it, acquiring a reputation for curing lepers and other saintly deeds, as well as for never washing above her ankles. Beatification came after her death in 1271, and a belated canonization in 1943, by which time her name had already been bestowed on the **Margit híd**, built by a French company in the 1870s. Linking Margit-sziget to Buda and Pest, it's an unusual bridge in the form of a splayed-out V, with a short arm joined to the southern tip of the island. In November 1944 it was blown up by the Nazis, killing hundreds of people including the German sappers who had detonated the explosives by mistake. Photos of the result can be seen in the underpass at the Pest end.

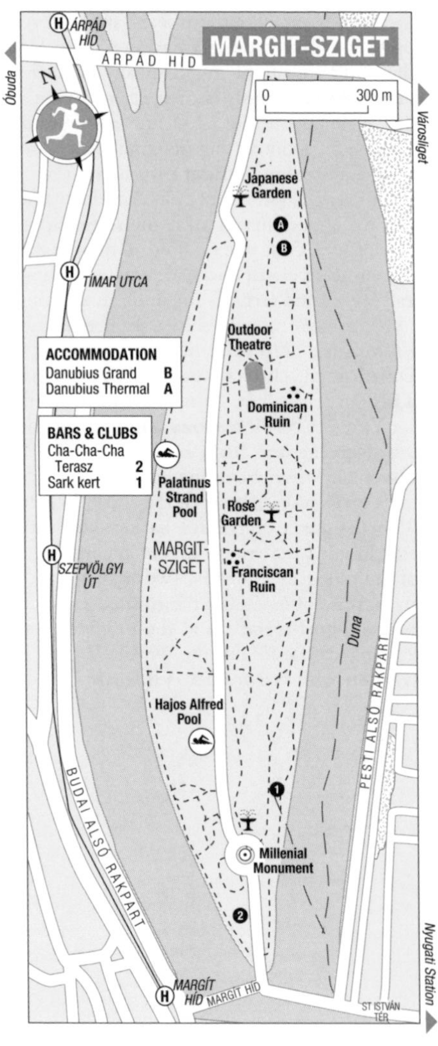

The island

There are two entrances to the island: from Árpád híd at the northern end and Margit híd to the south. Trams #4 and #6 stop at the southern entrance, tram #1 stops at the northern entrance, and bus #26 (from Nyugati tér, by Nugati pu. metro) runs up the middle of the island and finishes at the Árpád híd metro (both stations are on the blue metro line). Motorists can only approach from the north of the island, via the Árpád híd, at which point they must leave their vehicles at a paying car park. Near both entrances you can rent **bikes**, **pedaloes** and **electric cars**, which tend to be rather battered but will get you around. Runners will love the low-impact **jogging** path around the island's circumference.

Walking down from the tram stop on Margit híd, you'll find picnickers unloading cars and, as summer nights wear on, people streaming in to party in

the woods or at outdoor bars and clubs like *Cha-cha-cha* and *Sárk kert* (see pp.173–174). Revellers are greeted by a Millennial Monument and a **fountain** that emits bursts of grand music. Further on, behind trees to the left, is the **Hajós Alfréd Pool** (known as the "Sport"; see p.191), named after the winner of the 100-metre and 1200-metre swimming races at the 1896 Olympics. Hajós was also an architect and designed the indoor pool, but the main attractions here are the all-season outdoor fifty-metre pool, where the national swimming team trains on weekdays from 9am. Another swimming venue, the **Palatinus Strand** (see p.192), lies nearly a kilometre further north. With a monumental entrance from the 1930s, it can hold as many as ten thousand people at a time in numerous open-air thermal pools, complete with a water chute, wave machine and segregated terraces for nude sunbathing.

Off to the east of the road between the two pools are the ruins of a **Franciscan church** from the late thirteenth century, while a ruined **Dominican church and convent** stands in the vicinity of the **Outdoor Theatre** (Szabadtéri Színpad) further north along the main road, which hosts plays, operas, fashion shows and concerts during summer. The café here makes a convenient stop for a beer and a snack, and is easily located by the **water tower** that rises above the complex.

A short way northeast of the tower is a **Premonstratensian Chapel**, whose Romanesque tower dates back to the twelfth century, when the order first established a monastery on the island. The tower's fifteenth-century bell is one of the oldest in Hungary. Two luxury **spa hotels** can be found beyond, across an expanse of lawn: the refurbished *fin-de-siècle Ramada Grand*, with an inviting café and beer terrace, and the modern, less appealing *Thermal*, which replaced the spa damaged during World War II. Beside the *Thermal* is a **Japanese Garden** with warm springs that sustain tropical fish and giant water lilies.

9

The Buda Hills

A densely wooded arc around a sixth of Budapest's circumference, the **Buda Hills** are as close to nature as you can get within the city limits. The hills are a favourite place for walking in all seasons, with trails marked with the distance or the duration ("ó" stands for hours; "p" for minutes). While some parts can be crowded with walkers and mountain-bikers at the weekend, it's possible to ramble for hours during the week and see hardly a soul. The most rewarding destinations for those with limited time are the "**railway circuit**", using the Cogwheel and Children's railways and the **chairlift**, and the **Bartók Memorial House**. Further south is the **Farkasréti Cemetery**, noted for its architecture as well as the personages buried here.

Moszkva tér is the easiest starting point for all the destinations in the hills: several buses and trams go up to the Cogwheel Railway, and services go to the chairlift and the Farkasréti Cemetery. Exploring the Buda Hills **by trail-bike** is a more ambitious option, if you've got a day to spare and the stamina. Velo-Touring (XI, Előpatak utca 1 ⓣ1/319-0571, ⓦwww.velo-touring.hu) rents 21-gear bikes (3530Ft/5hr; 23,540Ft deposit) and can advise on routes; their office is about 1km from Farkasréti Cemetery. Bikes can be carried on the Cogwheel and Children's railways.

The railway circuit

This is an easy and enjoyable way to visit the hills that will especially appeal to kids. The whole trip can take under two hours if connections click, or a half-day if you prefer to take your time. You begin at the lower terminal of the **Cogwheel Railway** (Fogaskerekűvasút, now designated tram #60), which is two stops from Moszkva tér on tram #18 or #56 or bus #22, #56 and others heading up Szilágyi Erzsébet fasor; alight opposite the cylindrical *Budapest Hotel*. The train was the third such railway in the world when it was inaugurated in 1874, and was steam-powered until its electrification in 1929. Running every ten minutes or so (daily 5am–11pm; BKV fares and passes apply), its cogs fitting into a notched track, the train climbs 300m over 3km through the villa-suburb of **Svábhegy**; for the best view, take a window seat on the right-hand side, facing backwards.

From the upper terminal on **Széchenyi-hegy**, it's a minute's walk to the **Children's Railway** (Gyermekvasút). A narrow-gauge line built by Communist youth brigades in 1948, it's almost entirely run by 13- to 17-year-old members of the Scouts and Guides movement, enabling them to get hands-on experience if they fancy a career with MÁV, the Hungarian Railways company. Watching

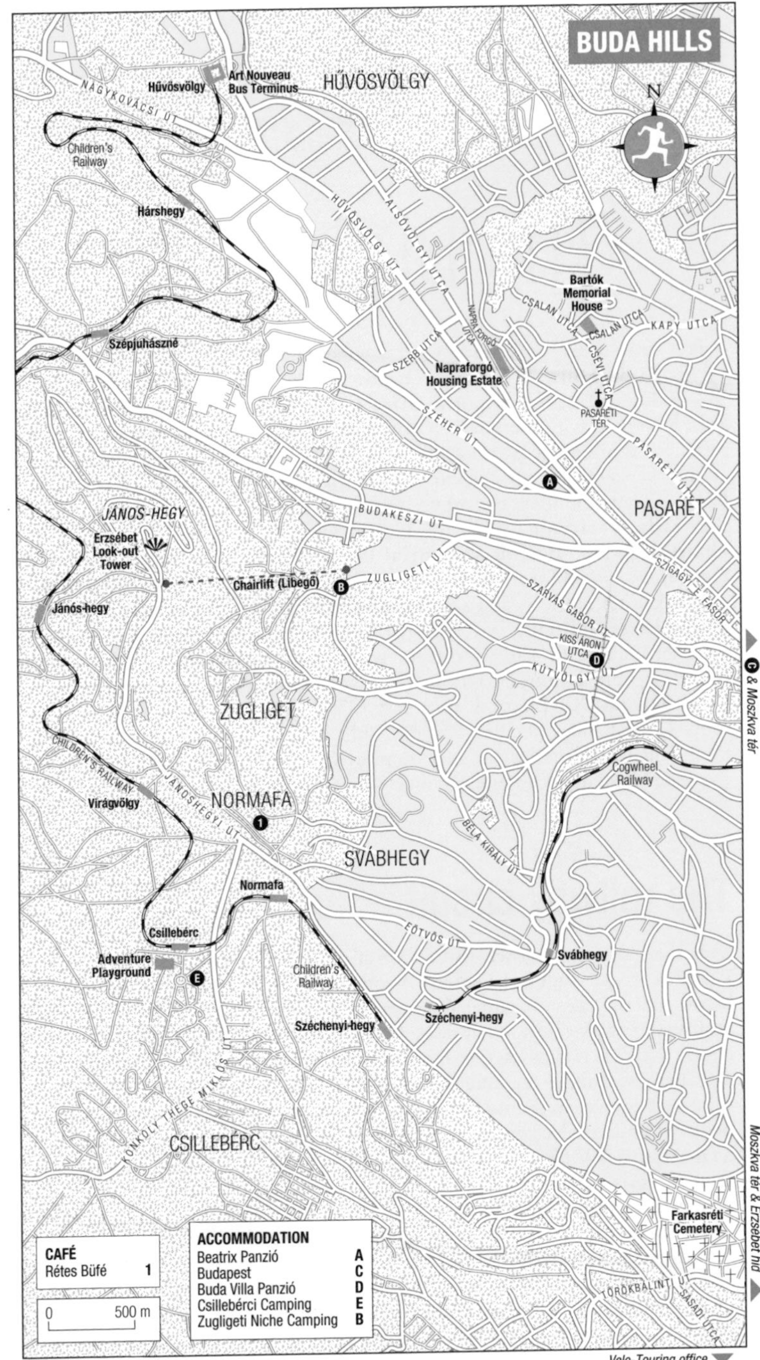
BUDA HILLS
N
HŰVÖSVÖLGY
Hűvösvölgy
Art Nouveau Bus Terminus
NAGYKOVÁCSI ÚT
Children's Railway
Hárshegy
HŰVÖSVÖLGY ÚT
ALSÓVÖLGYI UTCA
Bartók Memorial House
CSALAN UTCA
CSALAN UTCA
KAPY UTCA
CSÉVI UTCA
NAPRAFORGÓ UTCA
SZERB UTCA
Szépjuhászné
Napraforgó Housing Estate
PASARÉTI TÉR
SZÉHER ÚT
PASARÉTI ÚT
PASARÉT
BUDAKESZI ÚT
JÁNOS-HEGY
Erzsébet Look-out Tower
Chairlift (Libegő)
ZUGLIGETI ÚT
SZILÁGYI E. FASOR
SZARVAS GÁBOR ÚT
KISS ÁRON UTCA
KÚTVÖLGYI ÚT
János-hegy
ZUGLIGET
C & Moszkva tér
Cogwheel Railway
CHILDREN'S RAILWAY
JÁNOSHEGYI ÚT
Virágvölgy
NORMAFA
SVÁBHEGY
BÉLA KIRÁLY ÚT
Normafa
EÖTVÖS ÚT
Csillebérc
Svábhegy
Adventure Playground
Children's Railway
Széchenyi-hegy
Széchenyi-hegy
KONKOLY THEGE MIKLÓS ÚT
CSILLEBÉRC
Moszkva tér & Erzsébet híd
Farkasréti Cemetery
TÖRÖKBÁLINTI ÚT
SASADI UTCA
CAFÉ
Rétes Büfé 1
0 500 m
ACCOMMODATION
Beatrix Panzió A
Budapest C
Buda Villa Panzió D
Csillebérci Camping E
Zugligeti Niche Camping B
Velo-Touring office

them wave flags, collect tickets and salute departures with great solemnity, you can see why it appealed to the Communists. Trains depart for the 11km, 45-minute journey to Hűvösvölgy every 45–60 minutes (Tues–Sun 9am–5pm, June–Aug also Mon; 450Ft to any mid-station, 600Ft from terminus to terminus). In summer, they sometimes run heritage trains, pulled by a steam engine or vintage diesel loco, for which a 200Ft supplement is charged.

The first stop, **Normafa** (more quickly reached on bus #90 or #90A from Moszkva tér), is a popular excursion centre with a modest **ski-run** and sledging slopes. Its name comes from a performance of the famous aria from Bellini's *Norma* given here by the actress Rozália Klein in 1840. At the next stop, **Csillebérc**, there's an **adventure playground** (Mon–Fri 10am–6pm, Sat & Sun 9am–7pm; 1700–2800Ft/hr ⓦwww.kalandpalya.com), with tree-top walkways and wire-slides – a smaller version of the tree-top canopy at Visegrád (see p.139).

Alighting at **János-hegy**, one stop on, you can either strike out down through woods to the town of **Budakeszi**, from where bus #22 takes you back to Moszkva tér, or make the fifteen-minute climb from the station to the top of **János-hegy** (527m), the highest point in Budapest. The Romanesque-style **Erzsébet lookout tower** (daily 8am–8pm; free) on the summit offers a panoramic view of the city and the Buda Hills. By the buffet below the summit is the upper terminal of the **chairlift** or **Libegő**, meaning "floater" in Hungarian (May–Sept 10am–5pm; Oct–April 9.30am–4pm; closed every other Mon; 500Ft), which wafts you down over trees and gardens to the suburb of **Zugliget**, from where #158 buses return to Moszkva tér.

Wild boar, which prefer to roam during the evening and sleep by day, are occasionally sighted in the forests above **Hárshegy**, one stop before the terminus at Hűvösvölgy. **Hűvösvölgy** (Cool Valley) is a rapidly expanding suburb spreading into the hills and valleys beyond, also linked directly to Moszkva tér by #56 buses. The **Art Nouveau bus terminus**, with its covered stairways leading to the train station, has been restored to its original elegance.

The Bartók Memorial House and Napraforgó utca

The **Bartók Memorial House** (Bartók Béla Emlékház; Tues–Sun 10am–5pm; 500Ft; ⓦwww.bartokmuseum.hu) at Csalán utca 29, in a leafy suburb below Láto-hegy, was the residence of Béla Bartók, his wife and two sons from 1932 until their emigration to America in 1940, by which time Bartók despaired of Hungary's right-wing regime. It can be reached by taking bus #29 from the Szemlőhegyi Cave to the Nagybányai út stop, which leads to Csalán utca, or bus #5 from Március 15 tér in Pest or Moszkva tér to the Pasaréti tér terminus, and then a ten-minute walk uphill (take the first left along Csévi utca).

The museum has an extensive range of Bartók memorabilia, including some of his original furniture and possessions; displays may include such items as the folk handicrafts he collected during his ethno-musical research trips to Transylvania with Zoltán Kodály, and the shirt cuff on which Bartók wiped his pen-nibs when composing scores. Chamber music **concerts** (1500Ft) are held here from March until June (ⓣ1/394-2100 for information).

Before you return to Moszkva tér, it's worth a brief detour to see the delightful **Napraforgó utca housing estate**, built in 1931. Its 22 houses –

▲ View of the city from the Buda Hills

designed by as many architects – embody different trends in Modernist architecture, from severe Bauhaus to folksy Arts and Crafts-style. The estate is signposted from **Pasaréti tér**, near the #5 bus terminus; follow Pasaréti út till you reach a playing field and cross the bridge on the left. For refreshment afterwards, head for the café in the listed 1930s **bus shelter** on Pasaréti tér. The shelter's curving horizontal form contrasts with slender vertical lines of the Franciscan Church of St Antal across the road – both were designed by the architect Géza Rimanóczy as a single project for the square.

Farkasréti Cemetery

Two kilometres west of Gellért-hegy in the hilly XI district is the **Farkasréti Cemetery** (Farkasréti temető; daily 7.30am–5pm; free), easily reached by riding tram #59 from Moszkva tér to the penultimate stop or by catching bus #8 from Március 15 tér in Pest – flower stalls and funerary masons indicate that you've arrived. Among the 10,000 graves in the "Wolf's Meadow Cemetery" are those of **Béla Bartók** (whose remains were ceremonially reburied in 1988 following their return from America, where he died in exile in 1945); his fellow composer **Zoltán Kodály**; and the conductor **Georg Solti**, who left Hungary in 1939 to meet Toscanini and thus escaped the fate of his Jewish parents.

Less well-known abroad are the actress Gizi Bajor, Olympic-medal winning boxer László Papp and some infamous figures from the Communist era: Hungary's Stalinist dictator **Mátyás Rákosi** (as a precaution against vandalism, only the initials on his grave are visible), his secret police chief Gábor Péter (see box, p.66), and András Hegedüs, the Politburo member who asked the Soviets to crush the Uprising. Also look out for the many wooden grave markers inscribed in the ancient runic Székely alphabet.

However, the real attraction is the amazing **mortuary chapel** by architect Imre Makovecz – one of his finest designs, and dating from 1975 – whose wood-ribbed vault resembles the inside of a human ribcage, with a casket for corpses where the heart would be. Be discreet, as the chapel is in constant use by mourners. Visitors keen to see more of Makovecz's work could pay a visit to Visegrád (p.139), an hour's journey north of the capital.

The city limits

While the centre of Budapest is hardly short of attractions, it would be a shame to overlook some others out towards or just beyond the city limits. In Pest, the **Railway History Park** – where visitors can drive steam trains – is popular with Hungarian tourists, while the **New Public Cemetery** completes the roll-call of illustrious Hungarian dead begun at Kerepesi. In Buda, the **Memento Park**, with its exiled Communist memorials, is the prime destination for foreigners, and children will also enjoy the **Tropicarium**, with its rainforest creatures and sharks – leaving the **Nagytétényi Castle Museum** to devotees of stately homes. You can reach any of these places from the city centre within an hour; for locations, see the colour maps "Budapest" and "Budapest and around" at the back of this book

Railway History Park

The engagingly hands-on **Hungarian Railway History Park**, or Hungarian Railway Museum (Magyar Vasúttörténeti Park; Tues–Sun: April–Oct 10am–6pm; late March & Nov to mid-Dec 10am–3pm; 950Ft, child 300Ft, family 1900Ft; Ⓦwww.mavnosztalgia.hu), lurks in the freight yards of the XIV district. Its roundhouse and sidings house over seventy locomotives and carriages from 1870 onwards, including the Árpád railcar that set the 1934 speed record from Budapest to Vienna in just under three hours, and a 1912 teak dining carriage from the Orient Express. Many of the museum's staff are ex-employees of MÁV (Hungarian State Railways), proud of a tradition inherited from the Royal Hungarian Railways. Between April and October (10am–4pm), you can **drive** a steam train (1000Ft), luggage cart (300Ft) or engine simulator (500Ft), ride a horse-drawn tram (100Ft) or a turntable used for turning locomotives around (200Ft), and operate a model-railway (200Ft) – wear old clothes. **Children's Day** (May 25) and **Transport Day** (June 7–8) see all kinds of events, with free admission for under-18s.

From April to October, the ticket price includes travel to the museum by vintage train (*különvonat*) from Nyugati Station (9.40am, 10.40am, 1.40pm & 3.40pm), for enthusiasts who don't mind being choked by diesel fumes for half an hour. Tickets are available from the MÁV Nosztalgia office next to platform 10 in the station. Otherwise, the park gates at Tatai út 95 are a short walk from the Rokolya utca stop, which is a longish ride by bus #30 from Keleti Station or Hősök tere.

New Public Cemetery

The **New Public Cemetery** (Új köztemető; daily 8am–dusk; free) is located in the X district of Pest beyond the breweries of Kőbánya, near the end of one of the longest tram rides in town (#28 or #37 from Népszínház utca, near Blaha Lujza tér). Budapest's largest cemetery – reflecting the city's growth in the latter half of the nineteenth century – its significance lies in the fact that it was here that **Imre Nagy** and 260 others, executed for their part in the Uprising, were secretly buried in unmarked graves in 1958. Any flowers left at **Plot 301** were removed by the police until 1989, when the deceased received a state funeral on Hősök tere. The plot is 2km from the main gates on Kozma utca; minibuses shuttle back and forth every twenty minutes. Near the graves, an ornate wooden gateway and headposts mark a mass grave now designated as a **National Pantheon** – as opposed to the Communist pantheon in Kerepesi (see p.85).

The adjacent **Jewish cemetery** (Mon–Fri & Sun 8am–2pm; free) is the burial place of Ernő Szép (author of *The Smell of Humans*, a searing Holocaust memoir), as well as many rabbis and industrialists. Beside the wall on Kozma utca stand the grand crypts of the Goldberger and Kornfeld manufacturing dynasties, and the dazzling blue-and-gold tiled Art Nouveau tomb of shopkeeper **Sándor Schmidl**, designed by Ödön Lechner and Béla Lajta (who later became supervisor of Budapest's Jewish cemeteries). The gates to the Jewish cemetery are 700m up the road from the New Public Cemetery; tram #37 runs past.

Memento Park (Statue Park)

Easily the most popular site on the outskirts, the **Memento Park** or Statue Park (Szoborpark; daily 10am–dusk; 1500Ft; Ⓦwww.mementopark.hu) brings together 42 of the monuments that glorified Communism in Budapest, to celebrate its demise. The park is way out beside Balatoni út in the XXII District, 15km southwest of the city centre; getting there involves taking bus #49-49v from Deák tér to Etele tér, and then a Volán bus from stand 7 or 8 towards Diósd-Érd, which takes ten minutes to reach the park. More expensive but simpler is the Memento Park bus that leaves from in front of *Le Meridien* hotel by Deák tér at 11am daily throughout the year, with an additional service at 3pm in July and August (3950Ft including entry to the park – tickets from the Volánbusz office across the road from the *Meridien*).

Built in stages (1994–2004) as an "unfinished project" by architect Ákos Eleőd, the complex is an anti-temple to a bankrupt ideology. Visitors are greeted by a replica of the **Stalin grandstand**, from which Party leaders reviewed parades; the giant boots recall the 8m-high Stalin statue toppled in 1956. Beyond lies Witness Square, representing all those squares in Eastern Europe where people defied Communism; it's flanked by buildings with Socialist Realist facades. Of these, the **Barrack Hall** is used to screen *Life of an Agent*, a montage of ÁVO training films on how to bug or search premises and recruit informers. Across the way, the **Red Star Store** sells Lenin and Stalin candles, model Trabant cars and selections of revolutionary songs, which can be heard playing from a 1950s' radio set.

The park proper lies behind a bogus Classical facade framing giant statues of **Lenin**, **Marx** and **Engels**. Lenin's once stood beside the Városliget, while Marx's and Engels' are carved from granite quarried at Mauthausen, a Nazi concentration

camp in Austria, later used by the Soviets. Inside the grounds, you'll encounter the **Red Army soldier** that guarded the foot of the Liberation Monument on Gellért-hegy, and dozens of other statues and memorials, large and small. Here are prewar Hungarian Communists like Béla Kun (secretly shot in Moscow on Stalin's orders) and Jenő Landler (afforded a place in the Kremlin Wall); Dimitrov, hero of the Comintern; and the Lenin statue from outside the Csepel ironworks. Artistically, the best works are the **Republic of Councils Monument** – a giant charging sailor based on a 1919 revolutionary poster – and Imre Varga's **Béla Kun Memorial**, with Kun on a tribune surrounded by a surging crowd of workers and soldiers (plus a bystander with an umbrella).

Budapestis fondly remember the statue of **Captain Ostapenko**, which once stood on the highway to Lake Balaton, where hitchhikers would arrange to meet their friends (a locality still known as "Ostapenko"), while the decision to move to the park the monument commemorating the Hungarian contingent of the International Brigade in the Spanish Civil War (three robotic figures with fists clenched to their heads) provoked a heartfelt debate that few of the others engendered.

Tropicarium

A must-see for kids, Budapest's **Tropicarium** (daily 10am–8pm; 1900Ft, children 1200Ft; Ⓦwww.tropicarium.hu) is the largest aquarium-terrarium in Central Europe, covering three thousand square metres. Its saltwater section has an eleven-metre-long glass tunnel for intimate views of sand, tiger and brown **sharks**, clownfish, triggerfish and wrasses; you can even feed stingrays. The freshwater part has piranhas, mouth-breeding cichlids from Africa's Great Lakes, and an outdoor pool to show fish lying dormant when it freezes over. Even better is the mini-**rainforest**, complete with macaws, marmoset monkeys, iguanas and alligators, kept steamy by a downpour with thunder and lightning effects every fifteen minutes. The Tropicarium is in the Campona Shopping Centre, Nagytétényi út 37–43, in Buda's XXII district; take bus #3 from Móricz Zsigmond körtér, or #14 or #144 from Kosztolányi Desző tér. The mall is named after a Roman fort that guarded the riverside, where excavations yielded a cult-statue of Mithras, now in the Aquincum Museum (see p.117).

Nagytétényi Castle Museum

Further out in the XXII district, the **Nagytétényi Castle Museum** (Nagytétényi Kastélymúzeum; Tues–Sun 10am–6pm; 600Ft, 800Ft for temporary exhibitions; Ⓦwww.nagytetenyi.hu) is strictly for lovers of antique furniture. Though rendered as "castle" in English, "*kastély*" generally signifies a manor house or chateau without fortifications, which Hungarian nobles began building after the Turks had been expelled – in this case by converting an older, ruined castle into a Baroque residence. Nowadays, its 28 rooms display furniture from the Gothic to the Biedermeier epochs, owned by the Applied Arts Museum; the most outstanding exhibit is a walnut-veneered refectory from Trencsen Monastery. In July and August, **historical dances** and **concerts**

▲ The Tropicarium

are held in the grounds (☎1/207-0005 for details). To get there, take bus #3 from Móricz Zsigmond körtér (30–45min) or the Tropicarium (15min) to the Petőfi utca stop; cross the road and follow Hugonnay utca down past the children's playground to the *kastély*.

11

Excursions from Budapest

The attractions in this chapter are all within an hour or so of the city, and appear on the "Budapest and around" map at the end of this book. Foremost are three sites on the picturesque **Danube Bend** to the north of Budapest. **Szentendre** is a historic Serbian settlement and artists' colony with a superb open-air ethnographic museum. Further to the north, **Visegrád** boasts medieval ruins, splendid scenery, "organic" buildings, and a treetop zip-slide in the hills, while across the Danube from Slovakia, the cathedral town of **Esztergom** is steeped in history. While each site merits a full day (though don't go on a Monday, when most attractions are closed), you could cram seeing two into one long day. For a short afternoon trip, there's the former Habsburg palace at **Gödöllő**, east of Budapest, where classical concerts are held over summer. Other **festivals** include the International Palace Games at Visegrád, the Fesztergom pop festival at Esztergom, and a plethora of folk events at Szentendre – any of which will add to your enjoyment of a visit.

Szentendre and Gödöllő are easily accessible by **HÉV** train from (respectively) Batthyány tér and Örs Vezér tere metro stations. BKV tickets are valid as far as the city limits; punch extra tickets to cover the remaining cost, or show a BKV pass when buying a ticket at the station. While Volán **buses** from the Árpád híd terminal (Árpád híd metro) are the fastest way to reach Visegrád or Esztergom, you can also make the leisurely journey via excursion **boats** (April–Oct) or speedier **hydrofoils** (June–Sept) from the Vigadó tér dock, operated in the summer by Mahart Passnave (Ⓦwww.mahartpassnave.hu). See the accounts of each town for more detailed transport information.

Szentendre

Szentendre (St Andrew), 20km north of Budapest, is both the most popular tourist destination in the vicinity of the capital and the easiest to reach. Despite a rash of souvenir shops, the centre remains a delightful maze of houses in autumnal colours, with secretive gardens and lanes winding up to hilltop churches, and plenty of museums and craft stalls; you should also allow at least a couple of hours for the open-air village museum outside town (see p.133).

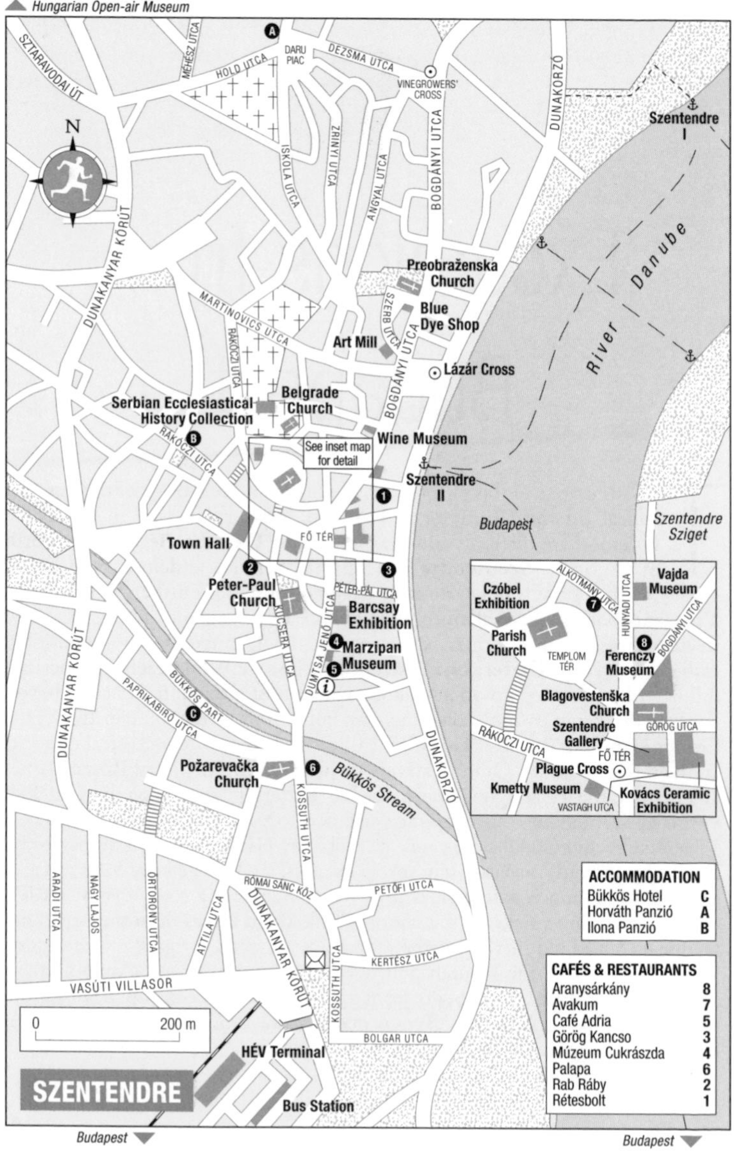

Szentendre's location on the lower slopes of the Pilis Hills is not only beautiful, but ensures that it is one of the sunniest places in Hungary, making it a perfect spot for an artists' colony – though most of the artists there today seem to be turning out tourist tat.

Before artists moved in during the first decades of the twentieth century, Szentendre's character had been forged by waves of refugees from Serbia. The first followed the catastrophic Serb defeat at Kosovo in 1389; the second, the Turkish recapture of Belgrade in 1690, causing 30,000 Serbs and Bosnians to flee. Six thousand settled in Szentendre, which became the seat of the Serbian Church in exile. Prospering through trade, they replaced their wooden churches with stone ones and built handsome town houses, but as Habsburg toleration waned and phylloxera (vine-blight) and floods ruined the local economy they trickled back to Serbia, so that by 1890 less than a quarter of the population was Serb. About seventy families of Serbian descent remain today.

Arrival and orientation

HÉV trains from Budapest (every 20min 6.30am–10pm; 40min) terminate near the **bus station**, ten-minutes' walk south of the town centre: cross Dunakanyar körút by subway and continue along Kossuth utca. Excursion **boats** (1hr 30min; 1490Ft) sailing from Vigadó tér at 9am (April Sat & Sun; May–Aug daily; Sept Fri; Oct Fri–Sun) and 10.30am (May–Sept daily; April & Oct Sat & Sun) dock at the Szentendre II landing near the heart of town, and at Szentendre I, near the crossing for the local ferry to Szentendrei-sziget (hourly; 250Ft).

Walking into the centre from the HÉV station, you can drop into **Tourinform** at Dumsta Jenő utca 22 (June–Aug Mon–Fri 9.30am–7pm, Sat & Sun 9am–4pm; Sept–May Mon–Sat 9.30am–4.30pm, Sun 10am–2pm; ⓣ26/317-965, ⓦwww.szentendre.hu) to obtain a map of town and information on concerts and festivals. ATMs and currency exchanges cluster around Fő tér. If you want to **stay** the night, there are lots of rooms for rent (look for "Zimmer frei" signs), plus numerous hotels and pensions.

Accommodation

Bükkös Hotel **Bükkös part 16 ⓣ26/312-021, ⓔgyorfbukkos.@freemail.hu.** Comfy rooms with TV, phone and minibar, in an idyllic location by a stream lined with weeping willows. Double rooms from 14,000Ft.

Horváth Panzió **Daru piac 2 ⓣ&ⓕ26/313-950.** Small pension in the quieter, northern part of the old town, with a bar, satellite TV and en-suite double rooms furnished with traditional folk crafts, from 4700Ft.

Ilona Panzió **Rákóczi utca 11 ⓣ&ⓕ26/313-599.** Ideally located pension, tucked away a couple of minutes' walk from the centre of town, with a breakfast terrace. Rooms – on the small side – start at 7700Ft.

The Town

Heading up Kossuth utca, you'll encounter the first evidence of a Serbian presence just before the Bükkos Stream in the form of an Orthodox church. Like many others in Szentendre, the slender **Požarevačka Church** (Sat & Sun 11am–5pm; 200Ft) was built from stone in the late eighteenth century to replace an older wooden structure in a grove of trees. Beyond the stream, Dumtsa Jenő utca heralds the onset of the tourist-zone with the chintzy *Múzeum Cukrászda* (see p.135) and a **Marzipan Museum** (daily 9am–7pm; 400Ft) showcasing confections by the family firm Szabo, including portraits of Princess Diana, busts of Emperor Franz Josef and Sissi, and a model of the Hungarian Parliament. Just uphill, the **Barcsay Exhibition** (Barcsay Kiállítás; Wed–Sun 10am–6pm; 400Ft) strikes a sterner note, with dark Cézanne-ish canvases and Quattrocentro anatomical studies by Jenő Barcsay (1900–88), a longstanding resident and teacher at Szentendre's artists' colony. A bit further on, the road is crossed by Péter-Pál utca, where a left turn brings you to the **Peter-Paul Church**, a yellow and white Baroque edifice built in 1708, whose original furnishings were taken back to Serbia after

World War I. Since then, it has served as a Catholic church, noted for its organ recitals (ask Tourinform for details).

Around Fő tér

Beyond the church, Triangular **Fő tér** swarms with horse-drawn carriages and sightseers milling around an ornate **Plague Cross**, erected by the merchants' guild after Szentendre escaped infection in 1763. The square and streets running off it have more galleries and museums than anyone could visit; the Pest County Museum Agency's website (Ⓦwww.pmmi.hu) gives a glimpse of each artist's work and lists current exhibitions, events and opening hours (though in Hungarian only). The **Szentendre Gallery** (Szentendrei Keptár; Wed–Sun 2–6pm; 400Ft), Fő tér 2–5, is the main commercial outlet for contemporary work; its ticket office (10am–5pm) sells admission tickets for other museums in the vicinity , which can only be bought there.

While some of the artists associated with Szentendre have their finest works hanging in the Hungarian National Museum in Budapest, others are better represented here – for instance János Kmetty (1889–1975) of the avant-garde movement centred around the journal *MA* (Today), whose hyperactive pen-and-ink or charcoal drawings fusing Cubism with the style of El Greco and Leonardo fill the **Kmetty Museum** (Kmetty Múzeum; Wed–Sun 2–6pm; 400Ft), across the square at no. 21. Tickets (sold at the gallery) are also valid for the Ferenczy Museum (see below).

Unjustly overlooked in the National Museum, the sculptor and ceramicist Margit Kovács (1902–1977) left a legacy that's by far the most popular of Szentendre's art collections. The **Kovács Ceramic Exhibition** (Kovács Margit Kerámia Kiállitás; daily 10am–6pm; 700Ft) never fails to delight, the themes of legends, dreams, religion, love and motherhood giving her graceful sculptures and reliefs universal appeal. The exhibition is tucked away down Vastagh György utca, off the square beside the Blagovestenska Church. You need to buy a ticket from the Szentendre Gallery beforehand, as they're not available on site.

Framing the north side of Fő tér, the **Blagovestenska Church** (Tues–Sun 10am–5pm; 250Ft), or Church of the Annunciation, is the most accessible of the town's Orthodox churches. Painted by Mihailo Zivkovia of Buda in the early eighteenth century, its icons evoke all the richness and tragedy of Serbian history. Look out for the tomb of a Greek merchant of Macedonian origin to the left of the entrance, and the Rococo windows and gate facing Görög utca (Greek Street), en route to the Kovács exhibition.

Next door to the church, a portal carved with emblems of science and learning provides the entrance to a former Serbian school, now the **Ferenczy Museum** (Ferenczy Múzeum; Wed–Sun 10am–6pm; 400Ft; ticket also valid for the Kmetty Museum). While the National Museum owns the pick of works by Impressionist Károly Ferenczy (1862–1917), this is the place to see art by his eldest son Valér and younger twins Nóemi and Béni, who branched out into Expressionism, textiles and bronzeware.

Templom tér and beyond

Just off Fő tér, an alley of steps ascends from Rákóczi utca to **Templom tér**, a walled hilltop with a great view of Szentendre's rooftops and gardens; **craft fairs** are regularly held here outside the Catholic **Parish Church** (Tues–Sun 10am–6pm; 200Ft). Of medieval origin with Romanesque and Gothic features, it was rebuilt in the Baroque style after falling derelict in Turkish times. The frescoes in its sanctuary were collectively painted by members of the town's artists' colony – among them Béla Czóbel (1883–1976), whose Bonnard-like portraits hang in the **Czóbel Exhibition** (Czóbel Béla Kiállitás; Wed–Sun 2–6pm; 400Ft) at no. 12, behind the church.

North of Templom tér, the rust-red spire of the Orthodox cathedral or **Belgrade Church** (April–Oct Tues–Sun 10am–6pm; 500Ft) rises above a walled garden on Alkotmány utca. Built during the late eighteenth century, it has a lavishly ornamented interior with icons depicting scenes from the New Testament and saints of the Orthodox Church. The old tombstones with Cyrillic inscriptions in the churchyard bear witness to a tale of demographic decline, echoed by the **Serbian Ecclesiastical History Collection** (mid-March to Oct Wed–Sun 10am–4pm; Nov to mid-March Fri–Sun 10am–4pm; 500Ft) in the Episcopal palace, whose hoard of icons, vestments and crosses comes from churches in Hungary that fell empty after the Serbs returned to the Balkans and the last remaining parishioners died out. From the Belgrade Church you can follow Alkotmány utca back down towards Fő tér, passing another artist's legacy on Hunyadi utca. The **Vajda Museum** (Wed–Sun 10am–2pm; 400Ft) pays homage to Lajos Vajda (1908–41), whose playful fusion of Serbian, Jewish and Swabian traditions with Cubism and Surrealism gave way to anguished charcoal drawings in the years before his death in a Nazi labour camp.

Sloping gently downhill from Fő tér inland of the river, **Bogdányi utca** is packed with craft stalls and folk-costumed vendors – souvenir heaven, or enough to drive you into the **Wine Museum** (Bor Múzeum; daily 10am–10pm; 100Ft) at no. 10. Housed in the cool cellars of the *Labirintus* restaurant, it does a fair job of describing Hungary's wine-making regions via maps, wine-bottle labels and other artefacts, with an English-speaking sommelier on hand for **wine-tasting** (1500Ft for five different types). Further on, the street opens onto a square where the small iron **Lázár Cross** – easy to miss behind parked cars – honours the Serb king Lázár, whom the Turks beheaded after the battle of Kosovo to avenge the death of Sultan Murad. Lázár's body was brought here by the Serbs and buried in a now long-gone wooden church, before being taken back to Serbia in 1774. Between March and October, horse-drawn carriages can be rented on the square for rides round town (from 1000Ft per person for 30min) ; bargain hard.

Continuing along Bogdányi utca, you can detour off to see what's on at the **ArtMill** (Művészeti-Malom; Tues–Sun 10am–6pm; 400Ft), a converted watermill hosting installations and performance art events, or admire the deep blue hues of clothes, tablecloths and bedspreads at the Kovács **Blue Dye Shop** (no. 36), showcasing a traditional style of folk dyeing once popular with ethnic Germans, and now with Hungarians. The **Preobraženska Church**, a bit further along, was erected by the tanners' guild in 1741–76, and its stoutness enhanced by a Louis XVI gate the following century. During the Serbian festival on August 19 it hosts the Blessing of the Grapes ceremony, recalling Szentendre's past as a wine-producing centre, as does the **Vinegrowers' Cross** at the end of Bogdányi utca.

The Hungarian Open-Air Museum

Set in rolling countryside 4km north of town, the amazing **Hungarian Open-Air Museum** (Szabadtéri Néprajzi Múzeum; late March–Oct Tues–Sun 9am–5pm; Nov to mid-Dec Sat & Sun 10am–3pm; 1000Ft, child 500Ft, family 2500Ft, or 1400Ft/700Ft/3500Ft respectively for festivals; ⓦ www.skanzen.hu) should not be missed. Hungary's largest outdoor museum of peasant architecture (termed a *skanzen*, after the first such museum, founded in a Stockholm suburb in 1891) can be reached by buses from stand 7 at the Szentendre bus station, leaving at ten minutes past the hour on weekdays and forty minutes past the hour at weekends (note that there's no service between 10am and 1pm). On festival days, special buses run all the way there from the Árpád híd bus station in Budapest.

It takes at least two hours to tour the naturalistic village ensembles transported here from six ethnographic regions of Hungary, representing rural life from the nineteenth century up until the 1920s and complete with dwellings, demonstrations of cottage industries and traditional breeds of livestock in barns. Each building has a custodian who can explain everything in detail, though usually only in Hungarian.

Downhill to the right from the entrance, a village from the isolated **Upper Tisza** region reveals that the homes of the poorest squires were barely superior to those of their tenants, yet rural carpenters produced highly skilled work, such as the circular "dry mill", the wooden bell tower, and the Greek Catholic church (on a hilltop beyond). Walking up past the Calvinist graveyard with its boat-shaped grave-markers, signs point you to the scant remains of a Roman village and on to **Western Transdanubia**, a poor region of clay soil and heavy rainfall, where houses were linked by covered verandas. Here, a schoolroom is equipped with benches, slates for writing on, a towel and basin for washing, and home-spun schoolbags. The section representing the ethnic German communities of the **Small Plain** seems far more regimented: neatly aligned whitewashed houses filled with knick-knacks and embroidered samplers bearing homilies like "When the Hausfrau is capable, the clocks keep good time".

Large adobe dwellings were also typical of villages in **Southern Transdanubia**, inhabited by Germans, Hungarians and Székely – their carved gateways big enough for haywains – and market towns on the **Great Plain**. A Baroque cottage from Sükösd has its visitors' room or "clean room" laid out for Christmas celebrations with a nativity crib and a church-shaped box. Beyond the houses are stables and pastures for long-horned cattle and Rácka sheep, and a windmill built in 1888, its sails still operating. A water-powered mill and grape-press, a washhouse and a fire station comprise the "centre" of a village from the **Bakony and Balaton Uplands**, where stone and hornbeam were used for building.

Demonstrations of **crafts** such as pottery, weaving and boot-making occur in each section at weekends and during **festivals**, when folk music and rituals, grape-pressing, children's games and other activities enliven the museum. Easter, the Pentecostal Games (May 27–28), a culinary Feast of the Soil (Aug 11) and two wine festivals (Sept and Nov) are among the highlights of the events calendar, listed on the museum's website. Additionally, **plays** are staged at the outdoor Amphitheatre during the Theatre Evenings of June and July, as advertised on the spot.

Visitors can sample dishes and wines from the different regions at the huge *Jöszörokszöllös* **restaurant** (daily 10am–10pm), open year-round. Freshly-baked scones, gingerbread and loaves are sold at a **bakery** in the Great Plain section.

Eating and drinking

Restaurants in Szentendre – particularly the ones on Fő tér used by coach parties – are relatively pricey by Hungarian standards. You'll do better in the backstreets or on **Dunakorzó** (though it's no less crowded in summer), or in **cafés** on the periphery of the centre. Look out for traditional local dishes such as Serbian *pljeskavica* and *cevapi* (lamb and beef burgers or meatballs served in thick, soft pittas), Dalmatian *prsut* (wafer-thin wind-cured ham), Greek moussaka and tzatziki, and Croatian fish recipes. For afters or mid-morning refreshment, head for the *Múzeum Cukrászda* (daily 10am–8pm) on Dumsta Jenő utca, where **cakes and ices** have been served in the beautifully tiled salon since 1889.

Restaurants, cafés and bars

Aranysárkány **Alkotmány utca 1a ⓣ26/311-0670, ⓦwww.aranysarkany.hu.** The award-winning "Golden Dragon" serves Hungarian nouvelle cuisine from an open kitchen, and is a/c. Try the goose-liver pâté with rose-petal jam, trout fillet with mashed potatoes and Campari sauce, and an Opium pudding of poppy-seed, cinnamon and vanilla with whipped cream and kiwi sauce. Pricey but worth it; booking advisable. Daily noon–10pm.

Avakum **Alkotmány utca 14.** Just uphill from the Aranysárkány, this cool cellar café is a nice place to refresh yourself with a glass of wine or a herbal tea. Mon–Thurs 11am–10pm, Fri & Sat 11am–11pm.

Café Adria **Kossuth utca 4.** A laid-back spot beside the Bükos Stream to nibble vine-leaves, aivar (paprika puree) and other Balkan snacks. Daily 10am–10pm.

Görög Kancsó **Dunakorzó 9 ⓣ26/303-178.** A lively, affordable taverna with tables outside, serving seafood, pizzas and Greek specialities. Daily noon–midnight.

Palapa **Dumsta Jenő utca 14a, ⓣ26/302-418, ⓦwww.palapa.hu.** A brilliant Mexican bar-restaurant with high-quality food, great service, fine cocktails and regular live music in the yard. Book ahead or arrive early to bag a table. Mon–Fri 5pm–midnight, Sat & Sun noon–midnight.

Rab Ráby **Kucsera utca 1a.** This vintage restaurant, decorated with suits of armour, is more traditionally Hungarian in style than the Aranysárkány and a touch cheaper, with a meat- and fish-heavy menu. Daily noon–11pm.

Rétesbolt **Bercsényi utca.** A takeaway snack-bar selling pizzas, hot dogs and delicious strudels. Daily 9am–6pm.

Visegrád

Approaching **Visegrád** from Szentendre, the hillsides start to plunge and the river twists shortly before you catch first sight of the citadel and ramparts of the ancient fortified site whose Slavic name means "High Castle". The view hasn't changed much since 1488, when János Thuroczy described its "upper walls stretching to the clouds floating in the sky, and the lower bastions reaching down as far as the river". At that time, courtly life in Visegrád was nearing its apogee and the palace of King Mátyás and Queen Beatrice was famed throughout Europe. The papal legate Cardinal Castelli described it as a "paradiso terrestri", seemingly unperturbed by the presence of Vlad the Impaler, who resided here under duress between 1462 and 1475. Today, Visegrád is a mere village, where the ferry docks and a few bars and restaurants round the church are the hub of local life. Tourists tend to focus on the **historic sites** north of the centre: the Royal Palace and Solomon's Tower near the river, and the hilltop citadel. All the river sites are in easy walking distance of each other but you might prefer taking a bus up to the citadel, thus saving your energy for gung-ho **activities** in the **Visegrád Hills**.

Each year (usually on the second weekend in July), Visegrád hosts the **International Palace Games**, an orgy of medieval pageantry, jousting and archery tournaments, craft workshops and plenty of eating and drinking, held in the grounds of the Royal Palace, Solomon's Tower and the Citadel; the Royal Palace website (see p.137) or Tourinform in Szentendre (see p.131) have more

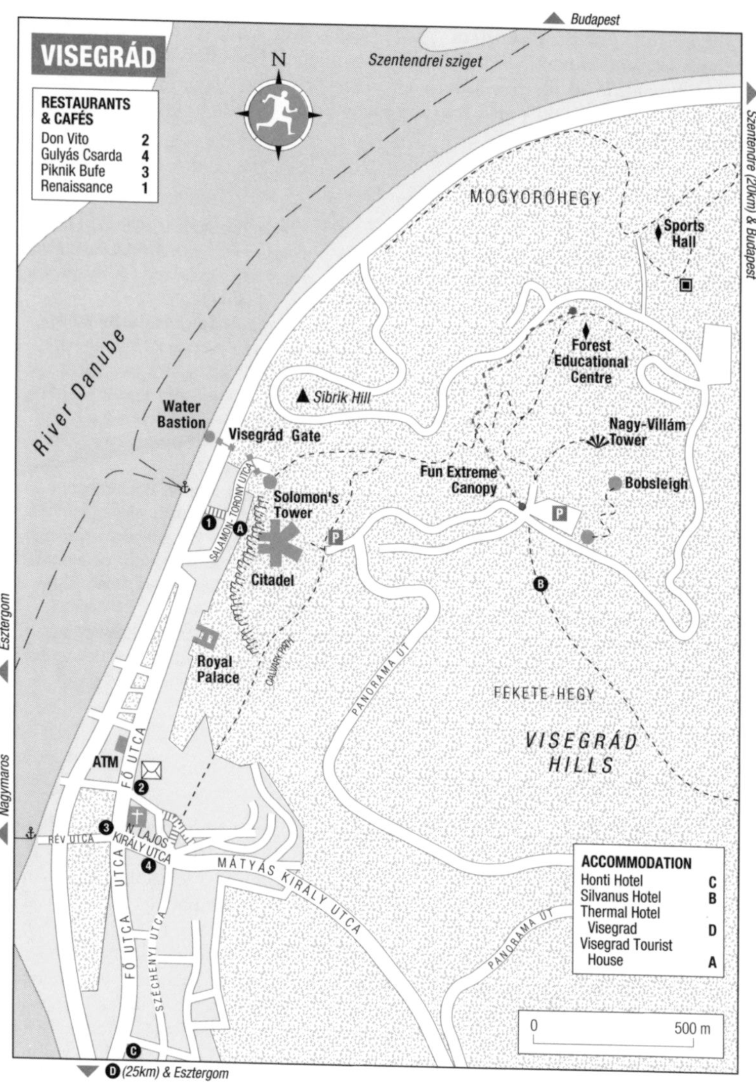

information. During the second half of June, the **Danube Bend Summer Games** see sports, musical and cultural events in all the villages between Szentendre and Visegrád; for details, visit Ⓦ www.dunakanyar.org.

Arrival and information

Given the majestic scenery of the Danube Bend, the best way to get to Visegrád is by river. **Boats** leave Budapest's Vigadó tér at 8am (May Fri–Sun; June–Aug daily; Sept Sat & Sun) and 9am (April Sat & Sun; May–Aug daily; Sept Fri; Oct Fri–Sun) take three and a half hours to make the journey upriver (1hr less back to Budapest); a one-way trip costs 2385Ft, or 1485Ft from Szentendre (2hr). **Hydrofoils** at 9.30am (June–Aug daily; May & Sept Sat & Sun) and 11.30am (July–Aug Sat & Sun) cost 3990Ft and take only an hour from Budapest. The landing stage in Visegrád is by the highway, just below Solomon's Tower. Alternatively, #800 **buses** leaving from stand 3 at Budapest's Árpád híd terminal (every 40–90min; 1hr 20min) stop at Szentendre's bus station, Visegrád's landing stage and by the local ferry stop before running on to Esztergom.

Visegrád has no tourist office as such, but staff at the Royal Palace, the Fun Extreme Canopy and the *Visegrád Tourist House* are all useful sources of **information**. There's an **ATM** on Fő utca.

Accommodation

Honti Hotel **Fő utca 66 ⓣ20/460-2134, ⓔhonti@mail.ohb.hu.** Set in a large garden at the southern end of town, with eight cosy en-suite doubles with balconies, costing 17,500Ft; breakfast is included.

Silvanus Hotel **Fekete-hegy ⓣ26/398-311.** An ageing three-star, close to the zip-ride and bobsleigh terminals and with splendid views of the Visegrád Hills. En-suite doubles are 21,250Ft.

Thermal Hotel Visegrád **Lepence, 25km south of Visegrád ⓣ26/801-900, ⓦwww.thv.hu.** A swanky four-star spa whose guests have unlimited use of its wellness centre, thermal pools and gym – come for a long weekend. Air-conditioned rooms with balconies from 46,000Ft, breakfast included.

Visegrád Tourist House **Salamon-torony utca 5 ⓣ20/923-8124, ⓦwww.visegradturistahaz.hu.** An Alpine chalet near Solomon's Tower, newly refurbished as an all-year hostel, with six to ten beds per room, clean bathrooms, a kitchen, and English-speaking management. A bed costs 2700Ft.

The Town

The layout of the **ruins** dates back to the thirteenth century, when Béla IV began fortifying the north against a recurrence of the Mongol invasion, while the construction of a royal palace below the hilltop citadel was a sign of greater security during the reign of the Angevins. However, its magnificence was effaced by the Turkish conquest, and later mud washing down from the hillside gradually buried the palace entirely. Subsequent generations doubted its existence until archeologist János Schulek had a lucky break after searching in vain for years. At a New Year's Eve party in 1934, the wine ran out and Schulek was sent to get some more from the neighbours. An old woman told him to go down to the wine cellar, and there he found clues in the stones that convinced him the palace was there, beneath Fő utca 23.

Now excavated and tastefully reconstructed, the **Royal Palace** (Királyi Palota; Tues–Sun 9am–5pm; 1000Ft; ⓦwww.visegradmuzeum.hu) spreads over four terraces. Founded in 1323 by the Angevin king Charles Robert, it was the setting for the Visegrád Congress of 1335, attended by the monarchs of Central Europe and the Grandmaster of the Teutonic Knights. Although nothing remains of this palace, the **Court of Honour** constructed for his successor Louis, which provided the basis for additions by kings Sigismund and Mátyás, is still to be seen on the second terrace. A pilastered **Renaissance loggia** surrounds a replica of the famous **Hercules Fountain**, which cools the tiled, gilded uppermost storey, overlooking the court. On the third terrace, where Mátyás and Beatrice resided, stands a copy of the **Lion Fountain**, bearing his raven crest and standing on leg-rests in the form of sleepy-looking lions and dogs. A bathhouse with underfloor heating, the huge tiled stoves in the dining rooms and a reconstruction of the palace herb gardens all contribute to the impression of courtly life.

Leaving the palace, turn right along Fő utca and then follow Salamon-torony utca up through a fortified gate to reach **Solomon's Tower** (Salamon-torony; May–Sept daily 9am–5pm; 600Ft). Named after an eleventh-century Hungarian king once thought to have been imprisoned there after being deposed, this mighty hexagonal keep is buttressed on two sides by unsightly concrete slabs. Its **Mátyás Museum** exhibits finds from the palace, including a copy of the white Anjou Fountain of the Angevins and the red marble *Visegrád Madonna*, a Renaissance masterpiece that shows many similarities to the works of Tomaso Fiamberti, an Italian employed by Beatrice to carve other statues at Visegrád, fragments of which are also displayed here. From the top of the tower you can see ramparts plunging down from the Citadel to the riverside **Water Bastion**, a squat, long-derelict structure with a fortified arch spanning the highway.

The Citadel

Visegrád's hilltop **Citadel** (Fellegvár; mid-March to mid-Nov daily 9.30am–6pm; rest of the year Sat & Sun 10am–3pm; closed when it snows; 1400Ft) is only partly restored but mightily impressive nonetheless, commanding a superb

▲ Visegrád's Citadel

view of the Börzsöny Mountains across the Danube. Besides two **museums** devoted to medieval hunting, fishing, punishment and torture, there are outdoor displays of **archery** and **falconry** in the summer. You can get there by a steep path through the woods from the rear gate of Solomon's Tower (40min), or an easier climb (20min) via the Calvary **footpath** behind Visegrád's church, which gets its name from bas-reliefs of the Stations of the Cross en route. There are also three **buses** a day (April–Sept 9.30am, 12.30pm & 3.30pm), which stop at both the boat and ferry stations and follow the scenic Panorama út up to a car park near the Citadel.

The Visegrád Hills

A popular rambling spot with fantastic views, the densely wooded **Visegrád Hills** offer thrill-seekers the chance to zip through the treetops or enjoy bobsleighing at Nagy-Villám, 400m up the road from the Citadel car park, from where paths radiate from another car park. One leads up to the **Nagy-Villám lookout tower** (kiáltó; 10am–5pm: April–Oct daily; Nov–March Sat & Sun; 100Ft), at the highest point on the Danube Bend (377m), with wonderful views as far as Slovakia. Just downhill from the car park is a **bobsleigh run** (Bobpálya; March Mon–Fri 11am–4pm, Sat & Sun 10am–5pm; April–Aug Mon–Fri 9am–6pm, Sat & Sun 9am–7pm; Sept–Oct Mon–Fri 10am–5pm, Sat & Sun 10am–6pm; Nov–Feb daily 11am–4pm; 350Ft, child 280Ft; Ⓦwww.bobozas.hu), where kids of all ages (and adults) can whiz down a one-kilometre-long track and chute; note that it's closed on rainy days, when the sleds' brakes are ineffective – call Ⓣ26/397-397 to check.

More thrilling is the **Fun Extreme Canopy** (Canopy pálya; mid-March to late Oct or mid-Nov Tues–Sun 10am–5pm; 3800F; Ⓣ30/246-3381, Ⓦwww.canopy.hu), inspired by the treetop walkways in Costa Rica's Monteverde Cloud Forest National Park. Eleven platforms, 14m high, are linked by wires to form an amazing zip-ride through the forest, which takes about 50 minutes to complete, sliding at speeds of up to 50km an hour. Guides, safety harnesses and helmets are provided; nerve rather than strength is needed. Trips require a minimum of four people and groups can't exceed twenty; individuals who turn up at weekends can be put with a group, but it's wiser to book ahead. Under-14s are excluded. The zip-wire's upper terminus is by the *Hunter's Inn*, on the far side of the car park from the bobsleigh run. Riders end up on a lower hill, Mogyoróhegy, from which they can return by minibus or walk up through the woods to Nagy-Villám. However, you may wish to linger a while and take a look at a trio of wooden buildings, just 200m from the lower terminus, by **Imre Makovecz**, the Hungarian guru of "organic architecture". After creating the breathtaking crypt at Farkasréti Cemetery (p.124), he was branded a troublemaker for his outspoken nationalism and "exiled" to Visegrád's forestry department, where he acquired a following by teaching summer schools on how to construct buildings using low-tech methods and materials such as branches and twigs. In the 1980s he built here a campsite **restaurant** with a roof like a nun's wimple, the yurt-like, turf-roofed **Forest Education Centre**, and a **Sports Hall** resembling a Viking church, before being allowed to work elsewhere and given the honour of designing the Hungarian Pavilion at the 1992 Seville Expo. Though Makovecz's work is now widely acclaimed, his lavish use of wood vexes some environmentalists, and his dabbling in right-wing politics makes his call for a return to a "real" Hungarian style of building somewhat suspect.

Eating and drinking

Don Vito **Fő utca 83 ☎26/397-230.** An enjoyable, inexpensive pizzeria themed on The Godfather; Luca Brasi or Don Corleone would approve of the dishes cooked in their name, in a wood-fired oven. Daily noon–midnight.

Gulyás Csárda **Nagy Lajos király utca 4.** This 1980s'-style inn does hearty, affordable Hungarian and German dishes, and has a beer garden. Daily noon–11pm.

Piknik Bufe **Rév utca.** A self-service snack bar with tables outside, where locals hang out drinking beer. Daily 10am–10pm.

Renaissance **Fő utca 9 ☎26/398-081.** A medieval-themed restaurant mainly frequented by coach parties, where diners can feast on suckling pig, while wearing a cardboard crown and being serenaded by a lute-player. Daily noon–10pm.

Esztergom

Beautifully situated in a crook of the Danube facing Slovakia, **Esztergom** is dominated by its basilica, whose dome is visible for miles around – a richly symbolic sight, as it was here that Prince Géza and his son Vajk (the future king and saint Stephen) brought Hungary into the fold of Christendom. Even after the court moved to Buda following the Mongol invasion, Esztergom remained the centre of Catholicism until the Turkish conquest, and resumed this role in the 1820s – as the poet Mihály Babits (who lived there) remarked, "this is the Hungarian Rome". Persecuted in the Rákóczi era but increasingly tolerated by the regime from the 1960s onwards, the Church regained much of its former property and influence under Christian governments in the post-Communist era, making Esztergom an obligatory stop for politicians in election year. For tourists, Esztergom makes an ideal day-trip, combining historic monuments and small-town charm in just the right doses, with the bonus of being within strolling distance of the Slovak town of Štúrovo.

Esztergom is big on summer **festivals**. Fesztergom (Ⓦwww.fesztergom.hu) is a three-day rock festival held in the Sports Centre on Prímás-sziget towards the end of June, while August kicks off with a folk and children's festival, followed by a two-day wine festival, outdoor art exhibitions and jazz concerts – dates are posted (in Hungarian) on Ⓦwww.esztergomprogram.hu.

Arrival and information

Unless you can afford to travel by hydrofoil, Esztergom is best reached by road. **Buses** from Budapest's Árpád híd terminal (every 40–90min) run via Visegrád (#880 from stand 3; 2hr) or Dörög, west of the Pilis Hills (#800 from stand 6; 1hr 20min), a less scenic but faster route. Arriving from Visegrád, get off near Basilica Hill rather than riding on to the bus station in the south of town. The train station, 1km further south, is linked to the centre by bus #1 and #5. The 8am **ferry** (May Fri–Sun; June–Aug daily; Sept Sat & Sun; 1900Ft; 5hr 30min; 4hr back) and 11.30am **hydrofoil** (June–Aug Fri–Sun; May & Sept Sat & Sun; 3290ft; 1hr 30min either way) from Budapest tie up at Prímás-sziget, fifteen-minutes' walk from the centre.

For **information**, head for Gran Tours, on the corner of Rákóczi tér (June–Aug Mon–Fri 8am–5pm, Sat 9am–noon; Sept–May Mon–Fri 8am–4pm; ☎33/502-001). They also change money (till 3.30pm), as does the K&H bank across the square, and sell tickets for local festivals.

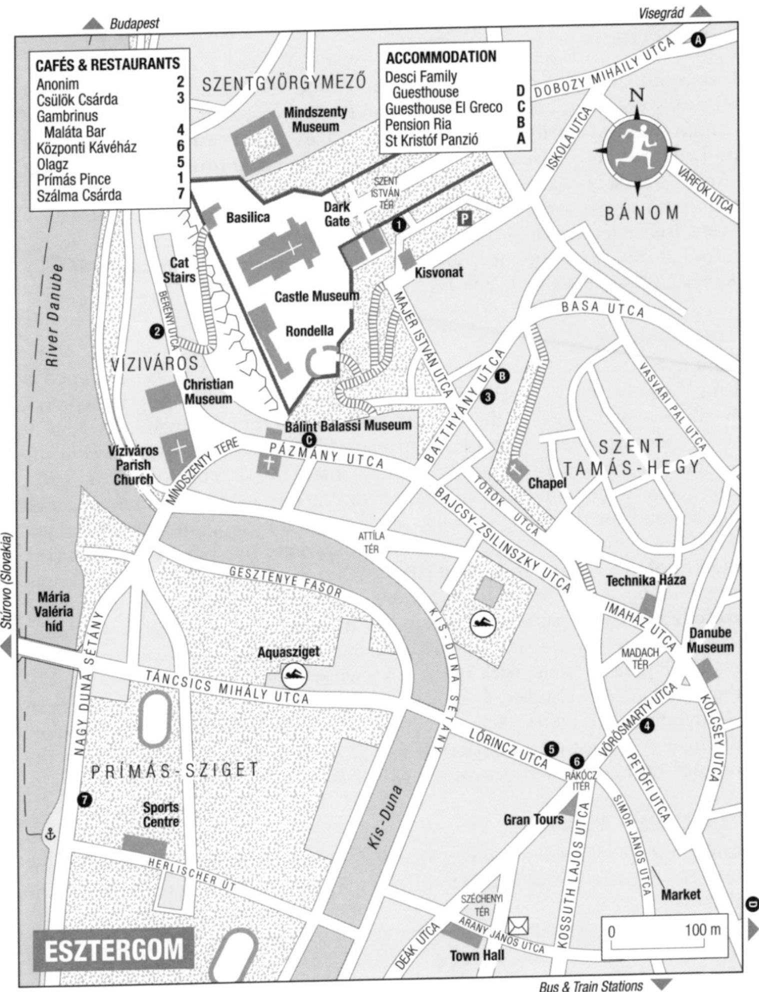

Accommodation

Decsi Family Guesthouse **Babits Mihály utca 8** **T 30/500-3350, E info@cometohungary.com.** 10min walk from the centre of the lower town, this friendly B&B has en-suite doubles for 10,000Ft.

Guesthouse El Greco **Pázmány Péter utca 15** **T 33/311-525, E info@elgrecocafe.hu.** A delightful B&B in the heart of the Víziváros, offering en-suite doubles with fridges and modems for 12,500Ft, and discounted tickets for Aquasziget.

Pension Ria **Batthyány utca 11–13** **T 33/313-115, W www.riapanzio.com.** Within easy walking distance of all the sights, offering rooms with showers from 6500Ft; there's also a sauna, mini-gym, internet, bike rental and a beer garden on site.

St Kristóf Panzió **Dobozy Mihály utca 11** **T 33/414-153, E kristoph@vnet.hu.** 10min walk from the Basilica, this charming pension has a/c rooms and apartments from 13,000Ft, plus a restaurant and a garden.

The Town

Esztergom consists of an upper town beside the Basilica, the waterfront Víziváros below it, and a sprawling lower town separated from the island of Prímás-sziget by a tributary of the Danube. Basic **orientation** is simple, but if pushed for time you might be tempted by a sightseeing **tour** on the **Kisvonat** (April–Oct daily 10am–5pm; 950Ft, child 500Ft; Ⓦwww.kisvonat.com), a road train with open carriages that runs every half hour from the car park below Szent István tér, down to Rákóczi tér, around Prímás-sziget and back to the terminus. Alternatively, you could rent a **bicycle** for the day from the *Pension Ria* (see p.141) for about 2000Ft.

The Basilica

Built upon the site of the first cathedral in Hungary, where Vajk was crowned as King Stephen by a papal envoy on Christmas Day 1000 AD, Esztergom's **Basilica** is the largest in the country, measuring 118m in length and 40m in width, and capped by a dome 100m high. Liszt's *Gran Mass* (Gran being the German name for Esztergom) was composed for its completion in 1869. Admission to the cathedral (daily 7am–6pm; enter by an entrance under the arch on the south side) is free, but tickets are required for the spooky **crypt** (krypta; daily 9am–5pm; 150Ft), where Cardinal Mindszenty (see box below) is buried; the **cupola** (May–Oct daily 9am–5pm; 300Ft), reached by three hundred steps and offering a superb view of Esztergom; and the collection of bejewelled crosiers and kitsch papal souvenirs in the **treasury** (kincstár; March–Oct daily 9am–4.30pm; Nov & Dec Tues–Fri 11am–3.30pm, Sat & Sun 10.30am–3.30pm; 600Ft). The last is at the back of the nave, whose main altarpiece was painted by the Venetian Michelangelo Grigoletti, based on Titian's *Assumption* in the Frari Church in Venice. Don't miss the red and white marble **Bakócz Chapel** (below the relief of Christ on a donkey), whose Florentine altar was salvaged from the original basilica that was destroyed by the Mongols.

The Castle Museum

On higher ground 30m south of the Basilica are the red-roofed, reconstructed remains of the palace founded by Prince Géza, now presented as the

Cardinal Mindszenty

When the much-travelled body of **Cardinal József Mindszenty** was finally laid to rest with state honours in 1991, it was a vindication of his uncompromising heroism – and the Vatican realpolitik that he despised. As a conservative and monarchist, Mindszenty had stubbornly opposed the postwar Communist takeover, warning that "cruel hands are reaching out to seize hold of our children, claws belonging to people who have nothing but evil to teach them". Arrested in 1948, tortured for 39 days and nights, and sentenced to life imprisonment for treason, Mindszenty was freed during the Uprising and took refuge in the US Embassy, where he remained for the next fifteen years – an exile in the heart of Budapest.

When the Vatican struck a deal with the Kádár regime in 1971, Mindszenty had to be pushed into resigning his position and going to Austria, where he died in 1975. Although his will stated that his body should not return home until "the red star of Moscow had fallen from Hungarian skies", his reburial occurred some weeks before the last Soviet soldier left, in preparation for Pope John Paul II's visit. Nowadays the Vatican proclaims his greatness, without any hint of apology for its past actions.

Castle Museum (Vármúzeum; Tues–Sun 10am–6pm; 1500Ft). A royal seat for almost three hundred years, it was here that Béla III entertained Philip of France and Frederick Barbarossa on their way to the Third Crusade, while the Renaissance prelate János Vitéz made it a centre of humanist culture, where Queen Beatrice spent her widowhood. Despite being sacked by the Turks and twice besieged before they were evicted in 1683, enough survived to be excavated in the 1930s.

Though foreigners are expected to join a tour in Hungarian, you can slip away to the rooms displaying visualizations of the palace in various epochs to reach the royal suite ahead of the crowd. Traces of the frescoes that once covered every wall can be seen in the vaulted living hall from Béla III's reign, from which stairs ascend to the study of Archbishop Vitéz – known as the **Hall of Virtues** after its allegorical murals. Beyond lies the **royal chapel**, whose Gothic rose window and Romanesque arches were executed by craftsmen brought over by Béla's French wives, while the rooftop offers a panoramic view of Esztergom and the river.

During June and July, **plays** and **dances** are staged in the **Rondella** bastion on the hillside. From here, steps descend to the Kisvonat terminus, the former primate's wine cellars – now the *Prímás Pince* restaurant (see p.145) – and the monumental **Dark Gate**. This imposing tunnel was built in the 1820s as a short-cut between church buildings on either side of the hill. It emerges opposite a Catholic seminary housing the small **Mindszenty Museum** (Mindszenty Múzeum; Tues–Sun 10am–5pm; free), with photos, personal effects and writings devoted to the Cardinal's memory.

The Víziváros and Prímás-sziget

Cut into the hillside overlooking the Danube, the precipitous **Cat Stairs** (Macskalépcső) offer a dramatic way down from the heights, and provide a splendid view of the river and Štúrovo. At the bottom lies the **Víziváros**, a Baroque enclave of churches and seminaries lining a serpentine street that changes its name as it goes. The old Primate's Palace at Berényi utca 2 houses the **Christian Museum** (Keresztény Múzeum; Tues–Sun 10am–6pm; 250Ft), Hungary's richest hoard of religious art, featuring the largest collection of Italian prints outside Italy; Renaissance paintings and wood carvings by German, Austrian and Hungarian masters; and a wheeled, gilded catafalque once used in Easter Week processions. Next door, the Italianate Baroque **Víziváros Parish Church** stands guard over a wedge-shaped plaza named after Mindszenty; the next stretch of the main street commemorates the sixteenth-century cardinal Péter Pázmány. At no. 13, the **Bálint Balassi Museum** (Balassi Bálint Múzeum; Tues–Sun 9am–5pm; 200Ft) mounts temporary historical exhibitions rather than dwelling on the poet Bálint Balassi (1554–94), who died trying to recapture Esztergom from the Turks: a half-crazed philanderer, he was famous for sexually assaulting women and then dedicating verses to them.

From Mindszenty tere, you can cross a bridge to **Prímás-sziget** (Primate's Island), a popular recreation spot separated from the mainland by the narrow Kis-Duna (Small Danube). Lined with chestnut trees and weeping willows, Gesztenye fasor and Kis-Duna sétány form a lovely shady promenade frequented by lovers and anglers, where outdoor **art exhibitions** are held during the week-long Arts Promenade festival in mid-August. Elsewhere, the main attraction is **Aquasziget** (Mon–Fri 10am–8pm, Sat 9am–8pm, Sun 9am–8pm; 1800Ft, children 1100Ft; Ⓦwww.aquasziget.hu), a superbly equipped water park and wellness centre offering all kinds of treatments from collagen refreshment to honey massages.

Further west along Táncsics Mihály utca, the reconstructed **Mária Valéria híd** links Esztergom with Slovak Štúrovo, five minutes' stroll across the river. Blown up by retreating Germans at the end of World War II, the bridge was left in ruins until an agreement to rebuild it was finally signed in 1999 after years of bilateral negotiations, with the European Union footing the bill. It seems only fair that EU citizens can **walk into Slovakia** with barely a flourish of their passports – other nationalities may need visas. Bring your passport anyway.

The lower town

From Prímás-sziget, it's an easy walk into the lower town, whose civic focus is **Széchenyi tér**, framed by an imposing **Town Hall** with Rococo windows that once belonged to Prince Rákóczi's general, János Bottyán. With its elaborate fountains and flowerbeds, the plaza is the setting for concerts each August, but otherwise it's quieter than nearby Rákóczi tér, the hub of everyday life with its supermarkets, banks and outdoor **market** running off along Simor János utca.

Stop for cake and coffee at the Art Nouveau *Központi Kávéház* (see below) on the corner of Vörösmarty utca before exploring the backstreets beyond. At Kölcsey utca 2, the **Danube Museum** (Duna Múzeum; daily except Tues: May–Oct 10am–6pm; Nov–April 9am–4pm; closed Jan; free; ⓦwww.dunamuzeum.hu) mounts a visitor-friendly exhibition on the history and hydrology of Hungary's great rivers, the Danube and the Tisza. Interactive models, videos and a children's section explain the principles of fluid hydraulics, regulating rivers and disaster relief during floods, the most recent of which occurred in 2002.

To get a final overview of the lower town, walk up Imaház utca past a flamboyant, Moorish-style edifice that was once Esztergom's synagogue and is now a science club, or **Technika Háza**. Shortly afterwards you'll find a flight of steps leading to **Szent Tamás-hegy** (St Thomas's Hill), a rocky outcrop named after the English martyr Thomas à Becket. A **chapel** was built here in his honour by Margaret Capet, whose English father-in-law, Henry II, prompted Thomas's assassination by raging "Who will rid me of this turbulent priest?" Even after her husband died and Margaret married Béla III of Hungary, her conscience would not let her forget the saint. The existing chapel (postdating the Turkish occupation) is fronted by a trio of life-size statues representing Golgotha.

Eating and drinking

Anonim Berényi utca 4 ⓣ33/411-880. Opposite the Cat Stairs in the Víziváros, this romantic restaurant specializes in game dishes. Try the *cserhat* (saddle of lamb braised with saurkraut) or *racponty* (fried carp fillet layered with paprika and sour cream). You can eat well for 4000Ft. Mon–Sat noon–10pm.

Csülök Csárda Batthyány utca 11–13 ⓣ33/412-420. Popular with tourists and locals alike, the "Knuckle Inn" serves hearty Hungarian, Czech and German dishes, including pig's knuckle, at reasonable prices. Daily noon–midnight.

Gambrinus Maláta Bar Vörösmarty utca 3. A late-night hang-out for ageing rockers and smooching teenagers, with dance music on its jukebox and an overhead tangle of varnished branches. Mon–Thurs 1pm–1am, Fri 1pm–3am, Sat 3pm–2am, Sun 3pm–midnight.

Központi Kávéház Vörösmarty utca 2 ⓦwww.kozpontikavehaz.hu. A stylishly revamped Art Nouveau coffee house, with tables outside and jazz piano indoors most evenings. Mon–Fri noon–10pm, Sat & Sun noon–midnight.

Olagz Lőrincz utca 5 ⓣ33/312-952. An inexpensive, no-frills pizzeria located midway between Rákóczi tér and Prímás-sziget. Mon–Fri 11am–10pm, Sat & Sun 11am–midnight.

Prímás Pince **Majer István utca.** Touristy but by no means bad, this restaurant occupies the cavernous former Primate's wine-cellars dug into the side of Basilica Hill, and serves decent Hungarian food at slightly inflated prices. Daily 10am–10pm.

Szálma Csárda **Prímás-sziget.** A rustic-style eatery near the island's hydrofoil dock, serving vast, tasty portions of poultry, fish and game at affordable prices. Daily noon–9pm.

Gödöllő

The small town of **GÖDÖLLŐ** boasts a former Habsburg summer palace and a famous artists' colony, but being 30km northeast of Budapest rather than on the Danube Bend, it gets far fewer tourists than Szentendre, despite a reliable HÉV service from Örs Vezér tere (the terminus of metro line 2) that means you can enjoy an evening concert and return easily to the capital afterwards.

The Royal Palace

The **Royal Palace** (Gödöllői Királyi kastély; Tues–Sun: Feb, March, Nov & Dec 10am–5pm; April–Oct 10am–6pm; 1800Ft; last tickets sold 40min before closing; Ⓦwww.kiralyikastely.hu) was commissioned by a confidante of Empress Maria Theresa's, Count Antal Grassalkovich, and designed by András Mayerhoffer, who introduced the Baroque style of mansion to Hungary in the 1740s. The palace suffered as a result of both world wars, being commandeered as a headquarters first by the Reds and then by the Whites in 1919–20, and pillaged by both the Nazis and the Red Army in 1944. One wing was later turned into an old people's home, while the rest was left to rot until 1985, when the restoration of the palace finally began.

Don't bother paying 3300Ft for a guided tour in English, as the 26 rooms on display are all captioned and described in a guidebook (1500Ft) sold in the palace shop. The formal **state rooms**, reached by a grand staircase, precede the private apartments used by Emperor Franz Josef and his wife Sissi – his decorated in grey and gold, hers draped in her favourite colour, violet. Sissi stayed two thousand nights here, preferring it to Vienna. While her possessions are reverentially displayed – right down to a horseshoe from her stallion – there's no sign to identify the secret staircase that she had installed as a means of getting some privacy in a relentlessly public life. Sissi's later years were blighted by tragedy – the death of her siblings and the suicide of her son Rudolf at Mayerling – before she herself was stabbed to death by an anarchist in 1898. Mourned throughout Hungary, she became the focus of a cult that outlasted all attempts to stifle it under Communism.

The **Baroque Theatre** (Barokk színház) that Count Grassalkovich established in a side-wing – used for only two weeks each year when he was in residence – and the **Royal Hill Pavilion** (Királydombi pavilion) and **Baths** (Fürdő) in the Palace's upper park can only be seen on pre-booked **tours** (3300Ft for all; 900Ft for the theatre alone; minimum 25 people; Ⓣ28/410-124). The baths were last enjoyed by Admiral Horthy, who used Gödöllő as a holiday home from 1920 till 1944, installing a swimming pool and an air-raid shelter (both removed when the park was restored). Musical and cultural programmes are staged within the palace throughout the year, including classical **concerts** in the Ornamental Yard over summer – ask Tourinform (see p.146) for details; tickets cost 1500–3500Ft.

The Town Museum

Leaving the palace, cross the main road and HÉV tracks and follow the signposts to Szabadság tér, where the delightful **Town Museum of Gödöllő** (Gödöllői Városi Múzeum; Tues–Sun 10am–6pm; 600Ft) focuses on the **Gödöllő Artists' Colony**. Founded in 1901, the colony was inspired by the English Pre-Raphaelites and the Arts and Crafts movement of William Morris and John Ruskin, whose communal, rural ethos it took a stage further. Members included Aladár Körösfői-Kriesch, who wrote a book about Ruskin and Morris; Sándor Nagy, whose home and workshop may eventually become a separate museum; and the architect Károly Kós. Though the colony dispersed in 1920, its stamp on the decorative arts persisted until the 1950s, while Kós's work has been a major influence on Imre Makovecz and his protegés, who dominate today's architectural scene. Captioned in English throughout, the museum's displays include a terrific exhibition of regional history, including mock-up rooms illustrating the life of the Gödöllő estate and artefacts from New Guinea donated by the local naturalist and explorer Ferenc Ignácz.

Practicalities

HÉV trains from Örs Vezér tere (every 45min; BKV passes and tickets valid as far as the city limits) take about forty minutes to reach Gödöllő; get off at the Szabadság tér stop, bang opposite the palace. For **information**, ask at the Tourinform booth inside the palace (Tues–Sun: Feb, March, Nov & Dec 10am–4pm; April–Oct 10am–5pm; ⓣ28/415-402, ⓦwww.gkrte.hu). If you're feeling peckish, try the humble *Palazzo Pizzeria* (no phone; daily 11am–11pm) beside the HÉV stop; alternatively, the *Galéria* **restaurant** on Szabadság tér (ⓣ28/510-860; daily 11am–9pm) has an inexpensive menu that includes exotic choices such as deer stew and grilled shark. Almost next door, there's also the *Sulyán Cukrászda* (daily 9am–7pm), for cakes, ices and coffee.

Listings

Listings

⓬ Accommodation 149

⓭ Restaurants 157

⓮ Coffee houses and patisseries 167

⓯ Bars and clubs 170

⓰ Gay Budapest 175

⓱ Entertainment 177

⓲ Sports 185

⓳ Baths and pools 188

⓴ Kids' Budapest 193

㉑ Shopping 197

12

Accommodation

In recent years, Budapest's **accommodation** has improved markedly in terms of availability, so much so that the surplus of rooms has brought a halt to the get-rich-quick price hikes that once afflicted the city. Rooms are most in demand at Christmas, New Year, the Spring Festival in March/April and the Grand Prix in August, when rates are marked up as much as twenty percent in some hotels. Even so, it should always be possible to find somewhere that's reasonably priced, if not well situated.

Budget travellers will find most hotels expensive even during low season (Nov–March, excluding New Year). Pensions are a cheaper alternative, often with much the same facilities as small hotels, such as en-suite bathrooms. If you're on a tight budget, your safest bet is a private room, where low prices should make up for what's often a poor location. However, these are getting harder to find – the trend nowadays is for self-contained studio flats or apartments rented through internet-based companies.

Hostels vary in price: some represent the cheapest accommodation in the city, while others are more expensive than private rooms. Another inexpensive option are **campsites**, where tent space can usually be found, even if all the **bungalows**, which some have, are taken.

Accommodation rates are usually quoted in **euros**; where prices are given in forints, we have followed suit, but note that you can always pay in forints. In the reviews here, the prices given refer to double rooms in the **high seasons** detailed above, and include taxes where applicable. Note that some hotels do not include twenty percent VAT (*Áfa*) and three percent tourist tax in quoted prices, so check before you commit yourself.

Hotel booking agencies and websites

Useful online accommodation sites include Ⓦwww.hotelinfo.hu, which lists the city's hotels and pensions and has information about Hungary Card discounts, but doesn't allow you to make bookings. If you want to book accommodation online, try the following sites: Ⓦwww.budapesthotelreservation.hu, Ⓦwww.hotels.hu, Ⓦwww.travelport.hu and Ⓦwww.hungarytourism.hu.

Ibusz V, Ferenciek tere 10, on the corner of Petőfi Sándor utca Ⓣ1/501-4910, Ⓦwww.ibusz.hu. Mon–Fri 9am–6pm, Sat 9am–1pm. Handles all forms of accommodation.

Vista Visitor Center VI, Paulay Ede utca 7 Ⓣ1/429-9999, Ⓦwww.vista.hu. Mon–Fri 9am–8pm, Sat 9am–6pm. Books hotels and apartments.

Hotels and pensions

The greatest choice of hotels and pensions can be found in **Pest**, where there's also more in the way of restaurants and nightlife – and more traffic noise, too. The grand hotels that lined the river bank were all destroyed during World War II, and their replacements – the *Marriott*, *Sofitel* and *InterContinental* – don't have quite the same elegance, despite being top establishments with familiar brand names. In this city of baths, it's no surprise that several of the big hotels offer **spa packages**: the *Gellért* and the Margít-sziget hotels were built next to springs, while other five-star hotels in the centre have spa complexes.

In general, **star ratings** give a fair idea of standards, though facilities at some of the older three-star places don't compare with their Western equivalents, even if room prices are similar. A common trend these days is smoking and no-smoking floors in hotels; this distinction will be swept away when the expected smoking ban is introduced (though no one knows exactly when that will come into force). In terms of **facilities**, many (though not all), hotels have wi-fi in foyer areas or throughout. In general the prevalence of showers over baths and twin beds over double beds (*francia ágy*) mean that it is always advisable to ask according to your needs when booking.

The Belváros

For locations, see the map on p.46.

Hotel Art (Best Western) **V, Királyi Pál utca 12 ⓣ1/266-2166, ⓦwww.bwhotelart.hu.** A small hotel in a quiet backstreet. Rooms are quite cramped, but have a/c, minibar, phone and TV, and there's a sauna, fitness room and laundry service. Doubles €140.

Astoria **V, Kossuth utca 19 ⓣ1/889-6000, ⓦwww.danubiushotels.com/astoria.** Four-star vintage hotel which has given its name to the major junction in central Pest on which it's located. The good-sized rooms have a sofa, safe, minibar, phone and TV; half have baths while the rest have showers, and there are smoking and non-smoking floors. The hotel's *Mirror* coffee house (see p.166) and bar is a popular meeting point. Doubles from €185.

ELTE Peregrinus Vendégház **V, Szerb utca 3 ⓣ1/266-4911, ⓦwww.peregrinushotel.hu.** Friendly place on a quiet backstreet in central Pest. The 25 rooms are spacious (unlike the bathrooms) and have minibar and TV, and as the hotel belongs to the university, all have writing tables to meet the needs of academic visitors. Buffet breakfast included in the rates. 27,500Ft.

Kempinski Corvinus **V, Erzsébet tér 7–8 ⓣ1/429-3777, ⓦwww.kempinski-budapest.com.** A flashy five-star establishment on the edge of the Belváros, which counts Madonna and Lewis Hamilton among past guests, with tastefully furnished rooms offering every luxury. Swimming pool, sauna, solarium, fitness room and underground garage, and wi-fi throughout. Rooms from €370.

Le Méridien **V, Erzsébet tér 9–10 ⓣ1/429-5500, ⓦwww.lemeridien-budapest.com.** Originally built for the Adria insurance company at the turn of the twentieth century, this building housed the police headquarters in the Communist years until it was totally gutted and reopened as a luxury hotel in 2000 – a welcome rival for the *Kempinski* next door. It's magnificently furnished throughout, and the well-equipped rooms are perhaps the most tasteful in the city. Parking and swimming pool. Rooms from €480.

Zara Boutique **V, Só utca 6 ⓣ1/577-0700, ⓦwww.zarahotels.com.** New four-star boutique hotel off the bottom of Váci utca, close to the Main Market Hall. Its 74 rooms are very pleasingly furnished with smart, dark furniture set against light walls, and are well equipped. All have showers, and you can ask for double or twin beds. Wi-fi in the lobby. Doubles from €178.

Lipótváros and Újlipótváros

For locations, see the map on p.54.

Four Seasons **V, Roosevelt tér 5–6 ⓣ1/268-6000, ⓦwww.fourseasons.com/budapest.** A magnificent restoration of this Budapest landmark has produced a new level of luxury in the city; the rooms have Art Nouveau-style fittings (even down to the beautiful radiators) and are excellently equipped; those overlooking the Danube naturally have the best aspect. Both the restaurants are excellent – the *Kávéház* is slightly cheaper than the *Páva* but still a very good option – and the service throughout the hotel is superlative. Underground garage. Standard rooms from €340.

Starlight Suiten **V, Mérleg utca 6 ⓣ1/484-3700, ⓦwww.starlighthotels.com.** Incredibly good value given its location near the Lánchíd (right behind the *Four Seasons*), with 54 spacious smoking and non-smoking suites. Each has a kitchenette with a microwave, two televisions (one in each room), a sofa and a writing desk. There's wi-fi access throughout, and facilities include a sauna, steam bath and fitness rooms. Suites from €189.

Terézváros and Erzsébetváros

For locations, see the map on p.64.

Andrássy **VI, Andrássy út 111 ⓣ1/462-2100, ⓦwww.andrassyhotel.com.** Housed in a fine Bauhaus building near the Városliget, the *Andrássy* offers five-star accommodation without the corporate feel. Most double rooms have balconies and all mod cons, including safes big enough for your laptop, though the smaller Classic rooms have a shower and no balcony. Try for one away from Andrássy út, which is a busy thoroughfare. The *Baraka* restaurant has a good reputation, and the hotel has wi-fi access throughout and easy access to the Belváros. Doubles start at €150.

Béke Radisson **VI, Teréz körút 43 ⓣ1/889-3900, ⓦwww.danubiushotels.com/beke.** Large, vintage hotel in a handy location on the Nagykörút near Nyugati station. Facilities include a sauna, pool, business centre, underground garage and a good café on the ground floor. The 239 rooms have a/c, minibar, TV and safe, and start at €140.

Benczúr **VI, Benczúr utca 35 ⓣ1/479-5650, ⓦwww.hotelbenczur.hu.** Large, modern and functional hotel on a leafy street off Andrássy út, with a nice garden at the back and parking in the yard (850Ft extra). The 60 "superior" doubles in one wing are all no-smoking and come with shower, TV and a/c, while the slightly cheaper "standard" ones in the other wing have fewer frills but do have baths. There are also some apartments for families. The hotel website says that Pope John Paul II was a guest, but don't ask to stay in the same room – he didn't sleep here. Doubles from €100.

City Home Residency **VI, Ó utca 43–49 ⓣ1/354-7800, ⓦwww.cityhome.hu.** Newly built apartment hotel 5min walk from the Opera House, with good-size studio flats and one-bedroom apartments. All have minimalist interiors, baths and very well-equipped kitchens (toaster, microwave, oven etc), and you have access to the ground-floor sauna, flashy pool and a gym kitted out with the latest gear. The excellent *Segal* restaurant within the building provides breakfasts. Studios €160, one-beds €180.

Corinthia Grand Royal **VII, Erzsébet körút 43–49 ⓣ1/479-4000, ⓦwww.corinthiahotels.com.** Pleasant new five-star place on the main boulevard, with over four hundred comfortable rooms, two good restaurants and a luxury spa complex. This was one of the grand prewar hotels, but for forty years the building was used as offices, while the ballroom acted as the very grand Red Star cinema. The rebuilding – only the facade is original, as you discover when you tap on the grand pillars in the foyer – has been beautifully executed, using original drawings; even the gorgeous ballroom is totally reconstructed (except for the chandeliers). Standard doubles start at €196.

Délibáb **VI, Délibáb utca 35 ⓣ1/342-9301, ⓦwww.hoteldelibab.com.** Simply furnished but pleasant, the *Délibáb* stands right on Hősök tere, within walking distance of the sights on Andrássy út and the City Park, and has excellent transport links too. Most rooms no-smoking, and some have balconies, but none have a/c; try to avoid the ones looking towards the park over the busy Dózsa György út. Rooms from €83.

easyHotel **VI, Eötvös utca 25/a ⓣ1/411-1982, ⓦeasyhotel.com.** Brand new place near Oktogon with the same approach as easyJet, where cheapness and simplicity rule. The a/c rooms are all no-smoking and have one bright orange wall. They come in two sizes: small (7–9 square metres, enough room for a bed and your bag, as long as it's not too big); and standard, which has slightly more space and even a couple of hooks. The en-suite shower/toilets have the feel of an airplane cubicle, and you pay extra for TV and internet access. There are two rooms with disabled access – and much more room – on the ground floor. Bookable online only, rooms start at €15, according to demand, but are usually €60–70.

K&K Opera VI, Révay utca 24 ⓣ1/269-0222, ⓦwww.kkhotels.com. Smart, modern and fully a/c four-star hotel right by the Opera House, with underground parking. Its 206 rooms – all with minibar, TV, safe and phone – have been recently refurbished, and around half have baths, the others showers. Doubles from €140, including buffet breakfast.

King's VII, Nagy Diófa utca 25–27 ⓣ1/352-7675, ⓦwww.kingshotel.hu. Popular with Jewish visitors, located smack in the old Jewish ghetto and with a kosher restaurant next door. There are 79 a/c rooms with one to four beds, fridge, safe and internet access. No-smoking rooms available. You have to pay in advance for Sabbath meals. Doubles from €100.

Medosz VI, Jókai tér 9 ⓣ1/374-3001, ⓦwww.medoszhotel.hu. Overlooking a quiet square near Oktogon, this friendly hotel was a trade union hostel until 1989. Not much has changed – it's still an unappealing modern block from the outside, and the small rooms have the simple bathrooms and basic institutional furniture that resonates with Communist Hungary nostalgia – but the location, good prices and the helpful staff make it a popular choice. Rooms have TVs and twin beds – some have the two beds end to end, so ask if you want yours next to each other. Doubles cost around €59, including breakfast.

Pest VI, Paulay Ede utca 31 ⓣ1/343-1198, ⓦwww.hotelpest.hu. Pleasant hotel in an old Pest apartment block – the bared walls in the bar area and foyer reveal its eighteenth century origins – and it's well situated in a small street across Andrássy út from the Opera House. Its 25 good-size rooms have a/c and TV, and a bath or shower. Breakfast is included in the rates, and served in the glass-covered courtyard. From €130.

Radio Inn VI, Benczúr utca 19 ⓣ1/342-8347, ⓦwww.radioinn.hu. Spacious, simply furnished smoking and no-smoking apartments complete with a living room, TV, big twin beds and a small kitchen with two electric rings; no a/c, however. Situated in a leafy street by the Chinese and Vietnamese embassies, with a pleasant garden. From €80.

Józsefváros and Ferencváros

For locations, see the map on p.82.

Anna VIII, Gyulai Pál utca 14 ⓣ1/327-2000, ⓦwww.annahotel.hu Located in a quiet road and with off-street parking, this hotel offers 42 small, fairly basic rooms – twin beds only – with TV and shower. Some rooms have a/c, and there are also apartments with double beds and baths. From €125.

Mercure Museum VIII, Trefort utca 2 ⓣ1/485-1080, ⓦwww.mercure-museum.hu. Having established itself in an imaginatively transformed Pest apartment block on a quiet street behind the National Museum, the *Mercure* has now expanded into the next-door block and has 104 rooms. The new half is sleek and modern in design, but the older part has more appeal, set around a glass-roofed courtyard. Rooms are small but well-equipped, with en-suite bathrooms, hairdryer, satellite TV and minibar. Off-street parking available, and there's wi-fi throughout. From €140.

Nemzeti Hotel VIII, József körút 4 ⓣ1/477-2000, ⓦwww.mercure-nemzeti.hu. This Art Nouveau hotel overlooking the busy Blaha Lujza tér was undergoing a complete refurbishment at the time of writing, and is scheduled to reopen in mid 2009 – check the website for updates and rates. Period features include a magnificent staircase and glass-roofed room on the ground floor; note that the rooms facing on to the courtyard are quieter.

Várhegy and the Víziváros

For locations, see the maps on p.91 and p.92.

Art'otel I, Bem rakpart 16–19 ⓣ1/487-9487, ⓦwww.artotel.hu. Boutique hotel that combines eighteenth-century buildings – comprising beautiful, spacious rooms with original doors and high ceilings – with a modern wing overlooking the river, offering marvellous views. Rooms are well equipped (bright red dressing gowns are among the items provided). There's a wi-fi network all round the hotel, and the business centre offers internet use. From €129.

Astra I, Vám utca 6 ⓣ1/214-1906, ⓦwww.hotelastra.hu. Small hotel in a converted 300-year-old building at the foot of the Castle District near Batthyány tér. Twelve well-furnished rooms (including three apartments) with minibar and a/c, from €112.

Burg I, Szentháromság tér 7 ⓣ 1/212-0269, ⓦ www.burghotelbudapest.com. Modern, small hotel right in the middle of the Castle District, opposite the Mátyás Church. The recently renovated rooms are all no-smoking, have en-suite bathrooms, a/c, minibar, safe and TV. Wi-fi throughout the hotel. Doubles from €115.

Carlton I, Apor Péter utca 3 ⓣ 1/224-0999, ⓦ www.carltonhotel.hu. Modern hotel, well situated below the Castle District and by the Chain Bridge. The modern interior is comfy enough and is much improved by the recent refurbishment, but the hotel struggles to match its four-star rating. Six no-smoking floors, two smoking floors, and wi-fi throughout. All 95 rooms have twin beds; half have showers, the other half have baths. Parking available. Doubles from €110.

Hilton Budapest I, Hess András tér 1–3 ⓣ 1/889-6600, ⓦ www.danubiushotels.com/hilton. By the Mátyás Church in the Vár, with superb views across the river, this hotel incorporates the remains of a medieval monastery and hosts summertime concerts in the former church. Luxurious to a fault. Wi-fi all over, and smoking and no-smoking floors. Standard doubles from €160; excellent special offers available.

Kulturinnov I, Szentháromság tér 6 ⓣ 1/224-8102, ⓦ www.mka.hu. Well positioned for sightseeing in a large neo-Gothic building right by Mátyás Church, and on the first floor of the Hungarian Cultural Foundation, which hosts cultural events, concerts and exhibitions. The quiet and spacious rooms have a minibar. Some rooms have a TV, and about half have a/c – but the thick walls offer some protection against the heat. Wi-fi throughout. Breakfast included. Doubles from €80.

Lánchíd 19 I, Lánchíd utca 19 ⓣ 1/419-1900, ⓦ www.lanchid19hotel.hu. The Hungarian debut of the worldwide Design hotel chain lies just below the Royal Palace, close to the Chain Bridge. Its award-winning design – all the work of local architects and artists – includes such features as an exterior facade of moving panels, as well as stylish lobby furniture and glass walkways leading to the 45 well-equipped rooms, which have striking bathrooms and individual decor themed on a wedding, a film or the like. Wi-fi throughout. From €150

Victoria I, Bem rakpart 11 ⓣ 1/457-8080, ⓦ www.victoria.hu. Small, very friendly hotel on the embankment directly below the Mátyás Church. The rooms have excellent views of the Lánchíd and the river, and are equipped with minibar, TV and a/c. Sauna and garage facilities. From €123.

Gellért-hegy and the Tabán

For locations, see the map on p.109.

Ábel Panzió XI, Ábel Jenő utca 9 ⓣ 1/209-2537, ⓦ www.abelpanzio.hu. Perhaps the most appealing pension in Budapest, a 1913 villa with beautiful Art Nouveau fittings in a quiet street, 20min walk from the Belváros. There are just ten rooms, two with twin beds, so it's essential to book in advance; there's a discount if you pay in cash. Doubles from €70.

Charles Hotel XI, Hegyalja út 23 ⓣ 1/212-9169, ⓦ www.charleshotel.hu. On the hill up from the Erzsébet híd on the main road to Vienna, this friendly apartment hotel was one of the first of its kind in the city. It has 73 rooms and apartments (you can choose double or twin beds, bath or shower) which come with cooking facilities, minibar and TV; those facing the inner yard are better, as the road is very busy. Some of the cheaper rooms have no a/c. Wi-fi all over, and bikes available for rent. Parking costs €8. From €65.

Citadella I, Citadella sétány ⓣ 1/466-5794, ⓦ www.citadella.hu. Breathtaking views of the city from this hotel inside the hulk of the old citadel, but note that at the weekend the neighbouring disco can be a bit noisy. The entrance gate is beside the restaurant outside the walls – you'll need to press the buzzer. To get here, take bus #27 from Móricz Zsigmond körtér, then it's a 10min walk from the Busuló Juhász stop. Double rooms with shared facilities (10,500Ft), private showers (11,500Ft) or baths (12,500Ft).

Flamenco XI, Tas vezér utca 3–7 ⓣ 1/889-5600, ⓦ www.danubiushotels.com/flamenco. In the leafy district behind Gellért Hill, this is a large, modern conference hotel, with two floors at the top for independent travellers. The rooms are of a good size, complemented by a pool, sauna and fitness room downstairs, and wi-fi access throughout. Rooms from €118.

Gellért XI, Szent Gellért tér 1 ⓣ 1/889-5500, ⓦ www.danubiushotels.com/gellert. Large, light corridors and lots of character at this well-established hotel. The facade, especially when floodlit, is magnificent, and so is the thermal pool, to which residents have their own lift down (and free entry, which comes

▲ Gellért Hotel

with a bathrobe). A large number of single rooms are available; all rooms are en suite. The cheaper rooms look on to the courtyard and don't have the views – or the sound of the trams, which blight the others, in spite of double-glazing. The beer hall (*söröző*) serves good food, and the coffee shop is excellent. Note that impending renovation may close all or part of the hotel from January 2009. Rooms start at €170.

Orion I, Döbrentei utca 13 ⓣ 1/356-8583, ⓦ bestwestern-ce.com/orion. Small modern block in the Tabán district, just south of the Vár. The simple rooms have TV and minibar – those at the front can be noisy – and guests can make use of a sauna. Doubles €125.

Óbuda and Margit-sziget

Danubius Grand and Danubius Thermal XIII, Margit-sziget ⓣ 1/889-4700, ⓦ www.danubiushotels.com/grandhotel, ⓦ www.danubiushotels.com/thermalhotel. See map, p.119. Both hotels are at the northern end of the island and provide a very wide range of spa facilities from mud spas to massages, as well as medical and cosmetic services from pedicures to plastic surgery, and have wi-fi access (for a fee). Rates include access to the thermal baths, pool, sauna, gym and other facilities. The *Grand* is the island's original, *fin-de-siècle* spa hotel; rooms here have balconies and high ceilings, and have been totally refurbished, with period furniture. The *Thermal* is the big modern one, with balconies offering views over the island. Doubles in the *Grand* start at €200, while those in the *Thermal* start at €215.

Pál Panzió III, Pálvölgyi köz 15 ⓣ 1/388-7099. See map, p.115. Four double rooms in this small, welcoming pension, situated in the hills near the Pálvölgy Stalactite Cave. Doubles from €60.

The Buda Hills

For locations, see the map on p.122.

Beatrix Panzió II, Szehér út 3 ⓣ 1/275-0550, ⓦ www.beatrixhotel.hu. Friendly eighteen-room pension in the villa district northwest of Moszkva tér – take tram #56. There's a bar on the ground floor, a sauna, and parking too. Doubles €70.

Budapest II, Szilágyi Erzsébet fasor 47 ⓣ 1/889-4200, ⓦ www.danubiushotels.com/budapest. Cylindrical tower facing the Buda Hills, opposite the lower terminal of the Cogwheel Railway, 500m from Moszkva tér. Rooms come with a/c, TV and minibar, and there's a sauna, fitness room and business centre too. The lobby's decor is rather 1970s, but at least there are excellent views over the city from the upper floors. Doubles from €94.

Buda Villa Panzió XII, Kiss Áron utca 6 ⓣ 1/275-0091, ⓦ www.budapansio.hu. Up in the hills above Moszkva tér, and a 10min ride from there on bus #156 (note that the last bus leaves about 10.45pm), this comfortable and friendly pension has a small garden that's perfect for relaxing in after a day's sightseeing, and a bar in the lounge on the first floor. Ten rooms, with doubles from €64, including breakfast.

Hostels

If you don't have a tent, a dormitory bed in a **hostel** is the cheapest alternative. Dorms tend to be mixed-sex, but many hostels also have private rooms at much the same price as hotel or pension accommodation, though often with very basic student furniture. Still, at least there are no surcharges of the sort levied in private rooms for staying fewer than four nights, and the hostels offer 24-hour information from English-speaking staff at the reception desk.

Unless stated otherwise, the hostels listed here are open year-round. Student dormitories – many of them located in the university area south of Gellért-hegy

– are open during July and August only. You can't be sure of getting a bed in the hostel of your choice in summer without **booking** in advance.

The Mellow Mood group runs some excellent year-round hostels in the city and also handles some of the university accommodation open during the summer. Staff at offices in Keleti Station (daily: June–Aug 7am–midnight; Sept–May 7am–8pm; ⓣ1/343-0748 or 1/413-2062, ⓦwww.mellowmood.hu), on the right of the glass doors at the far end as you arrive, can give information, make bookings and organize transport to their hostels from the station.

Finally, note that as many of Pest's hostels are in residential blocks – exceptions being *Marco Polo* and *Ráday* – they particularly frown on rowdy guests.

Pest

Astoria City VII, Rákóczi út 4.III.27 ⓣ1/266-1327, ⓦwww.astoriacityhostel.com. See map, p.64. On the third floor (with a lift), this is a pleasant small hostel in the heart of the city, with two eight-bed dorms, one six-bed and one en-suite double room. The six-bed overlooks a quiet inner courtyard, the others to the noisy main road. They also have apartments in the same block, and rooms a few doors along. Prices includes breakfast and internet access. Laundry service available. Dorm beds from €12, double rooms from €36.

Caterina VI, Teréz körút 30.III.28 ⓣ1/269-5990, ⓦwww.caterinahostel.hu. See map, p.64. Long-established hostel that has moved to a new venue, above the Művész cinema near the Oktogon, and although it's on the third floor with no lift, the small set-up gives it a friendly feel. There are rooms of six, eight and ten bunk beds, as well as a room for three, and three apartments in neighbouring streets. The eight-bed room is the quietest, looking on to the courtyard – the others overlook the noisy boulevard. They have a laundry service, a kitchen and free internet access. Dorm beds from 2500Ft, including breakfast.

Green Bridge V, Molnár utca 22 ⓣ1/266-6922, ⓦwww.greenbridgehostel.com. See map, p.46. Small hostel in a quiet street near the Danube in the Belváros. Run by a helpful young couple, it's on the ground floor and has rooms of five to eight beds, plus two double rooms and apartments for groups. There's a laundry service, and free internet access and coffee. They can also book places on cave tours. Beds from €10, doubles €50.

Marco Polo VII, Nyár utca 6 ⓣ1/413-2555, ⓦwww.marcopolohostel.com. See map, p.64. Big, busy and clean hostel close to Blaha Lujza tér, with simply furnished four- and twelve-bed dorms with bunks, as well as 36 double rooms, and a bar in the cellar. IYHF cardholders get a discount. Dorm beds 4500Ft, doubles 17,000Ft.

Ráday IX, Ráday utca 43–45 ⓣ06-20/443-2883, ⓦwww.agapetours.hu. See map p.82. Under its new name City Hostel Pest, the hostel on this buzzing street has rooms of one to four beds with basic student hostel furniture. Open July & Aug only. Beds from €24.

Red Bus V, Semmelweis utca 14 ⓣ1/266-0136, ⓦwww.redbusbudapest.hu. See map, p.46. Friendly and relaxed hostel on a quiet back street close to Deák tér, with rooms of two to five beds. Breakfast and the use of the kitchen are included in the price; internet use and laundry service are extra. As it's set in a residential block, this is not a place for partying. See website for special offers; otherwise 3600Ft for dorm beds, 9900Ft for doubles.

Buda

For locations, see the map on p.109.

Back Pack XI, Takács Menyhért utca 33 ⓣ1/385-8946, ⓦwww.backpackbudapest.hu. Charming fifty-bed hostel with a shaded garden, about 20min from the centre (tram #49 or bus #7 to Tétényi út stop). The staff provide lots of information on the city, sport and fitness, and also organize cave trips. Dorm beds from 3000Ft, doubles 9000Ft.

Landler XI, Bartók Béla út 17 ⓣ1/463-3621. Tram #47 or #49 from Deák tér. One of the older hostels, housed in the Baross Gábor Kollégium, near the Gellért Baths. Basic two- and three-bed rooms, with high ceilings and basins, and shared bathrooms down the corridor. Open July & Aug only. A bed in a three-bed room is 3400Ft; two-bed rooms are 4000Ft per head or 5900Ft for single occupancy.

Private rooms and apartments

Self-contained **studio flats** or **apartments** are available to rent through agencies such as Ibusz (see box, p.149) or To-Ma at V, Október 6 utca 22 (Mon–Fri 9am–noon, Sat–Sun 9am–5pm; ⓣ1/353-0819, ⓦwww.tomatour.hu), and internet-based companies such as Budapest Lets (ⓦwww.budapestlets.com), a UK-Hungarian venture managing about forty well-equipped properties, from one-room studio flats on Ráday utca to luxury apartments on Várhegy.

The budget option is a **private room** – the downsides being that you have less choice and you are less independent of the owners. The two agencies above handle rooms, too – getting one via one of the touts at the train stations may be cheaper but carries more risk. Depending on location and amenities, **prices** for a double room start at 6000Ft a night, while apartments go from 8000Ft. Rates can be up to thirty percent higher if you stay fewer than four nights.

The *Budapest Atlasz* is invaluable for checking the location of sites and access by public transport. For atmosphere, you can't beat the nineteenth-century blocks where spacious, high-ceilinged apartments surround a courtyard with wrought-iron balconies. For these, the best areas to choose are Pest's V, VI and VII districts – you're best keeping inside or near the Nagykörút – and the parts of Buda nearest the Vár. Avoid the rundown VIII and IX districts unless you can get a place inside the Nagykörút. Elsewhere – particularly in Újpest (IV), Csepel (XXI) or Óbuda (III) – you're likely to end up in a box on the twelfth floor of a *lakótelep* (housing estate). Some knowledge of Hungarian facilitates **settling in** to private rooms; guests normally receive an explanation of the boiler system and multiple door keys (*kulcs*), and may have use of the washing machine (*mosógép*), which might itself require a demonstration.

Camping

Budapest's **campsites** are generally well equipped and pleasant, with trees, grass and sometimes even a pool. They can get crowded between June and September, when smaller places might run out of space. It is illegal to camp anywhere else, and the parks are patrolled to enforce this.

The campsites listed here are all in Buda, since the Pest ones are not very inviting.

Csillebérci Camping XII, Konkoly Thege Miklós út 21 ⓣ1/395-6537, ⓦwww.csilleberciszabadido.hu. See map, p.122. Large, well-equipped site up in the Buda Hills, with space for 1000 campers and a range of bungalows. Bus #90 from Moszkva tér to the Csillebérc stop or bus #90A to Normafa, then a short walk. Open all year.

Római Camping III, Szentendrei út 189 ⓣ1/388-7167, ⓦwww.romaicamping.hu. See map, p.115. Huge site beside the road to Szentendre in Rómaifürdő (25min by HÉV from Batthyány tér), with space for 2500 campers. They also have wooden bungalows, and the price includes use of the neighbouring Rómaifürdő lido. Open year-round.

Zugligeti Niche Camping XII, Zugligeti út 101 ⓣ1/200-8346, ⓦwww.campingniche.hu. See map, p.122. At the end of the #158 bus route from Moszkva tér, opposite the chairlift up to János-hegy, this is a small, terraced ravine site in the woods with space for 260 campers and good facilities, including a pleasant little restaurant occupying the former tram station at the far end. April–Oct.

13

Restaurants

Hungarian cuisine was born on the plains, and centres around good solid meals you could cook up over a fire that would last you the day. The staples are meat (especially pork), paprika, bread and lard, all washed down with wine or *pálinka* (the harsh Hungarian fruit brandy), and unsurprisingly, traditional local fare is heavy and calorific.

This basic truth still survives in spite of the dramatic transformation of the Budapest dining scene in recent years. The range of cuisines represented continues to grow, with excellent Italian, French, Chinese and fusion cooking around, as well as modern – lighter – takes on the heavy Hungarian classics. The standard of the top restaurants has also changed beyond recognition as they vie for Budapest's first Michelin star, with *Lou Lou* and *Café Kör* making it into the top 100 restaurants in the world, by one reckoning in 2007.

And finally, prices have rocketed – there are now plenty of wealthy businessmen, Hungarian and foreign, eager to indulge, and sadly too many new restaurants think that pretentious decor, a few gimmicks and of course some nouvelle cuisine are a recipe for ridiculous prices. This has put many places out of reach of the locals, but the past couple of years have brought a welcome

Restaurant Gypsy bands

▲ Restaurant Gypsy band

A traditional accompaniment to a Hungarian meal is the Gypsy band, dressed in blue and red waistcoats and displaying astonishing skill – one favourite piece of music imitates the sound of the lark (*pacsirta*). This music arouses strong passions – and not just among the diners who stand up and sing with the band: tell a Hungarian that these schmaltzy tunes are Hungarian folk and you'll be informed, in no uncertain terms, that this is Gypsy music. The rural Vlach Roma will say exactly the opposite: that the songs are a Hungarian entity, quite different to what the Roma play for themselves (see *Hungarian music* colour section). In fact, the tunes you'll hear in the restaurants are popularized versions of the old folk songs – **magyar nóta** – composed in the nineteenth century (and played today) by Romungro Gypsy dynasties. To get the full charm of this entertainment try the *Rézkakas* in the Belváros, or the *Kéhli* in Óbuda – the latter has a big local following and the atmosphere is great on Friday nights. If you ask for a tune when the *prímás* (the lead violinist in the all-blue waistcoat) comes round the tables, bear in mind that you'll be expected to pay for the privilege.

Hungarian wine

Hungary's **wines** are a delight, thus far under-appreciated in the global market. In general, the country's climate favours whites, especially crisp and floral varieties, but its reds are also delicious and offer more complexity and variation, including light and spicy vintages that are often chilled before drinking, as well an emerging number of fine rosés.

In the Communist era **wine production** emphasized quantity over quality, throwing any number of different grapes together and shipping as much as possible to an undemanding Soviet market. Since 1989, however, there has been a huge investment in wine production, especially by foreign concerns in the internationally recognised Tokaj region, but also by native vintners in other regions. These smaller producers have turned their quality around extremely quickly, reviving older grape varieties and introducing new treatments, such as barrique (ageing the wine in small oak barrels).

Although Hungary has twenty official wine regions, the best producers are concentrated in a few areas. For **reds** seek out Eger in the north (Vilmos Thummerer is a name to look out for), Szekszárd to the south (Ferenc Vesztergombi, Takler, Tamás Dúzsi and others) and Villány near the Croatian border (the long list of producers here includes József Bock, Attila Gere and Tiffán and Vylyan). The last two regions also produce excellent **rosés** – those of Bock and Dúzsi are particularly recommended. For **whites**, the best regions are located around Lake Balaton to the southwest of Budapest (Huba Szeremley, Jásdi and Otto Légli), and of course Tokaj, the wine region famed for its incredibly sweet Aszú wines.

Many of the grape varieties used in Hungarian wines will be familiar, even if their Hungarian names are less so, but there are also some indigenous grapes that are worth trying. Among red wines, alongside the well-known Cabernet Franc and Cabernet Sauvignon and others, the **Kadarka** yields a light, spicy, cherry-coloured wine that has undergone a revival in the past decade. It is a common ingredient in Bull's Blood, the famous blend made in Eger and Szekszárd. Many producers turn out cuvées – special blends that, like the barrique wines, tend to be more expensive than varietal wines.

Alongside the familiar whites of Sauvignon Blanc and Olaszrizling (Italian Riesling) are Irsai Olivér, which produces a floral, aromatic wine, and Cserszegi Fűszeres which has a slightly smoother, spicier flavour. Among **Tokaj** wines Aszú is the best known, but the drier Furmint and the honeyed Hárslevelű (lime or linden leaf), less cloying than the Aszú, are both worth looking for.

For a sophisticated white, try the Taposó-kút 2005 from the Szent Ilona Borház, a blend that captures the characteristics of the Furmint and Hárslevelű with Olaszrizling grapes. Taposó-kút hails from Somló, a hill west of Balaton whose volcanic soil produces fascinating results, just as it does around Tokaj; this is a crisp yet rich wine with a minerally character.

reaction, with a revival in cheap eateries and self-service restaurants offering generous portions of cheap food.

Hungarian cuisine

For foreigners, the archetypal Magyar dish is still goulash – historically the basis of much **Hungarian cooking**. The ancient Magyars relished cauldrons of this *gulyás* (pronounced "gou-yash"), a soup made of potatoes and whatever meat was available, which was later flavoured with paprika and beefed up into a variety of stews, modified over the centuries by the various foreign influences which helped diversify the country's cuisine. Hungary's Slav visitors probably introduced native cooks to yogurt and sour cream – vital ingredients in many dishes – while the influence of the Turks, Austrians and Germans is apparent in a variety of sticky pastries and strudels, as well as in recipes featuring sauerkraut or dumplings. There's a lot of fish, too – fish soup (*halászlé*) is one of the national dishes, a marvellously spicy bouillabaisse in the right hands – but it's worth remembering that landlocked Hungary's fish, such as the very bony carp and the more palatable catfish, all come from lakes and rivers – anything else will be imported. For a glossary of **food and drink terms** see p.228.

Traditionally, Hungarians take their main meal at **lunchtime**. While some restaurants offer a bargain set menu (*napi menű*) – some places call them business lunches – the majority of places are strictly *à la carte*. The menu (*étlap*) usually kicks off with **cold and hot starters** (*hideg* and *meleg előételek*), **soups** (*levesek*) and then the **main courses** (*főételek*) – sometimes divided into meat (*hús*) and fish (*hal*). These are followed by vegetables (*zöldségek*), salads (*saláták*) and sometimes pasta (*tészták*). Finally, there are the desserts (*édességek* or *desszertek*). Bread is provided automatically, on the grounds that "a meal without bread is no meal". **Drinks** are under the heading *italok* – or may be on a separate drinks or wine menu (*itallap* or *borlap*). If you don't want a full meal, you might just order a filling soup, such as a fish or bean soup like *Jókai bableves*, along with a salad.

Despite the emergence of *vegetáriánus* restaurants in Budapest, and a growing understanding of the concept, **vegetarians** are still poorly catered to, and it's only in the more upmarket places that the choices become anything close to tempting. In most restaurants, you'll find yourself existing on a diet of vegetables and cheese fried in breadcrumbs known as *rántott gomba* (with mushrooms), *rántott karfiol* (cauliflower), or *rántott sajt* (cheese). *Gomba paprikás* (mushroom paprika stew) is also fine, though check if it has been cooked in oil rather than in lard. Alternatively there are eggs – fried (*tükörtojás*), soft-boiled (*lágy tojás*), scrambled (*tojásrántotta*), or in mayonnaise (*kaszinótojás*) – or salads, though Hungary is surprisingly weak in the latter, given the excellent produce you can see in the shops.

It's wise to **reserve** a table if you're determined to eat somewhere in particular, though you can usually find an alternative within a couple of blocks. We've included phone numbers where booking is advisable, though of course not all staff will speak English. While more and more restaurants have introduced no-smoking sections, **smoking** is generally accepted (though a total ban in restaurants is expected sometime soon). Many of the places listed here take **credit cards** – a surprising exception is the excellent *Café Kör*.

A final note of caution: waiters in Budapest are known to make "mistakes" with your bill, and foreign visitors are especially easy targets for overcharging. Other more common tactics include offering expensive "specials of the day", overcharging or demanding exorbitant amounts for the wine. Insist on a proper menu (including prices for drinks), don't be shy about querying the total, and avoid the seedier tourist joints in the Belváros (see p.39).

Breakfast and brunch

A nation of early risers, Hungarians traditionally have a calorific **breakfast** (*reggeli*). Commonly, this includes cheese, eggs or salami together with bread and jam, washed down with coffee; in rural areas it's often accompanied by a shot of *pálinka* (brandy) to "clear the palate" or "aid digestion". **Sunday brunch** is a popular development in the restaurant scene, usually an all-you-can-eat buffet for a fixed price. Brunch at *Gundel* (see p.164) is a great way to taste its cuisine without the usual formality, and will set you back 5800Ft; most of the top hotels also lay on a spread. Prices can be slightly higher there, but most of the hotels have children's play areas. Brunch usually starts around noon and lasts till about 3pm; booking is advisable.

In addition to the places below, two breakfast favourites are *Vian* on Liszt Ferenc tér (p.173) and the laid-back *Kiadó* nearby on Jókai tér (p.171).

Bambi I, Frankel Leó utca 2–4. See map, p.91. This excellent old bar with its stern waitresses and red plastic-covered seats, is also a good breakfast venue for omelettes and coffee. Mon–Fri from 7am, Sat & Sun from 9am.

Nothin' But the Blues VIII, Krúdy Gyula utca 6. See map, p.82. Serves a full English breakfast of baked beans, bacon, Cumberland sausage and hash browns, with unlimited tea or coffee (1100Ft) – a rarity in Budapest – with tables outside. Daily from 8.30am.

Princess Outlets at the exits of metro stations all over the city. Sweet and savoury puff pastries to go – try a mushroom or cheese-filled *bürek*. Mon–Fri from 6am, Sat from 9am.

Sir Morik IX, Ráday utca 15. See map, p.82. Popular with neighbourhood expats for its range of freshly-brewed coffees from around the world and for its croissants and pastries – which you have to carry to the tables outside if you don't want to perch on a stool indoors. Daily from 10am.

Sandwich bars, cafeterias and fast-food diners

Budapest has taken to fast food in a big way, and you'll have little trouble finding a *McDonald's*, *Pizza Hut*, *Subway* or *Burger King* if you want one. For a quick bite in a less commercial setting, the Chinese stand-up joints and Turkish kebab outlets all over town are cheap, though you may wonder what goes into some of the food. The recent economic hardships have encouraged a revival of cheap local eateries, and if you want to eat like the average Hungarian, look out for a *önkiszolgáló étterem* (self-service restaurant), a *főzelék* establishment (dishes of creamed vegetables, *főzelék*, which taste much better than they sound) or another Hungarian pecularity, the *étkezde* – a small lunchtime diner where customers sit at shared tables and eat hearty home-cooked food.

Bombay Express VI, Andrássy út 44. See map, p.64. Pop into this self-service Indian place two blocks from the Oktogon for vegetable samosa, dahl, chicken tikka masala, lamb Hyderabad or spicy kebabs, to eat in or take out. Daily 11am–11pm.

Duran Sandwich Bar V, Október 6 utca 15 & XII, Retek utca 18. See maps, p.46 and 91. A sandwich and coffee chain – filling a surprising gap in Budapest. Their artistic open sandwiches (180–250Ft) of caviar, pureed paprika, smoked beef, pickled herring and such like really zap your taste-buds. Both branch are open Mon–Fri 8am–5.30pm, Sat 9am–1pm; the Retek utca is open until 2pm on Sat.

Falafel VI, Paulay Ede utca 53. See map, p.64. Budapest's most popular falafel joint for years, and they haven't changed their formula or expanded to new glossy premises. You just pay your money and stuff your pitta breads as full as you can. Seating upstairs. Mon–Fri 10am–8pm, Sat 10am–6pm.

Kádár Étkezde VII, Klauzál tér 10. See map, p.64. Diner with delicious home cooking; traditional Budapest Jewish food (non-kosher) on Fri. Mon–Sat 11.30am–3.30pm; closed mid-July to mid-Aug.

Kis Mama Konyhája IX, Lonyay utca 7. See map, p.82. Self-service lunchtime joint near the Great Market Hall, offering decent and very cheap food – mostly Hungarian, but there's also pasta and pizza. Mains from 600Ft. Mon–Fri 10am–6pm, Sat 10am–3pm.

Marie Kristensen Sandwich Bar IX, Ráday utca 7. See map, p.82. The Danish flavour the name implies is hard to spot – this is simply a decent, regular sandwich bar, just off Kálvin tér. Mon–Fri 8am–9pm, Sat 11am–8pm.

Sahara VIII, József körút 82. **See map, p.82.** Close to the Corvin cinema at Ferenc körút metro station, this bright joint has a wide range of tasty Middle Eastern food, eaten at shared tables. The freshest, tastiest Turkish/Middle Eastern food in the city. No smoking downstairs – you can smoke shishas upstairs. No alcohol. Also does takeaways. Daily 10am–midnight.

Vapiano V, Bécsi utca 5. **See map, p.46.** Fast food Italian-style near Deák tér in central Pest, and what style it is. Excellent pastas and salads made with fresh ingredients before your eyes. You are given a card as you enter, then head to the pizza, pasta, salad or dessert counter to order; your purchases are recorded on your card and you pay as you leave. Pasta and pizzas 1200–2000Ft. Daily 10.30am–midnight.

Restaurants

Despite the plethora of tourist traps in the Vár, **Buda** offers some excellent eating possibilities. There is no typical style of Buda restaurant: establishments here range from grand villas in the hills to small friendly local concerns. **Pest** has a much wider range of places, particularly within the Nagykörút. You can generally reckon that those further from the Belváros or the Vár are likely to be cheaper.

The Belváros

The places reviewed here appear on the map on p.46.

Gerlóczy V, Gerlóczy utca 1 ⓣ1/235-0953, ⓦwww.gerloczy.hu. This atmospheric corner café on quiet Károly Kammermayer tér, not far from the busy Károly körút, gets packed at lunchtime with office staff popping in for a quick lunch. The food is adequate bistro fare. Daily 8am–11pm.

Károlyi V, Károlyi Mihály utca 16 ⓣ1/328-0240. It's the courtyard setting in the heart of the city, inside the gates of the Petőfi Museum and backing onto the Károlyi garden behind, that makes this place so special. The interior is also pleasant, and even nicer when the piano player takes his breaks. Good-sized portions of trad Hungarian fare with mains 1700–3500Ft. Daily 11am–midnight.

Rézkakas V, Veres Pálné utca 3 ⓣ1/318-0038, ⓦwww.rezkakasrestaurant.com. The smart "Golden Cockerel" (as the name translates) is one of the best places to eat in traditional Hungarian style, with an excellent Gypsy band playing away in the corner. Popular with foreign visitors, so expect to pay from 3000Ft up to 7000Ft for a main course. Daily noon–midnight.

Trattoria Toscana V, Belgrád rakpart 13, ⓣ1/327-0045, ⓦwww.toscana.hu. On the Danube riverfront near Szabadság Bridge, this is a favourite spot for authentic Italian cuisine at reasonable prices, and with appealing faux Tuscan surroundings. The atmosphere is relaxed despite the smart business clientele. On Sun from Sept–June, a clown offers entertainment for the kids. Mains from 2400Ft. Daily noon–midnight.

Lipótváros and Újlipótváros

The places reviewed here appear on the map on p.54.

Café Kör V, Sas utca 17 ⓣ1/311-0053, ⓦwww.cafekor.com. Buzzy place near the basilica, with a very relaxed feel and English-speaking staff. Its wines and grilled meats are excellent, as are the salads, and the specials of the day (displayed on a board) are recommended – the roasted pike-perch in garlic is always a favourite. Main courses 2000–4000Ft. The only downside to the intimacy of the place is that smoking is allowed throughout. Booking essential. No credit cards. Mon–Sat 10am–10pm.

Csarnok V, Hold utca 11 ⓣ1/269-4906. Good, down-to-earth Hungarian restaurant that used to serve the workers at the market a few doors along; the clientele is now more upmarket, but its unpretentious feel has been preserved. Specialities are mutton, lamb and bone marrow dishes from 1400Ft upwards, and there are also traditional dishes such as *pacal* (tripe). Mon–Fri 9am–11pm.

Firkász **XIII, Tátra utca 18 ☎1/450-1118.** Done up like a journalists' haunt from the turn of the last century, *Firkász* serves decent traditional Hungarian food, with creamed veg stews and the like at reasonable prices – mains from 2000Ft. Daily noon–midnight.

Govinda **V, Vigyázó Ferenc utca 4 ☎1/473-1310.** Hare Krishna vegetarian restaurant serving good, inexpensive set meals (1800Ft for a large plate), accompanied by the whiff of soporific incense. Mon–Fri 11.30am–8pm, Sat noon–9pm.

Kispozsonyi **XIII, Pozsonyi út 18.** Atmospheric (and smoky) local joint with filling Hungarian dishes; its popularity means you may have to wait for a table. The small terrace affords an escape from the fumes in the summer. Mains 1000–1800Ft. Daily 10am–midnight.

Lou Lou **V, Vigyázó Ferenc utca 4 ☎1/312-4505, ⓦwww.loulourestaurant.com.** A leading contender for Budapest's first Michelin star, and (naturally) expensive. The select French-influenced menu is strong on duck, liver and fish, accompanied by top Hungarian wines. Presentation is excellent, as is the service. Non-smoking section. Mains from 4700Ft, lunch menus 4900Ft. Mon–Fri noon–3pm & 7–11pm, Sat 7–11pm.

Okay Italia **XIII, Szent István körút 20.** A relaxed, lively restaurant that's an old favourite with expats and locals alike, serving up very good pasta and pizza at reasonable prices. Daily noon–midnight.

Pomo D'Oro **V, Arany János utca 9 ☎1/302-6473, ⓦwww.pomodorobudapest.com.** A large, rustic Italian restaurant at the river end of this street, where the interior is split into many different levels, giving it a cosy feel. The woodburning oven turns out excellent pizzas from 1400Ft, while mains are from 1900Ft. A wide range of Italian wines, and some Hungarian too, though all are quite pricey. They serve a small portion – *kisadag* – for children and will provide pencils and paper on request. The deli next door also has seating and serves pasta dishes from 1300Ft. Daily noon–midnight.

Via Luna **V, Nagysándor József utca 1 ☎1/312-8058.** Popular Italian-style restaurant – its name referring to the neighbouring Hold (moon) utca – close to Arany János utca metro station, serving pizzas (from 1400Ft) and good, filling salads. Daily noon–11.30pm.

Terézváros and Erzsébetváros

The places reviewed here appear on the map on p.64.

Belcanto **VI, Dalszínház utca 8 ☎1/269-2786, ⓦwww.belcanto.hu.** Right across from the Opera House, this is a smart place whose distinctive feature is that in the course of the evening the waiters join together for bursts of song, making for a lively atmosphere. They serve good international fare, but with mains starting at 5000Ft, this isn't a cheap evening out. Daily noon–3pm & 6pm–midnight.

Bock Bisztró **VII, Erzsébet körút 43–49 ☎1/321-0340, ⓦwww.bockbisztro.hu.** A great place to eat, both classy and relaxed, with friendly staff and delicious, reasonably priced food (mains 2800–4400Ft), and children's portions at 70 percent of full price. Meat takes pride of place here, in true Hungarian fashion, but there are also modern takes on classic dishes: the Esterházy chicken and smoked duck breast are both recommended. Located within the *Grand Corinthia* hotel, the *Bock* takes its name from one of Hungary's top vintners, József Bock, and its stock includes many labels that you won't find elsewhere in the city. A number of wines can be ordered by the glass. Booking essential. Unobtrusive live guitar or accordion music in the evenings. Mon–Sat noon–midnight.

Bouchon **VI, Zichy Jenő utca 33 ☎1/353-4094.** Pleasant restaurant set up by former Café Kör staff. Matching the Kör would be a challenge, but the friendly manager runs a cheerful place serving traditional Hungarian fare. Mains from 2300Ft, and you can order a wide selection of wines by the glass. Small portions are available at 70 percent of full price. Mon–Sat 9am–11pm.

Carmel **VII, Kazinczy utca 31 ☎1/322-1834, ⓦwww.carmel.hu.** Long-established Jewish restaurant that turned *glatt* kosher in 2008. Their food has improved recently, the decor classier with a/c, and in Aug & Sept they have *klezmer*-style concerts (2000Ft) on Thurs from 8pm. Sun–Thurs noon–11pm, Fri noon–4pm.

Chez Daniel **VI, Szív utca 32 ☎1/302-4039.** Fresh ingredients, including fish, are a plus at this pricey French restaurant run by idiosyncratic master chef Daniel Labrosse, who is brilliant and friendly when in form. In summer things move out into the atmospheric courtyard. Booking recommended. Daily noon–10.30pm.

Eklektika VI, Nagymező utca 30 ⓣ1/266-1226, ⓦwww.eklektika.hu. Laid-back café-restaurant with a youngish clientele and a strong arty feel, with changing displays by local artists on the walls. It's open all day, serving buffet breakfasts, all-you-can-eat lunches, and great suppers at very reasonable prices – mains from 1800Ft. Occasional live jazz, a DJ every Tues, and on Sat the owners promise a surprise event at 9pm. Mon–Fri 10am–midnight, Sat–Sun noon–midnight.

Fausto's Osteria VII, Dohány utca 5 ⓣ1/269-6806, ⓦwww.osteria.hu. This excellent and elegant Italian restaurant was originally opened by master chef Fausto DiVora. Even though he has moved to his new, more upmarket *Fausto's*, off Andrássy út, the service and cooking here remain outstanding. Mains start at 2600Ft, but the three-course chef's menu is just 2800Ft. Both restaurants have the same opening times: Mon–Sat noon–3pm & 5–11pm.

Fészek VII, Kertész utca 36 ⓣ1/322-6043. Housed in an artists' club on the corner of Dob utca, this has a wonderful arcaded courtyard shaded by a huge chestnut tree, and it is worth visiting in summer for the setting alone. Shame the food on the huge menu does not match the surroundings. In winter the restaurant moves into the sparse but elegant interior, and the menu is much shorter. Main courses from 1600Ft. Daily noon–11pm.

Giero VI, Paulay Ede utca 58. The food is almost a sideshow at this highly atmospheric cellar restaurant run by a Roma family, who also provide the music. There are just three tables, as a third of the space is given over to the musicians – who play for themselves, their friends, or for customers if the band likes the look of them. The restaurant's very relaxed with a small menu (which may not be that relevant to what they have on the day) and the prices are also flexible – and cheap. The food is sometimes marvellous and fresh, sometimes less so, but that's beside the point. In summer the *Giero* occasionally turns into a jazz bar. Daily noon–midnight (times flexible).

Il Terzo Cerchio VII, Dohány utca 40 ⓣ1/354-0788. The Third Circle of Dante's hell was full of gluttons, and this Florentine-run pizzeria has its share. It has moved to larger and more elegant premises on the corner of Nyár utca, where the ceiling has been stripped back to reveal the fine brick vaulting. It's popular with Italian visitors, which must be a good sign, and serves up good food at reasonable prices: pastas and pizzas from 1600Ft. Seafood is a speciality – try the linguine with octopus, at 2900Ft. Daily noon–11.30pm.

Két Szerecsen VI, Nagymező utca 14 ⓣ1/343-1984, ⓦwww.ketszerecsen.com. Buzzy place just off Andrássy út, good for coffee and breakfast but also for supper. Excellent starters, including an aubergine spread served on toast. Mains start at 1900Ft and include the interesting breast of duck in a red wine chocolate sauce with mashed potato (2700Ft). They offer a starter and main course, plus half a bottle of wine, for 7500Ft, but the wine list is small and surprisingly expensive. Mon–Fri 8am–1am, Sat–Sun 9am–1am.

Klassz VI, Andrássy út 41 ⓣ1/413-1545. This strikingly decorated restaurant-cum-wine bar is one of the best places in Budapest – *klassz* means "super", which describes it well. Since it's small, popular and does not take reservations, you'll need to arrive early to be sure of a table. Its links with the Budapest Wine Society ensure a choice of top Hungarian vintages, most of which are available by the glass, and the staff can advise on what goes well with what. The duck in honey sauce is delicious (2400Ft), and they also have *mangalica* – a Hungarian breed of hairy pig that's rather in vogue on Budapest menus, but may be a touch fatty for some tastes. Mon–Sat 11.30am–11pm, Sun 11.30am–6pm.

Kőleves VII, Dob utca 26 ⓣ1/322-1011, ⓦwww.koleves.com. The latest incarnation of this restaurant on the corner of Kazinczy utca has a relaxed, art-house vibe but slow service. Mains cost 1500–3700Ft and include veal and chicken dishes (with olive or goat's cheese stuffings, for example) and smoked turkey leg with *sólet* (Jewish baked beans). Menu of the day 900Ft. Mon–Sat 11am–midnight, Sun till 11pm.

Krizia VI, Mozsár utca 12 ⓣ1/331-8711. Small and elegant Italian restaurant, not far from the Opera, that serves fabulous food with mains from 2600Ft and good three-course menus for just 1200–2600Ft. The owner makes his own salami and jams. Mon–Sat noon–3pm & 6.30pm–midnight.

M VII, Kertész utca 48 ☎1/322-3108. Small, wood-panelled place, near the Music Academy and spread over two floors. Boho atmosphere, slow service and pleasant enough food. The menu includes lots of salads and chicken dishes; a starter, main and wine will cost about 3700Ft. Daily noon–midnight.

Marquis de Salade VI, Hajós utca 43 ☎1/302-4086. Cuisine with a strong Azerbaijani flavour, served up in generous portions in this basement restaurant decorated with beautiful Persian carpets. The starters are particularly tasty, and the lamb main dishes are outstanding. The wine list is surprisingly limited and the bottled water is among the most expensive in the city. Expect a three-course meal with wine to come to 8000Ft a head. Daily 11am–midnight.

Menza VI, Liszt Ferenc tér 2 ☎1/413-1482. Good, moderately priced establishment with stylish retro decor, and retro Hungarian dishes too, such as *hagymás rostélyos* (braised steak piled high with onions; 1890Ft) and *kolozsvári töltött káposzta* (stuffed cabbage; 1490Ft) which evoke nostalgic memories among the locals. There's also a two-course lunch menu for 890Ft. It's on popular drinking square Liszt Ferenc tér, however, and some of the area's loud swagger seems to have rubbed off on *Menza*. Daily 10am–midnight.

Olimpia VII, Alpar utca 5 ☎1/321-2805. Small place by the Garay tér market hall with nothing Greek about it except the decor: the new management have concentrated purely on the food, which they serve up in a quirky, personable manner. There is no menu, just a choice of three to six-course meals for up to just 6000Ft, and the rest you leave to them. The dishes are small but the combinations are fascinating and delicious, while wines are spectacular, though not cheap: you can buy by the bottle or ask for a glass of wine to accompany each course. The service is very laid-back – a six-course meal may end up stretching to eight, and can take four hours or more, though lunches are quicker. Booking absolutely essential.

The Városliget

The places reviewed here appear on the map on p.74.

Bagolyvár XIV, Állatkerti körút 2 ☎1/468-3110, ⓦwww.bagolyvar.com. Sister to the *Gundel* (see below), but offering traditional Hungarian family-style cooking at far lower prices. Housed in an intriguing Károly Kós-style building, it aims to recreate the atmosphere of the interwar middle-class home, both in its menu and its service (all the staff are women – reflecting the quaint idea that in those days all women stayed at home). It's an excellent introduction to Hungarian cooking. Mains 2000–3300Ft, with a three-course menu at 3000Ft. Daily noon–11pm.

Gundel XIV, Állatkerti körút 2 ☎1/321-3550, ⓦwww.gundel.hu. Budapest's most famous restaurant offers plush surroundings and an expensive – but good – menu (mains from 5700Ft). The all-you-can-eat Sun brunch (5800Ft) is the cheapest way of getting a taste. Smart dress is required, though ties aren't compulsory for brunch. Booking essential. Daily noon–4pm & 7pm–midnight, Sun brunch 11.30am–3pm. At the side of the building, the *1984 Wine Bar* (Mon–Sat 5–11pm) offers a cheaper selection of *Gundel* cuisine, to accompany a good selection of vintages.

Józsefváros and Ferencváros

The places reviewed here appear on the map on p.82.

Fülemüle VIII, Kőfaragó utca 5 ☎1/266-7947, ⓦwww.fulemule.hu. Popular and relaxed restaurant a few minutes' walk from Rákóczi út, serving typical dishes of middle-class secular Jewish Budapest: *sólet* (beans), goose soup with matzo dumplings, and duck leg with cabbage and "broken" potato. Prices are reasonable, with mains from 2600Ft. Mon–Thurs noon–10pm, Fri–Sat noon–11pm.

Lanzhou VIII, Luther utca 1b ☎1/314-1080. Popular with the local Chinese community – always a good sign in a Chinese restaurant – the *Lanzhou* is excellent value with a large menu of specialities such as spicy tripe. Daily noon–11pm.

Múzeum VIII, Múzeum körút 12 ☎1/267-0375, ⓦwww.muzeumkavehaz.hu. This grand nineteenth-century restaurant, with ceiling frescoes and Zsolnay tiles, is under new management, which can hopefully give its old-school approach a modern twist without losing the high standards in the kitchen. Part of the restaurant has been turned back into a coffee house, serving

▲ Műzeum restaurant

lighter fare and sandwiches. Mains from 2700Ft. Sat lunch menu 3300Ft. Mon–Sat noon–midnight, coffee house section open from 9am.

Soul Café IX, Ráday utca 11–13 ⓣ1/217-6986, ⓦwww.soulcafe.hu. One of the better places to eat on Ráday, offering European fusion cooking - Hungarian, French, Italian and a *soupçon* of North African - and a good selection of Hungarian wines (try the Tüske Pince rosé). Day menu 980Ft, business menu 1980Ft. Daily noon–1am.

Trattoria IX, Ráday utca 16 ⓣ1/215-2888. Another reliable option on Ráday, serving tasty pizza, pasta and antipasto with gusto. Tables outdoors, a/c inside and free wi-fi. Daily noon–midnight.

Várhegy, central Buda and the Tabán

Arcade XII, Kiss János altábornagy utca 38 ⓣ1/225-1969, ⓦwww.arcadebistro.hu. See map, p.91. Upmarket place, with a low-key modern interior and a small terrace, serving excellent international cuisine with a strong French influence. There's also a range of good Hungarian wines. A meal will set you back 9000Ft a head with half a bottle of wine, unless you go for more expensive corks such as the Gere Kopár. Mon–Sun 11am–11pm.

Café Pierrot I, Fortuna utca 14 ⓣ 1/375-6971. See map, p.92. A rare elegant hangout in the Communist era, *Pierrot* remains one of the better places in the Castle area today. It serves good, well-presented food, though the prices are steep by local standards and the easy-listening piano music can get a bit much. Salads from 2800Ft, mains from 3500Ft. Daily 11am–midnight.

Carne di Hall II, Bem rakpart 20 ⓣ1/210-8137, ⓦwww.carnedihall.com. See map, p.91. Under the same management as *Lou Lou* in Pest (see p.162), and serving food that's just as good, even if the pun in the name (a reference to Carnegie Hall) doesn't quite work. Service is leisurely. Delicious steaks and chocolate torte. Mains 2500–4500Ft. Daily noon–midnight.

Csalogány 26 I, Csalogány utca 26 ⓣ1/210-7892, ⓦwww.csalogasny26.hu. See map, p.91. Another excellent new bistro down the hill towards the river from Moszkva tér that has avoided the temptation to go for showiness and high prices. Opened by a former *Lou Lou* chef, it has immediately picked up a deserving reputation for its menu. You may have to wait for your meal, as the exacting chef oversees everything in a very small kitchen. Mains from 2800Ft, lunchtime menu 1200ft for two courses, 1400Ft for three. Booking essential. Mon–Fri noon–3pm & 7pm–midnight, Sat 7pm–midnight.

Gusto's II, Frankel Leó utca ⓣ1/316-3970. See map, p.91. Near the Buda side of Margit híd, this charming little bar serves light meals (and very good tiramisu) at moderate prices – main dishes start at 1500Ft. Booking essential. Mon–Fri 10am–10pm, Sat 10am–4pm.

Horgásztanya I, Fő utca 27 ⓣ1/489-0236, See map, p.91. An enjoyable fish restaurant with a regular clientele and decor that has has remained unchanged for many years – thankfully it's resisted the forces of modernization. Some of the best fish soups in the city are served in generous portions from 900Ft; mains start at 1900Ft. Daily noon–11pm.

Márkus Vendéglő II, Lövőház utca 17 ⓣ1/212-3153. See map, p.91. Close to Moszkva tér, this is a great no-frills place option after a long walk in the Buda Hills. Large portions of traditional Hungarian dishes, including an excellent *Jókai bableves* (a filling, smoky bean soup) and various stuffed turkey dishes. Prices are still pretty reasonable, with soup, a main course and glass of wine at 4100Ft. Menus in English available. Daily noon–midnight.

Rivalda I, Színház utca 5–9 ⓣ1/489-0236. See map, p.92. Unlike so many other places on Várhegy, the *Rivalda* attracts a loyal local clientele. Prices are fairly steep, but in return you get cooking of a high standard (the chicken with mustard maple syrup and the chocolate gateau are especially recommended) and wacky, theatrically inspired decor. Mains from 3400Ft, and two- or three-course lunch menus at 4000Ft. Daily 11.30am–11.30pm.

Tabáni Terasz I, Apród utca 10 ⓣ1/201-1086, ⓦwww.tabaniterasz.hu. See map, p.109. An excellent setting, with the summer terrace offering views up to the Buda Palace, and a cosy interior in winter, too. Large portions, with refreshing variations on traditional dishes, such as duck steak grilled with honey and smoked salt at 3100Ft. Daily noon–midnight.

Óbuda

Kéhli III, Mókus utca 22 ⓣ1/368-0613, ⓦwww.kehli.hu. See map, p.115. One hundred years ago this was the favourite haunt of one of Hungary's great gourmands, the turn-of-the-century writer Gyula Krúdy, and today the *Kéhli* still serves the dishes he loved, such as beef soup with bone marrow on garlic toast (a starter, for 2000Ft). Set in one of the few old buildings in Óbuda to survive the 1960s planning blitz, it's a big place and does attract large groups, but there are plenty of local regulars, too. Most main courses are 3000–4000Ft, and portions are generous; you eat your fill to the accompaniment of a lively Hungarian Gypsy band (from 8pm). Daily noon–midnight.

Kerék III, Bécsi út 103 ⓣ1/250-4261. See map, p.115. There is an unchanging feel to the "Wheel", a small place just near the amphitheatre in southern Óbuda. It serves traditional Hungarian food, such as *bableves füstölt csülökkel* (bean soup with smoked pork knuckle; 750Ft) and *vasi pecsenye* (pork marinated in garlic and milk; 1400Ft) at very reasonable prices. No haute cuisine here, just locals out for a meal. *Srámli* (accordion) music is provided by a couple of old musicians (Mon–Sat from 6pm), and there's outside seating in summer. Daily noon–11pm.

Kisbuda Gyöngye III, Kenyeres utca 34 ⓣ1/368-6402. See map, p.115. Excellent Hungarian food in the elegant surroundings of the "Pearl of Little Buda", which is filled with furniture from a *fin-de-siècle* well-to-do Budapest home. Gentle piano music and small courtyard at the back. Booking essential. Mains 2300–4000Ft. Daily noon–midnight.

14

Coffee houses and patisseries

Daily life in Budapest is still punctuated by the consumption of black coffee drunk from little glasses, though cappuccinos and white coffee are becoming ever more popular. These quintessentially Central European coffee breaks are less prolonged these days than before the war, when the **coffee house** (*kávéház*) was the social club, home and haven for its clientele. Free newspapers were available to the regulars – writers, journalists and lawyers (for whom the cafés were effectively "offices") or posing revolutionaries – with sympathy drinks or credit to those down on their luck. Today's coffee houses and **patisseries** (*cukrászda*) are less romantic but still full of character, whether fabulously opulent, with silver service, or homely and idiosyncratic. However, the tendency to aim at either the rich business visitor and charge high prices (such as at the *Lukács*) or a younger clientele lured in via loud music (at the *Angelika*) is driving away the older regulars and cutting off these institutions from their roots.

The Belváros

The locations of places reviewed below are on the map on p.46.

Astoria Kávéház V, Kossuth utca 19. The *Astoria* hotel's Mirror coffee house/bar dates from the turn of the last century and is still a popular meeting place. Daily 7am–11pm.

Azték V, in the Röser-bazár, a courtyard running between Károly körút 22 and Semmelweis utca 19 ⓦ www.choxolat.hu. Perhaps the best place in the city for chocolate gourmands, selling home-made chocolate as well as imported products (all made with a minimum of sugar) and fabulous hot chocolate – ask for the extra thick variety, which will warm you up on a winter's day. You can sit at the tables inside, or outside in summer in the courtyard. Mon–Fri 7am–7pm, Sat 9am–2pm.

Centrál Kávéház V, Károlyi Mihály utca 9. In its heyday, the decades around World War I, this large coffee house was a popular venue in Budapest's literary scene, and after many years as a dowdy university club, it has now been restored to its former grandeur. Serves a wide range of food throughout the day, from cheap favourites such as creamed spinach to more expensive dishes. Daily 8am–midnight or 1am.

Gerbeaud V, Vörösmarty tér 7. A Budapest institution with a gilded salon and terrace, and good service; always packed with tourists. Daily 9am–9pm.

Lipótváros

See the map on p.54 for the locations of places reviewed here.

Bedő Ház V, Honvéd utca 3. This restored Art Nouveau gem of a building just north of Szabadság tér is a delightful spot for a coffee break. Mon–Fri 8am–6pm, Sat 9am–6pm.

▲ Centrál Kávéház

Europa V, Szent István körút 7. Excellent cakes at this popular coffee house near the Margit híd. Daily 9am–10pm, May–Oct till 11pm

Sport V, Bank utca 5. Seventies furniture and service and good cakes in this fine example of an *ancien-régime* café. Mon–Fri 9am–5pm.

Szalai V, Balassi Bálint utca 4. Old-style cake shop, one of the few remaining in Budapest, serving pastries baked on the premises. Beneath its large gilt-framed mirrors are a few tables where the regulars watch the world pass by. Daily except Tues 9am–7pm, Nov–April closed Mon.

Terézváros, Erzsébetvaros and Józsefváros

See the map on p.64 for the locations of places reviewed below.

Fröhlich VII, Dob utca 22. Excellent kosher patisserie 5min walk from the Dohány utca synagogue, and a great people-watching place. Specialities include the best *flódni* (apple, walnut and poppyseed cake) in the city. Mon–Thurs 9am–6pm, Fri 7.30am–3pm, Sun 10am–4pm; closed Sat & Jewish holidays.

Godot VII, Madách út 8. Lively café serving snacks at lunchtimes, with a comedy theatre upstairs. Mon–Fri 9am–midnight, Sat–Sun 4pm–midnight.

Király VII, Király utca 19. Small patisserie with a few tables, serving excellent pastries, cakes and ice cream. Mon–Fri 9am–8pm, Sat–Sun 10am–7pm.

Lukács VI, Andrássy út 70. One of the city's old coffee houses, this was beautifully restored by the bank with which it now shares the building. However, prices have shot up, sadly ending its status as a popular locals' haunt. Daily 9.30am–7pm.

Mai Manó VI, Nagymező utca 20. Small, friendly, smoky café that spills out onto the street from underneath the Mai Manó Photography Museum. Serves sandwiches, croissants and good coffees. Daily 10am–1am.

Művész VI, Andrássy út 29. There's an air of faded grandeur in this coffee house that's more notable for its decor – chandeliers and gilt – than its rather standard cakes. In summer the inside room gets very stuffy and smoky, with no a/c. Still, the presence of elderly ladies in fur hats bears witness to the venue's success in retaining a loyal clientele over the years. Daily 8am–midnight.

Múzeum Cukrászda VIII, Múzeum körút 10. See map, p.82. Friendly hangout near the National Museum that is usually packed with students. Fresh pastries arrive early in the morning. Open daily 24hr.

New York VII, Erzsébet körút 9-11. This fabulous coffee house was a popular haunt of writers in the early 1900s. Recently restored as part of the *Boscolo* hotel, it has lost none of its magnificence, but high prices mean it has struggled to win back its place among today's impoverished intelligentsia. Daily 10am–midnight.

Buda

See the maps on p.91 and p.122 for the locations of places reviewed below.

Ági Rétes II, Retek utca 19. Best *rétes* in town, all baked on the cosy premises of this patisserie a few yards from the Fény utca market by Moszkva tér. For such a minute place – there is just one table – the range of strudels is impressive: down a coffee as you try the plum (*szilva*), cheese, (*túrós*) cherry (*meggyes*) or poppyseed (*mákos*) in different combinations. Mon–Fri 10am–6pm, Sat 10am–2pm.

Angelika I, Batthyány tér 7. Atmospheric old coffee house in a former convent – even the funky refit with new furniture, staff and music can't totally destroy the place, though you are less likely to get old ladies meeting for their regular coffees these days. Also has a lively terrace. Mon–Sat 9am–11pm, Sun 9am–midnight.

Artigiana Gelati XII, Csaba utca 8. Exotic ice cream flavours and the best quality in town, a couple of minutes up the road from Moszkva tér. Tues–Sun 10.30am–8pm.

Cziniel III, Nánási út 55. Large, popular café just north of the Roman ruins at Aquincum, with excellent ice creams and chestnut *puré*. A good place to bring children too, as it has its own play area, and handy if you've been on the riverbank enjoying the bars and restaurants on the Római-part or want to head further out from Aquincum. Daily May–Sept 9am–10pm, Oct–April 9am–7.30pm.

Daubner III, Szépvölgyi út 29. It is a trek to get to this patisserie in Óbuda, and it has no tables, but the place is always crowded, especially at weekends, when people will patiently queue up for its delicious cakes, such as the plum slipper (*szilvás papucs*) or pumpkin-seed scone (*tökmagos pogácsa*). The family was said to have sold the whole business off in 2008 – recipes and all. It remains to be seen if standards fall. Tues–Sun 9am–7pm.

Rétes Büfé XII, Normafa. This hut at the top of the Buda Hills by the old tree where Bellini's aria was sung (see p.123) is a place of pilgrimage for families, walkers and (in winter) skiers who flock to the hills. You can expect to queue for the excellent *rétes* on fine days. The *Rétes Kert* across the road is run by the same crowd. Daily 10am–5pm.

Ruszwurm I, Szentháromság tér 7. Near the Mátyás Church in the Castle District, this diminutive Baroque coffee house can be so packed that it's almost impossible to get a seat in summer. Delicious cakes and ices. Daily 10am–8pm.

15

Bars and clubs

Budapest's nightlife scene is small – spend a few evenings drinking and clubbing and you'll be spotting familiar faces. The scene centres on two main areas in Pest: **Liszt Ferenc tér** (the place to see and be seen, where most of the larger bars have big screens for football) and semi-pedestrianized **Ráday utca**, running down from Kalvin tér, which, with its innumerable cafés and terraces, styles itself "Budapest's Soho". There's also another concentration of bars in the VII district, set up in condemned buildings: most of them move from year to year, but they have become an established feature. Finally, there are the outdoor bars, mainly on Margit-sziget and around the river.

Budapest's bars can be divided into three kinds: the *borozó* (wine bar), the *söröző* (beer bar) and the newer, livelier places that don't bother with such distinctions. The majority of **wine bars** are nothing like their counterparts in the West, being mainly working men's watering holes offering such humble snacks as *zsíros kenyér* (bread and pork dripping with onion and paprika). Conversely, **beer halls** (*söröző*) are often quite upmarket, striving to resemble an English pub or a German *bierkeller*, and serving full meals. And then there are the *kert* bars, "garden bars"' often based in derelict houses with a cheerful bohemian feel. These may have live music or DJs, table football (*csocsó*), film screenings and other attractions, and they serve whatever people are drinking, as well as *pálinka*, the powerful Hungarian schnapps (see p.232). Many of the *kert* bars are in the VII and VIII district, where a plentiful supply of wrecked buildings stand waiting the developer's hammer – places such as *Szimplakert* that have managed to survive in spite of local protests at the noise levels. Enduringly popular places such as *West Balkán* move from site to site but retain their name – a look in the listings magazines (see p.32) will usually reveal their new location should they move. Of the **outdoor summer bars**, you'll find several at the southern end of Margit-sziget, while *Zöld Pardon* is down near Petőfi híd – many of them have dancefloors, and charge a small entry fee.

The **club** scene is especially varied in the summer, when it expands into several large outdoor venues, and there are also one-off events held in the old Turkish baths or sites further out of town (advertised via promotional posters at bus stops). **DJs** to look out for include Sterbinszky and Kühl, the more alternative Naga and Mango, and anything with the Tilos Rádió stamp on it. Expect to pay 500Ft upwards to get into a club, and be warned that it's worth keeping on the right side of the bouncers.

Most places open around lunchtime and stay open until after midnight, unless otherwise stated, though bars in residential areas have to close their terraces at 10pm. There is a good network of night buses (see p.28) that can help you make your way home, taxis are easy to flag down, and the streets are generally safe.

Drinking etiquette

Hungarian has a variety of tongue-twisting ways to **toast** fellow drinkers. *Egészségedre*! ("Your health") is the most common, but it's usually said to one person whom you know well. To a group, you might use *Egészségetekre*!; if your acquaintance is more formal, it would be *Egészségére*! To friends, a simple *Szia*! is fine. For more on language, see p.232.

Clinking glasses of **beer** used to be frowned upon, as it was said that this was how the Austrians celebrated the execution of the Hungarian generals in 1849; the "right" Hungarian way was to bang your glass on the table before raising it to your lips. These days, though, people say that there was a 150-year time limit on that taboo, and clinking beer-glasses is back.

See p.159 for warnings about **rip-offs** in restaurants, which apply equally to bars. Most bars do not take **credit cards**. Bear in mind that Budapest's bars are very **smoky** – the average Hungarian adult gets through more than 3000 cigarettes a year, and most of them seem to be smoked in late-night bars. Hungary is expected to follow the EU line on smoking bans in the near future, but the government is dithering over when this will happen. Note that the gay and lesbian scene is covered separately, in chapter 16.

The Belváros

For the locations of the places reviewed here, see the map on p.46.

Mélypont V, Magyar utca 23. A retro basement bar with a strong flavour of 1970s Hungary, "Rock Bottom" is full of memorabilia that won't mean much to the average non-Hungarian. Popular with a youngish crowd, and has table football. Mon–Fri 4pm–1am, Sat 6pm–1am, Sun 6pm–midnight.

Spoon V, on the river by the Inter-Continental hotel, ⓦwww.spooncafe.hu. Set in a boat on the Danube in a great setting, looking across to the Lanchíd and the Buda Palace; the men's toilets have grandstand views of the Royal Palace. There's also a restaurant, which is good but expensive. Daily noon–2am.

Lipótváros

For the locations of the places reviewed here, see the map on p.54.

Tokaji Borozó V, Falk Miksa utca 32. Lively, smoky old-style cellar wine bar serving wines from the Tokaj region in northeast Hungary – at 100Ft for a small glass this is not top-end stuff – as well as snacks such as *lepcsánka* (potato pancakes) and *zsíros kenyér*. Mon–Fri noon–9pm.

Trocadero Café V, Szent István körút 15. Excellent Latin music and dancing at this club just up from Nyugati Station. Entry fee varies. Daily 9pm–5am.

Terézváros and Erzsébetváros

For the locations of the places reviewed here, see the map on p.64.

Castro Bistro VII, Madách tér 3. This smoky bar with a misleadingly Cuban name has moved to a new location very close to Deák tér. Good music, beer and Serbian food attract a mixed crowd of Hungarians and foreigners. Free wi-fi. Mon–Thurs 10am–midnight, Fri 10am–1am, Sat noon–1am, Sun 2pm–midnight.

Ellátó VII, Klauzál tér 2. Set up in 2007 and an instant success, its dilapidated look of bare bricks and old paintwork gives it a relaxed feel. The kitchen serves up decent retro dishes, here too with a strong Serbian flavour. Mon–Wed noon–2am, Thurs–Fri noon –4am, Sat–Sun 5pm–4am.

Gül Baba Szeráj VI, Paulay Ede utca 55. Furnished with Turkish kelims, cushions and lamps, with shishas, wine-tasting nights with food (3500Ft) and muted reggae music, this is a nice place to chill out and talk. Daily 10am–midnight.

Katapult VII, Dohány utca 1. Small, popular and very red bar opposite the big synagogue. Mon–Sat 10am–2am, Sun 2pm–midnight.

Kiadó VI, Jókai tér 3. This popular new bar is across Andrássy út from the places around Liszt Ferenc tér, but feels as though it's in another city – much more laid back than its neighbours, with few pretensions. The ground floor rooms are open all day from 10am, breakfast and snacks are served during the day; the other door to the right leads downstairs to a cosy bar with sofas, open from 5pm. Both upstairs and downstairs are divided into smaller intimate sections, giving the place a friendly feel. Open daily till 1am.

Kuplung VI, Király utca 46. A surprisingly large bar down a narrow alleyway in what was once a police stable and later a moped repair shop (the name means "clutch"). Has table football (*csocsó*) and in its highly soundproofed side-room hosts regular live music and DJs. Daily till 4am.

Morrison's VI, Révay utca 25 ⓦ www.morrisons.hu. A long-established dance bar that's very popular with students who clearly like its heaving, sweaty atmosphere. The opening of an off-shoot, *Morrison's II*, at V, Honvéd utca 40, has hardly helped to alleviate the crush. Entry 500Ft after 9pm. Mon–Sat 7pm–4am.

Moyo VI, Liszt Ferenc tér 10 ⓦ www.moyocafe.hu. One of the smaller bars on the north side of this popular partying square that distinguishes itself from its bigger rivals by its friendly staff and good food. Outside seating, too. Daily 11am–midnight.

Old Man's Music Pub VII, Akácfa utca 13 ⓦ www.oldmans.hu. Large, popular joint near Blaha Lujza tér, with live local bands every evening 9–11pm. Daily 3pm–dawn.

Piaf VI, Nagymezo utca 25. This old favourite is basically a small ground-floor bar and cellar frequented by the odd Hungarian film star and lots of wannabes, with occasional jazz or rock live sets. Entry 800Ft. Daily 10pm–6am.

Pótkulcs VI, Csengery utca 65b ⓦ www.potkulcs.hu. There's no sign on the small metal door from the street at 65b, but go through and you'll find yourself in a shaded yard, with the bar straight ahead, and a room with sofas and table football off to the left. The "Spare Key" is a laid-back place that attracts a good range of visitors, and the music is excellent too, ranging from *klezmer* and Roma bands to underground, folk and jazz. Gets very smoky in winter, but has outside seating when it gets warmer. Mon–Wed & Sun 5pm–1.30am, Thurs–Sat 5pm–2.30am.

Sark VII, Klauzál tér 14. Small, heaving bar, decorated with massive murals. DJs and good live music (world/*klezmer*/Roma) downstairs from Sept–May. From June–Sept much of the action moves to the *Sark kert* at the southern tip of Margit-sziget – ask at the bar for directions. Daily noon–3am.

Sirály VI, Király utca 50 ⓦ www.siraly.co.hu. The "Seagull" bar is located in one of those unoccupied buildings that could at any time be closed down, part of an arty cultural centre which seems to rev up the bohemian, lefty feel. Regular jazz and theatre downstairs. Daily 10am–midnight.

Sixtus VII, Nagy Diófa utca 26. The "Sistine Chapel" has long been a smoky favourite with sections of the expat community, but has a good local following, too. It's a cosy place, with just two rooms. Mon–Fri 5pm–2am, Sat 8am–2am.

Szimplakert VII, Kazinczy utca 14 ⓦ www.szimpla.hu. One of the oldest *kert* bars, spilling over from room to room and with good music, regular film showings (600Ft) in the garden and free wi-fi access (noon–7pm). It has become a standard stop for stag parties, and the main courtyard is packed and noisy at night from mid-May onwards, though it makes a delightful and quiet refuge by day. Several bars (one for cocktails) and bicycle storage. Daily noon–midnight.

▲ Szimplakert

Szóda VII, Wesselényi utca 18 ⓦ www.szoda.com. Busy bar with a retro look behind the main synagogue, with pleasantly laid-back music from the DJs and inexpensive drinks; they also serve food and have free wi-fi access. Mon–Fri 9am–midnight, Sat & Sun 2pm–midnight or later.

Vian VI, Liszt Ferenc tér 11. Less pretentious than the others on this posiest of squares, with pleasant staff, a relaxed atmosphere and good food. Free wi-fi access. Daily 9am–midnight.

Joszefváros and Ferencváros

For the locations of the places reviewed here, see the map on p.82.

Corvintető VIII, Blaha Lujza tér 1–2 ⓦwww.corvinteto.hu. Inspired rooftop bar above the old Corvin department store on this busy square, this is a popular new venture that will stay open until the building is redeveloped, which could be any time in the next couple of years. You take a lift on the left-hand side of the building – on the way up the lift attendant offers shots of Unicum, the medicinal national drink. Live music or DJs from 9pm. Daily 6pm–5am.

Csiga VIII, Vásár utca 2. By the Rákóczi tér market hall, this friendly, smoky corner bar is popular with locals and expats. Good food and occasional live music. Mon–Sat 11am–1am.

Jelen VIII, Márkus Emilia utca 2–4. Another in a succession of great, friendly bars run by Dutch resident Hans, with high ceilings and good music; gets packed as the evening progresses. Live music on Thurs, funk DJs on Fri, and good *pálinka* and food. It's in the far right-hand corner of the same former department store as *Corvintető* (see above). Sun–Wed 4pm–2am, Thurs–Sat 4pm–4am.

Paris-Texas IX, Ráday utca 22. Stylish bar with pool tables and a good atmosphere. Mon–Fri 10am–3am, Sat & Sun 1pm–3am.

Trafó Bar Tangó IX, Liliom utca 41 ⓦwww.trafo.hu. The cellar bar at the vibrant Trafó arts centre has live music and DJs, and gets very crowded. Daily 6pm–4am.

Buda

Bambi I, Frankel Leó utca 2–4. See map, p.91. One of the few surviving socialist-realist bars, with stern waitresses and red plastic-covered seats. They serve breakfast, omelettes, snack lunches, cakes and alcohol all day long. Mon–Fri 7am–9pm, Sat & Sun 9am–8pm.

Kecskeméti Borozó II, Széna tér. See map, p.91. By Moszkva tér, on the corner of Retek utca, this is a crowded, sweaty and smoky stand-up wine bar. A notice on the wall reads "We do not serve drunks", but that would rule out most of the people inside. However, they do serve that staple of Hungarian bar fare, *zsíros kenyér*. Mon–Sat 9am–11pm.

Lánchíd Söröző I, Fő utca 4. See map, p.91. Atmospheric little bar, handily placed at the Buda end of the Lánchíd. It's a quiet place in daytime, frequented by tourists and the odd regular, but in the evening Robi, the manager, brings in concert DVDs – he loves his music, as the photos of him with BB King and others on the walls testify. Excellent toasted sandwiches. Daily 10am–midnight.

Libella XI, Budafóki út 7. See map, p.109. Friendly unmarked spot near the *Gellért Hotel*. Popular with the student crowd from the nearby Technical University for its bar snacks, chess and draughts. Mon–Fri 8am–1am, Sat–Sun noon–1am.

Móri Borozó I, Fiáth János utca 16. See map, p.91. Cheap neighbourhood venue just up from Moszkva tér, with darts and bar billiards in the room at the far end. June–Aug daily 4–11pm; Sept–May Mon–Sat 2–11pm, Sun 2–9pm.

Platán I, Döbrentei tér. See map, p.109. Popular meeting place near the river, under the plane trees at the foot of the Tabán, with outdoor tables. Serves sandwiches and has wi-fi access. Daily till 10pm.

Zöld Pardon XI, Goldmann György tér ⓦwww.zp.hu. See map, p.82. Camden Lock by the Danube: a large, heaving outdoor club near the Petőfi bridgehead, where you can dance to drum 'n' bass, deep house and jungle. With an average age of 16 (lots of 14-year-olds), the clientele is all about texting and posing. Live music at 9pm, six bars (one cocktails-only). Bring some 100Ft coins to get through the turnstiles; entry 200Ft. Daily 9am–6am.

Óbuda and Margit-sziget

Cha-Cha-Cha Terasz XIII, Athletics Club, Margit-sziget. See map, p.119. The best of the Margit-sziget outdoor bars, at the southern end of the island: turning off Margit híd it is the second bar along on the left. This buzzy place is the summer venue of an established bar on Bajcsy-Zsilinszky út, and plays 1970s and 1980s music (Hungarian and Western) for dancing and Sgt Pepper style videos (or sports TV) on the big screen.

Stag tourism

"Kindly do not vomit from the balcony", plead signs in Krakow, Bratislava and Tallinn, where locals are tired of the drunken antics of **stag-party tourists**, but even though Budapest is an increasingly popular destination for stag and hen trips, it's yet to be spoiled by their presence. The city offers plenty of activities, from pub crawls and wine-tastings to tank-driving and paint-ball, to keep groups entertained. Pole-dancing lessons and spa makeovers are more likely to be of interest to **hen parties**.

If you're visiting as part of a stag party, bear in mind taxi drivers have an infallible nose for stags and rob them blind given a chance, so arrange a hotel and a transfer from the airport before you arrive. Telling a driver to "take us to a club" is a sure way to end up at a Mafia-run joint with rip-off prices – only ask for clubs or bars by name. Many tour operators offer a guided pub crawl for stag groups that ends in a lap dancing club; the *4Play Lounge* (VIII, József körút 60, Ⓦwww.4playlounge.com) and *Marilyn's* (VIII, Baross utca 4) have free entry, the lowest-priced drinks (from 3000Ft) and no trouble, unlike most other such places. Packages can be arranged through Budapest-based Stag Republic (Ⓦwww.stagrepublic.co.uk).

Though it opens mid-May, it doesn't really come alive till mid-June. Late May–Sept, daily, 6pm–2am.

Római-part III, Rómaifürdő. See map, p.115. This is not one bar, but a whole string of open-air bars and cheap eateries lining the riverbank north of Óbuda; the food is mainly of the deep-fried meat and fish with chips variety. Take the HÉV train from Batthyány tér to Rómaifürdő and it is a 10min walk down to the river. Noon until 10pm.

Sark kert XIII, Margit-sziget. See map, p.119. Another summer island bar: walking up from Margit híd it's on the right after *Cha-Cha-Cha*. Can feel like an unfinished campsite at a Red Sea resort: fairly basic in its seating and facilities, but it's a lively place once the crowds arrive. Has occasional live music. Late May–Sept, daily, 6pm–2am.

16

Gay Budapest

Budapest's **gay scene** has taken wing in recent years, with new overtly gay clubs replacing the old covert meeting places, and the appearance of a trilingual monthly listings magazine, *Mások* ("Outsiders"). This greater prominence is also reflected in law – the age of consent is 14 for homosexuals and heterosexuals alike, and Parliament is moving towards a legal framework for homosexual couples, though if the conservative Fidesz party gets back into power, expect that to be delayed.

These changes are gradual rather than radical, though; while Budapest is a cosmopolitan city, Hungarian society at large is socially conservative. Gays must still tread warily and lesbians even more so. The Hungarian word for gay is *meleg* – "warm"; *buzi* is the commonly used pejorative term – it derives from the word *buzeráns*, which has the same roots as "bugger".

The Budapest gay scene is very male-dominated. Perhaps the best spot for lesbians is the *Eklektika* bar (see p.176), though there is also a women-only lesbian group, Ösztrosokk, that meets at Tűzoltó utca 22 on the last Saturday of every month (7pm–4am; entry 500–600Ft; Ⓦwww.osztrosokk.femfatal.hu). The **website** Ⓦwww.gayguide.net has the latest on gay accommodation, bars, clubs, restaurants, baths and events in the city. The largest gay and lesbian organization in town is **Háttér** (Ⓦwww.hatter.hu), which runs a **helpline** (daily 6–11pm; Ⓣ1/329-3380) that can give advice and information on events – although some of the operators only speak Hungarian.

The major event in the gay calendar is **Gay Pride Budapest**, a well-established four-day festival taking place in late June or early July. Incorporating a varied programme of film screenings, public discussion forums and gay parties, it culminates in the colourful Pride March at the weekend, which wends its way along Andrássy út, down to the Danube – or more recently up to the Városliget. The march was disrupted in 2007 and 2008 by right-wing extremists – this may well happen again so, if you're planning to be there, watch out for any signs of trouble.

Bars and restaurants

Most of the bars listed on the next page levy an **entry fee** or set a minimum consumption level – being gay in Budapest is an expensive privilege. Some venues give you a card when you enter, on which all your drinks are written down; you pay for your drinks and the entry fee as you leave. Be warned that if you lose the card, you'll have to pay a lot of money. You can find listings for places and events in English in the gay freebie monthly *Na Végre*, found at most gay venues.

The Belváros

The places reviewed here appear on the map on p.46.

Action V, Magyar utca 42 ⓦwww.action.gay.hu. The most hardcore of the gay bars, full of young men looking for one-night stands. The entrance is hard to find – it's 15m along from the big "A" sign on the door. Dark room, video room and live shows on Fri (700Ft entry). Minimum consumption 1600Ft. Daily 9pm–5am.

Amstel River Café V, Párizsi utca 6. Not on the river but in the middle of the Belváros, this friendly Dutch-style pub-restaurant attracts a large foreign clientele and is popular with gays. Daily noon–midnight.

Capella V, Belgrád rakpart 23 ⓦwww.capellacafe.hu. Drag queens and lots of kitsch, with decor as outrageous as the acts. It's become a well-known haunt, and prices are highish. Popular with straights, though more gays come on Wed. Drag shows start at midnight and 1am. Entry 500Ft Wed & Thurs, 1500Ft Fri & Sat, up to 3500Ft on special occasions. Daily 10pm–5am.

Club 93 V, Vas utca 2. A cheap pizzeria just off Rákóczi út, popular with gays and lesbians. The gallery and window seating make it a good place to people-watch. Daily 11.30am–midnight.

CoXx (formerly Chaos) V, Dohány utca 38 ⓦwww.coxx.hu. The most cultured of the gay bars, this men-only venue is a friendly place to meet. The ground floor is a gallery and internet café; downstairs holds a dancefloor, video rooms and numerous other spaces. Minimum consumption 1000Ft. Daily 9pm–4am.

Elsewhere in the city

Eklektika VI, Nagymező utca 30 ⓣ1/266-1226, ⓦwww.eklektika.hu. See map, p.64. Laid-back lesbian-run café/restaurant that has moved to new, larger premises with a more turn-of-the-century feel. It serves great food all day and at very reasonable prices, and has occasional jazz and a DJ every Tues; on Sat the owners promise a surprise event at 9pm. No entry fee. Mon–Fri 10am–midnight, Sat–Sun noon–midnight.

Fenyögyöngye II, Szépvölgyi út 155 ⓣ1/325-9783. See map, p.115. This restaurant is gay-owned, not that many who go there know that. It's at the last stop of the #65 bus from Kolosy tér in Óbuda. Good Hungarian food, polite service. Daily noon–11pm.

Le Café M V, Nagysándor József utca 3, ⓦwww.lecafem.com. See map, p.54. The former *Mystery Bar* is a small, friendly place near the Arany János utca metro, for talking rather than dancing (there's no disco). It's a good place to start or end the evening. Internet café too, with wi-fi. Free entry. Mon–Fri 4pm–4am, Sat & Sun 6pm–4am.

Baths

Budapest's first private gay **bath** is Magnum Sauna & Gym at VIII, Csepreghy utca 2 (Mon–Thurs 1pm–1am, Fri 1pm–4am and open continuously Sat 1pm–Mon 1am; 1800–2500Ft; ⓣ1/267-2532, ⓦwww.magnumszauna.hu), near the Ferenc körut metro stop. It opened in 2001 and has a steam room and dry sauna, as well as a gym and numerous smaller spaces. Gay activity in the public steam baths was dealt a blow by a TV report in early 2005 showing video footage of gay encounters, taken secretly in the Király baths. Swimming costumes are at present compulsory at the Király and the baths are patrolled, so that action is not as widespread as it once was, but there's still more here than at the other public steam baths. The sun terrace at the Palatinus strand and the roof terrace at the Széchenyi remain popular gay meeting places. Note that increased entry fees mean that you see fewer young local men and more tourists in the baths.

From the dazzling Roma violinists who inspired Brahms *Hungarian Dances* to Márta Sebestyén's soaring voice in the *English Patient* film score, Hungarian music has long exerted a fascination over foreigners, and remains one of Budapest's greatest cultural assets. For the Hungarian people – a Magyar island in a sea of Slavs – music is a crucial means of expressing identity, while the constant exchange with the region's other musical genres – Slav, Germanic, Romanian, Jewish and Roma – has resulted in a fusion of styles that keeps the contemporary scene as vibrant as ever.

Art Nouveau entrance hall, Music Academy ▲

Statue of Liszt, Liszt Ferenc tér ▼

Iván Fischer ▼

Classical heights

Hungary's roll call of home-grown classical icons is out of all proportion to the size of the population: distinguished **conductors** such as Sir Georg Solti and George Széll, great **musicians**, from Joseph Szigeti to András Schiff, and the celebrated triumvirate of **composers**, Ferenc (Franz) Liszt, Béla Bartók and Zoltán Kodály, who shaped Hungary's old musical traditions into their modern form. In fact, it was **Liszt** – who considered himself a Hungarian despite not speaking the language – who founded Budapest's Music Academy, which still turns out the excellent musicians you can catch in the city's concert halls: see Chapter 17 for details of the best venues.

The pick of the larger orchestras are the privately funded **Budapest Festival Orchestra** (Ⓦwww.bfz.hu), which has won accolades all around the world under its conductor **Iván Fischer**; and the **National Philharmonic**, conducted by the pianist **Zoltán Kocsis**. Look out also for performances by three excellent chamber orchestras: the Liszt Ferenc, the Budapest Strings (*Budapesti Vonósok*) and the Weiner Száz Orchestra; and Budapest's leading Baroque group, the Orfeo Orchestra under György Vashegyi.

Probably the best known Hungarian **soloist** today is the pianist András Schiff, but you'll be lucky to catch him in Budapest as tickets for his concerts are hard to come by (and he's now based in Britain). Other internationally renowned pianists who regularly perform include Tamás Vasary, Péter Frankl, Desző Ránki, Gábor Csalog and Kocsis himself. The cellist Miklós Perényi is an old hand on Budapest's classical circuit while other names to look out for include the violinists Barnabás Kelemen and József Lendvai, the cellist László Fenyő and the brilliant pianist Gergely Bogányi. Finally, the organist Xavier Varnus deserves a special mention: his showy technique and unusual approach, performing variations on any tune the audience names, result in packed venues.

Living folk

Far from withering away with the peasant culture that spawned it, **folk** has proved a surprisingly resilient genre. Back in the 1960s, when the Communist party stifled any independent initiatives and when anything national in character smacked of anti-Communism, folk was reduced to sanitized performances by large ensembles. Come the gentle liberalization of the early 1970s, a group of musicians led by Béla Halmos and Ferenc Sebő decided to start a **táncház** or "dance house" in Budapest, modelled on traditional Hungarian village barn dances. Following in the footsteps of Bartók and Kodály, they recorded old folk tunes and traditional dance steps and recreated them in the *táncház*, teaching Budapestis the dances rather than just performing them on stage, and so reintroducing a whole generation to their roots.

The *táncház* quickly caught on, and developed as a kind of counter-culture for city dwellers; thirty years later, the fall of Communism has removed the movement's edgy, rebellious image (today's youth are more likely to go to a rave or catch a band at an outdoor venue like Zöld Pardon) but it's still going strong. The music is enticingly raw and earthy, and the atmosphere relaxed – you don't have to dress up, and anyone is welcome. Besides the weekly dance houses (see p.180), the biggest event in the folk calendar is the national dance gathering during the Budapest Spring Festival (see p.32).

▲ Táncház workshop

▼ Alvin és a Mókusok performing at Zöld Pardon

Roby Lakatos ▲

Restaurant Gypsy band ▼

Roma rhythms

One major development in Hungary's post-Communist music scene has been the emergence of **Roma (Gypsy) music**. Surprisingly, given the Roma's reputation as instrumental virtuosos, the traditional music in rural Vlach Gypsy communities uses no instruments, relying instead on oral gymnastics and percussion. It was first performed for a wider public by the band Kalyi Jag, and their distinctive sound has inspired many groups.

A very different Roma tradition is the music played in Hungarian restaurants by members of the urban Romungro Gypsies (see p.157). This style has spawned some brilliant instrumentalists outside the tradition, such as the cimbalom player Kálmán Balogh and the Brussels-based Roby Lakatos, the latest in a dynasty of fiddlers that dates back to the eighteenth century. However, in recent years a decline in demand for restaurant bands has sent younger Romungro musicians in a new direction: **Roma jazz**. Players in their early twenties or younger are taking the jazz world by storm; those in the know rate Gábor Bolla as one of the finest tenor saxophone players in Europe.

Besides, with the growth in world music the musical divisions that used to split the Romungro and Vlach Roma are far less distinct now, as musicians from both traditions get together to move in new directions: the violinist and accordionist Róbert Farkas and bands such as the fusion group Nomada are busy reshaping Roma urban traditions. Catch any of them while you are in Budapest, in venues such as the Gödör Klub (see p.180) and you'll see that the skills that fascinated Brahms are as strong as ever today.

Entertainment

Live **music** is one of Budapest's strengths: the country has a huge depth of talent (see *Hungarian music* colour section for more), and most evenings you can choose from classical, folk and jazz performances. The city also boasts some stunning **cinemas** and **theatres** that are worth visiting for their architecture alone. If you are undeterred by the language barrier, an evening at the theatre can be a rewarding experience. Language is less of a problem at cinemas, with foreign films often screened in their original language.

If you can't get tickets for a performance from one of the ticket offices it is always worth persevering with the staff at the venue's ticket office or door, as there is often some way in, even if it costs a bit extra – for instance, the Music Academy puts aside tickets each performance for a fire and a police officer, which are often not used, and it also has space on its top balcony.

Arts centres and multi-purpose venues

The venues listed below are used for a variety of concerts and other entertainment events. Bear in mind that many arts centres close for the summer.

A38 XI, Pázmány Péter sétány Ⓣ**1/464-3940,** Ⓦ**www.a38.hu.** Housed on a boat that was reputedly given to Hungary in return for writing off the Ukrainian debt and is moored on the Buda side of the river, just below Petőfi híd, it has a separate admission charge (500Ft) for each of its three decks, where top international and Hungarian performers play rock, jazz, folk and world music.

Ticket outlets

Tickets for most big music and theatre events are available from several outlets in the city – the most accessible ones are listed below. Note that there's often a small handling fee slapped onto ticket prices for major international shows.

Broadway ticket office XIII, Hollán Ernő utca 10. Ⓣ1/340-4040. Mon–Fri 11am–6pm.

Cultur-Comfort VI, Paulay Ede utca 31 Ⓣ1/322-0000 Ⓦwww.cultur-comfort.hu. Near the Opera and next door to the Hotel Pest. Mon–Fri 9am–6pm.

Rózsavölgyi Record Shop V, Szervita tér 5, near Deák tér. Mon–Fri 10am–6pm, Sat 10am–3pm.

Thália VI, Nagymező utca 19, next door to the Operetta Theatre Ⓣ1/428-0791. Mon–Fri 10am–6pm, Sat 10am–4pm.

TicketExpress VI, Andrássy út 18 Ⓣ06/30-3030999, Ⓦwww.tex.hu. A few doors down from the Opera House. Mon–Fri 10am–6.30pm, Sat 10am–3pm.

Millenáris Park II, Fény utca 20–22 ⓣ1/336-4000, ⓦwww.millenaris.hu. The Fogadó concert hall here regularly hosts good concerts and festivals, some featuring international acts. In summer, concerts are held on the park's outdoor stages.

Palace of Arts (Művészetek palotája) IX, Komor Marcell utca 1 ⓣ1/555-3000, ⓦwww.mupa.hu. This substantial complex on the riverbank in southern Pest has a top-of-the-range concert hall, theatre and museum, and as the shop-window for the capital's culture scene, it sees a superb range of concerts, attracting the top international classical, jazz and world music orchestras and acts.

Petőfi Csarnok XIV, Zichy Mihály út 14 ⓣ1/363-3730, ⓦwww.petoficsarnok.hu. On the edge of the Városliget, this big hall is often used by local and international rock and jazz groups, as well as hosting weekend flea markets and occasional craft fairs.

Trafó IX, Liliom utca 41 ⓣ1/215-1600, ⓦwww.trafo.hu. A dynamic contemporary arts centre in a former transformer station, it pulls in full houses with concerts and theatre and dance performances, by Hungarian and foreign artistes. Good bar downstairs.

Classical music, opera and ballet

The city offers a wide variety of **classical music** performances, with several concerts most nights, especially during the Budapest Spring and Autumn festivals (see pp.32–33 respectively). Hungary's strong traditions in classical music ensure that standards are high (see *Hungarian music* colour section).

You can enjoy **opera** and **ballet** in Budapest at a very reasonable price, even treating yourself to several glasses of (Hungarian) champagne in the bar during the interval. Most opera productions are in Hungarian, a custom introduced by Gustav Mahler when he was director of the Opera House, which remains the principal venue (the box office is inside the main doors or, if they are closed, round on the left-hand side of the building in Dalszinház utca; Mon–Sat 11am–5pm, Sun 4–7pm). Performances are also held at the nearby Thália Theatre, while the other big opera venue, the Modernist Erkel Theatre in Köztársaság tér, is undergoing restoration and may be open in time for its centenary in 2011.

One genre that has long appealed to the Hungarian spirit is **operetta**, with Hungarians making a major contribution to the turn-of-the-century Viennese tradition through composers such as Ferenc Lehár and Imre Kálmán. Lehár's *The Merry Widow* and Kálmán's *The Csárdás Princess* still draw the crowds with their combination of grand tunes, extravagant staging and romantic comedy in the suitably over-the-top Operetta Theatre.

Besides the key venues listed below, a few places of worship regularly host concerts, among them the church on **Kálvin tér** (see p.84); the **Lutheran Church** on Deák tér (see p.52; the programme includes free performances of Bach before Easter, details of which are posted by the church entrance); and the **Dohány utca synagogue** (see p.68). The **Mátyás Church** on Várhegy (see p.93) stages choral or organ recitals on Fridays and Saturdays between June and September (from 8pm), and less frequently the rest of the year.

The opera, theatre and concert halls take a **summer break** at the end of May, reopening in mid-September; there is a summer season of concerts at open-air venues, including the outdoor stage on Margit-sziget (see p.120), the **Dominican Yard** of the *Hilton* hotel (see p.95) in the Castle District, and the **Vajdahunyad Castle** in the Városliget (see p.77), though the music they offer is fairly mainstream.

A comprehensive listing, in Hungarian, of classical music events can be found at ⓦwww.koncertkalendarium.hu, and in the free monthly *Koncert Kalendárium*, available from ticket offices or in listings magazines (see p.32). Regular concerts are held at the following venues.

Bartók Memorial House (Bartók Emlékház) II, Csalán utca 29 ⓣ1/394-2100, ⓦwww.bartokmuseum.hu. Concerts – not just of the music of Bartók – are held in the villa where the composer used to live, most Fri at 6pm but also on other days. Tickets are either included in the entry fee or are up to a modest 2000Ft.

Budapest Operetta Theatre (Budapesti Operettszínház) VI, Nagymező utca 17 ⓣ1/312-4866, ⓦwww.operett.hu. The magnificently refurbished home of Hungarian operetta, where you can enjoy works by Lehár and Kálmán, as well as modern musicals.

Music Academy (Zeneakadémia) VI, Liszt Ferenc tér 8 ⓣ1/342-0179. Founded by Ferenc Liszt in 1875, it hosts nightly concerts and recitals in the magnificent gold-covered Nagyterem (Great Hall) or the smaller Kisterem. The music is excellent and the place has a real buzz.

National Concert Hall (Bartók Béla Nemzeti Hangversenyterem) in the Palace of Arts (see p.178). This new concert hall has superb acoustics and attracts world-class performers, not just in the classical arena.

Óbuda Music Society (Óbudai Társaskör) III, Kiskorona utca 7 ⓣ1/250-0288, ⓦwww.obudaitarsaskor.hu. Small concert hall on the edge of the housing estates south of the Árpád híd in Óbuda. The quality of performance is excellent, and big local ensembles such as the Liszt Chamber Orchestra, Budapest Strings and Auer String Quartet are based here. Also stages some jazz concerts.

Old Music Academy (Régi Zeneakadémia) VI, Vörösmarty utca 35. Performances by young musicians every Sat morning, in the concert hall of the Liszt Memorial Museum.

Opera House (Magyar Állami Operaház) VI, Andrássy út 22 ⓣ1/332-7914, ⓦwww.opera.hu. Budapest's grandest venue, with gilded frescoes and three-tonne chandeliers (dress tends towards smart), though plagued by internal conflicts and a lack of money. A new management team was appointed in 2007 with the task of raising standards – they would do well to cut the vast number of productions in the repertoire. You can still get cheap seats – tickets start at 800Ft, though they go up to 17,000Ft for the best seats at the best shows.

Thália Theatre (Thália Színház) VI, Nagymező 22 ⓣ1/331-0500, ⓦwww.thalia.hu. On Budapest's "Broadway", the Thália hosts operas and musicals, as well as theatre and dance.

Vigadó V, Vigadó tér 1. Another fabulously decorated hall, though the acoustics are inferior. Dating from 1865, it is the oldest of the major concert venues and several Liszt premiers were performed here. Closed for restoration at the time of writing.

Pop, rock and jazz

Budapest attracts every Hungarian **band** worth its amplifiers and a growing roll-call of international stars, appearances by whom are well covered in the media. Posters around town – particularly around Deák tér, Ferenciek tere and the Astoria underpass – publicize concerts by local bands. Concert ticket prices range from 1000Ft for local bands and up to as much as 15,000Ft for stadium gigs by international superstars. Apart from the venues listed below, performances take place at the places listed on pp.177–178; at the vast Puskás Ferenc Stadion, the smaller Kisstadion or the Papp László Sportaréna (all near Stadionok metro station). A number of bars also have live music, such as *Jelen*, *Kuplung*, *Pótkulcs*, *Sark* and *Simplakert* (see chapter 15 for details).

When it comes to **jazz** (or *dzsessz*, as it is sometimes becomes in Hungarian), don't be fooled by the small number of regular venues in Budapest. The country boasts some brilliant jazz musicians, such as György Vukán, György Szabados, Béla Szakcsi Lakatos and the award-winning pianist Kálmán Oláh. Now there is a new phenomenon, Roma jazz, spawning a fresh generation of brilliant players (see *Hungarian music* colour section) One jazz club to look out for is the Harmonia Jazz Workshop (Harmonia Jazz Műhely), which is looking for a new home and may hold sessions at the

Budapest Jazz Club (VIII, Múzeum utca 7, by the National Museum) and elsewhere. There are also occasional jazz concerts in theatres such as the MU Színház (see p.184).

The biggest venue of all is the Óbudai (or Hajógyári) sziget north of Margit-sziget, which in mid-August hosts the week-long **Sziget festival** (Ⓦwww.sziget.hu/fesztival), one of the major European music events. In 2008, over 200 international stars including REM, Iron Maiden, Alanis Morissette and The Killers, and almost 500 Hungarian performers (such as Péterfy Bori & Love Band and Little Cow-Kistehén), attracted 385,000 people, served by 74 bars and 27 buffets. Day tickets cost €32, weekly tickets €150. Going by foot, you take the HÉV from Batthyány tér to the Filorigát stop and follow the crowds across the bridge to the island. Slightly less crowded is the bus from Deák tér and the boats from Batthyány tér or Jászai Mari tér, at the Pest end of the Margít híd (see the festival website for more information).

Benczúr House (Benczúr Ház) VI, Benczúr utca 27 ⓣ1/321-7334, Ⓦwww.benczurhaz.hu. Mainstream jazz venue in a very grand nineteenth-century villa off the top of Andrássy út that today houses the Post Office Cultural Centre.

Columbus Jazz Club V, Vigadó tér ⓣ1/266-9013, Ⓦwww.majazz.hu. Jazz venue on a boat moored in central Pest that hosts top Hungarian as well as international players.

Gödör Klub V, Erzsébet tér ⓣ06-20/201 3868, Ⓦwww.godorklub.hu. Underground venue at the bottom of the steps in the middle of the square – this was once a huge hole (*gödör* in Hungarian) dug for the new National Theatre, but construction was abandoned after a change of government. Nicknamed the National Hole as years of vacillation followed, it was finally turned into a park and a music venue. It's not a very intimate space but it has a very good range of concerts – jazz, folk, alternative Hungarian pop and Roma acts.

If Kávézó IX, Ráday utca 19 Ⓦwww.ifkavezo.hu. Good musical events most nights at this relatively new upstairs venue on the popular Ráday utca.

Jazz Garden V, Veres Pálné utca 44A ⓣ1/266-7364, Ⓦwww.jazzgarden.hu. Cellar jazz bar and restaurant. Performers include Hungarian stars Béla Szakcsi Lakatos and Aladár Pege, as well as American blues guitarist Bruce Lewis, a local resident. Daily except Tues 6pm–2am.

Sirály VI, Király utca 50 Ⓦwww.siraly.co.hu. Regular jazz and theatre downstairs in this bohemian place, a very deluxe squat.

Take Five VI, Paulay Ede utca 2 ⓣ30-986-8856, Ⓦwww.take5.hu. Largish new basement venue below the Vista travel agency just off Deák tér that gets many of the top performers on its nightly programme. Most concerts start at 9pm.

Folk music and dance

Hungarian **folk music** and **dancing** underwent a revival in the 1970s, drawing inspiration from Hungarian communities in Transylvania, regarded as pure wellsprings of Magyar culture – see *Hungarian music* colour section for more on the dance house movement. The movement still exists today, and has been extended to other cultures – you'll also see adverts for Greek (*görög*), Roma and other dance houses. Visitors are welcome to attend the gatherings (350–800Ft admission; see Ⓦwww.tanchaz.hu for more) and learn the steps. Details of children's dance houses are on p.196.

Concerts of Hungarian folk music by the likes of Muzsikás, Téka, Tükrös, Ökrös, Csík and Kalamajka take place regularly, while there are also performances by groups such as Vujicsics, inspired by South Slav music from Serbia, Croatia and Bulgaria. Two singers to look out for on the circuit are Beáta Pálya, whose repertoire draws on her Hungarian and Roma roots as well as other

▲ Táncház, Petőfi Csarnok

cultures, and Ági Szalóki, who captures the traditional female folk sound – she accompanies bands such as the Ökrös Ensemble as well as performing solo. There has been a sudden growth in **Roma** groups (see *Hungarian music* colour section), while the old Jewish musical traditions are continued by *klezmer* performers such as Di Naye Kapelye, who are far closer to the original spirit than the ubiquitous easy-listening Budapest Klezmer Band. An entertaining blend of the two styles is offered by the Fellegini Klezmer Gipsy band, led by Balázs Fellegi. Apart from the venues listed below, performances take place at the venues listed on pp.177–178 and in bars and clubs listed in chapter 15, such as Pótkulcs and Sirály.

A38 See p.177. This floating venue attracts top international and Hungarian folk and world music performers.

Aranytíz Cultural Centre V, Arany János utca 10 ⓦwww.aranytiz.hu. The Kalamajka ensemble plays here to a packed dancefloor on Sat nights from late Sept through to early June, with dance teaching from 7pm; the children's session begins at 5pm (see p.196). As the evening rolls on a jamming session often develops with other bands joining in. The cultural centre's programme includes Hungarian and international theatre performances and jazz concerts, too.

Fonó Music Hall (Fonó Budai Zeneház) XI, Sztregova utca 3 ⓣ1/206-5300, ⓦwww.fono.hu. Lively international folk and world music venue, 2km south of Móricz Zsigmond körtér – four stops from there on tram #18 or #47. Every Wed evening there's a dance house led by Téka, Méta or Tükrös.

Gödör Klub See p.180. It's always worth seeing what's on at this club underneath Erzsébet tér, with its mix of live Hungarian folk, jazz and Roma – it is one of the best venues for Hungarian Roma acts such as Romano Drom, who play here every month. In June the club hosts a big international Roma arts festival.

Millenáris Park See p.178. The folk band Muzsikás and the top local ethno-jazz group, the Dresch Quartet, are among the Hungarian bands regularly performing here, but they also have international stars of all music genres.

Cinema

Hollywood blockbusters and Euro soft-porn films dominate Budapest's mainstream **cinemas**, though the city has a chain of art-house cinemas that specialize in the latest releases and obscure European films – *angol* indicates a British film, *lengyel* Polish, *német* German, *olasz* Italian, and *orosz* Russian. A host of multiplexes showing the latest Hollywood blockbusters and mainstream fare can be found across the city: the Corvin listed below is a free-standing **multiplex**, but they can also be found in the big shopping malls (see p.199).

Cinema **listings** appear in the *mozi* section of the free Hungarian weekly *Pesti Est*. The times of shows are cryptically abbreviated: *n8* or *1/4 8* – short for *negyed 8* – means 7.15; *f8* or *1/2 8* (*fél 8*) means 7.30; and *h8* or *3/4 8* (három*negyed 8*) means 7.45pm. "*Mb*." indicates the film is dubbed – as many are – and *fel*. or *feliratos* means that it has Hungarian subtitles.

Cinema-going is cheap, with tickets costing from 800Ft in the smaller cinemas, 1400Ft or more in the multiplexes. In the summer some of the outdoor bars, such as the *Szimplakert* (see p.172), show films a couple of times a week; there are also summer outdoor and drive-in cinemas on the edge of town – for more details of these contact Tourinform (see p.41).

The main **film festivals** are the Hungarian Film Festival (Ⓦwww.szemle.film.hu), a parade of the year's new films in February (tickets from the Corvin

Hungary on film

Hungarians have an impressive record in film, and many of the Hollywood greats were **Hungarian emigrés** – Michael Curtiz, Sir Alex Korda, George Cukor, and actors Béla Lugosi, Tony Curtis and Leslie Howard to name but a few. In the Communist years Hungarian film continued to make waves, with Miklós Jancsó, Károly Makk, István Szabó, Márta Mészáros and others directing films that managed to say much about the oppressive regime in spite of its restrictions. Now the main constraint on film makers is chronic underfunding, but what the Hungarian film industry lacks in money it makes up for in ideas.

Established directors to look out for are Péter Gothár, with his absurd humour and love of the fantastic (*Time Stands Still*, *Let Me Hang Vaska*), Ildikó Enyedi (*My Twentieth Century* and *Simon the Magician*), Béla Tarr (*Werckmeister Harmonies* and the epic eight-hour *Satan Tango*) and János Szász, whose film *The Witman Boys* won the best international film at Cannes in 1997. Other younger stars are Kornél Mundruczó, Szabolcs Hajdú, Ferenc Török and Nimród Antal, whose first film, the black comedy *Kontroll*, was a big hit abroad; as well as György Pálfi, whose *Hukkle* similarly won international acclaim. Two new names making feature films are Szabolcs Tolnai, whose film *Sand Glass* about the writer Danilo Kis won widespread praise; and Péter Fazakas, whose first feature film, *Para*, was released in 2008.

Budapest has been a popular **location** for films, both for its looks and its cheapness – though the EU has now blocked the Hungarian tax loophole that made it so appealing – serving as Buenos Aires in *Evita* and as Paris in the *Maigret* TV series; in the latter, the view towards the Basilica down Lázár utca behind the Opera House acts as the view of the Sacré-Coeur, and Paris developed a hill rising on one bank of the Seine rather like that in Budapest. But it also serves as itself: the American documentary *Divan* by Pearl Gluck captures some of the characters and atmosphere of the old Jewish quarter in its interviews.

DVDs, most of them subtitled, have made Hungarian films much more accessible, making it possible to enjoy classics such as Géza Radványi's *Valahol Európában* (1947) and Zoltán Fábri's *Körhinta* (1955).

Filmpalota), and the Titanic International Film Festival (Ⓦwww.titanicfilmfest.hu) in April, an alternative festival of Hungarian and foreign films that has been going for more than fifteen years.

Cirko-gejzir V, Balassi Bálint utca 15–17. One of the best alternative cinemas, with a regular selection of movies from around the globe – in any given week they might be showing films by Almodóvar, Tarkovsky, Jarmusch, Wenders and Rohmer.

Corvin Budapest Film Palace (Corvin Filmpalota) VIII, Corvin köz 1, Ⓦwww.corvin.hu. This glitzy multiplex, near the Ferenc körút metro, is a modern jungle of cinemas, popcorn and drinks. It's a good place to catch the latest foreign releases, and in Feb it hosts the Hungarian Film Festival. Reduced-price tickets on Wed.

Muvész VI, Teréz körút 30, Ⓦwww.artmozi.hu. Art-house cinema near the Oktogon, with one large and several smaller rooms named after big film personalities.

Puskin V, Kossuth Lajos 18, Ⓦwww.artmozi.hu. Complex of three cinemas in the centre of town, with a large café attached. The coffered ceiling of the turn-of-the-century main screen is magnificent.

Toldi V, Bajcsy-Zsilinszky út 36–38 Ⓦwww.artmozi.hu. Next door to Arany János utca metro station, the Toldi is one of the more dynamic alternative cinemas in town, with a bar and a bookshop where people congregate. One of the venues for the annual Titanic Film Festival.

Uránia National Film Theatre (Uránia Nemzeti Filmszínház) VIII, Rákóczi út 21, Ⓦwww.urania-nf.hu. With its magnificent Venetian-Moorish decorations, this might seem a strange choice of location for Budapest's main showcase of Hungarian films. But it was in this cinema, built in the 1890s as a dance hall, that the first Hungarian feature film was shot in 1901. While it places special emphasis on local films, its programme is international.

Theatre and contemporary dance

Hungarians usually show great sophistication when it comes to building theatres: take the splendid mass of the **Vígszínház** up the road from Nyugati Station, or the **New Theatre** opposite the Opera House. However, if the newly constructed **National Theatre** is anything to go by (see p.89), the theatre world is suffering a lapse in taste that extends to the stage as well. The new showcase for Hungarian theatre is a sad mish-mash of styles, mainstream Hungarian **theatre** is in the doldrums, and its melodramatic and unsubtle productions offer little to tempt the visitor – but look out for those by the provincial theatre company from the town of **Kaposvár**, in southwest Hungary, or by Hungarian companies from outside the borders, such as from Cluj, Romania.

Alternative theatre tends to be more interesting – and since music and dance play a greater part here, language can be less of a barrier. One Hungarian group that has received considerable critical acclaim abroad are **Krétakör**, who were a big hit at the 2005 Edinburgh Festival with their interpretation of Chekhov's *The Seagull*, by the young director Árpád Schilling. Other names to look out for are **László Hudi**, **Frenák Pál** and **Péter Halász**, who have all spent time with foreign ensembles, bringing fresh new ideas back to Hungary. Two promising names in dance are **Réka Szabó**, who runs the Tünet (Symptom) group, and **Krisztián Gergye**. And finally, Hungary has a strong puppet tradition and the shows in the two **puppet** theatres can be interesting (see p.184).

To find out what's on, look out for flyers and check out the theatre listings publication *Súgó* (published in English in July & Aug) or the listings magazines (see p.32).

Besides the venues below, there's the outdoor theatre on Margit-sziget (see p.120), which hosts colourful musicals in summer.

Budapest Bábszínház **VI, Andrássy út 69 ⓣ1/342-2702, ⓦwww.budapest-babszinhaz.hu.** Budapest Puppet Theatre has a lot of shows for adults – masked grotesqueries or renditions of Bartók's *The Wooden Prince* and *The Miraculous Mandarin* and Mozart's *Magic Flute*. Open all year round.

Kolibri Pince **VI, Andrássy út 77 ⓣ1/311-0870, ⓦwww.szinhaz.hu/kolibri.** Puppet shows and live performances for adults as well as children at three venues (see p.196 for the other two); this is the best one for grown-up performances. Closed early June–Aug.

Merlin Theatre **V, Gerlóczy utca 4 ⓣ1/317-9338, ⓦwww.merlinbudapest.org.** In the centre of Pest, this often hosts visiting British theatre companies.

MU Színház **XI, Körösy József utca 17 ⓣ1/466-4627, ⓦwww.mu.hu.** Alternative theatre venue that also hosts jazz concerts. It has a popular smoky bar in the foyer.

National Theatre **(Nemzeti Színház) IX, Bajor Gizi park 1 ⓣ1/476-6800, ⓦwww.nemzetiszinhaz.hu.** The proud flagship of Hungarian theatre. Some shows are in English, put on by local troupes.

New Theatre **(Új Színház) VI, Paulay Ede utca 35 ⓣ1/351-1406, ⓦwww.szinhaz.hu/ujszinhaz.** This stunning Art Nouveau building across the road from the Opera House is one of the better mainstream theatres, offering reliably polished performances.

Sirály **VII, Király utca 50 ⓣ06/20-248 2261, ⓦwww.siraly.co.hu.** Alternative theatre and jazz downstairs at this bohemian bar.

Szkéné Színház **XI, Műegyetem rakpart 3 ⓣ1/463-2451, ⓦwww.szkene.hu.** A small theatre housed in the main building of the Technical University near the *Gellért Hotel*, this has been an alternative venue for many years, dating back to the bad old days of Communism.

Thália Theatre **See p.179.** Musicals, theatre and dance, such as shows by Réka Szabó's Tünet dance group.

Trafó **See p.178.** Dynamic contemporary arts centre that has theatre performances by Krétakör and other groups, as well as many good international companies.

Vígszínház **XIII, Szent István körút 14 ⓣ1/329 2340, ⓦwww.vigszinhaz.hu.** Great for people-watching, as the locals dress up in their finest to attend performances, which are very much in the mainstream Hungarian style. Visiting companies also perform here.

18

Sports

Hungarians are passionate about sport. **Spectator sports** such as Grand Prix racing, soccer and horse-racing are very popular, though years of underfunding and mismanagement have brought the last two nearly to their knees. Hungary's strongest showing on an international level is in kayaking, shooting, waterpolo and fencing – for its size it performs very well in the Olympic medal charts. Sports **facilities** have suffered similarly from a lack of funding, but you can find a reasonable range of sports and activities to choose from around the capital. Information about the city's extensive bath and swimming facilities is given in chapter 19; there's information about bike rental on p.31, while if you want to go exploring the Buda Hills by trail-bike, see p.121.

One activity (rather than a sport) that you can easily join in is **chess**: Hungary has a long tradition of great chess players, and you can see the game being keenly played by elderly men in many parks.

Soccer

Hungary's great footballing days are long past – the golden team of the 1950s that beat England 6–3 with stars such as Ferenc Puskás and József Bozsik is a world away from today's national squad, struggling to qualify for big tournaments. The club scene is also in deep crisis, with teams floundering in a financial desert.

While **international matches** are held at the Puskás Ferenc Stadium – generally filling just a third of its 76,000 seats – club football revolves around the turf of three **premier league teams** listed below; see the daily paper *Nemzeti Sport* for details of fixtures. The **season** runs from late July to late November and late February to mid-June. Most matches are played on Saturday afternoons, with tickets costing 800–3000Ft.

Ferencváros (aka FTC or Fradi) IX, Üllői út 129 ⓦwww.ftc.hu. Népliget metro. Fradi is the biggest club in the country and almost a national institution; its supporters, dressed in the club's colours of green and white, are the loudest presence at international matches too. The club has long had right-wing ties: this was the fascists' team before the war, and in recent years it has attracted a strong skinhead – and anti-Semitic – element. Fradi's recent history has been one of tragi-comedy, having been first taken over by a second-rate demagogic politician, then by a Jewish businessman. Financial difficulties have now relegated the club to the second division, and it's in the process of being bought by the businessman Kevin McCabe, who also owns the British club Sheffield United.

MTK VIII, Salgótarján utca 12–14, ⓦwww.mtkhungaria.hu. Tram #37 from Blaha Lujza tér. Fradi's big local rival, "Em-tay-kah" – as it is popularly known – has traditionally had strong support among the Jewish community, and unlike its neighbour it is still a major contender in the top division. MTK's ground was the setting for scenes in the film *Escape to Victory*.

Újpest IV, Megyeri út 13, Ⓦ www.ujpestfc.hu. Four stops on bus #30 from Újpest Központ metro station. Formerly the police's team, Újpest's purple strip is a regular contender for the Hungarian championship. Its 13,000 all-seater stadium was completed in 2001.

Horse-racing

Horse-racing was introduced from England by Count Széchenyi in 1827 and flourished until 1949, when flat racing (*galopp*) was banned by the Communists. For many years punters could only enjoy trotting races, but in the mid-1980s flat racing resumed at **Kincsem Park**, X, Albertirsai út 2–6 (Pillangó utca on the red metro, and then either walk or catch #100 bus). **Flat racing** takes place here on Sundays from spring to autumn; **trotting** – *ügető*, where the horse it harnessed to a light carriage – is all year round, mostly on Saturdays. Races are advertised in *Fortuna* magazine. Both types have a devoted and excitable following, which makes attending the races entertaining; the atmosphere at the tracks is informal, but photographing the racegoers is frowned upon, since many attend unbeknownst to their spouses or employers.

Betting operates on a tote system, where your returns are affected by how the odds stood at the close of betting. The different types of bet comprise *tét*, placing money on the winner; *hely*, on a horse coming in the first three; and the popular *befutó*, a bet on two horses to come in either first and second or first and third. Winnings are paid out about fifteen minutes after the end of the race.

Grand Prix racing

The **Hungarian Grand Prix** takes place in summer – usually mid-August – at the purpose-built Formula One racing track, the **Hungaroring**, at **Mogyoród**, 20km northeast of Budapest. The event was first held in 1986, but every year financial uncertainties surrounding the event spark rumours concerning its future. Assuming it's going ahead as normal, you can get details from Tourinform, any listings magazine or the website Ⓦ www.hungaroring.hu.

Tickets are available from Ostermann Forma-1, V, Apáczai Csere János utca 11, third floor (Ⓣ 1/266-2040), online at the address above; or from booths in Ferenciek tér. Prices range from €40-100 for the first day to €100–360 for the final day, and €110–400 for a three-day pass – the price being partly determined by the location, and whether you book in advance or (risking disappointment) on the day. You can reach the track by special buses from the Árpád híd bus station; trains from Keleti Station to Fót, and then a bus from there; or by HÉV train from Örs vezér tere to the Szilasliget stop, which is 1800m northeast of Gate C.

Participatory sports

Canoeing Taking a canoe or kayak out on the Danube can be exhilarating – you just have to remember to head upstream first. The Béke Boathouse is a 10min walk from the Rómaifürdő HÉV station (or take bus #34 to the door from the Árpád híd station) at III, Római-part 51–53, Ⓣ 1/388-9303. Open April to mid-Oct.

Caving The Buda Hills are peppered with a cave system about 100km long. You can walk round a couple of them (see p.118) without any special equipment, or you can go on more adventurous visits with Caving under Budapest (☎06/20 928-4969, Ⓦbarlangaszat.hu). The group leads two- to three-hour tours – you don't need caving experience, but you do need to be fit and fairly agile, as you'll be climbing on walls and squeezing through passageways. You are given helmets, headlights and overalls. English-speaking tours are on Mon, Wed and Fri and start at the Pálvölgyi cave (see p.118). The Hungarian Association of Speleologists, at the Szemlőhegyi Cave (see p.118; ☎1/346-0494) can put you in touch with groups exploring caves in the Buda Hills and elsewhere in Hungary.

Fitness centres and gyms Most of the larger hotels and some of the shopping malls (see p.199) have them – they are properly regulated, unlike some of the backstreet ones, and are open to non-residents.

Ice-skating There's an ice rink by Hősök tere in the Városliget (Nov–March Mon–Fri 9am–1pm, 4–8pm, Sat–Sun 10am–2pm, 4–8pm); entry costs 700–970Ft, and skates can be rented.

Skiing If it's a snowy winter, you can ski at Normafa in the Buda Hills, best reached on bus #90 or #90A from Moszkva tér. Equipment can be rented from Suli Sí by the entrance of the Császár Komjádi pool at II, Árpád Fejedelem utca 8 (☎1/212-0330, Ⓦwww.sulisi.hu), or Bikebase at VI, Podmaniczky utca 19 (daily 9am–7pm; ☎1/269-5983, Ⓦwww.bikebase.hu), where the friendly staff can advise you on other places to ski.

Squash Try City Squash Club, II, Marcibányi tér 13 (☎1/336-0408, Ⓦww.squashtech.hu; prices for court rental start at 2200Ft), 5min walk from Moszkva tér; or Top Squash Club, on the fourth floor of the nearby Mammut Mall I (☎1/345-8193, Ⓦwww.top-squash.hu; prices start at 2500Ft an hour).

Tank-driving If you've got a day and lots of cash to spare, why not try tank-driving at Baj, near Tata, where 55 acres of muddy terrain and obstacles can be negotiated in a range of ex-Soviet armoured vehicles. Popular with stag parties – they also do paint-balling. See Ⓦwww.tank.hu for details.

Tennis Courts can be booked all year round at the Városmajor Tennis Academy in Városmajor Park, near Moszkva tér (☎1/202–5337) and at the *Thermal Hotel Helia* in Angyalföld, XIII, Kárpát utca 62 (☎1/889-5800). Racquets are available for rent.

19

Baths and pools

With more than a hundred springs offering an endless supply of hot water at temperatures of up to 76°C, Budapest is deservedly known as a **spa city**, and visiting one of the many baths should not be missed. Housed in some of Budapest's finest buildings, the baths are impressive sights in their own right; with their medicinal properties, the thermal waters are reputed to cure myriad ailments – and of course there's the swimming itself.

The smaller Rudas and Király baths are first and foremost **steam baths**, with saunas and small pools fed by thermal springs. In the larger baths, such as the Gellért or Széchenyi, you can alternate between brisk dips in the swimming pool and leisurely soaks in the steam section. Finally – and this contributes to the appeal of the baths – they are an important social hub, where people come to sit and chat as they follow the rituals. As you admire the light filtering through the dome in the Rudas, watch the chess players ponder their next move in the outdoor pool of the Széchenyi or peer through the mists in the steam rooms at the Gellért, there's a real sense of being part of a tradition that has lasted centuries.

Bath house history

Even though the sulphurous content of Budapest's waters mean that they don't always smell very pleasant, their therapeutic qualities have long been exploited. The earliest remains of baths here date back to the Bronze Age, and a succession of invaders have since capitalized on the benefits of the healthy waters. The **Romans**, who appreciated a good bath, set up camp along the banks of the Danube – you can see the ruins of their bath houses in Óbuda. After their arrival from the east, the **Hungarian tribes** also recognized the value of the thermal springs, as testified by the remnants of a hospital bath house from 1178 found near the Lukács.

During their occupation, the **Ottomans** played a vital role in the development of Budapest's baths – the precept, under Islamic law, for washing five times a day before prayers is thought to have engendered a popular bathing culture here. The oldest baths that survive today are the Turkish baths on the Buda side of the river: built in the late sixteenth century, the Király and the Rudas baths have preserved their original layout, with a central bathing pool surrounded by smaller pools that lie below the old Turkish cupolas.

The next **golden age of bathing** occurred in the late nineteenth and early twentieth centuries, as a fashion for spas swept across Europe. Budapest's existing baths were dressed up in a new magnificence, and splendid buildings such as the

▲ Gellért Baths

neo-Baroque Széchenyi Baths in the Városliget and the Art Nouveau Gellért Baths were erected. During the **Communist era**, the baths were as popular as ever – a place to meet and gossip in the murky mists – but they suffered prolonged neglect. In recent years, however, major investments have seen the buildings restored and their facilities upgraded by way of new features such as whirlpools – Budapest's baths are now far more salubrious places to visit. And it's not just people who have benefited from the thermal waters. The success of the hippopotamus breeding programme at Budapest Zoo is thought to be partly due to the constant supply of hot water from the Széchenyi Baths across the road – the hippos clearly benefit from wallowing in lovely thermal pools. The hot springs also saved them during the bitter winter siege of the city in 1944–45, when most of the zoo's other animals died in the freezing temperatures.

There are three types of bath: *gyógyfürdő*, a **thermal bath** in its original Turkish form, as at the Rudas and Király, or the magnificent nineteenth-century settings of the Gellért and Széchenyi; *uszoda*, a proper swimming pool such as the Sport; and *strand*, a lido in a verdant setting, such as the Palatinus. Most baths are divided into a **swimming** area and a separate section for **steam baths** (*gőzfürdő* or the *gőz*, as they are popularly known). The website for the Budapest Baths Directorate, Ⓦwww.spasbudapest.com, has general information on all the main baths.

A new feature on the bathing scene is the **Thai spa** – proper massage parlours rather than sex joints. These offer massages with all sorts of exotic oils, much in demand in this city, where every self-regarding Budapesti woman makes regular visits to her cosmetician for a little pampering.

Bathing essentials

The Budapest bathing experience can be a little daunting, as little is written in English once you are inside and attendants are unlikely to speak more than Hungarian and a smattering of German. However, the basic system of attendants and cabins is the same in most steam baths and swimming pools, and once you get the hang of the rituals, a visit to the baths becomes most rewarding. A standard **ticket** purchased from the ticket office (*pénztár*) gets you into the pools as well as the sauna and steam rooms; you'll often have the choice between changing in a communal room and using a locker (*szekrény*), or a slightly more expensive cubicle (*kabin*) – the latter gives you more privacy and, in the mixed-sex baths, this allows couples to change together. Supplementary tickets will buy you a massage (*masszázs*), a soak in a private tub (*kádfürdő*) or a mud bath (*iszapfürdő*) – a list by the office will detail the available services.

Recently, attempts have been made to control the numbers of visitors to the baths: the Király and Rudas impose limits on the length of your stay, while several of the big baths offer a small refund if you stay less than three hours – the shorter the visit, the higher the refund. As you go into the baths, you're given a counter to feed into the turnstile at the entrance – there is usually a member of staff standing around to show you what to do as it can be confusing. When you leave, put your counter into the turnstile at the exit; this feeds out a chit, which you take to the *pénztár* for your refund.

Once inside the **changing room** (*öltöző*), an attendant will direct you to a cabin or locker. In most single-sex steam baths, the wearing of swimsuits is still rare – the authorities do sometimes make them compulsory, as they have done in the Király, but it's up to you in the other baths. In the steam baths, the attendant will give you a *kötény* – a small loincloth for men or an apron for women – which offers a vestige of cover. Once you've changed, you need to find the attendant again; they will lock your locker or cabin door and give you a tag (or another key with which to double lock your door for security). You tie the tag or key to your swimming costume or the strings of your *kötény*, making a note of your cabin number and taking with you any supplementary tickets (if you're booked in for a massage, bring a couple of hundred forints for tipping the masseur). In all baths bring flip-flops if you have them, as well as your own soap and shampoo; in the steam baths, you don't need a towel as you're given a sheet to dry yourself with.

The best way to enjoy the **steam baths** is to go from room to room, moving on whenever the heat gets too much. A popular sequence is: sauna (dry steam – often divided into three rooms, the furthest being the hottest), cool pool, steam room, cold plunge (if you can bear it), hot plunge (this makes your skin tingle wonderfully, but don't stay in for long), followed by a wallow in the larger, warmer pools that are usually at the centre of the baths. Most people then repeat the whole thing again, but the sequence you choose is entirely up to you – the main thing is not to stay in any one section if you feel uncomfortable.

When you're completely finished, take a sheet from the pile to dry yourself. Relax in the rest room if you feel exhausted – certainly don't plan on anything too strenuous afterwards – and then find the attendant to unlock your cabin or locker. It's usual to tip the attendant a couple of hundred forints.

In many **pools**, bathing caps (*uszósapka*) are compulsory: in the Széchenyi, they're only required in the middle of the three outdoor pools (the one reserved for swimming proper); go in without a cap and you'll be whistled at by the attendant and told to get out. Like swimsuits and towels, caps can be rented at the *pénztár* – though at the Gellért you can pick up an unattractive blue plastic one inside for free. Another tip in the swimming pools: some, such as the main inside pool of the Gellért, have an anti-clockwise swimming policy: you may be whistled at if you don't follow the arrows.

Császár Komjádi Uszoda II, Árpád fejedelem útja 8. A large, modern pool complex just north of Margit híd on the Buda side – the entrance faces the river. The large outdoor swimming pool (bathing caps compulsory) is covered over in winter. The complex is one of the major waterpolo venues in Budapest, which means one of its pools may be given over to the players on weekdays. Daily 6am–6pm; 1320Ft.

Gellért Gyógyfürdő XI, Kelenhegyi út 4. The most popular of the city's baths, and also one of the oldest – although nothing remains of the medieval buildings – the Gellért has it all: a magnificent main pool for swimming, hot pools for sitting around in both inside and outside on the terrace, fabulous Art Nouveau steam baths, and a large outdoor area, including a wave machine in the main pool (May–Aug) and shaded terraces. Of course there's also a restaurant where you can get your daily dose of meat fried in breadcrumbs. The Gellért attracts a lot of foreigners, and many of the attendants speak German or English. To enjoy the waters you must first reach the changing rooms by a labyrinth of passages; staff are usually helpful with directions. At the far end of the pool are steps leading down to the separate thermal baths, with segregated areas and ornate plunge pools for men and women. Tickets cover both sections; towels, bathrobes and swimsuits can be rented, though you can get free blue plastic bathing caps at the exit from the changing-rooms. May–Sept daily 6am–7pm (the swimming pool often opens later – check at the entrance); Oct–April Mon–Fri 6am–7pm, Sat & Sun 6am–5pm. Tickets cost 2800ft with locker, 3100Ft with cubicle, with 400Ft refunded if you leave within 2hr, 200Ft in 3hr.

Hajós Alfred Sport Uszoda XIII, southern end of Margit-sziget. One of the nicest places for proper swimming, this is a beautiful 1930s lido renovated for the 2001 European waterpolo championships. There's a small sauna, and two large outdoor pools against a backdrop of trees; one is normally given over to waterpolo. In the winter you can swim out along a channel to the larger of the pools without walking outside. Mon–Fri 6am–4pm, Sat–Sun 6am–6pm; 1320Ft.

Király Gyógyfürdő II, Fő utca 84. Fabulous Turkish baths, in the Viziváros in Buda, easy to spot thanks to the four copper cupolas. This was the most popular of the steam baths with the gay community until Feb 2005, when a television reporter secretly filmed the goings-on in the pool among the naked bathers. When the scenes were broadcast on national news, the bath authorities immediately imposed a compulsory swimming trunks order on bathers, and began to patrol the bathing areas, severely cramping gay bathers' style. The main pool under the cupola is surrounded by smaller – hotter and cooler – pools, with doors leading off to the steam massage rooms. Women Mon, Wed & Fri 7am–6pm; men Tues, Thurs & Sat 9am–8pm. Tickets cost 1300Ft (last tickets 1hr before closing); the maximum stay is 1hr 30min Mon–Fri, 1hr Sat.

Lian Thai Massage and Spa VII, Wesselényi út 9 ⓣ1/235-0745, ⓦwww.lianmassage.hu. One of the new Thai spas in the city that offers chocolate (10,500Ft), honey (10,500Ft), aromatic oil (9500Ft) and other massages.

Lukács Fürdő II, Frankl Leó út 25–29. This spa complex just north of the Margit híd in Buda has four small but delightful open-air pools, as well as mud baths and a medical treatment section – its waters are said to be good for rheumatism, arthritis and other complaints. The open-air facilities, including a thermal pool, a cooler and smaller swimming pool, and a bubbling pool with whirling currents, are in two intimate courtyards. If the folly-like ticket hall by the road is only selling tickets for the steam baths, you may be directed to the ticket hall at the entrance to the swimming complex: go into the courtyard and head round to the left (past plaques declaring gratitude in different languages from those who have benefited from the medicinal waters), following the signs for the *uszoda* (pool). The swimming pool and adjacent baths are mixed. Mon–Sat 6am–7pm, Sun 6am–5pm; 1700Ft for a locker, 1900Ft for a cabin, with a refund of 400Ft if you leave within 2hr, 200Ft within 3hr.

Palatinus Strand XIII, Margit-sziget. Halfway up the island on the west side, the Palatinus has a large outdoor set of pools, including a wave pool and children's pools, all set in a big expanse of grass. The sunroof above the changing rooms is something of a gay centre. May–Aug daily 9am–7pm; 1800Ft (you pay more for a changing cabin, and more again at weekends).

Rác Gyógyfürdő I, Hadnagy utca 8–10. One of the oldest baths – the medieval King Mátyás is said to have used the baths on this site in the Tabán – but nothing remains from those times. Closed for redevelopment at time of writing, and due to reopen in 2009 as part of a luxury *Baglioni* spa hotel complex. ⓦwww.baglionihotels.com.

Rudas Gyógyfürdő I, Döbrentei tér 9. One of the city's original Turkish baths, at the Buda end of the Erzsébet híd, this is at its best when the sun shines through the holes in the dome to light up the beautiful interior, which has just undergone major restoration. The steam baths were for many years a male preserve, but women now get a day to themselves. There's an apron system in the steam section on single-sex days, but swimming costumes are compulsory on mixed days. There is also a nineteenth-century swimming pool, open to both sexes, to the left of the main entrance – normal swimwear compulsory here. During the winter months, the Rudas sometimes hosts all-night "cinetrip" raves, with silent films and DJs. Women only Tues 6am–8pm; men only Mon & Wed–Fri 6am–8pm; mixed Fri 10pm–4am, Sat & Sun 6am–5pm & 10pm–4am. Maximum stay is 1hr 30min Mon–Fri, 1hr Sat. Steam bath 2200Ft, with 400Ft refunded if you leave within 2hr, 200Ft in 3hr.

Széchenyi Fürdő XIV, Állatkerti körút 11. A magnificent nineteenth-century complex in the Városliget, with its entrance opposite the entrance to the Budapest Circus. There are sixteen pools in all, including the various medicinal sections, but you'll probably use just the three outdoor ones: the hot pool where people play chess (bring your own chess set if you want to play); a pool for swimming (bathing caps compulsory); and a whirlpool. Across the far side of the hot pool from the changing rooms is a mixed sauna with a maze of hot and cold pools. It is becoming a popular spot for yuppie evening parties. Daily 6am–10pm; 2400Ft for locker, 2800Ft for cabin, with 400Ft refunded if you leave within 2hr, 200Ft in 3hr.

20

Kids' Budapest

Budapest offers a healthy range of activities for kids, from state-of-the-art playgrounds to roller-skating parks, with concessions on most entry tickets for under-14s. Don't expect anything especially hi-tech, however, as a lack of cash dogs the facilities, but many of the city's playgrounds have been refurbished in recent years, and plenty of places have activities specifically for children, from the **Palace of Arts**, which has events most weekends, to **restaurants** such as *Trattoria Toscana*, which has a clown to entertain children at weekends.

Budapest's **public transport** – under-6s travel free – will keep children happily entertained. **Trams** are an endless source of fun, the best ride being along the embankment in tram #2. Across the water, the **Sikló** (see p.104) is a great experience, rising up above the rooftops from the Lánchíd to the Royal Palace. A popular way for families to spend an afternoon in the Buda Hills is to go on the "**railway circuit**" – the Cogwheel Railway, the Children's Railway and the chairlift (see p.121). From April to October there's the added thrill of **boat rides** on the Danube – either short tours of the city up to Margit-sziget and back, or further afield to Szentendre and on to Esztergom – though for young children, boredom is less likely to kick in on the shorter rides. Another summertime source of delight are the **steam trains** that run from Nyugati

▲ Children's Railway, Buda Hills

Station to the Railway History Park Visegrád and Esztergom. Finally the **Summer on the Chain Bridge** festival, every weekend from mid-June to mid-August on the Lánchíd, has regular events aimed at children (see p.33).

If you want more ideas for keeping children occupied, you might want to track down *Benjamin in Budapest*, a very enthusiastic city guide for children that you can find in larger bookshops in Budapest.

Playgrounds, parks and outdoor activities

Caves Underground Buda is good fun for children as long as they aren't scared of the dark. The caves under the Várhegy (see p.97) offer some exciting exploration, while the Pálvölgyi Stalactite Caves and the Szemlőhegyi Caves (p.118) display dramatic geological formations. Note the Pálvölgyi doesn't admit children under 5.

Challengeland (Kalandpálya) XII, Konkoly Thege Miklós út 21 ⓦwww.kalandpalya.com. Up in the Buda Hills and offering some of the city's best in outdoor fun, this is a real adventure playground, where children aged 3–12 can go on ropewalks and swing from tree to tree. The website has films showing what's on offer: click on *belépés*. To get there, take the Children's Railway to Csillebérc Station, or catch the #90 bus from Moszkva tér. Entry 1700–2800Ft for the first hour, depending on the height of child, then 500Ft an hour. May–Oct Mon–Fri 10am–6pm, Sat & Sun 10am–7pm.

Görzenál Skatepark III, Árpád fejedelem útja ⓦwww.gorzenal.hu. Space to rollerblade, skateboard and cycle, with ramps and jumps, all to your heart's content. You can get here by taking the Szentendre HÉV to Timár utca. Entry is 400–600Ft; it's cheaper in term-time and on weekdays. Mon–Thurs & Sun 9am–6pm, Fri & Sat 9am–7pm.

Kids' Park (Kölyökpark) II, Mammut 2 (shop 328), Lövőház utca 1–5 ⓣ1/345-8512 (see p.199). Indoor play area (for ages 1–11) in a city mall that comes into its own on wet days. You pay 700Ft for half an hour's use of slides, climbing walls and more – parents can leave the kids here to do their shopping, too.

Margit-sziget See p.118. The island in the middle of the Danube is a great open space where you can rent bikes and four-person trikes, or take a trip on the train on wheels, leaving from the strange sculpture at the southern end of the island. The Palatinus open-air baths (see p.192) have a wave machine and lots of small pools for kids. The low point of the island is the zoo across on the east – a smelly and sorry-looking place. Otherwise, the varied scenery and open areas for frisbee and ball games all create a very pleasant atmosphere.

Playgrounds Since central Budapest is still very residential, there are a lot of playgrounds in squares and parks, such as the Károlyi kert near the Astoria (Belváros), Szabadság tér (Lipótváros), Klauzál tér (Erzsébetváros), on the Margit-sziget and at several locations in the Városliget, one of the best being near Dembinsky utca, while in Buda you can find them at the Millenaris Park near Moszkva tér (see p.107), on the Gellért-hegy and at the Feneketlen tó (see map, p.109).

Tropicarium See p.127. You can get close to the sharks, feed the stingray and experience the rainforests in this huge aquarium-terrarium in southern Buda.

Városliget See p.77. The park has the largest concentration of activities and attractions for children: playgrounds, the zoo (see below), a circus and a fairground; the latter includes Kisvidám Park, a summertime section for younger kids with suitably tame rides. The Széchenyi Baths (see p.192) are popular with bigger children – especially the large outdoor hot pool and the whirlpool. For those who prefer to stay above water level, there's also rowing in summer and ice-skating in winter (Nov–March Mon–Fri 9am–1pm & 4–8pm, Sat & Sun 10am–2pm & 4–8pm, depending on the weather) on the lake by Hősök tere.

Zoo (Állatkert) See p.80. With its visionary director, the zoo gets better every year. Kids can feed the camels and giraffes, tickle the rhinos or stroke the farm animals in the petting farm, and explore attractions such as the restored Palm House with its tropical birds and alligators, or the new Crocodile House. There are also family-friendly features such as, by the playground, women's toilets that have children's toilets in the adult cubicles. There's also the **Zoo Funhouse (Állatkert Játszóház ⓦwww.jatekmester.hu)**, a brilliant indoor playcentre for babies, toddlers and children aged up to 10. In addition to a well-constructed activity centre, there's also the chance to be taken by the zookeepers to see the animals being fed. You can enter from the zoo (500Ft an hour in addition to the zoo ticket), or from the street entrance between the zoo and the circus (1000Ft an hour – includes visit to the zoo). Prices are higher at weekends. Daily 9am–8pm.

Museums

Hospital in the Rock **See p.97**. With gory waxworks, spooky Cold War bunkers and an excellent guided tour, this could be great fun for kids (especially boys) – but unfortunately you can't run around or touch anything and admission charges are steep.

Hungarian Open-Air Museum **See p.133.** Children's programmes every weekend, a playground and frequent folk-craft and folk-dancing displays in this museum outside Szentendre, north of the city.

Natural History Museum **See p.88.** Full of colour and activity, with interactive games and lots to look at, plenty of it at child height. Well thought-out, it certainly grabs children's attention.

Palace of Miracles **See p.107.** Now re-housed in the Millenáris Park, this great interactive playhouse has loads of activities for children which serve as a back-door way of explaining scientific principles, such as gravity. Good explanations in English.

Railway History Park **See p.125.** Strong child appeal here: lots of big old engines and carriages, and in summer you can even drive an engine yourself.

Telephone Museum **See p.96.** A hands-on museum, which is a rarity in Budapest; children enjoy sending faxes and calling one another on vintage phones.

Transport Museum **Városliget; see p.99.** Vehicles, trams, ships and trains of all kinds and sizes, plus a model train set that runs on the hour every hour until 5pm. Across the way, on the first floor of the Petofi Csarnok, is an Aviation and Space Flight display.

Theatre, dance and other activities

The fact that successful music ensembles such as the Budapest Festival Orchestra and the folk group Muzsikás hold regular events designed specifically for children says a lot about Hungarian attitudes to young people. Members of the orchestra introduce children to their musical instruments, while Muzsikás invite children to take their first steps in Hungarian folk-dancing – both of these events are conducted primarily in Hungarian but non-Hungarian speakers will still enjoy them. Budapest also has a strong tradition in **puppetry**, and many big Hungarian writers have contributed to its children's repertoire. There are some English-language performances, but again, puppet shows are good visual entertainment even without the language. Morning and matinée performances are for kids. Tickets are available from the puppet theatres (*bábszínház;* see p.196) or the ticket offices listed on p.177.

Budapest Festival Orchestra Cocoa Concerts **III, Selmeci utca 14–16, Óbuda (see p.115) and the Music Academy (see p.179)**. The ensemble, under its inspirational leader Iván Fischer, holds hour-long Sunday Cocoa concerts (*Kakaó koncert*) for children aged 5–12. Members of the orchestra introduce children to the music and the instruments – and give them a cup of cocoa, too. The concerts are usually at 2.30–4.30pm at the above venues. Tickets: ⓣ1/355-4015, ⓔrendeles@bfz.hu or at ⓦwww.bfz.hu; the website has details of dates.

Budapest Puppet Theatre (Budapest Bábszínház) VI, Andrássy út 69 ⓦwww.budapest-babszinhaz.hu (see p.64). One of the most established puppet theatres – it also does shows for adults.

Kalamajka Children's Dance House Aranytíz Club (see p.181). Children can take to the dancefloor and learn Hungarian folk dance steps to music played by leading musicians from the Kalamajka folk group. Afterwards it's the turn of the grown-ups. Late Sept–May Sat 5–6pm.

Kolibri Theatre (Színház) VI, Jókai tér 10 ⓣ1/311-0870 and Kolibri Nest (Fészek) VI, Andrássy út 74 ⓣ1/332-3720, ⓦwww.szinhaz.hu/kolibri. The Kolibri venues have shows for children of all ages, but those at the Kolibri Fészek are usually better for smaller children. Closed early June–Aug.

Millenáris Park See p.107. Regular children's programmes are put on in the *Fogadó* building here, including puppet shows, craft workshops and more.

Muzsikás Children's Dance House TEMI Fővarosi Művelődési Háza, XI, Fehérvári út 47 ⓦwww.muzsikas.hu. While members of the Muzsikás folk band – if they are not away on tour – play, two dancers take children (and their parents) through some basic steps, chanting Hungarian children's songs and rhymes – but non-Hungarian children will enjoy the dancing anyway. Sessions are held most Tues at 5.30pm from Sept–May, and cost 300Ft for children, 600Ft for adults; you pay at the door. The Capital Cultural Centre, as the venue is called in English, is a couple of stops beyond Móricz Zsigmond körtér on trams #18 and #47.

21

Shopping

Budapest's shopping scene has been transformed in recent years by the mushrooming of international chain stores and the opening of modern **shopping malls** across the city. The malls (many of which also have children's facilities such as play areas and nappy-changing rooms) have brought in long opening hours and a bright new style that sets the pace for other shops – not that many locals can afford to buy in the malls, where prices are high by Hungarian standards. Holding their own, however, against the international brands are numerous small backstreet shops, which continue to preserve **local crafts** and traditions. Budapest also has a set of distinguished **market halls** (*vásárcsarnok*) dating from the late nineteenth century, some of which still function as food markets; others have been turned into supermarkets, though you can still admire their structure. There are also some outdoor markets (*piac*), which are a more lively proposition, with smallholders coming into town to sell their produce. Most of the markets are busy, crowded places, so you should mind your pockets and bags at all times. And all of them sell some kind of refreshment – usually fried or alcoholic.

The main **shopping areas** are located to the south of Vörösmarty tér in central Pest, in particular in and around pedestrianized Váci utca, which has the biggest concentration of glamorous and expensive shops, as well as branches of popular Western stores including H&M, Mango, Springfield, Esprit and Zara. The nearby Deák Ferenc utca has been jazzed up as "Fashion Street" and attracted names such as Sisley, Tommy Hilfiger and Benetton. The main streets radiating out from the centre – Bajcsy-Zsilinszky út, Andrássy út and Rákóczi út – are other major shopping focuses, as are the Nagykörút (especially between Margit híd and Blaha Lujza tér) and the Kiskörút. Shops in the Várhegy are almost exclusively given over to providing foreign tourists with folksy souvenirs such as embroidered tablecloths, hussar pots and fancy bottles of Tokaj wine.

One feature of old Budapest that has survived is its **artisan shops**: whether it's the small jewellery workshops such as Wladis, the quirky brush shop in Dob utca and the old craftsmen and workshops in the backstreets inside the Nagykörút, or the growing number of young fashion designers whose work is deservedly attracting attention. Look out for Emilia Anda, Edina Farkas, Anikó Németh and Katti Zoób, whose clothes range from the trendy to the avant-garde and the eccentrically unwearable.

Most shops are **open** Monday to Friday between 10am and 6pm, and Saturday until 1pm, with food stores generally operating from 8am to 6pm or 7pm. Some shops in the centre of the city have extended hours on Saturdays, while the malls are open roughly 10am–8pm every day, but close around 6pm on Sunday. You can usually find a 24-hour outlet selling alcohol, cigarettes and some food in the centre of town, such as, at V, Október 6 utca 11 and at XIII,

Pozsonyi út 18. It's useful to recognize that "Azonnal jövök" or "Rögtön jövök" signs on shop doors both mean "back shortly".

Markets and market halls

Bio-piac XII, Csörsz utca 18 (see map, p.91). Organic market behind the Mom Cultural Centre (Mom Művelődési Központ), up the road from the Mom Park Mall. Great range of produce, especially in summer – the peaches, tomatoes and peppers are so much better than supermarket fare. There is also a playground for children. The odd right-wing nationalist stalls should not bother visitors. Sat 6.30am–noon.

Fény utca II, at the back of the Mammut mall, by Moszkva tér (see map, p.91). Popular market that has survived a transfer to a modern setting. There's an excellent cheese shop on the top floor, which is also where you'll find what is perhaps the best *lángos* in town – a popular stand-up snack of fried dough eaten with garlic, sour cream, cheese or all three together. Mon–Fri 6am–4pm, Sat 6am–1pm.

Great Market Hall (Nagycsarnok) IX, Vámház körút 2 (see map, p.82). By the Szabadság híd at the bottom end of Váci utca, the Nagycsarnok is the largest and finest market hall of them all, as well as being the most expensive. It also has good stalls upstairs, selling knives and wood craft amid the touristy embroideries and tat. Mon 6am–4pm, Tues–Fri 6am–6pm, Sat 6am–2pm.

Hold utca V, Hold utca 13 (see map, p.54). Right behind the American Embassy, this fine nineteenth-century market hall still has some smaller holders selling their produce. Mon–Fri 6am–5pm, Sat 6am–1pm.

▲ Paprika stall

Hunyadi tér VI (see map, p.64). Another of the old market halls, free of any modernization – though the local council is desperate to sell if off. Stalls spill out into the square in front. Mon–Fri 6am–5pm, Sat 6am–1pm.

Klauzál tér VII (see map, p.64). In the heart of the old Jewish quarter. A supermarket has squeezed the fruit and veg stands out into the entrance passage. Mon–Fri 6am–5pm, Sat 6am–1pm.

Lehel Hall XIII, Lehel tér (see map, p.54). Large, popular market housed in a wacky new market hall designed by the former dissident László Rajk – whatever you think of the exterior, it's a lively place inside with lots of small stalls. Mon–Fri 6am–5pm, Sat 6am–1pm, Sun 6am–noon.

Flea markets

Ecseri piac XIX, Nagykőrösi út (see Budapest colour map). On the southeast edge of the city, this has become a well-known spot for tourists – and for ripping them off (you'll need to bargain hard). Stalls sell everything from bike parts and jackboots to peasant clothing and hand-carved pipes, with a few genuine antiques among the tat. You can get here on bus #54 (red) from the Határ út metro stop on the blue line, or bus #54 (black) from Boráros tér by Petőfi híd. Mon–Fri 8am–4pm, Sat 8am–noon.

Petőfi Csarnok XIV, Zichy Mihály utca 14 (see map, p.74). A weekend flea market in and around the 'Pecsa', the ugly cultural centre in the Városliget, this is smaller than Ecseri, and less established. Lots of the wares are junk, but there are some good bargains too. Small entry fee. Sat & Sun 8am–2pm.

Malls

Mammut II, Széna tér ⓦ www.mammut.hu (see map, p.91). Close to Moszkva tér, and twice its original size since the opening of Mammut II next door, linked by a bridge. Amid the 320 shops, there's a cinema, fitness centre, squash courts, children's play area and nappy-changing room, as well as an excellent market at the back. Mon–Sat 10am–9pm, Sun 10am–6pm.

Mom Park XII, Alkotás utca 53 ⓦ www.mompark.hu (see map, p.91). One of the newer malls, up the road from Déli metro station, and with more than seventy shops, a cinema and a fitness centre. Mon–Sat 10am–8pm, Sun 10am–6pm.

WestEnd City Center VI, Váci út 1–3 (next to Nyugati station) ⓦ www.westend.hu (see map, p.64). Past the grand indoor waterfall cascading down at the southern entrance, you'll find brands such as Mango, Mexx and Springfield, as well as M&S. Mon–Sat 10am–9pm, Sun10am–6pm.

Antiques

Falk Miksa utca, running south off Szent István körút, near the Pest end of the Margit híd, is known as Budapest's "Street of Antiques", and is where you'll find the biggest collection of **antique stores** and galleries. Three or four times a year the street holds an evening festival of music, entertainment and, of course, antiques. There are also a couple of outlets on Kossuth Lajos utca, between Ferenciek tere and the *Astoria Hotel*.

Most antique specialists should be able to advise on what you can export from the country and how to go about it. Several shops organize **auctions**; the best months for these are April, May, September and December – check the free hotel magazine *Where Budapest* for dates. Another good source of antiques are the flea markets listed on p.198, though you'll need to be wary about parting with large sums of money, as stallholders can charge hugely inflated prices.

BÁV V, Ferenciek tere 10 (see map, p.46). One of numerous BÁV outlets in the city, this one specializes in paintings, jewellery and other treasures. They hold regular auctions at V, Bécsi utca 1. Mon–Fri 10am–6pm, Sat 9am–1pm.

Judaica VII, Wesselényi utca 13 (see map, p.64). Down the road behind the Dohány utca synagogue, and offering Jewish books, pictures and artefacts. It also organizes occasional auctions. Mon–Thurs 10am–6pm, Fri 10am–3pm.

Sóos V, József Attila utca 22 (see map, p.46). An excellent place to pick up some fine junk and secondhand photographic goods. Mon–Fri 9am–5pm, Sat 10am–1pm.

Art and photography galleries

ACB VI, Király utca 76 ⓣ 1/413-7608, ⓦ www.acbgaleria.hu (see map, p.64). Contemporary fine arts with a friendly, well-informed management, up the road from the Music Academy. Tues–Fri 2–6pm, Sat noon–4pm or by appointment.

Deák Erika Galéria VI, Jókai tér 1 ⓣ 1/302-4927, ⓦ www.deakgaleria.hu (see map, p.64). Contemporary Hungarian art gallery off Andrássy út. Wed–Fri noon–6pm, Sat 11am–6pm

Dovin Galéria V, Galamb utca 6 ⓣ 1/318-3673, ⓦ www.dovingaleria.hu (see map, p.46). Elegant gallery in central Pest selling contemporary Hungarian art. Tues–Fri noon–6pm, Sat 11am–2pm.

Knoll VI, Liszt Ferenc tér 10 ⓣ 1/267-3842 (see map, p.64). Run by the Viennese gallery owner Hans Knoll, this was the first private gallery in the city when it opened in 1989. Since then, it has built up a strong reputation, with shows by Hungarian and foreign contemporary artists. Tues–Fri 2–6.30pm, Sat 11am–2pm.

Mai Manó VI, Nagymező utca 20 ⓣ 1/473-2666 ⓦ www.maimano.hu

(see map, p.64). Contemporary and old Hungarian photographs, cards and books for sale in the shop on the first floor. The gallery above it is covered on p.85. Mon–Fri 2–7pm, Sat & Sun 11am–7pm.

Várfok Galéria I, Várfok utca 14 ⓣ1/213-5155 ⓦwww.varfok-galeria.hu (see map, p.91). The best-known of the three small galleries just off Moszkva tér, the gallery was founded in 1990 and displays work by the younger generation of Hungarian avant-garde artists. Tues–Sat 11am–6pm.

Books and maps

Hungarians love their books and Budapestis' homes tend to be crammed with literature – Book Week each June is a long-awaited event. Bookshops stock a good range of photographic albums, books about the city and foreign-language books. If it's old books and prints you want, one of the best places to head for is Múzeum körút, where there are several **secondhand bookshops** (*antikvárium*) clustered opposite the Hungarian National Museum – they have quite a selection of English and German books.

Alexandra V, Nyugati tér 7 ⓦwww.alexandrakonyveshaz.hu (see map, p.64). A vast new bookshop on five floors across from Nyugati Station, with long opening hours. There are regular, free literary and music events on its stage. Daily 10am–midnight. Its branch by the Dohány utca synagogue at Károly körút 3 (open daily till 10pm) has a secondhand section upstairs as well as a pleasant covered rooftop café.

Bestsellers V, Október 6 utca 11 ⓣ1/312-1295 (see map, p.46). Excellent range of English books, with English and Hungarian literature, travel and reference books, and newspapers too. Staff are friendly and can order books in. Mon–Fri 9am–6.30pm, Sat 10am–5pm, Sun 10am–4pm.

CEU bookshop V, Zrinyi utca 12 (see map, p.54). Attached to the Central European University, this has mainly academic books and a good selection of Hungarian literature in English. Mon–Fri 10am–6pm.

Földgömb-Térkép VI, Bajcsy-Zsilinszky út 37 (see map, p.64). A well-stocked map shop, but you have to ask the stern staff for the maps you want, which makes browsing difficult. Mon–Wed 9am–5pm, Thurs 9am–6.30pm, Fri 9am–3.30pm.

Honterus V, Múzeum körút 35 (see map, p.46). Engravings, postcards and secondhand books. Mon–Fri 10am–6pm, Sat 10am–2pm.

Írók Boltja VI, Andrássy út 45 (see map, p.64). On the premises of the prewar *Japán* coffee house, the "Writers' Bookshop" has a wide range of English-language books at the back, and a good selection of photography, art and architecture books in the main part of the shop. You can drink coffee and read at the tables in the front. Mon–Fri 10am–6pm, Sat 10am–1pm (July & Aug closed Sat).

Központi Antikvárium V, Múzeum körút 17 (see map, p.46). Large secondhand bookshop with some antiquarian books and prints too. Mon–Fri 10am–6.30pm, Sat 10am–2pm.

Libri V, Váci utca 22 and Rákoczi út 12 (see maps, p.46 & p.64). The *Studium* branch in Váci utca is a foreign language specialist store, and has a good stock of books on Hungary. English-language and travel books are upstairs at Rákoczi út 12, where you'll also find a small internet café. Mon–Fri 10am–7pm, Sat–Sun 10am–3pm.

Litea I, Hess András tér 4 (see map, p.92). A well-lit shop with a good stock of English books on Hungary, some CDs and cassettes, and a coffee bar with tables. Daily 10am–6pm.

Red Bus V, Semmelweis utca 14 ⓣ1/337-7453, ⓦwww.redbusbudapest.hu (see map, p.64). Up the road from *Astoria*, and a good place to pick up secondhand English paperbacks for your holiday reading. Mon–Fri 10am–6pm, Sat 10am–2pm.

Térképkirály VI, Bajcsy-Zsilinszky út 23 (see map, p.64). Range of maps and guidebooks across the road from Arany János utca metro station. Also sells BKV public transport tickets. Mon–Fri 9am–5.30pm.

Treehugger Dan VI, Csengery utca 48 ⓣ1/322-0774 ⓦwww.treehugger.hu (see map, p.64). Tiny and easy to miss shop just off Andrássy út that's packed with second-hand books. They're mainly in English, though there's a small French and German selection too – and its gay and lesbian section is possibly the only one in town. You can also loiter here over a smoke-free cup of organic Fairtrade tea, coffee or chocolate and use the wi-fi access. Dan is also an environmental activist, and organizes music and talks here and at his other outlet in the Discover Hungary office behind the Opera at VI, Lázár utca 16. Mon–Fri 10am–7pm, Sat 10am–5pm.

Clothes, jewellery and shoes

Eclectick V, Irányi utca 20 (see map, p.46). Clothes designed by Edina Farkas, and a retro shop – toys and more – in the basement. Mon–Fri 10am–6pm, Sat 11am–4pm.

Emilia Anda V, Váci utca 16/b and Galamb utca 4 (see map, p.46). Classy, well-designed day and evening wear for women, and a range of jewellery including chunky rings and beautiful pendants. Mon–Fri 11am–6pm, Sat 11am–2pm.

Fleischer Shirts VI, Paulay Ede utca 53 (see map, p.64). Old-fashioned shirt-maker selling handmade garments at good prices. On the corner of Nagymező utca, 5min walk from the Opera House. Mon–Fri 10am–6pm.

Havalda Leather VI, Hajós utca 23 ⓦwww.havalda.hu (see map, p.64). Leather belt shop, opened in 1938 by the grandparents of the present owner. Sells belts, purses, dog leads and collars and other leather goods. Open Mon–Fri 11am–7pm.

Iguana V, Krúdy Gyula utca 9 (see map, p.46). A packed, stuffy shop selling all kinds of 1950s, 1960s and 1970s retro fashion – clothes, bags, music, sunglasses and jewellery. Mon–Fri 10am–6pm, Sat 10am–1pm.

Clothing and shoe sizes

Women's dresses and skirts

American	4	6	8	10	12	14	16	18
British	8	10	12	14	16	18	20	22
Continental	38	40	42	44	46	48	50	52

Women's blouses and sweaters

American	6	8	10	12	14	16	18
British	30	32	34	36	38	40	42
Continental	40	42	44	46	48	50	52

Women's shoes

American	5	6	7	8	9	10	11
British	3	4	5	6	7	8	9
Continental	36	37	38	39	40	41	42

Men's suits

American	34	36	38	40	42	44	46	48
British	34	36	38	40	42	44	46	48
Continental	44	46	48	50	52	54	56	58

Men's shirts

American	14	15	15.5	16	16.5	17	17.5	18
British	14	15	15.5	16	16.5	17	17.5	18
Continental	36	38	39	41	42	43	44	45

Men's shoes

American	7	7.5	8	8.5	9.5	10	10.5	11	11.5
British	6	7	7.5	8	9	9.5	10	11	12
Continental	39	40	41	42	43	44	44	45	46

Katti Zoób V, Szent István körút 17 ⓦwww.kattizoob.com (see map, p.54). Among the band of young designers who've made a big splash with their products, Zoób is one of the most successful, and uses gorgeous fabrics. She has also collaborated with the porcelain company Zsolnay to produce jewellery. Her store is inside the courtyard to the right. Mon–Fri 10am–6pm, Sat 10am–1pm.
Manier V, Nyáry Pál utca 4 ⓦwww.manier.hu (see map, p.46). Zany, appealing clothes by Anikó Németh; the designs have calmed down from the Baroque early days but they retain plenty of inventiveness. The first-floor shop/workshop is just off the lower half of Váci utca, behind no. 48. Mon–Fri 10am–6pm.
Paróka bolt VII, Dob utca 31 (see map, p.64). Wig-makers in the heart of the old Jewish quarter. Wigs don't come much cheaper between here and Brooklyn. Mon–Fri 10am–6pm.
Tisza shoes VII, Károly körút 1 (see map, p.64). This Hungarian brand of trainers is an unlikely survivor of the Communist era, and the shop at the Astoria junction, Tisza Cipő, has won an international reputation for the hipness of the shoes. Mon–Fri 10am–6pm, Sat 10am–1pm.
Valéria Fazekas V, Váci utca 50 (see map, p.46). Another of the more creative places on the lower part of Váci utca, this small shop produces delightful hats, some wacky and some very wearable. Mon–Fri 10am–6pm, Sat 10am–4pm.
Vass V, Haris köz 2. A traditional shoemaker, just behind Ferenciek tere, producing handmade shoes to order and ready-to-wear. Mon–Fri 10am–6pm, Sat 10am–1pm.

Household goods

Brush shop VII, Dob utca 3 (see map, p.64). A wonderful little place: every kind of brush you can think of in this very traditional artisan's shop. Mon–Fri 10am–6pm, Sat 10am–1pm.
Kátay VI, Teréz körút 28 (see map, p.64). Just the place to add that Hungarian touch to your kitchen – whether it is a wooden spoon stand, a special noodle-making board or authentic Budapest café coffee glasses. Mon–Fri 10am–6pm, Sat 10am–1pm.

Pottery, jewellery and crafts

Haas & Czjzek VI, Bajcsy-Zsilinszky út 23, ⓦwww.porcelan.hu (see map, p.64). Full selection of Hungarian porcelain, including Hollóháza, Alföld and Zsolnay, and some glassware. The shop dates back to 1792, as the small display at the back documents. Mon–Fri 10am–7pm, Sat 10am–3pm.
Herend V, József nádor tér 11, ⓦwww.herend.com (see map, p.54). Very fancy – some would say twee – and expensive porcelain from the Herend factory in western Hungary, as collected by the likes of Queen Victoria. Mon–Fri 10am–6pm, Sat 10am–1pm.
Holló Folk Art Gallery V, Vitkovics Mihály utca 10 (see map, p.46). This beautiful early nineteenth-century shop near the Astoria is a very pleasant place in which to browse wares such as intricately iced gingerbread figures, and wooden furniture, boxes, eggs and candlesticks, all hand-painted with bird, tulip and heart folk motifs. Mon–Fri 10am–6pm, Sat 10am–1pm.
Intuita V, Váci utca 67 (see map, p.46). Amid the tourist tat at the main market hall end of Váci utca, this shop stands out for its quality Hungarian pottery and jewellery. Mon–Fri 10am–6pm, Sat 10am–1pm.
Ómama Bizsúja V, Szent István körút 1 (see map, p.54). A tiny treasure-trove of a shop – its entrance is tucked in to the left as you walk down the passageway that leads from the street at the Pest end of the Margit híd. Absolutely crammed full of jewellery – in amongst the more glitzy costume jewellery there are some stunning Deco-style pieces and good-quality paste. Mon–Fri 10am–6pm, Sat 10am–1pm.
Wladis Galéria V, Falk Miksa utca 13 ⓦwww.wladisgaleria.hu (see map, p.54). Founded by a lecturer at the Applied Arts College the workshop produces very appealing chunky silver jewellery at a price: rings from 20,000Ft and earrings from 29,000Ft. Mon–Fri 10am–6pm, Sat 10am–1pm.

Photos

Fotólabor VIII, Gyulai Pál utca 14 (see map, p.82). Good black and white prints done very cheaply, and photos developed and enlarged. Mon–Fri 8am–6pm.

Fotolux VII, Károly körút 21 (see map, p.46). Good-quality photographic developing and printing, and professional films. Mon–Fri 9am–9pm, Sat 9am–7pm.

Records and CDs

CD Bar VIII, Krúdy Gyula utca 6 (see map, p.82). Basement shop in an increasingly fashionable backstreet a couple of streets behind the Hungarian National Museum, selling classical and jazz records. Mon–Fri 10am–8pm, Sat 10am–4pm.

Fonó XI, Sztregova utca 3 (see map, p.109). It's a 20min tram ride from Deák tér on #47 to get to the shop in the bar of this folk club, but it's worth the effort for the range of jazz, ethno-jazz blues and world music and, above all, Hungarian folk CDs. Wed–Fri 5–10pm, Sat 7–10pm.

Kodály Zoltán Zeneműbolt V, Múzeum körút 21 (see map, p.46). Scores of CDs, tapes and secondhand Hungarian classical records, opposite the Hungarian National Museum. Mon–Fri 10am–6pm, Sat 10am–1pm.

Lemezdokk VIII, Horánszky utca 27 (see map, p.82). Just off Krúdy Gyula utca, with lots of old vinyl as well as some CDs; they have blues, rock and some jazz. Mon–Fri 11am–6pm Sat 10am–2pm.

MCD V, Sütő utca 2 (see map, p.46). CD megastore behind the Lutheran church on Deák tér. Mon–Fri 10am–6pm, Sat 10am–1pm.

MesterPorta I, Corvin tér 7 (see map, p.91). The outlet for Etnofon Records, one of the most active publishers of Hungarian and other folk music, and also sells instruments and sheet music. The shop is a tram stop down from Batthyány tér. Mon–Fri 10am–6pm.

Rózsavölgyi Zeneműbolt V, Szervita tér 5 (see map, p.46). Long-established record shop with a knowledgeable staff, near Vörösmarty tér. Classical music on the ground floor, rock and folk downstairs. It has a concert ticket office at the back, and is good for sheet music as well. Mon–Fri 9.30am–7pm (Wed 10am), Sat 10am–5pm.

Wave VI, Révay utca 4 (see map, p.54). Small CD shop off the bottom of Bajcsy-Zsilinszky út; staff are well-informed on its range of underground and Hungarian folk. They also sell tickets to concerts. Mon–Fri 11am–7pm, Sat 11am–3pm

Toys

Fajáték VII, Erzsébet körút 23 (see map, p.64). Small shop near the junction with Wesselényi utca, packed with wooden toys. Mon–Fri 10am–6pm, Sat 10am–1pm.

Fakopáncs VIII, Baross utca 46 ⓦwww.fakopancs.hu (see map, p.82). A massive array of wooden puzzles and toys in this "Woodpecker" shop, near the junction of Baross utca and the Nagykörút. They have a smaller outlet round the corner at József körút 50. Mon–Fri 9am–7pm, Sat 9am–4pm, Sun 9am–2pm.

Játékszerek anno VI, Teréz körút 54 (see map, p.64). Beautifully made reproductions of toys and games from the turn of the last century, including wooden tops, kaleidoscopes, and a spectacular wind-up duck on a bicycle. Mon–Fri 10am–6pm, Sat 9am–1pm.

Modell Makett VII, Erzsébet körút 51 (see map, p.64). Small shop selling models and do-it-yourself kits of buses, cars, trams and trains. Mon–Fri 10am–6pm, Sat 10am–1pm.

Food, wine and pálinka

Bio ABC V, Múzeum körút 19 (see map, p.46). Natural oils, organic fruits, juices, cheeses and snacks. Opposite the Hungarian National Museum. Mon–Fri 10am–7pm, Sat 10am–2pm.

Bio Centrum II, Széna tér 3, inside the Mammut I (see map, p.91). This is the city's only organic supermarket, on the first floor of the Mammut mall. Mon–Sat 10am–9pm, Sun 10am–6pm.

Budapest Wine Society V, Szent István tér 3 ⓣ1/328-0314 ⓦwww.bortarsasag.hu (see map, p.54). The most central branch of what's become the major distributor of Hungary's leading producers, with excellent wines and good advice in English. There are two more outlets in the centre: a larger store at Batthyány utca 59, up the hill from Moszkva tér, and a smaller one at Ráday utca 7, near Kálvin tér. Mon–Fri noon–8pm, Sat 10am–4pm.

Életház XII, Böszörményi út 13-15 (see map, p.91). One of the first organic shops in Budapest, this lies above Déli metro station and has a range of foods, cosmetics and other eco-products. Mon–Fri 10am–6pm, Sat 10am–1pm.

In Vino Veritas VII, Dohány utca 58–62 ⓣ1/341-3174, ⓦwww.borkereskedes.hu (see map, p.64). Friendly store close to Blaha Lujza tér, with an excellent range of wines as well as other produce. Mon–Fri 9am–8pm, Sat 10am–6pm.

La Boutique des Vins V, József Attila utca 12 ⓣ1/266-4397, ⓦwww.malatinszky.hu (see map, p.46). Founded by the former sommelier of the *Gundel* restaurant (see p.164) who now has a vineyard of his own. Strongest in wines from Villány and Tokaj. Mon–Fri 10am–6pm, Sept–May also Sat 10am–3pm.

Magyar Pálinka Háza VIII, Rákóczi út 17 (see map, p.64). A surprising range of flavours going far beyond the conventional pear and apricot *pálinkas* to include elderflower, paprika and many more. Mon–Sat 9am–7pm.

Rothschild VII, Dob utca 12 (see map, p.64). On the edge of the Jewish quarter, a couple of minutes' walk from the Dohány utca synagogue, this is one of the few shops in Budapest selling kosher Hungarian and imported wines and foods. Mon–Thurs 10am–6pm, Fri 9am–2pm. In town, there's another large outlet at Arany János utca 27–29 (Mon–Fri 7am–10pm, Sat 8am–6pm, Sun 9am–2pm.)

Contexts

Contexts

History......207

Books......215

History

Although Budapest has only formally existed since 1873, when the twin cities of Buda and Pest were united in a single municipality together with the smaller Óbuda – initially known throughout Europe as "Pest-Buda" – the locality has been settled since **prehistory**. *Homo sapiens* appeared here around 8000 BC, and a succession of peoples overran the region during the first Age of Migrations, the most important of whom were the **Celtic** Eravisci who settled on Gellért-hegy in about 400 BC.

In 35 BC the Danube Basin was conquered by the **Romans** and subsequently incorporated within their empire as the province of Pannonia, whose northern half was governed from the town of **Aquincum** on the west bank of the Danube. Ruins of a camp, villas, baths and an amphitheatre can still be seen today in Óbuda and Rómaifürdo. Roman rule lasted until 430 AD, when Pannonia was ceded to **Attila the Hun**. Attila's planned assault on Rome was averted by his death on his wedding night, and thereafter Pannonia was carved up by **Germanic tribes** until they were ousted by the Turkic-speaking **Avars**, who were in turn assailed by the Bulgars, another warlike race from the Eurasian steppes. Golden torques and other treasures from Hun, Goth and Avar burial sites – now on display in the National Museum – suggest that they were quite sophisticated rather than mere "barbarians".

The coming of the Magyars

The most significant of the invaders from the east were the **Magyars**, who stamped their language and identity on Hungary. Their origins lie in the Finno-Ugric peoples who dwelt in the snowy forests between the Volga and the Urals, where today two Siberian peoples still speak languages that are the closest linguistic relatives to Hungarian; along with Finnish, Turkish and Mongolian, these languages make up the Altaic family. Many of these Magyars migrated south, where they eventually became vassals of the Khazar empire and mingled with the Bulgars as both peoples moved westwards to escape the marauding Petchenegs.

In 895 or 896 AD, seven Magyar tribes led by Árpád entered the Carpathian Basin and spread out across the plain, in what Hungarians call the "**landtaking**" (*honfoglalás*). They settled here, though they remained raiders for the next seventy years, striking terror as far afield as France (where people thought them to be Huns), until a series of defeats persuaded them to settle for assimilating their gains. According to the medieval chronicler, known today simply as Anonymous, the clan of Árpád settled on Csepel-sziget, and it was Árpád's brother, Buda, who purportedly gave his name to the west bank of the new settlement.

The Árpád dynasty

Civilization developed gradually after Árpád's great-grandson **Prince Géza** established links with Bavaria and invited Catholic missionaries to Hungary. His son **Stephen** (István) took the decisive step of applying to Pope Sylvester for recognition, and on Christmas Day in the year 1000 AD was crowned as a Christian king. With the help of the Italian Bishop Gellért, he then set about converting his pagan subjects. Stephen was subsequently credited with the **foundation of Hungary** and canonized after his death in 1038. His mummified hand and the crown of St Stephen have since been revered as both holy and national relics, and are today some of Budapest's most popular tourist attractions.

Despite succession struggles after Stephen's death, a lack of external threats during the eleventh and twelfth centuries enabled the **development of Buda and Pest** to begin in earnest, largely thanks to French, Walloon and German settlers who worked and traded here under royal protection. However, the growth in royal power caused tribal leaders to rebel in 1222, and Andrew II was forced to recognize the noble status and rights of the **nation** – landed freemen exempt from taxation – in the Golden Bull, a kind of Hungarian Magna Carta.

Andrew's son **Béla IV** tried to restore royal authority, but the **Mongol invasion** of 1241 devastated the country and left even the royal palace of Esztergom in ruins. Only the timely death of Ghengis Khan spared Hungary from further ravages. Mindful of a return visit, Béla selected **Várhegy** as a more defensible seat and encouraged foreign artisans to rebuild Buda, which German colonists called "*Ofen*" after its numerous lime-kilns (the name Pest, which is of Slav origin, also means "oven").

Renaissance and decline

After the Árpád dynasty expired in 1301, foreign powers advanced their own claims to the throne and for a while there were three competing kings, all duly crowned. Eventually **Charles Robert** of the French Angevin (or Anjou) dynasty triumphed. Peacetime gave him the opportunity to develop the gold mines of Transylvania and northern Hungary – the richest in Europe – and Charles bequeathed a robust exchequer to his son **Louis the Great**, whose reign saw the population of Hungary rise to three million, and the crown territories expand to include much of what are now Croatia and Poland. The oldest extant strata of the Buda Palace on Várhegy date from this time.

After Louis' demise, the throne was claimed by **Sigismund of Luxembourg**, Prince of Bohemia, whom the nobility despised as the "Czech swine". His failure to check the advance of the Turks through the Balkans was only redeemed by the Transylvanian warlord **János Hunyadi**, whose lifting of the siege of Belgrade caused rejoicing throughout Christendom. Vajdahunyad Castle in the Városliget is a romantic nineteenth-century replica of Hunyadi's ancestral seat in Transylvania.

Hunyadi's nephew, **Mátyás Corvinus**, is remembered as the **Renaissance king** who, together with his second wife Beatrice of Naples, lured humanists and artists from Italy to their court. Mátyás was an enlightened despot, renowned for his fairness, but when he died in 1490, leaving no legitimate heir, the nobles took control, choosing a pliable successor and exploiting the peasantry. However in 1514 the peasants, led by **György Dózsa**, rebelled against the oppression. The savage repression of this **revolt** (over 70,000 peasants were killed and Dózsa was roasted alive) and subsequent laws imposing "perpetual serfdom" alienated the mass of the population – a situation hardly improved by the coronation of the 9-year-old **Louis II**, who was barely 16 when he had to face the full might of the Turks under Sultan Süleyman "the Magnificent".

The Turkish conquest: Hungary divided

The battle of **Mohács** in 1526 was a shattering defeat for the Hungarians – the king and half the nobility perished, leaving Hungary leaderless. After sacking Buda, the Turks withdrew to muster forces for their real objective, Vienna. To forestall this, Ferdinand of Habsburg proclaimed himself king of Hungary and occupied the western part of the country, while in Buda the nobles put János Zápolyai on the throne. Following Zápolyai's death in 1541, Ferdinand claimed full sovereignty, but the Sultan occupied Buda and central Hungary and made Zápolyai's son ruler of Transylvania, which henceforth became a semi-autonomous principality – a tripartite division known as the **Tripartium**, formally recognized in 1568. Despite various truces, warfare became a fact of life for the next 150 years, and national independence was not to be recovered for centuries afterwards.

Turkish-occupied Hungary was ruled by a Pasha in Buda, with much of the land either deeded to the Sultan's soldiers and officials, or run directly as a state fief. The towns, however, enjoyed some rights and were encouraged to trade, and the Turks were largely indifferent to the sectarian bigotry practised in Habsburg-ruled Hungary. The Habsburg **liberation of Buda** in 1686 was actually a disaster for its inhabitants, as the victors massacred Jews, pillaged at will and reduced Buda and Pest to rubble. The city's Turkish baths and the tomb of Gül Baba were among the few surviving buildings.

Habsburg rule

Habsburg rule was a bitter pill, which the Hungarians attempted to reject in the **War of Independence** of 1703–11, led by Prince **Ferenc Rákóczi II**. Though it was unsuccessful, the Habsburgs began to soften their autocracy with paternalism as a result. The revival of towns and villages during this time owed much to settlers from all over the empire, hence the Serb and Greek churches that remain in Pest and Szentendre. Yet while the aristocracy commissioned over two hundred palaces, and Baroque town centres and orchestras flourished, the masses remained all but serfs, mired in isolated villages.

Such contradictions impelled the Reform movement led by **Count István Széchenyi**. His vision of progress was embodied in the construction of the Lánchíd (Chain Bridge) between Buda and Pest, which proved an enormous spur to the development of the two districts. The National Museum, the Academy of Sciences and many other institutions were founded at this time, while the coffee houses of Pest became a hotbed of radical politics. Széchenyi's arch-rival was **Lajos Kossuth**, small-town lawyer turned member of parliament and editor of the radical *Pesti Hirlap*, which scandalized and delighted citizens. Kossuth detested the Habsburgs, revered "universal liberty", and demanded an end to serfdom and censorship. Magyar chauvinism was his blind spot, however, and the law of 1840, his greatest pre-revolutionary achievement, inflamed dormant nationalist feelings among Croats, Slovaks and Romanians by making Hungarian the sole official language.

When the empire was shaken by revolutions that broke out across Europe in **March 1848**, local radicals seized the moment. Kossuth dominated Parliament, while **Sándor Petőfi** mobilized crowds on the streets of Pest. A second war of independence followed, which again ended in defeat and Habsburg repression, epitomized by the execution of Prime Minister Batthyány in 1849, and the Citadella atop Gellért-hegy, built to intimidate citizens with its guns.

Budapest's Belle Époque

Gradually, brute force was replaced by a **policy of compromise**, by which Hungary was economically integrated with Austria and, as Austrian power waned, given a major shareholding in the Habsburg empire, henceforth known as the "Dual Monarchy". The compromise (*Ausgleich*) of 1867, engineered by **Ferenc Deák**, brought Hungary prosperity and status, but tied the country inextricably to the empire's fortunes. Buda and Pest underwent rapid expansion and formally merged. Pest was extensively remodelled, acquiring the Nagykörút (Great Boulevard) and Andrássy út, a grand approach to the Városliget, where Hungary's millennial anniversary celebrations were staged in 1896, marking a thousand years since the arrival of the Hungarian tribes in the Carpathian Basin. (In fact they arrived in 895 but preparations were late, so the official date was adjusted to 896.) New suburbs were created to house the burgeoning population, which was by now predominantly Magyar, though there were still large German and Jewish communities. Both elegance and squalor abounded, café society reached its apogee, and Budapest experienced a **cultural efflorescence** in the early years of the twentieth century to rival that of Vienna. Today, the most tangible reminders are the remarkable buildings by Ödön Lechner, Béla Lajta and other masters of Art Nouveau and National Romanticism – the styles that characterized the era.

The Horthy years

Dragged into **World War I** by its allegiance to Austria and Germany, Hungary was facing defeat by the autumn of 1918. The Western or Entente powers decided to dismantle the Habsburg empire in favour of the "**Successor States**" – Romania, Czechoslovakia and Yugoslavia – which would acquire much of their territory at Hungary's expense. In Budapest, the October 30 "Michaelmas Daisy Revolution" put the Social Democratic party of Count **Mihály Károlyi** in power, but his government avoided the issue of land reform, attempted unsuccessfully to negotiate peace with the Entente and finally resigned when France backed further demands by the Successor States.

On March 21, 1919, a **Republic of Councils** (*Tanácsköztársaság*) was proclaimed led by **Béla Kun**, which ruled through local Soviets. Hoping for radical change and believing that "Russia will save us", many initially supported the new regime, but enforced nationalization of land and capital and attacks on religion soon alienated the majority. After 134 days, the regime collapsed before the advancing Romanian army, which occupied Budapest.

Then came the **White Terror**, as right-wing gangs moved up from the south killing "Reds" and Jews, who were made scapegoats for the earlier Communist

"Red Terror" – especially in Budapest, the Bolshevik capital. **Admiral Miklós Horthy**, self-appointed regent for Karl IV, who had been exiled by the Western allies ("the Admiral without a fleet, for the king without a kingdom") entered what he called the "sinful city" on a white horse, and ordered a return to "traditional values". Meanwhile, at the Paris Conference, Hungary was obliged to sign the **Treaty of Trianon** (July 4, 1920), surrendering two-thirds of its historic territory and three-fifths of its total population (three million in all) to the Successor States. The bitterest loss was **Transylvania** – a devastating blow to national pride. Horthy's regency was characterized by gala balls and hunger marches, revanchism and growing **anti-Semitism**, enshrined in law from 1925. Yet Horthy was a moderate compared to the **Arrow Cross** Fascists waiting in the wings, whose power grew as **World War II** raged, and the Hungarian Second Army perished at Stalingrad.

Anticipating Horthy's defection from the Axis in October 1944, Nazi Germany staged a coup, installing an Arrow Cross government, which enabled them to begin the massacre of the **Jews** of Budapest. It was only thanks to the valiant efforts of foreign diplomats like Wallenberg and Lutz that half of them survived, when ninety percent of Hungary's provincial Jews perished. In late December, the Red Army smashed through the defensive "Attila Line" and encircled the capital, held by German troops. During the seven-week **siege of Budapest**, citizens endured endless shelling amidst a bitter winter, as street-fighting raged. In January the Germans withdrew from Pest, blew up the Danube bridges and holed up in Buda, where Várhegy was reduced to rubble as the Red Army battered the *Wehrmacht* into submission. Aside from the Jews in the ghetto – for whom it meant salvation from the Arrow Cross – the city's **liberation** on February 13, 1945 brought little joy to Budapestis, as the Red Army embarked on an orgy of rape and looting, followed by a wave of deportations to Siberia.

The Communist takeover and the 1956 Uprising

As Budapestis struggled to rebuild their lives after the war, the Soviet-backed **Communists** took control bit by bit – stealthily reducing the power of other forces in society, and using the threat of the Red Army and the **ÁVO secret police**, who took over the former Arrow Cross torture chambers on Andrássy út. By 1948 their hold on Hungary was total, symbolized by the red stars that everywhere replaced the crown of St Stephen, and a huge statue of Stalin beside the Városliget, where citizens were obliged to parade before Hungary's "Little Stalin", **Mátyás Rákosi**.

The power struggles in the Moscow Communist Party leadership that followed the death of Stalin in 1953 were replicated in the other eastern European capitals, and in Hungary Rákosi was replaced by **Imre Nagy**. Nagy's "New Course" allowed Hungarians an easier life before Rákosi struck back by expelling him from the Party for "deviationism". However, society had taken heart from the respite and intellectuals held increasingly outspoken public debates during the summer of 1956. The mood came to a head in October, when 200,000 people attended the funeral of László Rajk (a victim of the show trials in 1949) in Kerepesi Cemetery, and Budapest's students decided to march to the General Bem statue near the Margit híd.

On October 23, demonstrators chanting anti Rákosi slogans crossed the Danube to mass outside Parliament. As dusk fell, students demanding access to the Radio Building were fired upon by the ÁVO, and a spontaneous **1956 Uprising** began, which rapidly took hold throughout Budapest and spread across Hungary. The newly restored Nagy found himself in a maelstrom, as popular demands were irreconcilable with realpolitik – independence and withdrawing from the Warsaw Pact were anathema to the Kremlin. It was Hungary's misfortune that the UN was preoccupied with the Suez Crisis when the Soviets reinvaded on November 10, crushing all resistance in six days. An estimated 2500 Hungarians died and some 200,000 fled abroad; back home, hundreds were executed and thousands gaoled for their part in the uprising.

"Goulash socialism" and the end of Communism

After Soviet power had been bloodily restored, **János Kádár** gradually normalized conditions, embarking on cautious reforms to create a "**goulash socialism**" that made Hungary the envy of its Warsaw Pact neighbours and the West's favourite Communist state in the late 1970s. Though everyone knew the limits of the "Hungarian condition", there was enough freedom and consumer goods to keep the majority content. Decentralized management, limited private enterprise and competition made Hungary's economy healthy compared to other Socialist states, but in the 1980s it became apparent that the attempt to reconcile a command economy and one-party rule with market forces was unsustainable. Dissidents tested the limits of criticism, and even within the Party there were those who realized that changes were needed. Happily, this coincided with the advent of Gorbachev, which made it much easier for the reform Communists to shunt Kádár aside in 1988.

The **end of Communism** was heralded by two events the following summer: the ceremonial reburial of Imre Nagy, and the dismantling of the barbed wire along the border with Austria, which enabled thousands of East Germans to escape to the west while "on holiday". In October 1989, the government announced the legalization of other parties as a prelude to free elections, and the People's Republic was renamed the Republic of Hungary in a ceremony broadcast live on national television. Two weeks later this was eclipsed by the fall of the Berlin Wall, closely followed by the Velvet Revolution in Czechoslovakia and the overthrow of Ceauceşcu in Romania on Christmas Day.

Budapest today: the post-Communist era

Hungary's first **free elections** in the spring of 1990 resulted in a humiliating rejection of the reform Communists' Hungarian Socialist Party (MSzP), and the installation of a centre-right coalition government dominated by the **Hungarian Democratic Forum (MDF)** under Premier **József Antall**. Committed to a total break with Communism, the MDF aimed to restore the traditions and hierarchies of prewar Hungary and its former position in Europe. While this appealed to many, not everyone wanted the Catholic Church to regain its earlier power, and Hungary's neighbours were quick to suspect a revanchist claim on the lost lands of Trianon. For most Hungarians, however, inflation, unemployment, crime and homelessness were more pressing issues.

After Antall's premature death in 1993, his successor failed to turn the economy around and the 1994 elections saw the **Socialists** (under the **MSzP** party) return to power. To allay fears of a return to totalitarianism, they included the **Free Democrats** (**SzDSz**) in government, and reassured Hungary's foreign creditors with austerity measures that angered voters who had expected the Socialists to reverse the growing inequalities in society. It soon became obvious that they were riddled with corruption; some party members became millionaires almost overnight. The brash new entrepreneurial class and consumer culture were deeply unsettling to many, especially the older generation.

The 1998 elections were narrowly won by the **Fidesz-Hungarian Civic Party** of **Viktor Orbán**, a Tony Blair-like figure who repositioned his party to the right, stressing the need to revive national culture and using the buzzword *polgári* (meaning "civic", but redolent of bourgeois middle-class values) to appeal to a broad constituency. The youngest prime minister in Hungarian history, Orbán promoted a conservative Christian agenda with an acute understanding of national and religious symbolism. Like Admiral Horthy, he regarded Budapest with suspicion, trying to undermine its SzDSz mayor, Gábor Demszky, by halting the building of the National Theatre (whose foundations had already been laid at vast expense), and cancelling the city's planned fourth metro line.

With an expanding economy, falling inflation and low unemployment levels – plus the achievement of steering Hungary into Nato – Orbán anticipated victory in the parliamentary elections of 2002. Instead, after a vitriolic campaign, his Fidesz-MDF coalition was ousted, the electorate preferring a return to the centre-left alliance of Socialists and Free Democrats that had governed before. This time the premier was former banker **Péter Medgyessy**, who lacked Orbán's charisma but reaped the benefits of his tough negotiations over Hungary's accession to the **European Union**, which it joined on May 1, 2004. While most Hungarians were fervently committed to membership, there was a widespread wish to limit foreign ownership – contrary to EU directives – and anxiety about the allocation of agricultural subsidies.

Dissatisfaction at Medgyessy's performance led to his resignation in August 2004, the premiership passing to sports minister and millionaire businessman **Ferenc Gyurcsány**, who revitalised the Socialists by appointing a cabinet of fellow millionaires who got rich during the privatization of state assets in the 1990s. Like previous governments, however, they faced the dilemma that Hungary was living beyond its means – its budget deficit of ten percent of GDP was the highest in the EU – while voters opposed further belt-tightening or reforms of the health system. By promising better welfare while secretly running up deficits, Gyurcsány managed to delay a reckoning long enough to win the April 2006 election – the first time a government had been re-elected since democracy was restored.

In September 2006, however, national radio broadcast a tape-recording of him telling his cabinet that austerity measures were inevitable "because we fucked up. Not a little, a lot... We lied in the morning, we lied in the evening." A furore ensued, with weeks of demonstrations outside Parliament led by Fidesz and the MDF, which boycotted the state ceremony marking the fiftieth anniversary of the Uprising, staging their own rally on October 23. That night, **rioting** erupted, protesters battling police around Kossuth tér and Nyugati station. In a throwback to 1956, they waved Hungarian flags with a hole cut out, and even managed to activate an old Soviet tank from a museum (which stalled before it reached Parliament). While Fidesz blamed the rioting on police brutality and public anger at Gyurcsány's duplicity, the government accused Fidesz of colluding with far-right extremists in an attempted coup.

Incredibly, Gyurcsány not only weathered the storm but imposed many of the austerity measures that voters dreaded, thanks to a divided opposition lacking alternative remedies for Hungary's fiscal crisis, and an apathetic electorate deeply cynical about all politicians. After eighteen years of democracy, sociologists found Hungarians more disillusioned, and society more divided, than at any time since the Horthy era. Much publicized parades by uniformed **far-right groups** flaunting the "Árpád stripes" of the Arrow Cross – the Magyar Gárda (Hungarian Guard) and Jóbbik (Movement for Better Hungary) – dismay liberal Hungarians, but few seriously fear Fascism taking hold in what is now an EU state.

While governments have come and gone since the historic election of 1990, Budapest's administration has remained in the hands of **Mayor Gábor Demszky**, on his fifth term in office at the time of writing. A teenage Maoist turned democratic activist in the Kádár era, he is neither an *apparatchik* nor a nationalist, but has a record of competence and a dour image that chimes with the gritty cynicism of Budapestis. Demszky has steered the city forwards without any major upsets, finally securing state funding for a **fourth metro line**, running from Keleti station in Pest to Ételе tér in Buda. Scheduled for completion in 2012 but already over time and budget, its construction seems likely to be the headstone of his career as mayor of one of the great cities of Europe.

Books

There is a wide range of books on Budapest available in the city, particularly architecture titles, or translations of Hungarian literature. Books tagged with the ★ symbol are particularly recommended. For a gentle introduction to Hungarian current affairs and literature, look for the locally published *The Hungarian Quarterly* (Ⓦwww.hungarianquarterly.com). See p.200 for a list of Budapest's better bookshops, most of which can take orders.

Art, architecture and photography

Our Budapest. A very informative series of pocket-size books: written in Hungarian and English by experts in their fields, and published by Budapest City Hall, they cover the city's architecture, baths and parks, and are very cheap, though unfortunately the standard of English varies.

★ **Irén Ács** *Hungary at Home*. Excellent collection of photos covering all walks of life in postwar Hungary. Her other books, including *Rendezvous*, are also worth looking out for in bookshops.

★ **Bruno Bourel & Lajos Parti Nagy** *Lightscapes*. One of the most interesting collections of photos available. Taken around the city by Bourel, a sharp-eyed French photographer who has lived there for many years, they are accompanied by words from a leading contemporary Hungarian writer.

Györgyi Éri *et al A Golden Age: Art and Society in Hungary 1896–1914*. Hungary's Art Nouveau age captured in a beautifully illustrated coffee-table volume.

★ **János Gerle** *et al Budapest: An Architectural Guide*. The best of the small new guides to the city's twentieth-century architecture, covering almost 300 buildings, with brief descriptions in Hungarian and English.

Ruth Gruber *Jewish Heritage Travel: A Guide to Central and Eastern Europe*. The most comprehensive guide to Jewish sights in Budapest and elsewhere.

Edwin Heathcote *Budapest: A Guide to Twentieth-Century Architecture*. A useful and informative pocket guide to the city, though with some curious omissions.

Tamás Hofer *et al Hungarian Peasant Art*. An excellently produced examination of Hungarian folk art, with lots of good photos.

Imre Móra *Budapest Then and Now*. A personal and very informative set of accounts of life in the capital, past and present.

★ **László Lugo Lugosi** *et al Budapest – On the Danube*; *Walks In the Jewish Quarter*; *The Castle District*; *Jewish Budapest*; *Walks Around the Great Boulevard*. A series of small-format architectural guides – the last one is especially recommended.

Tamás Révész *Budapest: A City before the Millennium*. Excellent collection of black and white photographs of the city, though the text can be irritating.

Dora Wieberson *et al The Architecture of Historic Hungary*. Comprehensive illustrated survey of Hungarian architecture through the ages.

History, politics and society

Robert Bideleux & Ian Jeffries *A History of Eastern Europe: Crisis and Change.* An excellent and wide-ranging history of the region.

Judit Frigyesi *Béla Bartók and Turn-of-the-century Budapest.* Placing Bartók in his cultural milieu, this is an excellent account of the Hungarian intellectual world at the beginning of the century.

Jörg K Hoensch *A History of Modern Hungary 1867–1994.* An authoritative history of the country.

László Kontler *Millennium in Central Europe: A History of Hungary.* Another very thorough and reliable history of the country, although its archaic style lets it down somewhat.

Paul Lendvai *The Hungarians: 1000 Years of Victory in Defeat.* Refreshing and authoritative book on Hungary's complex and often tragic history, with particularly stimulating accounts of the Treaty of Trianon and the subsequent Nazi and Communist tyrannies – there are some fascinating pictures, too.

Bill Lomax *Hungary 1956.* Still probably the best – and shortest – book on the Uprising, by an acknowledged expert on modern Hungary. Lomax also edited *Eyewitness in Hungary*, an anthology of accounts by foreign Communists (most of whom were sympathetic to the Uprising) that vividly depicts the elation, confusion and tragedy of the events of October 1956.

John Lukács *Budapest 1900.* Excellent and very readable account of the politics and society of Budapest at the turn of the century, during a golden age that was shortly to come to an end.

John Man *Attila the Hun.* A beautifully written biography of the Magyars' mythical ancestor, illuminating horsemanship and warfare as practised by the Seven Tribes that later colonized the Carpathian basin.

George Schöpflin *Politics in Eastern Europe 1945–1992.* An excellent overview of the region by a political scientist who has since become an MEP for the centre-right Fidesz party.

Michael Stewart *The Time of the Gypsies.* This superb book on Roma culture is based on anthropological research conducted in a Roma community in south-eastern Hungary in the 1980s.

Peter Sugar (ed) *A History of Hungary.* A useful and not too academic survey of Hungarian history from pre-Conquest times to the close of the Kádár era, with a brief epilogue on the transition to democracy.

Tony Thorne *Countess Dracula.* An intriguing biography of the sixteenth-century "Blood Countess" Erzsébet Báthory, which argues that she was framed by her uncle to safeguard the Báthory fortune. For a fictional account, see Andrei Codrescu's *The Blood Countess* under "Literature".

Biography and travel writing

Magda Dénes *Castles Burning: A Child's Life in War.* A moving biographical account of the Budapest ghetto and postwar escape to France, Cuba and the United States, seen through the eyes of a Jewish girl. The author died in 1966, shortly before the book was published.

Ray Keenoy *Eminent Hungarians*. Everything you always wanted to know about Hungary's most renowned historical and contemporary figures – from Lajos Kossuth and Attila József, to Harry Houdini and Ernő Rubik, creator of the Rubik's cube.

Patrick Leigh Fermor *A Time of Gifts*; *Between the Woods and the Water*. In 1934 the young Leigh Fermor started walking from Holland to Turkey, reaching Hungary in the closing chapter of *A Time of Gifts*. In *Between the Woods and the Water* the inhabitants of the Great Plain and Transylvania – both gypsies and aristocrats – are superbly evoked. Lyrical and erudite.

Edward Fox *The Hungarian Who Walked to Heaven*. A brief account of the life of Sándor Kőrösi Csoma, the Hungarian who went in search of the roots of the ancient Hungarians and got sidetracked into making the first Tibetan dictionary.

John Paget *Hungary and Transylvania*. Paget's massive book attempts to explain nineteenth-century Hungary to the English middle class, and, within its aristocratic limitations, succeeds. Occasionally found in secondhand bookshops.

Giorgio and Nicola Pressburger *Homage to the Eighth District*. Evocative short stories about Jewish life in Budapest, before, during and after World War II, by twin brothers who fled Hungary in 1956.

Ernő Szép *The Smell of Humans*. A superb and harrowing memoir of the Holocaust in Hungary.

Rogan Taylor & Klára Jamrich (eds) *Puskás on Puskás*. Not only does this marvellous book depict the life of Hungary's – and one of the world's – greatest footballers, it also provides an intriguing insight into postwar Communist Hungary.

Literature

Hungary's fabulously rich **literary heritage** has been more widely appreciated in recent years thanks to the success of authors such as Sándor Márai and the Nobel-prize-winning Imre Kertész. A useful starting point is *Hungarian Literature* (Babel Guides), an informative guide to the best Hungarian fiction, drama and poetry in translation, with selected excerpts. There are also numerous collections of short stories published in Budapest, though the quality of translations varies from the sublime to the ridiculous. Works by nineteenth-century authors such as Mór Jókai are most likely to be found in secondhand bookshops (see p.200).

Anthologies

Loránt Czigány (ed) *The Oxford History of Hungarian Literature from the Earliest Times to the Present*. Probably the most comprehensive collection in print to date. In chronological order, with good coverage of the political and social background.

György Gömöri (ed) *Colonnade of Teeth*. In spite of its strange title, this is a good introduction to the work of young Hungarian poets.

Michael March (ed) *Description of a Struggle*. A collection of contemporary Eastern European prose, featuring four pieces by Hungarian writers including Nádas and Esterházy.

George Szirtes (ed) *An Island of Sound: Hungarian Poetry and Fiction Before and Beyond the Iron Curtain*. Superbly compiled anthology featuring the cream of Hungarian prose and poetry from the end of World War II through to 1989.

Poetry

Endre Ady *Poems of Endre Ady*. Regarded by many as the finest Hungarian poet of the twentieth century, Ady's allusive verses are notoriously difficult to translate.

George Faludy *Selected Poems 1933–80*. Fiery, lyrical poetry by a victim of both Nazi and Soviet repression. Themes of political defiance, the nobility of the human spirit, and the struggle to preserve human values in the face of oppression predominate.

Miklós Radnóti *Under Gemini: the Selected Poems of Miklós Radnóti, with a Prose Memoir*; *Foamy Sky: the Major Poems*. The two best collections of Radnóti's sparse, anguished poetry. His final poems, found in his coat pocket after he had been shot on a forced march to a labour camp, are especially moving.

Zsuzsa Rákovsky *New Life*. Well-received volume translated by the Hungarian-born English poet George Szirtes.

Fiction

Chico Barque *Budapest*. A Brazilian novel about a ghost-writer's romance with a Hungarian and her language. An intriguing play on storytelling that deftly captures the atmosphere of the city – all the more remarkable since the author has never been to Budapest.

Andrei Codrescu *The Blood Countess*. A lurid thriller juxtaposing the bloodstained life of Countess Báthory with far-right conspiracies in 1990s' Budapest, where her alter ego is resurrected.

Géza Csáth *The Magician's Garden and Other Stories*; *Opium and Other Stories*. Disturbing short stories written in the magic realist genre. The author was tormented by insanity and opium addiction, killing his wife and then himself in 1918.

Tibor Déry *The Portuguese Princess*. Wry short stories by a once-committed Communist, who was jailed for three years after the Uprising and died in 1977.

Péter Esterházy *Celestial Harmonies*. Written by a descendant of the famous aristocratic family, this is a dense and demanding book, chronicling the rise of the Esterházys during the Austro-Hungarian empire and their downfall under Communism. His latest novel (yet to be translated), was born of his shock at discovering that his father had been an informer for the Communist secret police.

Tibor Fischer *Under the Frog, A Black Comedy*. "Under a frog down a coalmine" is a Hungarian expression meaning "Things can't get worse", but this fictional account of the 1956 Uprising will have you in stitches. Fischer's parents fled to Britain in 1956.

Jenő Rejtő *The Blonde Hurricane*. Like Antal Szerb and Miklós Radnoti, Rejtő was a great Hungarian writer who was killed in the Holocaust for his Jewish descent: all three could have escaped, but they thought it would never happen in Budapest. He wrote a series of excellent romps – this translation succeeds far better than Jenő's *Quarantine in the Grand Hotel.*

Imre Kertész *Fateless.* Drawing from the author's own experiences as an Auschwitz survivor, this Nobel-prize winning book tells the tale of a young boy's deportation to, and survival in, a concentration camp. A brilliant translation by Tim Wilkinson.

Dezső Kosztolányi *Skylark.* A short and tragic story of an old couple and their beloved child by one of Hungary's top writers of the twentieth century, in a masterly translation by Richard Aczél.

Gyula Krúdy *Adventures of Sinbad.* Stories about a gourmand and womanizer by a popular Hungarian author with similar interests to his hero.

Sándor Márai *Embers.* An atmospheric and moving tale about friendship, love and betrayal by one of Hungary's most respected pre-World War II writers; a beautiful read. His *Conversations in Bolzano* is another character study, but its didactic, declamatory dialogue doesn't ring true.

Zsigmond Móricz *Be Faithful Unto Death.* This novel by a major late nineteenth-century Hungarian author sheds light on how Hungarians see themselves – both then and now.

Péter Nádas *A Book of Memories.* This translation of a novel about a novelist writing about a novel caused a sensation when it appeared in 1998. A Proustian account of bisexual relationships, Stalinist repression and modern-day Hungary in a brilliant translation by Iván Sanders.

Antal Szerb *Journey by Moonlight.* This Hungarian classic, written in 1937, tells the story of a Hungarian businessman on honeymoon in Italy who embarks upon a mystical and dazzling journey through the country. The superb translation by Len Rix ensures that the atmosphere of the original is beautifully retained. Szerb's *Martians' Guide to Budapest* is a delightful introduction to the city.

Food and wine

Susan Derecskey *The Hungarian Cookbook.* A good, easy-to-follow selection of traditional and modern recipes.

Stephen Kirkland *The Wine and Vines of Hungary.* Authoritative and accessible guide with tips on what to order. Covers the different wines of the country's regions, and their wine-makers too.

George Lang *The Cuisine of Hungary.* A well-written and beautifully illustrated work, telling you everything you need to know about Hungarian cooking, its history and how to do it yourself.

Language

Language

Hungarian..223

Basic grammar..223

Pronunciation..224

Words and phrases..224

Hungarian food and drink terms..228

Glossary of Hungarian terms...233

Hungarian

Hungarian is a unique, complex and subtle tongue, classified as belonging to the Finno-Ugric linguistic group, which includes Finnish and Estonian. If you happen to know those languages, however, don't expect them to be a help: there are some structural similarities, but lexically they are totally different. In fact, some scholars think the connection is completely bogus and have linked Hungarian to the Siberian Chuvash language and a whole host of other fairly obscure tongues. Essentially, the origins of Hungarian remain a mystery and, although a few words of Turkish have crept in, together with some German, English and (a few) Russian neologisms, there's not much that the beginner will recognize.

Consequently, foreigners aren't really expected to speak Hungarian, and locals are used to being addressed in **German**, the lingua franca of Hungarian tourism. However, **English** is gaining ground rapidly, and is increasingly understood. That said, a few basic Magyar phrases can make all the difference. Hungarians are intensely proud of their language and pleased when foreigners make an effort to learn a few courtesies. Note that **signage** is mostly in Hungarian only, though multi-lingual signs can be found on the metro, in most museums and in many restaurants.

The Rough Guides' *Hungarian for Travellers* is a useful **phrasebook** and, if you're prepared to study the language seriously, the best available book is *Colloquial Hungarian* (Routledge). As a supplement, invest in the handy little *Angol–Magyar/Magyar–Angol Kisszótár* dictionaries, available from bookshops in Hungary.

Basic grammar

Although its rules are complicated, it's worth describing a few features of **Hungarian grammar**, albeit imperfectly. Hungarian is an agglutinative language – in other words, its vocabulary is built upon **root-words**, which are modified in various ways to express different ideas and nuances. Instead of prepositions "to", "from", "in" etc, Hungarian uses **suffixes**, or tags added to the ends of genderless **nouns**. The change in suffix is largely determined by the noun's context: for example the noun "book" (*könyv*) will take a final "*et*" in the accusative (*könyvet*); "in the book" = *könyvben*; "from the book" = *könyvből*. It is also affected by the rules of vowel harmony (which take a while to get used to, but don't alter meaning, so don't worry about getting them wrong!). Most of the nouns in the vocabulary section below are in the nominative or subject form, that is, without suffixes. In Hungarian, "**the**" is *a* (before a word beginning with a consonant) or *az* (preceding a vowel); the word for "**a/an**" is *egy* (which also means "one").

Plurals are indicated by adding a final "k", with a link vowel if necessary, giving *-ek*, *-ok* or *-ak*. Nouns preceded by a number or other indication of quantity (eg, many, several) do *not* appear as plural: eg *könyvek* means "books", but "two books" is *két könyv* (using the singular form of the noun).

Adjectives precede the noun (*a piros ház* = the red house), adopting suffixes to form the comparative (*jó* = good; *jobb* = better), plus the prefix *leg* to signify the superlative (*legjobb* = the best).

Negatives are usually formed by placing the word *nem* before the verb or adjective. *Ez* (this), *ezek* (these), *az* (that) and *azok* (those) are the **demonstratives**.

Pronunciation

Achieving passably good **pronunciation**, rather than grammar, is the first priority (see below for general guidelines). **Stress** almost invariably falls on the first syllable of a word and all letters are spoken, although in sentences the tendency is to slur words together. Vowel sounds are greatly affected by the bristling **accents** (that actually distinguish separate letters) which, together with the "double letters" *cs*, *gy*, *ly*, *ny*, *sz*, *ty*, and *zs*, give the Hungarian **alphabet** its formidable appearance.

a o as in hot
á a as in father
b b as in best
c ts as in bats
cs ch as in church
d d as in dust
e e as in yet
é ay as in say
f f as in fed
g g as in go
gy a soft dy as in due
h h as in hat
i i as in bit, but slightly longer
í ee as in see
j y as in yes
k k as in sick
l l as in leap
ly y as in yes
m m as in mud
n n as in not
ny ny as in onion
o aw as in saw, with the tongue kept high
ó aw as in saw, as above but longer
ö ur as in fur, with the lips tightly rounded but without any "r" sound
ő ur as in fur, as above but longer
p p as in sip
r r pronounced with the tip of the tongue like a Scottish "r"
s sh as in shop
sz s as in so
t t as in sit
ty ty as in Tuesday or prettier, said quickly
u u as in pull
ú oo as in food
ü u as in the German "über" with the lips tightly rounded
ű u as above, but longer
v v as in vat
w v as in "Valkman," "vhiskey" or "WC" (vait-say)
z z as in zero
zs zh as in measure

Words and phrases

Basics

Do you speak …	beszél …
… English	… angolul
… German	… németül
… French	… franciául
yes	igen
OK	jó
no/not	nem
and	és

or	vagy	how are you?	hogy van? (more formal)
I (don't) understand	(nem) értem	could you speak more slowly?	elmondaná lassabban?
please	kérem	what do you call this?	mi a neve ennek?
excuse me (apology)	bocsánat, or elnézést	please write it down	kérem, írja le
excuse me (to attract attention)	legyen szives	today	ma
two beers, please	két sört kérek	tomorrow	holnap
thank you (very much)	köszönöm (szépen)	the day after tomorrow	holnapután
you're welcome	szívesen	yesterday	tegnap
hello/goodbye	szia (informal)	the day before yesterday	tegnapelőtt
good morning	jó reggelt	in the morning	reggel
good day	jó napot	in the evening	este
good evening	jó estét	at noon	délben
good night	jó éjszakát	at midnight	éjfélkor
goodbye	viszontlátásra		
see you later	viszlát (informal)		
how are you?	hogy vagy? (informal)		

Questions and requests

Hungarian has numerous interrogative modes whose subtleties elude foreigners, so it's best to use the simple *van?* ("is there?"), to which the reply might be *nincs* or *nincsen* ("there isn't"/"there aren't any"). In shops or restaurants you will immediately be addressed with the one-word *tessék,* meaning "Can I help you?", "What would you like?" or "Next!". To order in restaurants, shops and markets, use *kérek* ("I'd like …") plus accusative noun; *Kérem, adjon azt* ("Please give me that"); *Egy ilyet kérek* ("I'll have one of those").

I'd like/we'd like	Szeretnék/szeretnénk	Do you have a student discount?	van diák kedvezmény?
Where is/are …?	Hol van/vannak …?	Is everything included?	Ebben minden szerepel?
Hurry up!	Siessen!	I asked for …	Én … -t rendeltem
How much is it?	Mennyibe kerül?	The bill please	Fizetni szeretnék
per night	egy éjszakára	We're paying separately	Külön-külön fizetünk
per week	egy hétre	what?	mi?
a single room	egyágyas szoba	why?	miert?
a double room	kétágyas szoba	when?	mikor?
hot (cold) water	meleg (hideg) víz	who?	ki?
a shower	egy zuhany		
It's very expensive	Ez nagyon drága		
Do you have anything cheaper?	Van valami olcsóbb?		

Some signs

entrance	bejárat	open	nyitva
exit	kijárat	closed	zárva
arrival	érkezés	push	tolni
departure	indulás	pull	húzni

free admission	szabad belépés	**hospital**	kórház
women's toilet	női (or WC – "Vait-say")	**pharmacy**	gyógyszertár
men's toilet	férfi mosdó (or WC – "Vait-say")	**(local) police**	(kerületi) Rendőrség
shop	bolt	**caution/beware!**	vigyázat!/vigyázz!
market	piac	**no smoking**	tilos a dohányzás/ dohányozni tilos
room for rent	szoba kiadó or Zimmer frei	**no bathing**	tilos a fürdés/ füredni tilos

Directions

Where's the …?	Hol van a …?	**towards**	felé
campsite	kemping	**on the right (left)**	jobbra (balra)
hotel	szálloda/hotel	**straight ahead**	egyenesen előre
railway station	vasútállomás	**(over) there/here**	ott/itt
bus station	buszállomás	**Where are you going?**	Hova megy?
bus-stand	kocsiállás	**Is that on the way to …?**	Az a … úton?
(bus or train) stop	megálló	**I want to get out at …**	Le akarok szállni … -on/en
inland	belföldi	**please stop here**	itt álljon meg
international	külföldi	**I'm lost**	eltévedtem
Is it near (far)?	Közel (messze) van?	**arrivals**	érkező járatok (or érkezés)
Which bus goes to …?	Melyik busz megy … -ra/re	**departures**	induló járatok (or indulás)
a one-way ticket to … please	egy jegyet kérek … -ra/re csak oda	**to/from**	hova/honnan
a return ticket to …	egy retur jegyet … -ra/re	**change**	átszállás
Do I have to change trains?	Át kell szállnom?	**via**	át

Descriptions and reactions

nothing	semmi	**quick**	gyors
perhaps	talán	**slow**	lassú
very	nagyon	**now**	most
good	jó	**later**	később
bad	rossz	**beautiful**	szép
better	jobb	**ugly**	csúnya
big	nagy	**Help!**	Segítség!
small	kicsi	**I'm ill**	beteg vagyok

Numbers and measures

In shops and markets, items are priced per piece (*darab*, abbreviated to *db.*) or per kilogram. Shoppers commonly request purchases in multiples of ten grams (*deka*); one hundred grams is *tíz deka*. The measure for fluids is the *deci* (abbreviated to *dl.*) – see "Drinks" (p.232) for how this applies in bars and restaurants.

1	egy	50	ötven
2	kettő	60	hatvan
3	három	70	hetven
4	négy	80	nyolcvan
5	öt	90	kilencven
6	hat	100	száz
7	hét	101	százegy
8	nyolc	150	százötven
9	kilenc	200	kettőszáz
10	tíz	300	háromszáz
11	tizenegy	400	négyszáz
12	tizenkettő	500	ötszáz
13	tizenhárom	600	hatszáz
14	tizennégy	700	hétszáz
15	tizenöt	800	nyolcszáz
16	tizenhat	900	kilencszáz
17	tizenhét	1000	egyezer
18	tizennyolc	half	fél
19	tizenkilenc	a quarter	negyed
20	húsz	each/piece	darab (db.)
21	huszonegy	10 grams	egy deka
30	harminc	100 grams	tíz deka
40	negyven		

Time, days and dates

Luckily, the 24-hour clock is used for timetables, but on cinema programmes you may see notations like 1/4, 3/4, etc. These derive from the spoken expression of time which, as in German, makes reference to the hour approaching completion. For example 3.30 is expressed as *fél négy* – "half (on the way to) four"; 3.45 – *háromnegyed négy* ("three quarters on the way to four"); 6.15 – *negyed hét* ("one quarter towards seven"), etc. However, " … o'clock" is … *óra*, rather than referring to the hour ahead. Duration is expressed by the suffixes *-től* ("from") and *-ig* ("to"); minutes are *perc*; to ask the time, say "*Hány óra?*"

Monday	hétfő	on Wednesday	szerdán
Tuesday	kedd	on Thursday	csütörtökön
Wednesday	szerda	on Friday	pénteken
Thursday	csütörtök	on Saturday	szombaton
Friday	péntek	on Sunday	vasárnap
Saturday	szombat	day	nap
Sunday	vasárnap	week	hét
on Monday	hetfőn	month	hónap
on Tuesday	kedden	year	év

Hungarian food and drink terms

The food categories here refer to the general divisions used in menus. In cheaper places you will also find a further division of meat dishes: ready-made meals like stews (*készételek*), and freshly cooked (in theory) dishes such as those cooked in breadcrumbs or grilled (*frissensültek*).

Tészták is a pasta-doughy category that can include savoury dishes such as *turoscsusza* (pasta served with cottage cheese and a sprinkling of bacon), as well as sweet ones like *somlói galuska* (cream and chocolate covered sponge). Two popular **snacks** which are nicer than they sound are *zsirós kenyér* (bread spread with lard and sprinkled with paprika; often sold in old-fashioned wine bars); and *lángos* (fried dough served with soured cream or a variety of other toppings, and available in markets).

Basics

borraválo	tip
bors	pepper
cukor	sugar
ecet	vinegar
egészségedre!	Cheers!
étlap	menu
jó étvágyat!	Bon appétit!
kenyér	bread
kifli	croissant-shaped roll
méz	honey
mustár	mustard
rizs	rice
só	salt
tejföl	sour cream
tejszín	cream
vaj	butter
zsemle or péksütemeny	bread rolls

Cooking terms

comb	leg
mell	breast
angolosan	(English-style) underdone/rare
főtt	boiled
főzelék	basic vegetable stews
jól megsütve	well done (fried)
jól megfőzve	well done (boiled)
pörkölt	stewed slowly
rántott	deep-fried in breadcrumbs
roston sütve	grilled
sülve	roasted
sült/sütve	fried

Soups (levesek)

bakonyi betyárleves	"Outlaw soup" of chicken, beef, noodles and vegetables, richly spiced
csirke-aprólék leves	mixed vegetable and giblet soup
erőleves	meat consommé often served with noodles (*tésztával* or *metélttel*), liver dumplings (*májgombóccal*), or an egg placed raw into the soup (*tojással*)
gombaleves	mushroom soup
gulyásleves	goulash in its original Hungarian form as a soup, sometimes served in a small kettle pot (*bográcsgulyás*)
halászlé	a rich fish soup often served with hot paprika

húsleves	meat consommé
jókai bableves	bean soup flavoured with smoked meat
kunsági pandúrleves	chicken soup seasoned with nutmeg, paprika and garlic
lencseleves	lentil soup
hideg meggyleves	chilled sour cherry soup
palócleves	mutton, bean and sour cream soup
paradicsomleves	tomato soup
tarkonyos borjúraguleves	lamb soup flavoured with tarragon
ujházi tyúkleves	chicken soup with noodles, vegetables and meat
zöldségleves	vegetable soup

Appetizers (előételek)

These comprise both hot (*meleg*) and cold (*hideg*) dishes.

füstölt csülök tormával	smoked knuckle of pork with horseradish
hortobágyi palacsinta	pancake stuffed with minced meat and served with creamy paprika sauce
körözött	a paprika-flavoured spread made with sheep's cheese and served with toast
libamáj	goose liver
rakott krumpli	layered potato casserole with sausage and eggs
rántott gomba	mushrooms fried in breacrumbs, sometimes stuffed with sheep's cheese (*juhtúróval töltött*)
rántott sajt, Camembert, karfiol	Camembert or cauliflower fried in breadcrumbs
tatárbeefsteak	raw mince mixed with an egg, salt, pepper, butter, paprika and mustard, and spread on toast
velőcsont fokhagymás pirítóssal	bone marrow spread on toast rubbed with garlic, a special delicacy associated with the gourmet Gyula Krúdy

Salads (saláták)

Salads are not Hungary's strong point; they are usually simple, and are often served in a vinegary dressing, although other dressings include blue cheese (*rokfortos*), yogurt (*joghurtos*) or French (*francia*).

csalamádé	mixed pickled salad
fejes saláta	lettuce
idénysaláta	fresh salad of whatever is in season
jércesaláta	chicken salad
paradicsom saláta	tomato salad
uborka saláta	cucumber; can be gherkins (*csemege* or *kovászos*) or the fresh variety (*friss*)

Fish dishes (halételek)

csuka tejfölben sütve	fried pike with sour cream
fogas	a local fish of the pike-perch family
fogasszeletek Gundel modra	breaded fillet of *fogas*
harcsa	catfish
kecsege	sterlet (small sturgeon)

nyelvhal	sole
paprikás ponty	carp in paprika sauce
pisztráng	trout
pisztráng tejszínes mártásban	trout baked in cream
ponty	carp
ponty filé gombával	carp fillet in mushroom sauce
rántott pontyfilé	carp fillet fried in breadcrumbs
rostélyos töltött ponty	carp stuffed with bread, egg, herbs and fish liver or roe
süllő	another pike-perch relative
sült hal	fried fish
tonhal	tuna

Meat dishes (húsételek)

baromfi	poultry
bécsi szelet	Wiener schnitzel
bélszin	sirloin
bélszinjava	tenderloin
csirke	chicken
fácán	pheasant
fasírt	meatballs
hátszin	rumpsteak
kacsa	duck
kolbász	spicy sausage
liba	goose
máj	liver
marha	beef
nyúl	rabbit
őz	venison
pulyka	turkey
sertés	pork
sonka	ham
vaddisznó	wild boar
vadételek	game
virsli	frankfurter
borjúpörkölt	closer to what foreigners mean by "goulash": veal stew seasoned with garlic
cigányrostélyos	"gypsy-style" steak with brown sauce
csikós tokány	strips of beef braised in bacon, onion rings, sour cream and tomato sauce
csülök Pékné módra	knuckle of pork roasted with potatoes and onions
erdélyi rakott-káposzta	layers of cabbage, rice and ground pork baked in sour cream (a Transylvanian speciality)
hagymás rostélyos	braised steak piled high with fried onions
pacal	tripe (usually in a paprika sauce)
paprikás csirke	chicken in paprika sauce
rablóhús nyárson	kebab of pork, veal and bacon
sertésborda	pork chop
sült libacomb tört burgonyával és párolt káposztával	grilled goose leg with potatoes, onions and steamed cabbage
töltött káposzta	cabbage stuffed with meat and rice, in a tomato sauce
töltött paprika	peppers stuffed with meat and rice, in a tomato sauce
vaddisznó borókamártással	wild boar in juniper sauce
vasi pecsenye	fried pork marinated in milk and garlic

Sauces (mártásban)

bormártásban	in a wine sauce
ecetes tormával	with horseradish
fokhagymás mártásban	in a garlic sauce
gombamártásban	in a mushroom sauce
kapormártásban	in a dill sauce
meggymártásban	in a morello cherry sauce
paprikás mártásban	in a paprika sauce
tárkonyos mártásban	in a tarragon sauce
tejszínes paprikás mártásban	in a cream and paprika sauce
vadasmártásban	in a brown sauce (made of mushrooms, almonds, herbs and brandy)
zöldborsós	in a green-pea sauce
zöldborsosmártásba	in a green peppercorn sauce

Accompaniments (köretek)

galuska	noodles
hasábburgonya	chips, french fries
krokett	potato croquettes
petrezselymes	boiled potatoes
burgonya	served with parsley
rizs	rice
zöldköret	mixed vegetables (often of frozen origin)

Vegetables (zöldségek)

bab	beans
borsó	peas
burgonya/krumpli	potatoes
fokhagyma	garlic
gomba	mushrooms
hagyma	onions
káposzta	cabbage
karfiol	cauliflower
kelkáposzta	savoy cabbage
kukorica	sweetcorn
lecsó	tomato and green pepper stew that's a popular ingredient in Hungarian cooking
padlizsán	aubergine/eggplant
paprika (édes/erős)	peppers (sweet/hot)
paradicsom	tomatoes
sárgarépa	carrots
spárga	asparagus
spenót	spinach
uborka	cucumber
zöldbab	green beans
zöldborsó	peas
zukkini	courgette

Fruit and nuts (gyümölcsök és diók)

alma	apple
birsalma	quince
bodza	elderflower
citrom	lemon
dió	walnut
eper	strawberry
földi mogyoró	peanut
füge	fig
(görög) dinnye	(water) melon
körte	pear
málna	raspberry
mandula	almond
meggy	morello cherry
mogyoró	hazelnut
narancs	orange
őszibarack	peach
sárgabarack	apricot
szilva	plum
szőlő	grape
tök	marrow or pumpkin/squash

Cheese (sajt)

Cheeses made in Hungary are a rather limited selection, the most interesting being the soft *juhtúró*.

füstölt sajt	smoked cheese	**trappista**	rubbery, Edam-type cheese
juhtúró	sheep's cheese	**túró**	curd cheese
kecske sajt	goat's cheese		
márvány	Danish blue cheese		

Desserts (édességek)

aranygaluska	golden dumpling cake	**rétes**	strudel
gesztenye puré	chestnut purée	**szilva gombóc**	dumpling stuffed with a plum
palacsinta	pancake		

Drinks (*italok*)

The drinks list (*itallap*) is usually divided into wine, beer, spirits and soft drinks. **Wine** is often served by the *deci* (*dl.*), or 100ml, and may be charged as such, so that the sum on the drinks list may be multiplied by two or three times on the bill. To avoid ambiguity over glass sizes, you can specify *egy deci*, *két deci* or *három deci* (respectively, 100ml, 200ml or 300ml). Most places serve **spritzers** on request but seldom list them on the menu. Hungarians specify such oddly-named mixes as a *Hosszúlépés* ("long step": 2dl. soda water, 1dl. wine), *Viceházmester* ("deputy janitor": 3dl. soda, 2dl. wine) or *Haziúr* ("landlord":4dl. soda, 1dl. wine), though some prefer wine mixed with cola as a thirst-quencher. **Pálinka** is a popular aperitif, distilled from apricots (*barackpálinka*), plums (*szilva*), William's pears (*Vilmoskörte*) or other fruit; and **Unicum** a dark, bitter digestif that Hungarians swear is good for the stomach. Due to Hungary's abundant thermal springs there are numerous local brands of **mineral water**; it's sold with colour-coded bottle-caps for easy recognition of still (*szénsavmentes* – pink caps), mildly fizzy (*enyhe* – green) or sparkling (*szénsavas* or *buborékos* – blue).

ásányvíz	mineral water	**pezsgő bor**	sparkling wine
bor	wine	**pohár**	300dl. of beer, or a glass of wine
borsmenta teá	peppermint tea	**rosé**	rosé wine
csapalt sör	draught beer	**sima (csap) víz**	ordinary (tap) water
édes bor	sweet wine	**sör**	beer
fehér bor	white wine	**száraz bor**	dry wine
félédes bor	medium-dry wine	**teá**	tea
gyümölcslé	fruit juice	**tejeskávé**	coffee with milk
kávé	coffee (espresso)	**Unicum**	a bitter medicinal *digestif*
koffeinmentes kávé	decaffeinated coffee	**üveg**	bottle (of wine)
korsó	half-litre of beer	**vörös bor**	red wine
menta teá	mint tea	**vörösboros Kola**	red wine mixed with cola
narancslé	orange juice		
pálinka	schnapps-like fruit brandy, in a range of flavours		

Glossary of Hungarian terms

ÁFA Goods tax, equivalent to VAT.

Állatkert Zoo.

Arrow Cross see Nyilas.

Áruház Department store.

ÁVO The dreaded secret police of the Rákosi era, renamed the ÁVH in 1949.

Barlang Cave.

Belváros Inner city.

Biedermeier Heavy nineteenth-century style of Viennese furniture that became very popular in Budapest homes.

Borkostoló Wine tasting.

Borozó Wine bar.

Botanikuskert Botanical garden.

Büfé Snack bar.

Cigány Gypsy/Roma (can be abusive).

Cigánytelep Gypsy settlement.

Cigányzene Gypsy music.

Csárda Inn; nowadays, a restaurant with rustic decor.

Csárdás Traditional wild dance to violin music.

Cukrászda Cake shop.

Diszterem Ceremonial hall.

Domb Hill.

Duna River Danube.

Egyetem University.

Erdély The Hungarian word for Transylvania, the region of Romania where a large Hungarian minority lives.

Erdő Forest, wood.

Étterem Restaurant.

Fasor Avenue.

Fogadó Inn.

Folyó River.

Forrás Natural spring.

Fürdő Public baths.

Gőzfürdő Steam bath.

Gyógyfürdő Mineral baths fed by thermal springs with therapeutic properties.

Hajó Boat.

Hajóállomás Boat landing stage.

Halászcsárda/halászkert Fish restaurant.

Ház House.

Hegy Hill or low mountain.

HÉV Commuter trains running from Budapest.

Híd Bridge.

Honvéd Hungarian army.

Ifjúsági szálló Youth hostel.

Iskola School.

Kápolna Chapel.

Kapu Gate.

Kert Garden, park.

Kerület (*ker.*) District.

Kiállítás Exhibition.

Kiáltó Lookout tower.

Kincstár Treasury.

Kirakodó vásár Fair, craft or flea market.

Kollégium Student hostel.

Korzó Promenade.

Körönd Circus (road junction, as in Piccadilly Circus).

Körút (*krt.*) Literally, ring road, but in Budapest refers to the main boulevards surrounding the Belváros.

Körtér Circus (see *körönd*).

Köz Alley, lane; also used to define narrow geographical regions.

Kulcs Key.

Kút Well or fountain.

Lakótelep High-rise housing estate.

Lépcső Flight of steps.

Liget Park, grove or wood.

Lovarda Riding school.

Magyar Hungarian (pronounced "*mod*-yor").

Magyarország Hungary.

Malév Hungarian national airline.

MÁV Hungarian national railways.

Megálló Railway station or tram or bus stop.

Megye County; the county system was originally established by King Stephen to extend his authority over the Magyar tribes.

Mozi Cinema.

Műemlék Historic monument, protected building.

Művelődési ház/központ Arts centre.

Nádor Palatine, highest administrative office in Hungary in the Habsburg empire pre-1848.

Nyilas "Arrow Cross"; Hungarian Fascist movement.

Palota Palace; *püspök-palota*, a bishop's residence.

Pályaudvar (*pu.*) Rail terminus.

Panzió Pension.

Patak Stream.

Pénz Money.

Piac Outdoor market.

Pince Cellar.

Rakpart Embankment or quay.

Református The reformed church, which in Hungary means the Calvinist faith.

Rendőrség Police.

Repülőtér Airport.

Rév Ferry.

Rom Ruined building; sometimes set in a *romkert*, a garden with stonework finds.

Roma The romany word for gypsy, preferred by many Roma in Hungary.

Sétány "Walk" or promenade.

Skanzen Outdoor ethnographic museum.

Sor Row, as in *fasor*, row of trees, ie avenue.

Söröző Beer hall.

Strand Beach, open-air baths or any area for sunbathing or swimming.

Szabadtér Open-air.

Szálló or **szálloda** Hotel.

Szent Saint.

Sziget Island.

Szoba kiadó Room to let.

Tájház Old peasant house turned into a museum, often illustrating the folk traditions of a region or ethnic group.

Táncház Venue for Hungarian folk music and dance.

Temető Cemetery.

Templom Church.

Tér Square; *tere* in the possessive case.

Terem Hall.

Tilos Forbidden; *tilos a dohányzás* means "smoking is forbidden".

Tó Lake.

Torony Tower.

Türbe Tomb or mausoleum of a Muslim dignitary.

Uszoda Swimming pool.

Udvar Courtyard.

Út Road; in the possessive case, *útja*.

Utca (*u.*) Street.

Vár Castle.

Város Town.

Városháza Town hall.

Vásár Market.

Vásárcsarnok Market hall.

Vasútállomás Railway station.

Vendéglő Restaurant.

Verbunkos Folk dance, originally a recruiting dance.

Völgy Valley.

Zsidó Jew or Jewish.

Zsinagóga Synagogue.

Travel store

ROUGH GUIDES Complete Listing

UK & Ireland
Britain
Devon & Cornwall
Dublin **D**
Edinburgh **D**
England
Ireland
The Lake District
London
London **D**
London Mini Guide
Scotland
Scottish Highlands & Islands
Wales

Europe
Algarve **D**
Amsterdam
Amsterdam **D**
Andalucía
Athens **D**
Austria
Baltic States
Barcelona
Barcelona **D**
Belgium & Luxembourg
Berlin
Brittany & Normandy
Bruges **D**
Brussels
Budapest
Bulgaria
Copenhagen
Corsica
Crete
Croatia
Cyprus
Czech & Slovak Republics
Denmark
Dodecanese & East Aegean Islands
Dordogne & The Lot
Europe on a Budget
Florence & Siena
Florence **D**
France
Germany
Gran Canaria **D**
Greece
Greek Islands
Hungary
Ibiza & Formentera **D**
Iceland
Ionian Islands
Italy
The Italian Lakes
Languedoc & Roussillon
Lanzarote & Fuerteventura **D**
Lisbon **D**
The Loire Valley
Madeira **D**
Madrid **D**
Mallorca **D**
Mallorca & Menorca
Malta & Gozo **D**
Moscow
The Netherlands
Norway
Paris
Paris **D**
Paris Mini Guide
Poland
Portugal
Prague
Prague **D**
Provence & the Côte D'Azur
Pyrenees
Romania
Rome
Rome **D**
Sardinia
Scandinavia
Sicily
Slovenia
Spain
St Petersburg
Sweden
Switzerland
Tenerife & La Gomera **D**
Turkey
Tuscany & Umbria
Venice & The Veneto
Venice **D**
Vienna

Asia
Bali & Lombok
Bangkok
Beijing
Cambodia
China
Goa
Hong Kong & Macau
Hong Kong & Macau **D**
India
Indonesia
Japan
Kerala
Korea
Laos
Malaysia, Singapore & Brunei
Nepal
The Philippines
Rajasthan, Dehli & Agra
Shanghai
Singapore
Singapore **D**
South India
Southeast Asia on a Budget
Sri Lanka
Taiwan
Thailand
Thailand's Beaches & Islands
Tokyo
Vietnam

Australasia
Australia
East Coast Australia
Fiji
Melbourne
New Zealand
Sydney
Tasmania

North America
Alaska
Baja California
Boston
California
Canada
Chicago
Colorado
Florida
The Grand Canyon
Hawaii
Honolulu **D**
Las Vegas **D**
Los Angeles & Southern California
Maui **D**
Miami & South Florida
Montréal
New England
New York City
New York City **D**
New York City Mini
Orlando & Walt Disney World® **D**
Oregon & Washington
San Francisco
San Francisco **D**
Seattle
Southwest USA
Toronto
USA
Vancouver
Washington DC
Yellowstone & The Grand Tetons
Yosemite

Caribbean & Latin America
Antigua & Barbuda **D**
Argentina
Bahamas
Barbados **D**
Belize
Bolivia
Brazil
Buenos Aires
Cancùn & Cozumel **D**
Caribbean
Central America on a Budget
Chile
Costa Rica
Cuba
Dominican Republic
Ecuador
Guatemala
Jamaica
Mexico
Peru
Puerto Rico
St Lucia **D**
South America on a Budget
Trinidad & Tobago
Yucatán

D: Rough Guide **DIRECTIONS** for short breaks

Available from all good bookstores

Africa & Middle East
Cape Town & the Garden Route
Dubai **D**
Egypt
Gambia
Jordan
Kenya
Marrakesh **D**
Morocco
South Africa, Lesotho & Swaziland
Tanzania
Tunisia
West Africa
Zanzibar

Travel Specials
First-Time Africa
First-Time Around the World
First-Time Asia
First-Time Europe
First-Time Latin America
Make the Most of Your Time on Earth
Travel with Babies & Young Children
Travel Online
Travel Survival
Ultimate Adventures
Walks in London & SE England
World Party

Maps
Algarve
Amsterdam
Andalucia & Costa del Sol
Argentina
Athens
Australia
Barcelona
Berlin
Boston & Cambridge
Brittany
Brussels
California
Chicago
Chile
Corsica
Costa Rica & Panama
Crete
Croatia
Cuba
Cyprus
Czech Republic
Dominican Republic
Dubai & UAE
Dublin
Egypt
Florence & Siena
Florida
France
Frankfurt
Germany
Greece
Guatemala & Belize
Iceland
India
Ireland
Italy
Kenya & Northern Tanzania
Lisbon
London
Los Angeles
Madrid
Malaysia
Mallorca
Marrakesh
Mexico
Miami & Key West
Morocco
New England
New York City
New Zealand
Northern Spain
Paris
Peru
Portugal
Prague
Pyrenees & Andorra
Rome
San Francisco
Sicily
South Africa
South India
Spain & Portugal
Sri Lanka
Tenerife
Thailand
Toronto
Trinidad & Tobago
Tunisia
Turkey
Tuscany
Venice
Vietnam, Laos & Cambodia
Washington DC
Yucatán Peninsula

Phrasebooks
Croatian
Czech
Dutch
Egyptian Arabic
French
German
Greek
Hindi & Urdu
Italian
Japanese
Latin American Spanish
Mandarin Chinese
Mexican Spanish
Polish
Portuguese
Russian
Spanish
Swahili
Thai
Turkish
Vietnamese

Computers
Blogging
eBay
FWD this link
iPhone
iPods, iTunes & music online
The Internet
Macs & OS X
MySpace
PlayStation Portable
Website Directory

Film & TV
American Independent Film
British Cult Comedy
Chick Flicks
Comedy Movies
Cult Movies
Film
Film Musicals
Film Noir
Gangster Movies
Horror Movies
Sci-Fi Movies
Westerns

Lifestyle
Babies
Ethical Living
Pregnancy & Birth
Running

Music Guides
The Beatles
The Best Music You've Never Heard
Blues
Bob Dylan
Book of Playlists
Classical Music
Elvis
Frank Sinatra
Heavy Metal
Hip-Hop
Led Zeppelin
Opera
Pink Floyd
Punk
Reggae
The Rolling Stones
Soul and R&B
Velvet Underground
World Music

Popular Culture
Classic Novels
Conspiracy Theories
Crime Fiction
Cult Fiction
The Da Vinci Code
Graphic Novels
His Dark Materials
Poker
Shakespeare
Superheroes
Tutankhamun
Unexplained Phenomena
Videogames

Science
The Brain
Climate Change
The Earth
Genes & Cloning
The Universe
Weather

For more information go to www.roughguides.com

EXPERIENCE THE REAL BUDAPEST

QUALITY ACCOMMODATION
IN CLASSIC APARTMENT BUILDINGS

- SHORT AND LONG TERM BOOKINGS AVAILABLE
- WONDERFUL VALUE FOR INDIVIDUALS, COUPLES AND GROUPS
- ALL APARTMENTS CENTRALLY LOCATED
- GREAT SERVICE - AIRPORT COLLECTION, MEET AND GREET, LEFT LUGGAGE, TOUR GUIDING
- ENGLISH SPEAKING REPRESENTATIVES
- MAKE YOUR STAY IN BUDAPEST EXTRA SPECIAL WITH BUDAPEST LETS
- CHECK OUT OUR WEB SITE **WWW.BUDAPESTLETS.COM**

BUDAPEST LETS

BUDAPEST'S ACCOMMODATION SPECIALISTS

"The most accurate maps in the world"

San Jose Mercury News

CITY MAPS 25 titles

Amsterdam · Athens · Barcelona · Berlin · Boston · Brussels · Chicago · Dublin · Florence & Siena · Frankfurt · Hong Kong · Lisbon · London · Los Angeles · Madrid · Marrakesh · Miami · New York City · Paris · Prague · Rome · San Francisco · Toronto · Venice · Washington DC

US$8.99 Can$13.99 £4.99

COUNTRY & REGIONAL MAPS 48 titles

Algarve · Andalucía · Argentina · Australia · Baja California · Brittany · Crete · Croatia · Cuba · Cyprus · Czech Republic · Dominican Republic · Dubai · Egypt · Greece · Guatemala & Belize · Iceland · Ireland · Kenya · Mexico · Morocco · New Zealand · Northern Spain · Peru · Portugal · Sicily · South Africa · South India · Sri Lanka · Tenerife · Thailand · Trinidad & Tobago · Tuscany · Yucatán Peninsula and more.

US$9.99 Can$13.99 £5.99

waterproof • rip-proof • amazing value

BROADEN YOUR HORIZONS

Visit us online

www.roughguides.com

Information on over 25,000 destinations around the world

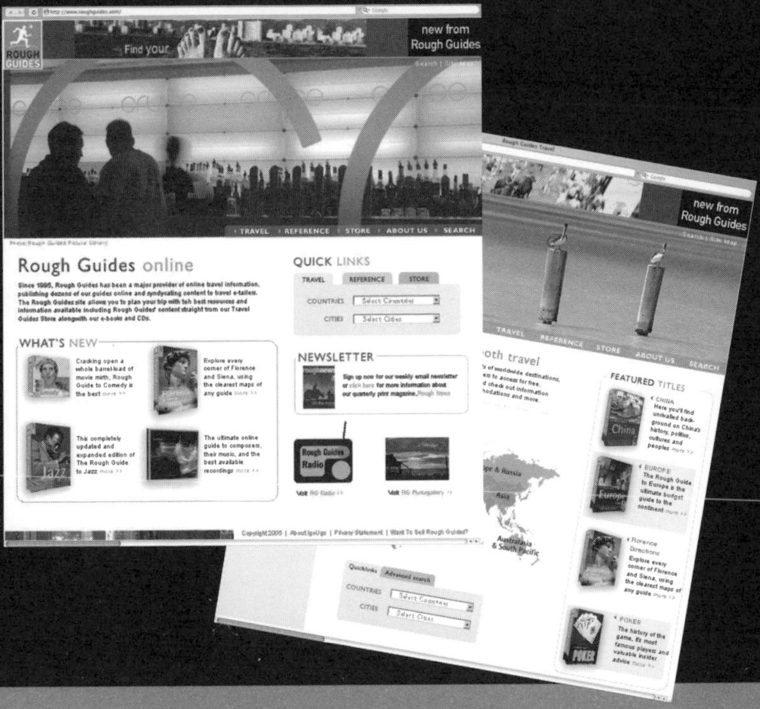

- **Read** Rough Guides' trusted travel info
- **Access** exclusive articles from Rough Guides authors
- **Update** yourself on new books, maps, CDs and other products
- **Enter** our competitions and win travel prizes
- **Share** ideas, journals, photos & travel advice with other users
- **Earn** points every time you contribute to the Rough Guide community and get rewards

BROADEN YOUR HORIZONS

NOTES

NOTES

NOTES

Small print and
Index

A Rough Guide to Rough Guides

Published in 1982, the first Rough Guide – to Greece – was a student scheme that became a publishing phenomenon. Mark Ellingham, a recent graduate in English from Bristol University, had been travelling in Greece the previous summer and couldn't find the right guidebook. With a small group of friends he wrote his own guide, combining a highly contemporary, journalistic style with a thoroughly practical approach to travellers' needs.

The immediate success of the book spawned a series that rapidly covered dozens of destinations. And, in addition to impecunious backpackers, Rough Guides soon acquired a much broader and older readership that relished the guides' wit and inquisitiveness as much as their enthusiastic, critical approach and value-for-money ethos.

These days, Rough Guides include recommendations from shoestring to luxury and cover more than 200 destinations around the globe, including almost every country in the Americas and Europe, more than half of Africa and most of Asia and Australasia. Our ever-growing team of authors and photographers is spread all over the world, particularly in Europe, the USA and Australia.

In the early 1990s, Rough Guides branched out of travel, with the publication of Rough Guides to World Music, Classical Music and the Internet. All three have become benchmark titles in their fields, spearheading the publication of a wide range of books under the Rough Guide name.

Including the travel series, Rough Guides now number more than 350 titles, covering: phrasebooks, waterproof maps, music guides from Opera to Heavy Metal, reference works as diverse as Conspiracy Theories and Shakespeare, and popular culture books from iPods to Poker. Rough Guides also produce a series of more than 120 World Music CDs in partnership with World Music Network.

Visit www.roughguides.com to see our latest publications.

Rough Guide travel images are available for commercial licensing at www.roughguidespictures.com

Rough Guide credits

Text editor: Polly Thomas
Layout: Anita Singh
Cartography: Alakananda Roy
Picture editor: Emily Taylor
Production: Rebecca Short
Proofreader: Anita Sach
Cover design: Chloë Roberts
Photographer: Eddie Gerald, Michelle Grant
Editorial: **London** Ruth Blackmore, Andy Turner, Keith Drew, Edward Aves, Alice Park, Lucy White, Jo Kirby, James Smart, Natasha Foges, Róisín Cameron, Emma Traynor, James Rice, Emma Gibbs, Kathryn Lane, Christina Valhouli, Monica Woods, Mani Ramaswamy, Alison Roberts, Harry Wilson, Joe Staines, Peter Buckley, Matthew Milton, Tracy Hopkins, Ruth Tidball; **New York** Andrew Rosenberg, Steven Horak, AnneLise Sorensen, Ella Steim, Anna Owens, Sean Mahoney, Paula Neudorf; **Delhi** Madhavi Singh, Karen D'Souza, Lubna Shaheen
Design & Pictures: **London** Scott Stickland, Dan May, Diana Jarvis, Mark Thomas, Chloë Roberts, Nicole Newman, Sarah Cummins; **Delhi** Umesh Aggarwal, Ajay Verma, Jessica Subramanian, Ankur Guha, Pradeep Thapliyal, Sachin Tanwar, Nikhil Agarwal
Production: Vicky Baldwin
Cartography: **London** Maxine Repath, Ed Wright, Katie Lloyd-Jones; **Delhi** Rajesh Chhibber, Ashutosh Bharti, Rajesh Mishra, Animesh Pathak, Jasbir Sandhu, Karobi Gogoi, Swati Handoo, Deshpal Dabas
Online: **London** George Atwell, Faye Hellon, Jeanette Angell, Fergus Day, Justine Bright, Clare Bryson, Áine Fearon, Adrian Low, Ezgi Celebi, Amber Bloomfield; **Delhi** Amit Verma, Rahul Kumar, Narender Kumar, Ravi Yadav, Debojit Borah, Rakesh Kumar, Ganesh Sharma, Shisir Basumatari
Marketing & Publicity: **London** Liz Statham, Niki Hanmer, Louise Maher, Jess Carter, Vanessa Godden, Vivienne Watton, Anna Paynton, Rachel Sprackett, Libby Jellie, Laura Vipond; **New York** Geoff Colquitt, Nancy Lambert, Katy Ball; **Delhi** Ragini Govind
Manager India: Punita Singh
Reference Director: Andrew Lockett
Operations Manager: Helen Phillips
PA to Publishing Director: Nicola Henderson
Publishing Director: Martin Dunford
Commercial Manager: Gino Magnotta
Managing Director: John Duhigg

ROUGH GUIDES

SMALL PRINT

Publishing information

This fourth edition published April 2009 by
Rough Guides Ltd,
80 Strand, London WC2R 0RL
345 Hudson St, 4th Floor,
New York, NY 10014, USA
14 Local Shopping Centre, Panchsheel Park,
New Delhi 110017, India
Distributed by the Penguin Group
Penguin Books Ltd,
80 Strand, London WC2R 0RL
Penguin Group (USA)
375 Hudson Street, NY 10014, USA
Penguin Group (Australia)
250 Camberwell Road, Camberwell,
Victoria 3124, Australia
Penguin Group (Canada)
195 Harry Walker Parkway N, Newmarket, ON,
L3Y 7B3 Canada
Penguin Group (NZ)
67 Apollo Drive, Mairangi Bay, Auckland 1310,
New Zealand

Cover concept by Peter Dyer.

Typeset in Bembo and Helvetica to an original design by Henry Iles.

Printed in China

© Charles Hebbert and Dan Richardson 2009

No part of this book may be reproduced in any form without permission from the publisher except for the quotation of brief passages in reviews.

256pp includes index

A catalogue record for this book is available from the British Library.

ISBN: 978-1-84836-048-8

The publishers and authors have done their best to ensure the accuracy and currency of all the information in **The Rough Guide to Budapest**, however, they can accept no responsibility for any loss, injury, or inconvenience sustained by any traveller as a result of information or advice contained in the guide.

1 3 5 7 9 8 6 4 2

Help us update

We've gone to a lot of effort to ensure that the fourth edition of **The Rough Guide to Budapest** is accurate and up to date. However, things change – places get "discovered", opening hours are notoriously fickle, restaurants and rooms raise prices or lower standards. If you feel we've got it wrong or left something out, we'd like to know, and if you can remember the address, the price, the hours, the phone number, so much the better.

Please send your comments with the subject line "**Rough Guide Budapest Update**" to ⓔmail@roughguides.com. We'll credit all contributions and send a copy of the next edition (or any other Rough Guide if you prefer) for the very best emails.

Have your questions answered and tell others about your trip at ⓦcommunity.roughguides.com

Acknowledgements

Charles Hebbert would like to thank firstly Rachel Appleby and Rozgonyi Zoltan for their additional research, my editors Polly Thomas, for her hard work at a busy time, and Monica Woods, for doing so much of the last minute extra stuff; and Bakonyi Ági, Biber Kriszta, Fenyő Krisztina, Gyene Gyöngyvér, Judith Heywood, Lőrinc Anna, Lucy Mallows, Alison Murchie, Nádori Péter, Pallai Peter, Helen Percival, Persanyi Miklos, Pulay Gergő, Szűcs Julia, Tolnai Lea and of course Caroline, Molly and Fergus.

Dan Richardson is grateful for the help and hospitality of Gordon Cross, Eszter Gomori, Lilla Farkas, Krisztina Novotta and Paul Evans, and the heroic editing of Polly Thomas and Monica Woods.

Readers' letters

Thanks to all the readers who have taken the time to write in with comments and suggestions (and apologies if we've inadvertently omitted or misspelt anyone's name):

Clare Abbott, Fergal Beirne, Micaela Blitz, G. Brewster, Marsha Brown, Hilary Clare, Mererid Puw Davies and Dan Gibson, I. Doak, Jane Doy, Katalin and Shaun Fisher, Edward Garston, Bren and Rob Golder, Kati Havasi, Mark Hilton, Geoff Holden, Ray and Ree Holmes, Mike Hounsell, Anita Isalska, Ryan James, Marion Janner, Andre Jordan, Mary Kauffman, Katherine Lieb, Steve Locke, Tiffany Madigan, Sue Middleton, Laura Mózes and Mark Kristóf, William Mulholland and Jan Hughes, Leslie Proudfoot, Gemma Rogers, Michel Rorai, Linda Shannon, Mirjam Schiffer, Frank Paul Silye, Bob Telfer, Melanie Trull, R. Vieira, Tom Walsh, Ronelle Ward, Wayne.

Photo credits

All photos © Rough Guides except the following:

Things not to miss
04 Folk music © Charles Hebbert
07 Budapest Spring Festival © Courtesy of Budapest Spring Festival
09 'Prince Eugene of Savoy' outside the Hungarian National Gallery © Dave G. Houser/Corbis
14 Sziget Festival © Courtesy of the Sziget Festival
19 Classical concerts © Manfred Horvath/DRR.Net

Hungarian Music colour section
Iván Fischer © DPA/Corbis
Roby Lakatos © Mladen Peric/Lebrecht

Black and whites
p.124 View of the city from the Buda Hills © Alamy
p.193 Children's Railway, Buda Hills © Sipa Press/Rex Features

Selected images from our guidebooks are available for licensing from:

ROUGHGUIDESPICTURES.COM

Index

Map entries are in colour.

A

accommodation ...149–156
addresses ...25
Agricultural Museum ...77
airport ...23
Almássy, László ...79
Andrássy út ...64–67
Anker Palace ...52
Anonymous statue ...78
Antall, József ...80, 113, 212
apartments ...154
Applied Arts Museum ...87, see also *Budapest's Art Nouveau* colour section
Aquincum ...117
Árpád, Prince ...73, 207
arrival ...23
Arrow Cross ...6, 58, 59, 105, 214
arts centres ...177
Astoria Hotel ...49, 150
Auction House ...47
Aviation and Space Flight Exhibition ...79
ÁVO secret police ...59, 66, 67, 110, 211, 212

B

Baba, Gül ...107
Bajcsy-Zsilinszky út ...56
Bajcsy-Zsilinszky, Endre ...56
Bálint Balassi Museum (Esztergom) ...143
Bandholtz, General ...57
banks ...40
Barcsay Exhibition (Szentendre) ...131
bars ...170–174
Bartók Memorial House ...123
Bartók, Béla ...67, 123, 124, see also *Hungarian music* colour section
Basilica (Esztergom) ...142
baths and pools
- Császár Komjádi ...107, 191
- Gellért ...109, 191
- Hajós Alfred (Sport) ...120, 191
- Király ...106, 191
- Lukács ...107, 192
- Palatinus Strand ...120, 192
- Rác ...112, 192
- Rudas ...112, 192
- Széchenyi ...79, 192

Batthyány tér ...105
Batthyány, Lajos ...50, 58, 85, 210
Bécsi kapu tér ...95
Bedő House ...57, see also *Budapest's Art Nouveau* colour section
Belgrád rakpart ...50
Belgrade Church (Szentendre) ...132
Belváros ...45–52
Belváros ...46
Belváros Parish Church ...50
Bem statue ...106
Bem tér ...106
bike rental ...31, 121
Blagovestenska Church (Szentendre) ...132
books ...200, 215–219
Botanical Garden ...89
bridges
- Chain Bridge ...103
- Erzsébet híd ...50
- Lánchíd ...103
- Margit híd ...119
- Mária Valéria híd (Esztergom) ...144
- Petőfi híd ...89
- Szabadság híd ...108

Bródy Sándor utca ...83
Buda Castle Labyrinth ...97
Buda, Várhegy and central ...91
Buda Hills ...121–124
Buda Hills ...122
Buda Palace ...98–108
Budakeszi ...123
Budapest Beach ...62
Budapest Card ...36
Budapest History Museum ...103
Budapest Plázs ...62
Budapest Spring Festival ...32
bus stations ...24
buses ...28
buses to Budapest ...20

C

camping ...154
Castle Hill ...90–108
Castle Museum (Esztergom) ...142
Castle Theatre ...98
Cathedral of the Dormition ...51
Cave Church ...110
Central European University (CEU) ...53
Centrál Kávéház ...49, 167
Chain Bridge ...103
chairlift ...123
children ...35, 193
children's activities ...193–196
Children's Railway ...121
Christian Museum (Esztergom) ...143
churches and cathedrals
- Basilica (Esztergom) ...142
- Belgrade Church (Szentendre) ...132
- Belváros Parish Church ...50
- Blagovestenska Church (Szentendre) ...132
- Cathedral of the Dormition ...51
- Cave Church ...110
- Church of St Anne ...106
- Church of the St Elizabeth Nuns ...106
- Franciscan Church ...48
- Lutheran Church ...52
- Mátyás Church ...93
- Peter-Paul Church (Szentendre) ...131
- Požarevačka Church (Szentendre) ...131
- Preobraženska Church (Szentendre) ...133
- Serbian Orthodox Church ...48
- Servite Church ...48
- St Stephen's Basilica ...55

cinema ...182
Circus ...79
Citadel (Visegrád) ...138
Citadella ...110
city tours ...30
city transport ...25–31
Civilian Amphitheatre ...117

Clark, Adam 105
classical music ....178, see also *Hungarian music* colour section
clubs 170–174
coffee houses 167–169
Cogwheel Railway 121
consulates 37
Contra-Aquincum 50
Coronation Regalia.........61
Corvin Cinema................87
costs 35
crime..............................36
Császár Komjádi Pool 107, 191
Csillebérc......................123
customs..........................37
cycling 31, 121
Czóbel Exhibition (Szentendre)..............132

D

dance houses ....180 see also *Hungarian music* colour section
Danube Museum (Esztergom)................144
Deák tér..........................52
Demszky, Gábor 214
disabled travellers 42
Dísz tér 98
Dohány utca Synagogue 68
Dózsa György út.............74
Drinking Hall 112
driving to Budapest 20
Duna-korzó.....................51

E

Economics University.....87
electricity 37
embassies 37
Eötvös Loránd Science University.....................81
Erkel Theatre 85
Ernst Museum 65
Erzsébet híd 50
Erzsébet look-out tower 123
Erzsébet tér 52
Erzsébetváros 68–69
Erzsébetváros, Terézváros and 64
Esztergom 140–145
Esztergom....................141
Eternal Flame (Báthori utca) 58
Eternal Flame (Kossuth tér) 59
etiquette 34

F

Farkasréti Cemetery 124
Ferenc Hopp Museum ...67
Ferenciek tere................48
Ferencváros 86–89
Ferencváros, Józsefváros and 82
Ferenczy Museum (Szentendre)..............132
Ferihegy airport 23
ferries.............................29
festivals 32–34
films 182
Fisher-girl fountain..........47
Fishermen's Bastion.......94
flat rental......................154
flea markets.................198
flights to Budapest 19
Fő tér (Óbuda) 115
Fő tér (Szentendre).......132
Fő utca (Víziváros) 105
folk music and dance...180, see also *Hungarian music* colour section
food............. 158, 228–232
football.........................185
Formula 1 186
Foundry Museum 106
Fountain of Hungarian Truth 84
Fradi (FTC).............86, 185
Franciscan Church 48
Fun Extreme Canopy (Visegrád)..................139
Funerary Museum 85
funicular (Sikló) 103

G

Garay tér.........................72
gay Budapest 175–176
Gay Pride......................175
Gellért Baths........109, 191, see also *Budapest's Art Nouveau* colour section
Gellért-hegy 108–111
Gellért-hegy and the Tabán.........................109
Gellért Hotel 108, 153
Geological Institute ....80, see also *Budapest's Art Nouveau* colour section
Geological Museum 80
Gerbeaud patisserie......47, 167
Glass House 58
glossary 233–234
Gödöllő 145–146
Gödöllő Artists' Colony ....102, 146, see also *Budapest's Art Nouveau* colour section
Gödöllő Palace 145
Gödöllő Town Museum 146
Golden Eagle Pharmacy Museum.......................97
Gozsdu-udvar.................71
Grand Prix 186
Great Market Hall 87
Gresham Palace ....53, see also *Budapest's Art Nouveau* colour section
Gül Baba's Tomb..........107
György Ráth Museum 67
Gypsy music................181, see also *Hungarian music* colour section
Gyurcsány, Ferenc........213

H

Hajós Alfréd Pool.........120, 191
Hárshegy 123
health.............................37
Hercules Villa................117
Heroes' Temple 69
HÉV trains......................29
history.................. 207–214
Hősök tere.............. 73–77
Holocaust 58, 59, 63, 67, 68–71, 88, 105
Holocaust Memorial (by the Danube) 59
Holocaust Memorial Centre 88
Holocaust Memorial (Dohány utca) 69
horse-racing 186
Horthy, Admiral.............60, 99, 108, 110, 145, 211

Hospital in the Rock.......97
hostels.........................154
hotels....................150–154
House of Terror...............66
House of the Future 107
Hűvösvölgy..................123, see also *Budapest's Art Nouveau* colour section
Hungarian Academy of Sciences......................55
Hungarian National Gallery................99–102
Hungarian National Gallery.......................100
Hungarian National Museum.......................83
Hungarian Natural History Museum.......................88
Hungarian Open-Air Museum (Szentendre) 133
Hungaroring..................186
Hunyadi tér.....................67
hydrofoils
from Vienna........................24
to the Danube Bend.........129

I

information 41
insurance........................38
international bus station 34
internet 38

J

János-hegy..................123
Japanese Garden.........120
jazz ....179, see also *Hungarian music* colour section
Jewish Cemetery (Kerepesi) 86
Jewish Cemetery (New Public).......................126
Jewish Museum 69
Jewish quarter....63, 68–71
Jews 58, 59, 63, 68–71, 88, 95, 105
Jókai tér.........................66
József körút....................84
József, Attila...................59
Józsefváros............ 81–86
Józsefváros and Ferencváros................82

K

Kádár, János...........85, 212
Kálmán statue 65
Kálvin tér 84
Kapisztrán tér.................95
Karolyi-kert (garden).......50
Károlyi, Mihály.........47, 49, 210
Károlyi Mihály utca.........49
Kassák Museum...........116
Kazinczy utca.................71
Keleti Station..................85
Kerepesi Cemetery.........85
Kerepesi Cemetery........86
kid's activities....... 193–196
Kilián Barracks 87
Kilometre Zero..............103
Király Baths..........106, 191
Király utca.......................68
Kiscelli Museum 118
Kisfaludi-Strobl, Zsigmond 110
Klothild Palaces..............48
Kmetty Museum (Szentendre)...............132
Kodály körönd................67
Kodály Memorial Museum 67
Kodály, Zoltán ....67, 123, 124, see also *Hungarian music* colour section
Kolosy tér 118
Kossuth Lajos utca.........48
Kossuth tér............. 59–61
Kossuth, Lajos.........59, 60, 85, 209
Kovács Ceramic Exhibition (Szentendre)..............132
Köztársaság tér 85
Kristóf tér........................47
Károlyi Mihály utca.........49
Kun, Béla.............127, 210
Kun Collection of Folk Art 116

L

Labyrinth, Buda Castle...97
Lajta, Béla........48, 65, 126, see also *Budapest's Art Nouveau* colour section
Lánchíd.........................103
language..............223–232
language courses...........39
laundry...........................38
Lechner, Ödön.........58, 66, 80, 87, 126, see also *Budapest's Art Nouveau* colour section
Lehel tér..........................62
Libegő..........................123
Liberation Monument...110
Lipótváros 53–61
Lipótváros and Újlipótváros................54
listings magazines..........32
Liszt Ferenc tér...............66
Liszt Memorial Museum 67
Liszt Music Academy....66, 179, see also *Hungarian music* colour section
Liszt, Ferenc (Franz)......66, 67, see also *Hungarian music* colour section
Little Princess statue......51
living in Budapest...........39
lost property 39
Ludwig Museum.............89
Lukács Baths........107, 192
Lutheran Church.............52
Lutheran Museum 52
Lutz, Carl..........58, 71, 211
Lutz monument 71

M

Magyar conquest 207
Mahler, Gustav 65
Mai Manó House............65
mail................................39
Makovecz, Imre....124, 139
maps...............................39
Március 15 tér 50
Margit híd 119
Margit körút..................107
Margít-sziget....... 118–120
Margít-sziget................119
Margít-sziget, Óbuda and 115
Mária Valéria híd (Esztergom)................144
markets........................198
Mary Magdalene Tower 96
Marzipan Museum (Szentendre)..............131
Mátyás Church 93
Mátyás Fountain...........102
Mátyás Museum (Visegrád) 138
media.............................31

INDEX

Medieval Jewish Prayer House ... 95
medieval wall of Pest ... 48, 82, 87
Memento Park ... 126
metro ... 26
Miksa Róth Museum ... 72
Mikszáth Kálmán tér ... 84
military amphitheatre ... 117
military baths ... 117
Military Court of Justice ... 106
Military History Museum ... 96
Millenáris Park ... 107, 178
Millenary Monument ... 73
Mindszenty, Cardinal ... 57, 142, 143
Mindszenty Museum (Esztergom) ... 143
Mogyoród ... 186
money ... 40
Monument to Hungarian Grief ... 57
Monument to the Uprising ... 75
Moszkva tér ... 107
Műcsarnok ... 74
museums
- Agricultural Museum ... 77
- Applied Arts Museum ... 87
- Aquincum Museum ... 117
- Aviation and Space Flight Exhibition ... 79
- Bálint Balassi Museum (Esztergom) ... 143
- Barcsay Exhibition (Szentendre) ... 131
- Bartók Memorial House ... 123
- Budapest History Museum ... 103
- Castle Museum (Esztergom) ... 142
- Christian Museum (Esztergom) ... 143
- Czóbel Exhibition (Szentendre) ... 132
- Danube Museum (Esztergom) ... 144
- Ernst Museum ... 65
- Ferenc Hopp Museum ... 67
- Ferenczy Museum (Szentendre) ... 132
- Foundry Museum ... 106
- Funerary Museum ... 85
- Geological Museum ... 80
- Gödöllő Town Museum ... 146
- Golden Eagle Pharmacy Museum ... 97
- György Ráth Museum ... 67
- Holocaust Memorial Centre ... 88
- Hospital in the Rock ... 97
- House of Terror ... 66
- House of the Future ... 107
- Hungarian National Gallery ... 99–102
- Hungarian National Museum ... 83
- Hungarian Natural History Museum ... 88
- Hungarian Open-Air Museum (Szentendre) ... 133
- Jewish Museum ... 69
- Kassák Museum ... 116
- Kiscelli Museum ... 118
- Kmetty Museum (Szentendre) ... 132
- Kodály Memorial Museum ... 67
- Kovács Ceramic Exhibition (Szentendre) ... 132
- Kun Collection of Folk Art ... 116
- Liszt Memorial Museum ... 67
- Ludwig Museum ... 89
- Lutheran Museum ... 52
- Mai Manó House ... 65
- Marzipan Museum (Szentendre) ... 131
- Mátyás Museum (Visegrád) ... 138
- Medieval Jewish Prayer House ... 95
- Memento Park ... 126
- Miksa Róth Museum ... 72
- Military History Museum ... 96
- Mindszenty Museum (Esztergom) ... 143
- Museum of Electrotechnology ... 71
- Museum of Ethnography ... 61
- **Museum of Fine Arts** ... 75–77
- Museum of Hungarian Art Nouveau ... 58
- Museum of Trade and Tourism ... 56
- Music History Museum ... 95
- Nagytétényi Castle Museum ... 127
- Óbuda Museum ... 116
- Palace of Miracles ... 107
- Petőfi Literary Museum ... 49
- Police History Museum ... 85
- Post Office Museum ... 65
- Railway History Park ... 125
- Royal Palace (Gödöllő) ... 145
- Semmelweis Medical Museum ... 112
- Serbian Ecclesiastical History Collection (Szentendre) ... 133
- Telephone Museum ... 96
- Transport Museum ... 79
- Underground Railway Museum ... 52
- Vajda Museum (Szentendre) ... 133
- Varga Museum ... 116
- Vasarely Museum ... 116
- Wine Museum (Szentendre) ... 133

Music Academy ... 66, 179, see also *Hungarian music* colour section
Music History Museum ... 95
Múzeum körút ... 81

N

Nagy statue ... 58
Nagy, Imre ... 58, 106, 126, 211, 212
Nagymező utca ... 65
Nagytétényi Castle Museum ... 127
names ... 40
Napraforgó utca housing estate ... 123, see also *Budapest's Art Nouveau* colour section
National Archives ... 95
National Bank ... 57
National Concert Hall ... 89, 178
National Pantheon ... 126
National Széchényi Library ... 102
National Theatre ... 89, 183
Neolog Judaism ... 68
New Public Cemetery ... 125
New Theatre ... 65, 184
New York Palace ... 71, 168
Normafa ... 123
Nyugati Railway Station ... 56

O

Óbuda Museum ... 116
Óbuda ... 114–118
Óbuda and Margít-sziget ... 115
Officers' Casino ... 48
Oktogon ... 66
Old Budapest City Hall ... 48
Old Father Danube statue ... 52
online booking agents ... 21
opening hours ... 40
opera ... 178
Opera House ... 65
Orbán, Viktor ... 213
Országház utca ... 96

Orthodox Synagogue 71
Outdoor Theatre 120

P

Palace of Arts 89, 178
Palace of Miracles 107
Palatinus Strand ... 120, 192
Pálvölgyi Stalactite Cave 118
Pantheon of the Working Class Movement 85
Papp László Sportaréna 80
Párisi udvar 48
Parliament 60
Pasaréti tér 124
Paul Street Boys 87
Pest Theatre 47
Peter-Paul Church (Szentendre) 131
Petőfi Csarnok 78
Petőfi Literary Museum 49
Petőfi, Sándor 50, 51, 83, 85, 210
Petőfi Sándor utca 48
Petőfi statue 51
Petőfi tér 50
phones 40
police 36
Police History Museum 85
pools, see baths
pop music 179
post 39
Post Office Museum 65
Post Office Savings Bank .... 58, see also *Budapest's Art Nouveau* colour section
Požarevačka Church (Szentendre) 131
Preobraženska Church (Szentendre) 133
private rooms 154
public holidays 40
Puskás, Ferenc 80
Puskás Ferenc Stadium 80, 185

R

Ráday utca 87
Railway circuit 121
Railway History Park 125
railway stations 24
Rákóczi, Ferenc 59, 209
Rákóczi tér 84
Rákosi, Mátyás 124, 211
Raoul Wallenberg Memorial Garden 69
religion 41
restaurants 157–169
Rippl-Rónai, József .... 66, 75, 102, see also *Budapest's Art Nouveau* colour section
Roma music .... 181, see also *Hungarian music* colour section
Rómaifürdő 117
Roosevelt tér 53
Róth, Miksa .... 48, 54, 72, see also *Budapest's Art Nouveau* colour section
Royal Palace (Visegrád) 137
Rózsadomb 107
Rózsavölgyi Building 48
Rudas Baths 112, 192
Rumbach utca Synagogue 70
Ruszwurm patisserie 93, 169

S

Sándor Palace 98
Semmelweis, Ignác 113
Semmelweis Medical Museum 112
Serbian Ecclesiastical History Collection (Szentendre) 133
Serbian Orthodox Church 48
Servite Church 48
shopping 197–204
Sikló (funicular) 103
Sissi (Empress Elizabeth) 65, 112, 145
soccer 185
Solomon's Tower (Visegrád) 138
Soros, George 53
Soviet Army Memorial 57
Sportaréna 80
sports 185–187
St Stephen's Basilica 55
St Stephen's Crown 6, 61
stag tourism 174
State Opera House 65
Statue Park 126
steam trains 125
Stephen, King/Saint 55, 94
Stock Exchange (former) 57
studying in Budapest 39
Svábhegy 121
swimming, *see* baths
Szabadság híd 108
Szabadság tér 56
Szabó Ervin Library 84
Szarvas tér 113
Széchenyi Baths 79, 192
Széchenyi, István 103, 209
Széchenyi-hegy 121
Szemlőhegyi Cave 118
Szent István Park 62
Szentendre 129–135
Szentendre 130
Szentháromság tér 93
Szervita tér 58
Szilágyi Dezső tér 105

T

Tabán 111–113
Tabán, Gellért-hegy and the 109
táncház .... 180–181, see also *Hungarian music* colour section
Táncsics Mihály utca 95
taxis 29
Telephone Museum 96
telephones 40
Terézváros 63–67
Terézváros and Erzsébetváros 64
theatre 183
time 41
Timewheel 74
Tóth Árpád sétány 96
tour operators 21
Tourinform 41
tourist offices 41
train stations 24
trains to Budapest 20
trams 28
Transport Museum 79
Trianon, Treaty of 57, 84, 211, 213
trolleybuses 28
Tropicarium 127
Turul statue 98

U

Újlipótváros....................62
Újlipótváros, Lipótváros and 54
Underground Railway.....47
Underground Railway Museum.......................52
Úri utca...........................96

V

Váci utca..................47–48
Vajda Museum (Szentendre) 133
Vajdahunyad Castle........77
Varga Museum 116
Várhegy.................90–108
Várhegy..........................92
Várhegy and central Buda 91
Várkert Bazár...............113
Várkert Kioszk...............113
Városliget................77–80
Városliget and the stadiums 74
Vasarely Museum.........116
Vidám Park.....................79
Vienna Gate....................95
Vigadó 51
visas 37
Visegrád..............135–140
Visegrád........................136
Visegrád Hills................139
Víziváros.............105–106
Vörösmarty, Mihály........47, 98, 102
Vörösmarty tér................45

W

Wallenburg monument...62
Wallenburg, Raoul.........62, 69, 103, 211
Washington statue..........78
websites 42
Weiss, Manfred..............86
WestEnd City Center.....56, 199
White Terror..................210
wine......................158, 232
Wine Museum (Szentendre) 133
working in Budapest......39

Y

Ybl Miklós tér 113

Z

Zoo ....80, see also *Budapest's Art Nouveau* colour section

Map symbols

maps are listed in the full index using coloured text

- Chapter division boundary
- International boundary
- Motorway
- Major road
- Minor road
- Pedestrianized street
- Steps
- Railway
- Tunnel
- Footpath
- River
- Ferry
- Wall
- Chairlift
- HÉV line and station
- Metro line and station
- Campsite
- Cave
- Ruins
- Mountain peak
- Rocks/cliff
- Accommodation
- Restaurant
- Parking
- Point of interest
- Internet access
- Tourist information
- Post office
- Airport
- Gate
- Bridge
- Bus stop
- Ferry port
- Synagogue
- Statue
- Monument
- Castle
- Viewpoint
- Hospital
- Baths/swimming pool
- Fountain
- Church (regional)
- Church (town)
- Building
- Market
- Stadium
- Jewish cemetery
- Christian cemetery
- Park/national park

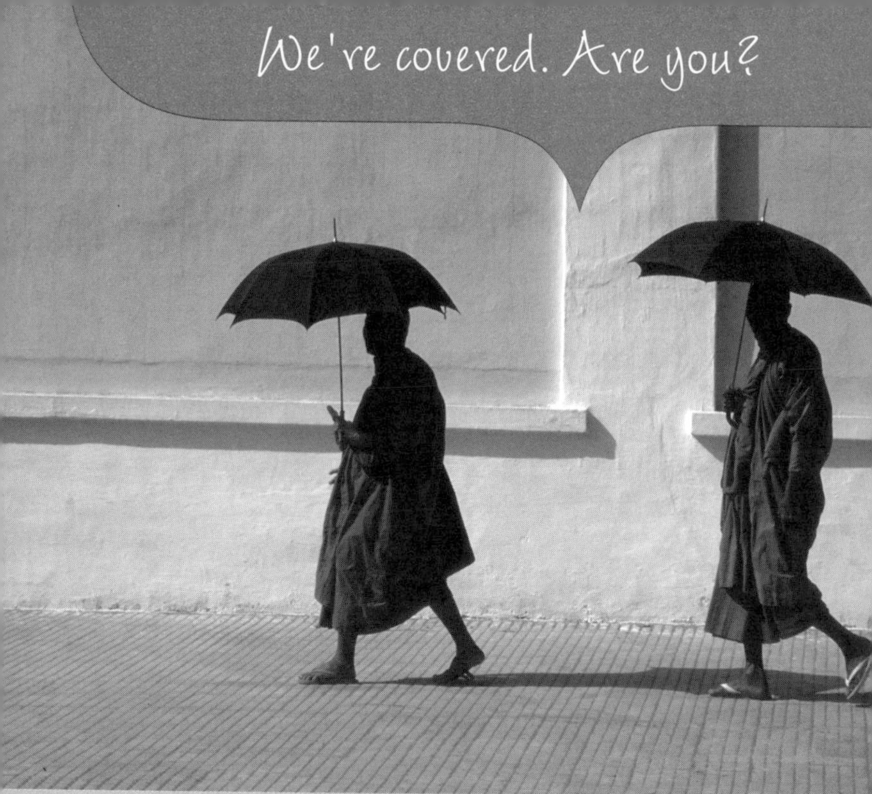

We're covered. Are you?

ROUGH GUIDES Travel Insurance

Visit our website at www.roughguides.com/website/shop or call:

UK: 0800 083 9507

Spain: 900 997 149

Australia: 1300 669 999

New Zealand: 0800 55 99 11

Worldwide: +44 870 890 2843

USA, call toll free on: 1 800 749 4922

Please quote our ref: ***Rough Guides books***

Cover for over 46 different nationalities and available in 4 different languages.

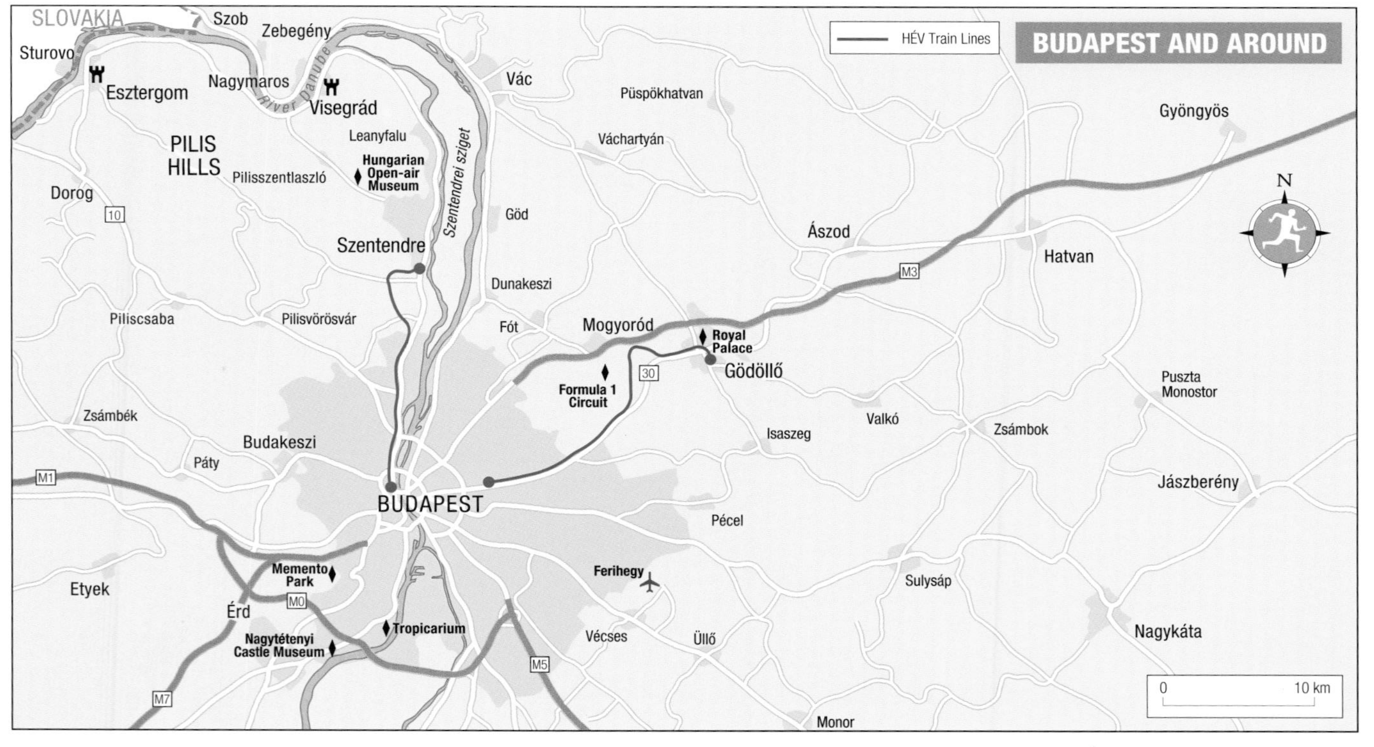
BUDAPEST AND AROUND
HÉV Train Lines
SLOVAKIA
Szob
Zebegény
Sturovo
Esztergom
Nagymaros
River Danube
Visegrád
Vác
Püspökhatvan
Gyöngyös
Leanyfalu
Váchartyán
PILIS
HILLS
Pilisszentlaszló
Hungarian
Open-air
Museum
Dorog
10
Szentendrei sziget
Göd
Ászod
N
Szentendre
Hatvan
M3
Dunakeszi
Piliscsaba
Pilisvörösvár
Fót
Mogyoród
Royal
Palace
30
Gödöllő
Formula 1
Circuit
Puszta
Monostor
Zsámbék
Valkó
Isaszeg
Zsámbok
Budakeszi
Páty
M1
Jászberény
BUDAPEST
Pécel
Memento
Park
Ferihegy
Etyek
Sulysáp
M0
Érd
Tropicarium
Nagytétenyi
Castle Museum
Vécses
Üllő
Nagykáta
M5
M7
0
10 km
Monor

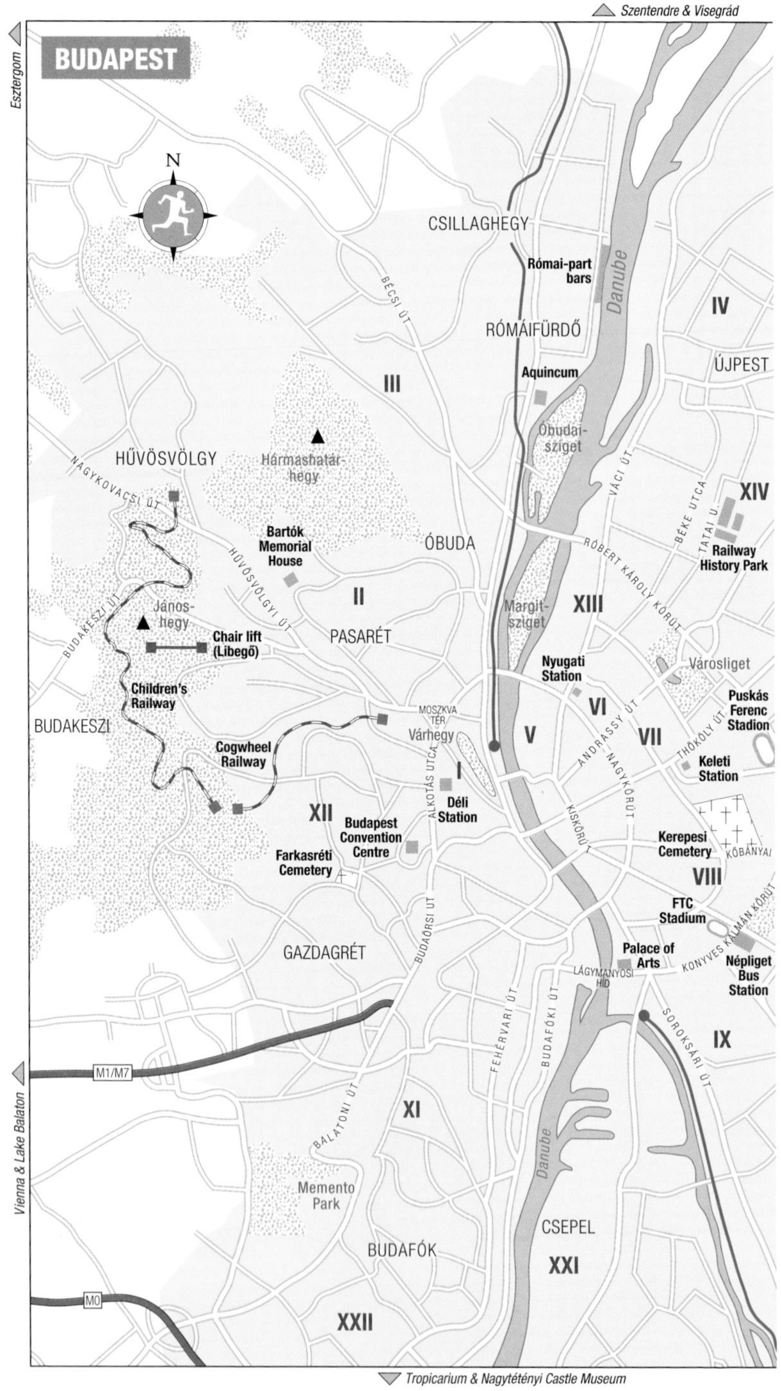

BUDAPEST
Szentendre & Visegrád
Esztergom
Vienna & Lake Balaton
Tropicarium & Nagytétényi Castle Museum
N
CSILLAGHEGY
Római-part bars
Danube
IV
RÓMÁIFÜRDŐ
ÚJPEST
Aquincum
III
Óbudai-sziget
HŰVÖSVÖLGY
Hármashatár-hegy
NAGYKOVÁCSI ÚT
VÁCI ÚT
BÉCSI ÚT
BÉKE UTCA
TATAI U.
XIV
Bartók Memorial House
ÓBUDA
RÓBERT KÁROLY KÖRÚT
Railway History Park
HŰVÖSVÖLGYI ÚT
II
Margit-sziget
XIII
BUDAKESZI ÚT
János-hegy
PASARÉT
Chair lift (Libegő)
Nyugati Station
Városliget
Children's Railway
VI
Puskás Ferenc Stadion
MOSZKVA TÉR
BUDAKESZI
Várhegy
V
ANDRASSY ÚT
VII
THÖKÖLY ÚT
Cogwheel Railway
ALKOTÁS UTCA
I
NAGYKÖRÚT
Keleti Station
Déli Station
XII
Budapest Convention Centre
KISKÖRÚT
Kerepesi Cemetery
KŐBÁNYAI
Farkasréti Cemetery
VIII
BUDAÖRSI ÚT
FTC Stadium
KÖNYVES KÁLMÁN KÖRÚT
GAZDAGRÉT
Palace of Arts
Népliget Bus Station
LÁGYMÁNYOSI HÍD
FEHÉRVÁRI ÚT
BUDAFOKI ÚT
SOROKSÁRI ÚT
IX
M1/M7
XI
BALATONI ÚT
Memento Park
CSEPEL
BUDAFÓK
XXI
M0
XXII

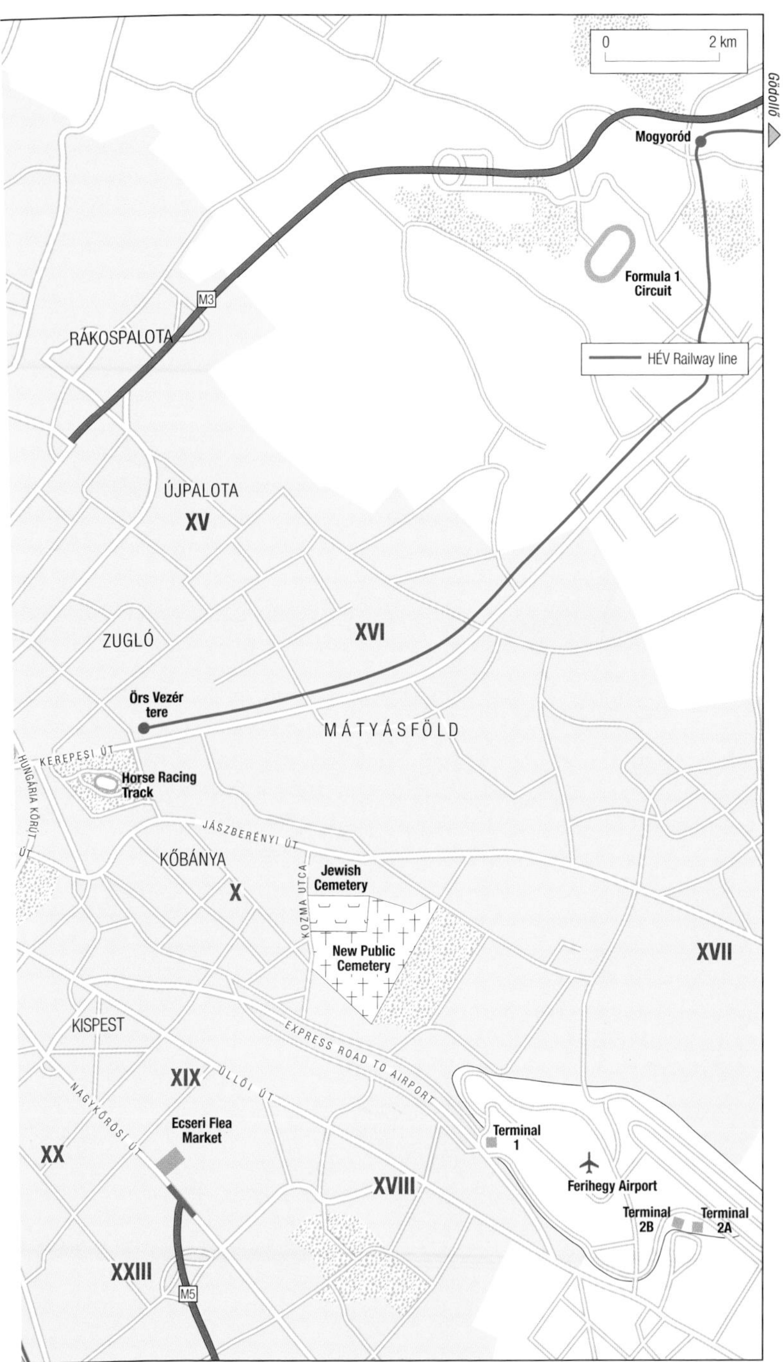
0
2 km
Gödöllő
Mogyoród
Formula 1
Circuit
HÉV Railway line
M3
RÁKOSPALOTA
ÚJPALOTA
XV
ZUGLÓ
XVI
Örs Vezér
tere
MÁTYÁSFÖLD
KEREPESI ÚT
HUNGÁRIA KÖRÚT
Horse Racing
Track
JÁSZBERÉNYI ÚT
KŐBÁNYA
X
KOZMA UTCA
Jewish
Cemetery
New Public
Cemetery
XVII
KISPEST
EXPRESS ROAD TO AIRPORT
XIX
ÜLLŐI ÚT
NAGYKŐRÖSI ÚT
Ecseri Flea
Market
XX
Terminal
1
Ferihegy Airport
XVIII
Terminal
2B
Terminal
2A
XXIII
M5

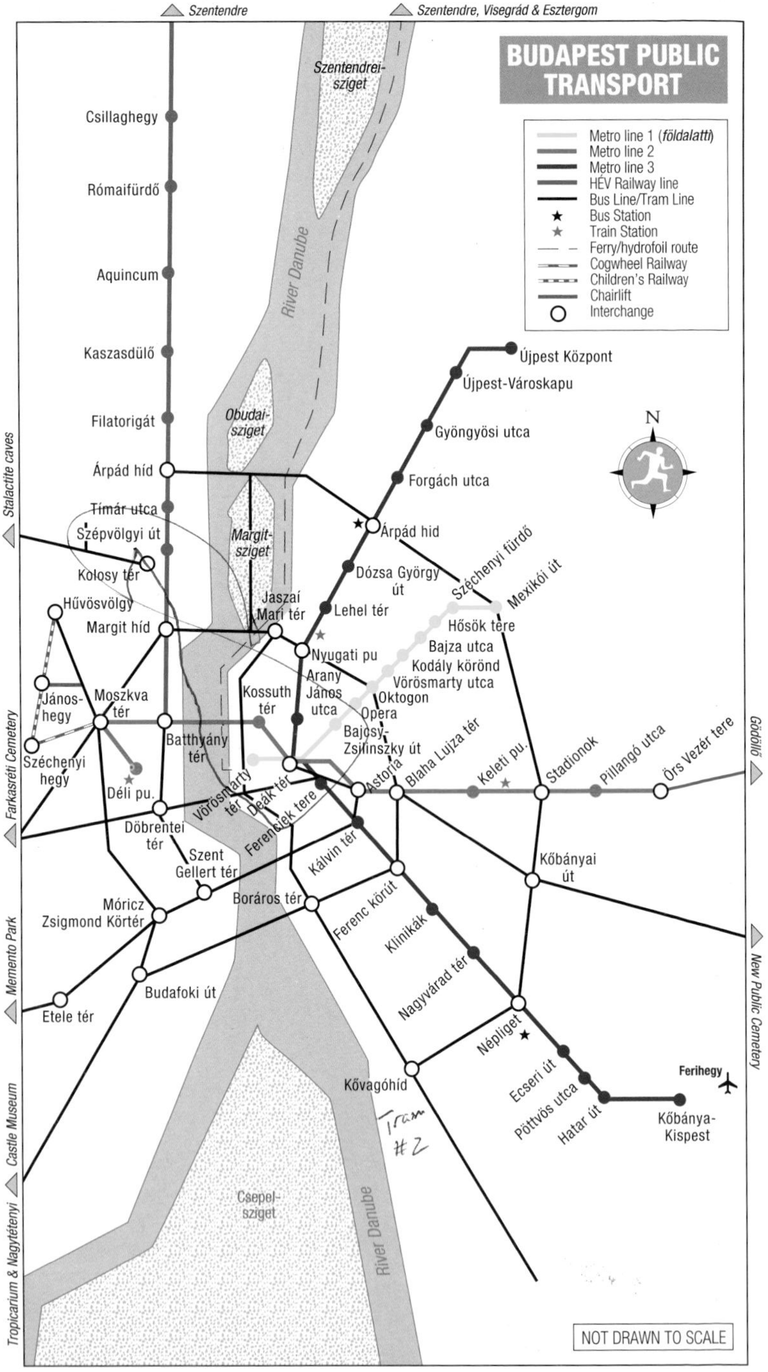

BUDAPEST PUBLIC TRANSPORT

Metro line 1 (*földalatti*)
Metro line 2
Metro line 3
HÉV Railway line
Bus Line/Tram Line
Bus Station
Train Station
Ferry/hydrofoil route
Cogwheel Railway
Children's Railway
Chairlift
Interchange

Szentendre
Szentendre, Visegrád & Esztergom
Szentendrei-sziget
River Danube
Óbudai-sziget
Margit-sziget
Csepel-sziget
Stalactite caves
Farkasréti Cemetery
Memento Park
Castle Museum
Tropicarium & Nagytétényi
Gödöllő
New Public Cemetery
Ferihegy
N

Csillaghegy
Rómaifürdő
Aquincum
Kaszasdülő
Filatorigát
Árpád híd
Tímár utca
Szépvölgyi út
Kolosy tér
Hűvösvölgy
Margit híd
János-hegy
Moszkva tér
Széchenyi hegy
Déli pu.
Batthyány tér
Döbrentei tér
Szent Gellert tér
Móricz Zsigmond Körtér
Budafoki út
Etele tér
Jaszai Mari tér
Kossuth tér
Vörösmarty tér
Deák tér
Ferenciek tere
Kálvin tér
Boráros tér
Ferenc körút
Klinikák
Nagyvárad tér
Népliget
Ecseri út
Pöttvös utca
Hatar út
Kőbánya-Kispest
Kővagóhíd
Újpest Központ
Újpest-Városkapu
Gyöngyösi utca
Forgách utca
Árpád hid
Dózsa György út
Lehel tér
Nyugati pu
Arany János utca
Széchenyi fürdő
Mexikói út
Hősök tere
Bajza utca
Kodály körönd
Vörösmarty utca
Oktogon
Opera
Bajcsy-Zsilinszky út
Astoria
Blaha Lujza tér
Keleti pu.
Stadionok
Pillangó utca
Örs Vezér tere
Kőbányai út

Tram #2

NOT DRAWN TO SCALE